Microsoft® Office 365™
ACCESS® 2016

INTRODUCTORY

Microsoft® Office 365™
ACCESS® 2016

INTRODUCTORY

Philip J. Pratt
Mary Z. Last

CENGAGE
Learning®

SHELLY CASHMAN SERIES®

Australia • Brazil • Japan • Korea • Mexico • Singapore • Spain • United Kingdom • United States

Microsoft® Access® 2016: Introductory
Philip J. Pratt and Mary Z. Last

SVP, GM Skills & Global Product Management:
Dawn Gerrain

Product Director: Kathleen McMahon

Senior Product Team Manager: Lauren Murphy

Associate Product Manager: William Guiliani

Senior Director, Development: Marah
Bellegarde

Product Development Manager: Leigh Hefferon

Managing Content Developer: Emma
F. Newsom

Developmental Editor: Amanda Brodkin

Product Assistant: Erica Chapman

Manuscript Quality Assurance: Jeffrey
Schwartz, John Freitas, Serge Palladino,
Susan Pedicini, Danielle Shaw, Susan Whalen

Senior Production Director: Wendy Troeger

Production Director: Patty Stephan

Senior Content Project Manager: Matthew
Hutchinson

Manufacturing Planner: Julio Esperas

Designer: Diana Graham

Text Designer: Joel Sadagursky

Cover Template Designer: Diana Graham

Cover image(s): karawan/Shutterstock.com;
Click Bestsellers/Shutterstock.com

Compositor: Lumina Datamatics, Inc.

Vice President, Marketing: Brian Joyner

Marketing Director: Michele McTighe

Marketing Manager: Stephanie Albracht

The material in this book was written using Microsoft Office 2016 and was Quality Assurance tested before the publication date. As Microsoft continually updates Office 2016 and Office 365, your software experience may vary slightly from what is seen in the printed text.

Mac users: If you're working through this product using a Mac, some of the steps may vary. Additional information for Mac users is included with the data files for this product.

For product information and technology assistance, contact us at
Cengage Learning Customer & Sales Support, 1-800-354-9706

For permission to use material from this text or product,
submit all requests online at **www.cengage.com/permissions.**
Further permissions questions can be e-mailed to
permissionrequest@cengage.com

Library of Congress Control Number: 2015955175

ISBN: 978-1-3058-7061-1

Cengage Learning
20 Channel Center Street
Boston, MA 02210
USA

Cengage Learning is a leading provider of customized learning solutions with employees residing in nearly 40 different countries and sales in more than 125 countries around the world. Find your local representative at:
www.cengage.com.

Cengage Learning products are represented in Canada by Nelson Education, Ltd.

To learn more about Cengage Learning, visit **www.cengage.com**

Purchase any of our products at your local college store or at our preferred online store **www.cengagebrain.com**

Printed in the United States of America
Print Number: 03   Print Year: 2017

Microsoft® Office 365™ ACCESS® 2016

INTRODUCTORY

Contents

Productivity Apps for School and Work

Corinne Hoisington

Lochlan keeps track of his class notes, football plays, and internship meetings with OneNote.

Zoe is using the annotation features of Microsoft Edge to take and save web notes for her research paper.

Nori is creating a Sway site to highlight this year's activities for the Student Government Association.

Hunter is adding interactive videos and screen recordings to his PowerPoint resume.

© Rawpixel/Shutterstock.com

Being computer literate no longer means mastery of only Word, Excel, PowerPoint, Outlook, and Access. To become technology power users, Hunter, Nori, Zoe, and Lochlan are exploring Microsoft OneNote, Sway, Mix, and Edge in Office 2016 and Windows 10.

In this Module

Learn to use productivity apps!
Links to companion **Sways**, featuring **videos** with hands-on instructions, are located on www.cengagebrain.com.

Introduction to OneNote 2016

notebook | section tab | To Do tag | screen clipping | note | template | Microsoft OneNote Mobile app | sync | drawing canvas | inked handwriting | Ink to Text

As you glance around any classroom, you invariably see paper notebooks and notepads on each desk. Because deciphering and sharing handwritten notes can be a challenge, Microsoft OneNote 2016 replaces physical notebooks, binders, and paper notes with a searchable, digital notebook. OneNote captures your ideas and schoolwork on any device so you can stay organized, share notes, and work with others on projects. Whether you are a student taking class notes as shown in **Figure 1** or an employee taking notes in company meetings, OneNote is the one place to keep notes for all of your projects.

Figure 1: OneNote 2016 notebook

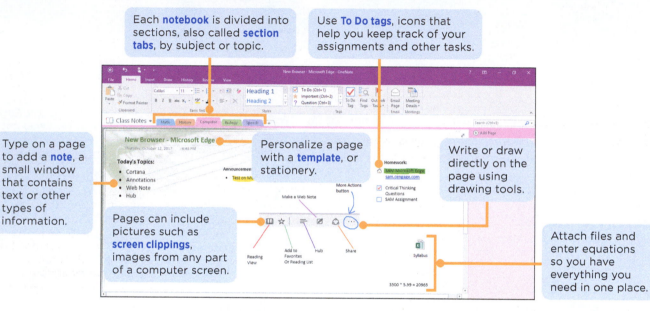

Each **notebook** is divided into sections, also called **section tabs**, by subject or topic.

Use **To Do tags**, icons that help you keep track of your assignments and other tasks.

Type on a page to add a **note**, a small window that contains text or other types of information.

Personalize a page with a **template**, or stationery.

Write or draw directly on the page using drawing tools.

Pages can include pictures such as **screen clippings**, images from any part of a computer screen.

Attach files and enter equations so you have everything you need in one place.

Creating a OneNote Notebook

OneNote is divided into sections similar to those in a spiral-bound notebook. Each OneNote notebook contains sections, pages, and other notebooks. You can use One-Note for school, business, and personal projects. Store information for each type of project in different notebooks to keep your tasks separate, or use any other organization that suits you. OneNote is flexible enough to adapt to the way you want to work.

When you create a notebook, it contains a blank page with a plain white background by default, though you can use templates, or stationery, to apply designs in categories such as Academic, Business, Decorative, and Planners. Start typing or use the buttons on the Insert tab to insert notes, which are small resizable windows that can contain text, equations, tables, on-screen writing, images, audio and video recordings, to-do lists, file attachments, and file printouts. Add as many notes as you need to each page.

Syncing a Notebook to the Cloud

OneNote saves your notes every time you make a change in a notebook. To make sure you can access your notebooks with a laptop, tablet, or smartphone wherever you are, OneNote uses cloud-based storage, such as OneDrive or SharePoint. **Microsoft OneNote Mobile app**, a lightweight version of OneNote 2016 shown in **Figure 2**, is available for free in the Windows Store, Google Play for Android devices, and the AppStore for iOS devices.

If you have a Microsoft account, OneNote saves your notes on OneDrive automatically for all your mobile devices and computers, which is called **syncing**. For example, you can use OneNote to take notes on your laptop during class, and then open OneNote on your phone to study later. To use a notebook stored on your computer with your OneNote Mobile app, move the notebook to OneDrive. You can quickly share notebook content with other people using OneDrive.

Figure 2: Microsoft OneNote Mobile app

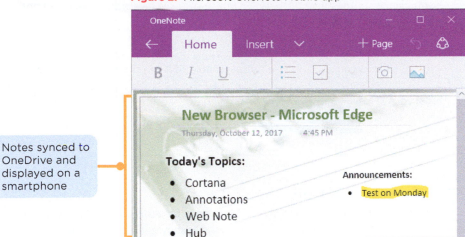

Notes synced to OneDrive and displayed on a smartphone

Taking Notes

Use OneNote pages to organize your notes by class and topic or lecture. Beyond simple typed notes, OneNote stores drawings, converts handwriting to searchable text and mathematical sketches to equations, and records audio and video.

OneNote includes drawing tools that let you sketch freehand drawings such as biological cell diagrams and financial supply-and-demand charts. As shown in **Figure 3**, the Draw tab on the ribbon provides these drawing tools along with shapes so you can insert diagrams and other illustrations to represent your ideas. When you draw on a page, OneNote creates a **drawing canvas**, which is a container for shapes and lines.

On the Job Now

OneNote is ideal for taking notes during meetings, whether you are recording minutes, documenting a discussion, sketching product diagrams, or listing follow-up items. Use a meeting template to add pages with content appropriate for meetings.

Figure 3: Tools on the Draw tab

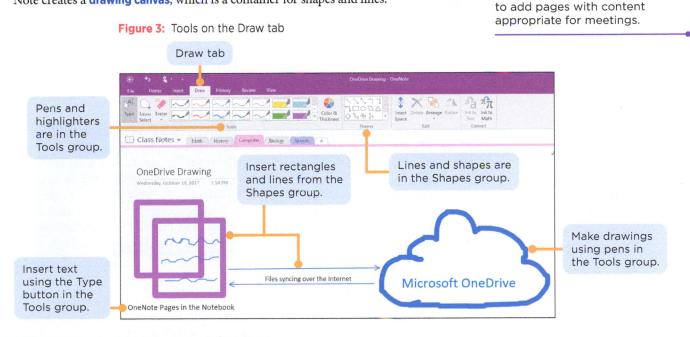

Draw tab

Pens and highlighters are in the Tools group.

Insert rectangles and lines from the Shapes group.

Lines and shapes are in the Shapes group.

Insert text using the Type button in the Tools group.

Make drawings using pens in the Tools group.

Converting Handwriting to Text

When you use a pen tool to write on a notebook page, the text you enter is called **inked handwriting**. OneNote can convert inked handwriting to typed text when you use the **Ink to Text** button in the Convert group on the Draw tab, as shown in **Figure 4**. After OneNote converts the handwriting to text, you can use the Search box to find terms in the converted text or any other note in your notebooks.

Figure 4: Converting handwriting to text

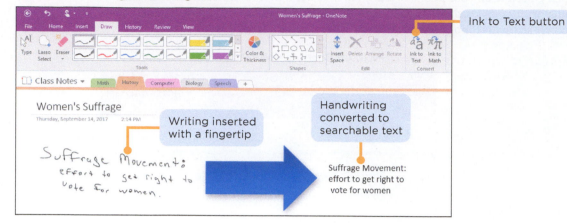

Ink to Text button

Women's Suffrage

Thursday, September 14, 2017   2:14 PM

Writing inserted with a fingertip

Handwriting converted to searchable text

Suffrage Movement: effort to get right to vote for women

Suffrage Movement: effort to get right to vote for women

On the Job Now

Use OneNote as a place to brainstorm ongoing work projects. If a notebook contains sensitive material, you can password-protect some or all of the notebook so that only certain people can open it.

Recording a Lecture

If your computer or mobile device has a microphone or camera, OneNote can record the audio or video from a lecture or business meeting as shown in **Figure 5**. When you record a lecture (with your instructor's permission), you can follow along, take regular notes at your own pace, and review the video recording later. You can control the start, pause, and stop motions of the recording when you play back the recording of your notes.

Figure 5: Video inserted in a notebook

Record Video button

Audio & Video Recording tab

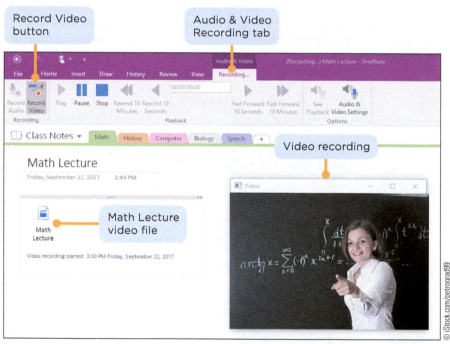

Video recording

Math Lecture

Friday, September 22, 2017   2:44 PM

Math Lecture video file

Video recording started: 3:00 PM Friday, September 22, 2017

© iStock.com/petrograd99

Try This Now

1: Taking Notes for a Week

Learn to use OneNote! Links to companion **Sways**, featuring **videos** with hands-on instructions, are located on www.cengagebrain.com.

As a student, you can get organized by using OneNote to take detailed notes in your classes. Perform the following tasks:

a. Create a new OneNote notebook on your Microsoft OneDrive account (the default location for new notebooks). Name the notebook with your first name followed by "Notes," as in **Caleb Notes**.

b. Create four section tabs, each with a different class name.

c. Take detailed notes in those classes for one week. Be sure to include notes, drawings, and other types of content.

d. Sync your notes with your OneDrive. Submit your assignment in the format specified by your instructor.

2: Using OneNote to Organize a Research Paper

You have a research paper due on the topic of three habits of successful students. Use OneNote to organize your research. Perform the following tasks:

a. Create a new OneNote notebook on your Microsoft OneDrive account. Name the notebook **Success Research**.

b. Create three section tabs with the following names:

- **Take Detailed Notes**
- **Be Respectful in Class**
- **Come to Class Prepared**

c. On the web, research the topics and find three sources for each section. Copy a sentence from each source and paste the sentence into the appropriate section. When you paste the sentence, OneNote inserts it in a note with a link to the source.

d. Sync your notes with your OneDrive. Submit your assignment in the format specified by your instructor.

3: Planning Your Career

Note: This activity requires a webcam or built-in video camera on any type of device.

Consider an occupation that interests you. Using OneNote, examine the responsibilities, education requirements, potential salary, and employment outlook of a specific career. Perform the following tasks:

a. Create a new OneNote notebook on your Microsoft OneDrive account. Name the notebook with your first name followed by a career title, such as **Kara - App Developer**.

b. Create four section tabs with the names **Responsibilities, Education Requirements, Median Salary**, and **Employment Outlook**.

c. Research the responsibilities of your career path. Using OneNote, record a short video (approximately 30 seconds) of yourself explaining the responsibilities of your career path. Place the video in the Responsibilities section.

d. On the web, research the educational requirements for your career path and find two appropriate sources. Copy a paragraph from each source and paste them into the appropriate section. When you paste a paragraph, OneNote inserts it in a note with a link to the source.

e. Research the median salary for a single year for this career. Create a mathematical equation in the Median Salary section that multiplies the amount of the median salary times 20 years to calculate how much you will possibly earn.

f. For the Employment Outlook section, research the outlook for your career path. Take at least four notes about what you find when researching the topic.

g. Sync your notes with your OneDrive. Submit your assignment in the format specified by your instructor.

Introduction to Sway

Sway site | responsive design | Storyline | card | Creative Commons license | animation emphasis effects | Docs.com

Expressing your ideas in a presentation typically means creating PowerPoint slides or a Word document. Microsoft Sway gives you another way to engage an audience. Sway is a free Microsoft tool available at Sway.com or as an app in Office 365. Using Sway, you can combine text, images, videos, and social media in a website called a **Sway site** that you can share and display on any device. To get started, you create a digital story on a web-based canvas without borders, slides, cells, or page breaks. A Sway site organizes the text, images, and video into a **responsive design**, which means your content adapts perfectly to any screen size as shown in **Figure 6**. You store a Sway site in the cloud on OneDrive using a free Microsoft account.

Figure 6: Sway site with responsive design

You can display a Sway presentation in a web browser.

Sway uses responsive design to make sure pages fit perfectly on any device.

© iStock.com/marinello, © iStock.com/marekuliasz

Creating a Sway Presentation

You can use Sway to build a digital flyer, a club newsletter, a vacation blog, an informational site, a digital art portfolio, or a new product rollout. After you select your topic and sign into Sway with your Microsoft account, a **Storyline** opens, providing tools and a work area for composing your digital story. See **Figure 7**. Each story can include text, images, and videos. You create a Sway by adding text and media content into a Storyline section, or **card**. To add pictures, videos, or documents, select a card in the left pane and then select the Insert Content button. The first card in a Sway presentation contains a title and background image.

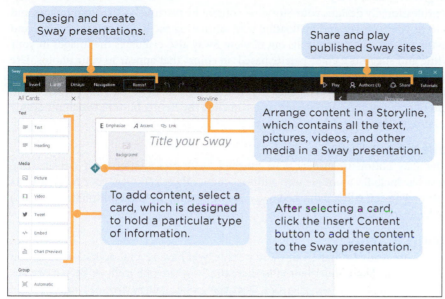

Design and create Sway presentations.

Share and play published Sway sites.

Arrange content in a Storyline, which contains all the text, pictures, videos, and other media in a Sway presentation.

To add content, select a card, which is designed to hold a particular type of information.

After selecting a card, click the Insert Content button to add the content to the Sway presentation.

Adding Content to Build a Story

As you work, Sway searches the Internet to help you find relevant images, videos, tweets, and other content from online sources such as Bing, YouTube, Twitter, and Facebook. You can drag content from the search results right into the Storyline. In addition, you can upload your own images and videos directly in the presentation. For example, if you are creating a Sway presentation about the market for commercial drones, Sway suggests content to incorporate into the presentation by displaying it in the left pane as search results. The search results include drone images tagged with a **Creative Commons license** at online sources as shown in **Figure 8**. A Creative Commons license is a public copyright license that allows the free distribution of an otherwise copyrighted work. In addition, you can specify the source of the media. For example, you can add your own Facebook or OneNote pictures and videos in Sway without leaving the app.

On the Job Now

If you have a Microsoft Word document containing an outline of your business content, drag the outline into Sway to create a card for each topic.

Figure 8: Images in Sway search results

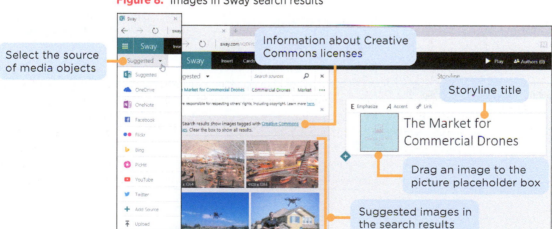

Select the source of media objects

Information about Creative Commons licenses

Storyline title

The Market for Commercial Drones

Drag an image to the picture placeholder box

Suggested images in the search results

Designing a Sway

Sway professionally designs your Storyline content by resizing background images and fonts to fit your display, and by floating text, animating media, embedding video, and removing images as a page scrolls out of view. Sway also evaluates the images in your Storyline and suggests a color palette based on colors that appear in your photos. Use the Design button to display tools including color palettes, font choices, **animation emphasis effects**, and style templates to provide a personality for a Sway presentation. Instead of creating your own design, you can click the Remix button, which randomly selects unique designs for your Sway site.

Publishing a Sway

Use the Play button to display your finished Sway presentation as a website. The Address bar includes a unique web address where others can view your Sway site. As the author, you can edit a published Sway site by clicking the Edit button (pencil icon) on the Sway toolbar.

Sharing a Sway

When you are ready to share your Sway website, you have several options as shown in **Figure 9**. Use the Share slider button to share the Sway site publically or keep it private. If you add the Sway site to the Microsoft **Docs.com** public gallery, anyone worldwide can use Bing, Google, or other search engines to find, view, and share your Sway site. You can also share your Sway site using Facebook, Twitter, Google+, Yammer, and other social media sites. Link your presentation to any webpage or email the link to your audience. Sway can also generate a code for embedding the link within another webpage.

Figure 9: Sharing a Sway site

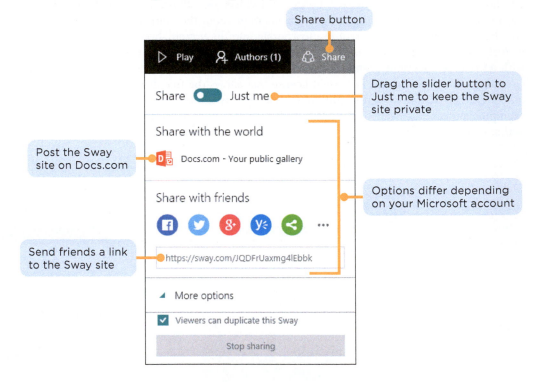

Try This Now

Learn to use Sway!
Links to companion **Sways**, featuring **videos** with hands-on instructions, are located on www.cengagebrain.com.

1: Creating a Sway Resume

Sway is a digital storytelling app. Create a Sway resume to share the skills, job experiences, and achievements you have that match the requirements of a future job interest. Perform the following tasks:

  a. Create a new presentation in Sway to use as a digital resume. Title the Sway Storyline with your full name and then select a background image.
  b. Create three separate sections titled **Academic Background, Work Experience**, and **Skills**, and insert text, a picture, and a paragraph or bulleted points in each section. Be sure to include your own picture.
  c. Add a fourth section that includes a video about your school that you find online.
  d. Customize the design of your presentation.
  e. Submit your assignment link in the format specified by your instructor.

2: Creating an Online Sway Newsletter

Newsletters are designed to capture the attention of their target audience. Using Sway, create a newsletter for a club, organization, or your favorite music group. Perform the following tasks:

  a. Create a new presentation in Sway to use as a digital newsletter for a club, organization, or your favorite music group. Provide a title for the Sway Storyline and select an appropriate background image.
  b. Select three separate sections with appropriate titles, such as Upcoming Events. In each section, insert text, a picture, and a paragraph or bulleted points.
  c. Add a fourth section that includes a video about your selected topic.
  d. Customize the design of your presentation.
  e. Submit your assignment link in the format specified by your instructor.

3: Creating and Sharing a Technology Presentation

To place a Sway presentation in the hands of your entire audience, you can share a link to the Sway presentation. Create a Sway presentation on a new technology and share it with your class. Perform the following tasks:

  a. Create a new presentation in Sway about a cutting-edge technology topic. Provide a title for the Sway Storyline and select a background image.
  b. Create four separate sections about your topic, and include text, a picture, and a paragraph in each section.
  c. Add a fifth section that includes a video about your topic.
  d. Customize the design of your presentation.
  e. Share the link to your Sway with your classmates and submit your assignment link in the format specified by your instructor.

Introduction to Office Mix

add-in | clip | slide recording | Slide Notes | screen recording | free-response quiz

Bottom Line

- Office Mix is a free PowerPoint add-in from Microsoft that adds features to PowerPoint.
- The Mix tab on the PowerPoint ribbon provides tools for creating screen recordings, videos, interactive quizzes, and live webpages.

To enliven business meetings and lectures, Microsoft adds a new dimension to presentations with a powerful toolset called Office Mix, a free add-in for PowerPoint. (An **add-in** is software that works with an installed app to extend its features.) Using Office Mix, you can record yourself on video, capture still and moving images on your desktop, and insert interactive elements such as quizzes and live webpages directly into PowerPoint slides. When you post the finished presentation to OneDrive, Office Mix provides a link you can share with friends and colleagues. Anyone with an Internet connection and a web browser can watch a published Office Mix presentation, such as the one in **Figure 10**, on a computer or mobile device.

Figure 10: Office Mix presentation

Adding Office Mix to PowerPoint

To get started, you create an Office Mix account at the website mix.office.com using an email address or a Facebook or Google account. Next, you download and install the Office Mix add-in (see **Figure 11**). Office Mix appears as a new tab named Mix on the PowerPoint ribbon in versions of Office 2013 and Office 2016 running on personal computers (PCs).

Learn to use Office Mix!

Links to companion **Sways**, featuring **videos** with hands-on instructions, are located on www.cengagebrain.com.

Figure 11: Getting started with Office Mix

Capturing Video Clips

A **clip** is a short segment of audio, such as music, or video. After finishing the content on a PowerPoint slide, you can use Office Mix to add a video clip to animate or illustrate the content. Office Mix creates video clips in two ways: by recording live action on a webcam and by capturing screen images and movements. If your computer has a webcam, you can record yourself and annotate the slide to create a **slide recording** as shown in **Figure 12**.

Figure 12: Making a slide recording

When you are making a slide recording, you can record your spoken narration at the same time. The **Slide Notes** feature works like a teleprompter to help you focus on your presentation content instead of memorizing your narration. Use the Inking tools to make annotations or add highlighting using different pen types and colors. After finishing a recording, edit the video in PowerPoint to trim the length or set playback options.

The second way to create a video is to capture on-screen images and actions with or without a voiceover. This method is ideal if you want to show how to use your favorite website or demonstrate an app such as OneNote. To share your screen with an audience, select the part of the screen you want to show in the video. Office Mix captures everything that happens in that area to create a **screen recording**, as shown in **Figure 13**. Office Mix inserts the screen recording as a video in the slide.

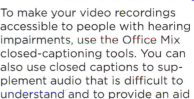
Figure 13: Making a screen recording

Inserting Quizzes, Live Webpages, and Apps

To enhance and assess audience understanding, make your slides interactive by adding quizzes, live webpages, and apps. Quizzes give immediate feedback to the user as shown in **Figure 14**. Office Mix supports several quiz formats, including a **free-response quiz** similar to a short answer quiz, and true/false, multiple-choice, and multiple-response formats.

Figure 14: Creating an interactive quiz

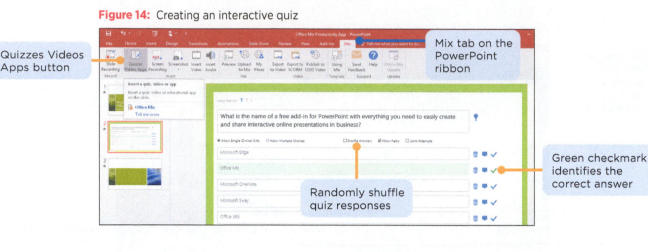

Quizzes Videos Apps button

Mix tab on the PowerPoint ribbon

Randomly shuffle quiz responses

Green checkmark identifies the correct answer

Sharing an Office Mix Presentation

When you complete your work with Office Mix, upload the presentation to your personal Office Mix dashboard as shown in **Figure 15**. Users of PCs, Macs, iOS devices, and Android devices can access and play Office Mix presentations. The Office Mix dashboard displays built-in analytics that include the quiz results and how much time viewers spent on each slide. You can play completed Office Mix presentations online or download them as movies.

Figure 15: Sharing an Office Mix presentation

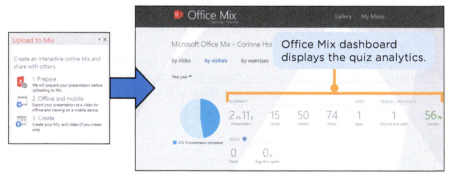

Office Mix dashboard displays the quiz analytics.

Try This Now

Learn to use Office Mix!
Links to companion **Sways**, featuring **videos** with hands-on instructions, are located on www.cengagebrain.com.

1: Creating an Office Mix Tutorial for OneNote

Note: This activity requires a microphone on your computer.

Office Mix makes it easy to record screens and their contents. Create PowerPoint slides with an Office Mix screen recording to show OneNote 2016 features. Perform the following tasks:

a. Create a PowerPoint presentation with the Ion Boardroom template. Create an opening slide with the title **My Favorite OneNote Features** and enter your name in the subtitle.
b. Create three additional slides, each titled with a new feature of OneNote. Open OneNote and use the Mix tab in PowerPoint to capture three separate screen recordings that teach your favorite features.
c. Add a fifth slide that quizzes the user with a multiple-choice question about OneNote and includes four responses. Be sure to insert a checkmark indicating the correct response.
d. Upload the completed presentation to your Office Mix dashboard and share the link with your instructor.
e. Submit your assignment link in the format specified by your instructor.

2: Teaching Augmented Reality with Office Mix

Note: This activity requires a webcam or built-in video camera on your computer.

A local elementary school has asked you to teach augmented reality to its students using Office Mix. Perform the following tasks:

a. Research augmented reality using your favorite online search tools.
b. Create a PowerPoint presentation with the Frame template. Create an opening slide with the title **Augmented Reality** and enter your name in the subtitle.
c. Create a slide with four bullets summarizing your research of augmented reality. Create a 20-second slide recording of yourself providing a quick overview of augmented reality.
d. Create another slide with a 30-second screen recording of a video about augmented reality from a site such as YouTube or another video-sharing site.
e. Add a final slide that quizzes the user with a true/false question about augmented reality. Be sure to insert a checkmark indicating the correct response.
f. Upload the completed presentation to your Office Mix dashboard and share the link with your instructor.
g. Submit your assignment link in the format specified by your instructor.

3: Marketing a Travel Destination with Office Mix

Note: This activity requires a webcam or built-in video camera on your computer.

To convince your audience to travel to a particular city, create a slide presentation marketing any city in the world using a slide recording, screen recording, and a quiz. Perform the following tasks:

a. Create a PowerPoint presentation with any template. Create an opening slide with the title of the city you are marketing as a travel destination and your name in the subtitle.
b. Create a slide with four bullets about the featured city. Create a 30-second slide recording of yourself explaining why this city is the perfect vacation destination.
c. Create another slide with a 20-second screen recording of a travel video about the city from a site such as YouTube or another video-sharing site.
d. Add a final slide that quizzes the user with a multiple-choice question about the featured city with five responses. Be sure to include a checkmark indicating the correct response.
e. Upload the completed presentation to your Office Mix dashboard and share your link with your instructor.
f. Submit your assignment link in the format specified by your instructor.

Introduction to Microsoft Edge

Reading view | Hub | Cortana | Web Note | Inking | sandbox

Bottom Line
- Microsoft Edge is the name of the new web browser built into Windows 10.
- Microsoft Edge allows you to search the web faster, take web notes, read webpages without distractions, and get instant assistance from Cortana.

Microsoft Edge is the default web browser developed for the Windows 10 operating system as a replacement for Internet Explorer. Unlike its predecessor, Edge lets you write on webpages, read webpages without advertisements and other distractions, and search for information using a virtual personal assistant. The Edge interface is clean and basic, as shown in **Figure 16**, meaning you can pay more attention to the webpage content.

Figure 16: Microsoft Edge tools

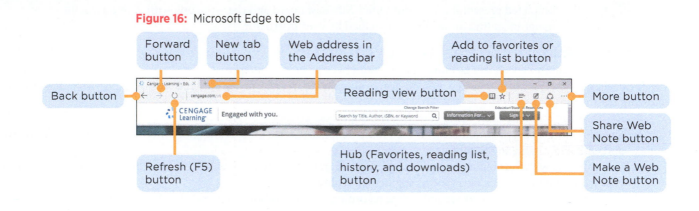

Learn to use Edge!
Links to companion **Sways**, featuring **videos** with hands-on instructions, are located on www.cengagebrain.com.

On the Job Now

Businesses started adopting Internet Explorer more than 20 years ago simply to view webpages. Today, Microsoft Edge has a different purpose: to promote interaction with the web and share its contents with colleagues.

Browsing the Web with Microsoft Edge

One of the fastest browsers available, Edge allows you to type search text directly in the Address bar. As you view the resulting webpage, you can switch to **Reading view**, which is available for most news and research sites, to eliminate distracting advertisements. For example, if you are catching up on technology news online, the webpage might be difficult to read due to a busy layout cluttered with ads. Switch to Reading view to refresh the page and remove the original page formatting, ads, and menu sidebars to read the article distraction-free.

Consider the **Hub** in Microsoft Edge as providing one-stop access to all the things you collect on the web, such as your favorite websites, reading list, surfing history, and downloaded files.

Locating Information with Cortana

Cortana, the Windows 10 virtual assistant, plays an important role in Microsoft Edge. After you turn on Cortana, it appears as an animated circle in the Address bar when you might need assistance, as shown in the restaurant website in **Figure 17**. When you click the Cortana icon, a pane slides in from the right of the browser window to display detailed information about the restaurant, including maps and reviews. Cortana can also assist you in defining words, finding the weather, suggesting coupons for shopping, updating stock market information, and calculating math.

Figure 17: Cortana providing restaurant information

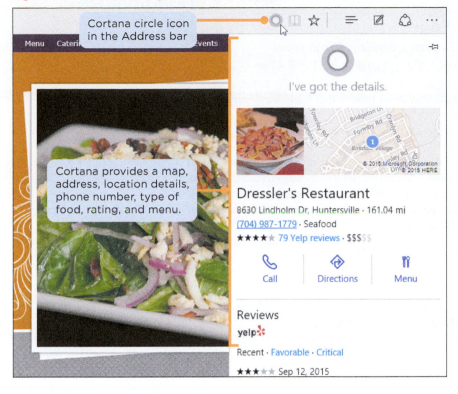

Cortana circle icon in the Address bar

Cortana provides a map, address, location details, phone number, type of food, rating, and menu.

I've got the details.

Dressler's Restaurant
8630 Lindholm Dr, Huntersville · 161.04 mi
(704) 987-1779 · Seafood
★★★★☆ 79 Yelp reviews · $$$$$

| Call | Directions | Menu |

Reviews
yelp

Recent · Favorable · Critical
★★★☆☆ Sep 12, 2015

Annotating Webpages

One of the most impressive Microsoft Edge features are the **Web Note** tools, which you use to write on a webpage or to highlight text. When you click the Make a Web Note button, an **Inking** toolbar appears, as shown in **Figure 18**, that provides writing and drawing tools. These tools include an eraser, a pen, and a highlighter with different colors. You can also insert a typed note and copy a screen image (called a screen clipping). You can draw with a pointing device, fingertip, or stylus using different pen colors. Whether you add notes to a recipe, annotate sources for a research paper, or select a product while shopping online, the Web Note tools can enhance your productivity. After you complete your notes, click the Save button to save the annotations to OneNote, your Favorites list, or your Reading list. You can share the inked page with others using the Share Web Note button.

On the Job Now

To enhance security, Microsoft Edge runs in a partial sandbox, an arrangement that prevents attackers from gaining control of your computer. Browsing within the **sandbox** protects computer resources and information from hackers.

Figure 18: Web Note tools in Microsoft Edge

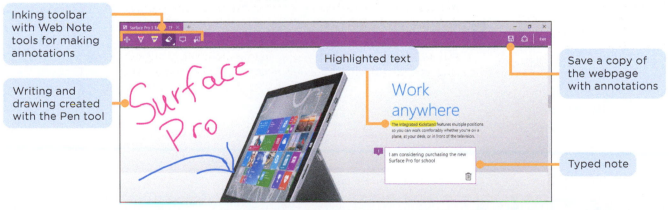

Inking toolbar with Web Note tools for making annotations

Writing and drawing created with the Pen tool

Highlighted text

Save a copy of the webpage with annotations

Work anywhere

The integrated Kickstand features multiple positions so you can work comfortably whether you're on a plane, at your desk, or in front of the television.

I am considering purchasing the new Surface Pro for school

Typed note

Try This Now

Learn to use Edge!
Links to companion **Sways**, featuring **videos** with hands-on instructions, are located on www.cengagebrain.com.

1: Using Cortana in Microsoft Edge

Note: This activity requires using Microsoft Edge on a Windows 10 computer.

Cortana can assist you in finding information on a webpage in Microsoft Edge. Perform the following tasks:

a. Create a Word document using the Word Screen Clipping tool to capture the following screenshots.

- Screenshot A—Using Microsoft Edge, open a webpage with a technology news article. Right-click a term in the article and ask Cortana to define it.
- Screenshot B—Using Microsoft Edge, open the website of a fancy restaurant in a city near you. Make sure the Cortana circle icon is displayed in the Address bar. (If it's not displayed, find a different restaurant website.) Click the Cortana circle icon to display a pane with information about the restaurant.
- Screenshot C—Using Microsoft Edge, type **10 USD to Euros** in the Address bar without pressing the Enter key. Cortana converts the U.S. dollars to Euros.
- Screenshot D—Using Microsoft Edge, type **Apple stock** in the Address bar without pressing the Enter key. Cortana displays the current stock quote.

b. Submit your assignment in the format specified by your instructor.

2: Viewing Online News with Reading View

Note: This activity requires using Microsoft Edge on a Windows 10 computer.

Reading view in Microsoft Edge can make a webpage less cluttered with ads and other distractions. Perform the following tasks:

a. Create a Word document using the Word Screen Clipping tool to capture the following screenshots.

- Screenshot A—Using Microsoft Edge, open the website **mashable.com**. Open a technology article. Click the Reading view button to display an ad-free page that uses only basic text formatting.
- Screenshot B—Using Microsoft Edge, open the website **bbc.com**. Open any news article. Click the Reading view button to display an ad-free page that uses only basic text formatting.
- Screenshot C—Make three types of annotations (Pen, Highlighter, and Add a typed note) on the BBC article page displayed in Reading view.

b. Submit your assignment in the format specified by your instructor.

3: Inking with Microsoft Edge

Note: This activity requires using Microsoft Edge on a Windows 10 computer.

Microsoft Edge provides many annotation options to record your ideas. Perform the following tasks:

a. Open the website **wolframalpha.com** in the Microsoft Edge browser. Wolfram Alpha is a well-respected academic search engine. Type **US$100 1965 dollars in 2015** in the Wolfram Alpha search text box and press the Enter key.

b. Click the Make a Web Note button to display the Web Note tools. Using the Pen tool, draw a circle around the result on the webpage. Save the page to OneNote.

c. In the Wolfram Alpha search text box, type the name of the city closest to where you live and press the Enter key. Using the Highlighter tool, highlight at least three interesting results. Add a note and then type a sentence about what you learned about this city. Save the page to OneNote. Share your OneNote notebook with your instructor.

d. Submit your assignment link in the format specified by your instructor.

Office 2016 and Windows 10: Essential Concepts and Skills

Objectives

You will have mastered the material in this module when you can:

- Use a touch screen
- Perform basic mouse operations
- Start Windows and sign in to an account
- Identify the objects in the Windows 10 desktop
- Identify the apps in and versions of Microsoft Office 2016
- Run an app

- Identify the components of the Microsoft Office ribbon
- Create folders
- Save files
- Change screen resolution
- Perform basic tasks in Microsoft Office apps
- Manage files
- Use Microsoft Office Help and Windows Help

This introductory module covers features and functions common to Office 2016 apps, as well as the basics of Windows 10.

Roadmap

In this module, you will learn how to perform basic tasks in Windows and the Office apps. The following roadmap identifies general activities you will perform as you progress through this module:

1. SIGN IN to an account
2. USE WINDOWS
3. USE Office APPS
4. FILE and Folder MANAGEMENT
5. SWITCH between APPS
6. SAVE and Manage FILES

7. **CHANGE SCREEN RESOLUTION**

8. **EXIT** Office **APPS**

9. **USE** Office and Windows **HELP**

At the beginning of the step instructions throughout each module, you will see an abbreviated form of this roadmap. The abbreviated roadmap uses colors to indicate module progress: gray means the module is beyond that activity, blue means the task being shown is covered in that activity, and black means that activity is yet to be covered. For example, the following abbreviated roadmap indicates the module would be showing a task in the Use Apps activity.

| 1 SIGN IN | 2 USE WINDOWS | **3 USE APPS** | 4 FILE MANAGEMENT | 5 SWITCH APPS |
| 6 SAVE FILES | 7 CHANGE SCREEN RESOLUTION | 8 EXIT APPS | 9 USE HELP |

Use the abbreviated roadmap as a progress guide while you read or step through the instructions in this module.

Introduction to the Windows 10 Operating System

Windows 10 is the newest version of Microsoft Windows, which is a popular and widely used operating system (Figure 1). An **operating system (OS)** is a set of programs that coordinate all the activities among computer or mobile device hardware.

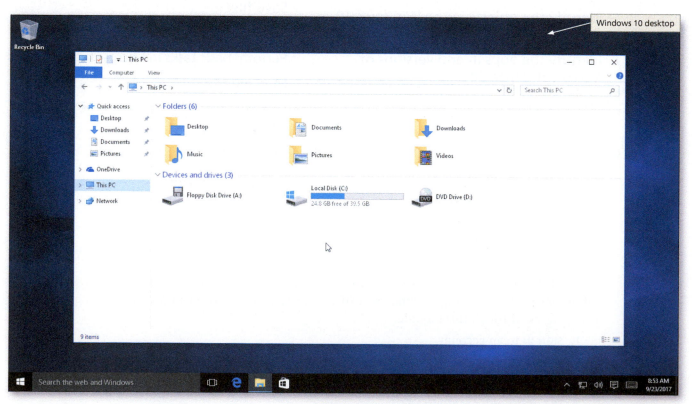

Figure 1

The Windows operating system simplifies the process of working with documents and apps by organizing the manner in which you interact with the computer. Windows is used to run apps. An application, or **app**, consists of programs designed to make users more productive and/or assist them with personal tasks, such as word processing or browsing the web.

Using a Touch Screen and a Mouse

Windows users who have computers or devices with touch screen capability can interact with the screen using gestures. A **gesture** is a motion you make on a touch screen with the tip of one or more fingers or your hand. Touch screens are convenient because they do not require a separate device for input. Table 1 presents common ways to interact with a touch screen.

If you are using your finger on a touch screen and are having difficulty completing the steps in this module, consider using a stylus. Many people find it easier to be precise with a stylus than with a finger. In addition, with a stylus you see the pointer. If you still are having trouble completing the steps with a stylus, try using a mouse.

CONSIDER THIS

Will your screen look different if you are using a touch screen?
The Windows and Microsoft Office interface varies slightly if you are using a touch screen. For this reason, you might notice that your screen looks slightly different from the screens in the module.

Table 1 Touch Screen Gestures

Motion	Description	Common Uses	Equivalent Mouse Operation
Tap	Quickly touch and release one finger one time.	Activate a link (built-in connection). Press a button. Run a program or an app.	Click
Double-tap	Quickly touch and release one finger two times.	Run a program or an app. Zoom in (show a smaller area on the screen, so that contents appear larger) at the location of the double-tap.	Double-click
Press and hold	Press and hold one finger to cause an action to occur, or until an action occurs.	Display a shortcut menu (immediate access to allowable actions). Activate a mode enabling you to move an item with one finger to a new location.	Right-click
Drag or slide	Press and hold one finger on an object and then move the finger to the new location.	Move an item around the screen Scroll.	Drag
Swipe	Press and hold one finger and then move the finger horizontally or vertically on the screen.	Select an object. Swipe from edge to display a bar such as the Action Center, Apps bar, and Navigation bar.	Drag
Stretch	Move two fingers apart.	Zoom in (show a smaller area on the screen, so that contents appear larger).	None
Pinch	Move two fingers together.	Zoom out (show a larger area on the screen, so that contents appear smaller).	None

Windows users who do not have touch screen capabilities typically work with a mouse that has at least two buttons. For a right-handed user, the left button usually is the primary mouse button, and the right mouse button is the secondary mouse button. Left-handed people, however, can reverse the function of these buttons.

Table 2 explains how to perform a variety of mouse operations. Some apps also use keys in combination with the mouse to perform certain actions. For example, when you hold down the CTRL key while rolling the mouse wheel, text on the screen may become larger or smaller based on the direction you roll the wheel. The function of the mouse buttons and the wheel varies depending on the app.

Table 2 Mouse Operations

Operation	Mouse Action	Example	Equivalent Touch Gesture
Point	Move the mouse until the pointer on the desktop is positioned on the item of choice.	Position the pointer on the screen.	None
Click	Press and release the primary mouse button, which usually is the left mouse button.	Select or deselect items on the screen or run an app or app feature.	Tap
Right-click	Press and release the secondary mouse button, which usually is the right mouse button.	Display a shortcut menu.	Press and hold
Double-click	Quickly press and release the primary mouse button twice without moving the mouse.	Run an app or app feature.	Double-tap
Triple-click	Quickly press and release the primary mouse button three times without moving the mouse.	Select a paragraph.	Triple-tap
Drag	Point to an item, hold down the primary mouse button, move the item to the desired location on the screen, and then release the mouse button.	Move an object from one location to another or draw pictures.	Drag or slide
Right-drag	Point to an item, hold down the right mouse button, move the item to the desired location on the screen, and then release the right mouse button.	Display a shortcut menu after moving an object from one location to another.	Press and hold, then drag
Rotate wheel	Roll the wheel forward or backward.	Scroll vertically (up and down).	Swipe
Free-spin wheel	Whirl the wheel forward or backward so that it spins freely on its own.	Scroll through many pages in seconds.	Swipe
Press wheel	Press the wheel button while moving the mouse.	Scroll continuously.	None
Tilt wheel	Press the wheel toward the right or left.	Scroll horizontally (left and right).	None
Press thumb button	Press the button on the side of the mouse with your thumb.	Move forward or backward through webpages and/or control media, games, etc.	None

Scrolling

A **scroll bar** is a horizontal or vertical bar that appears when the contents of an area may not be visible completely on the screen (Figure 2). A scroll bar contains **scroll arrows** and a **scroll box** that enable you to view areas that currently cannot be seen on the screen. Clicking the up and down scroll arrows moves the screen content up or down one line. You also can click above or below the scroll box to move up or down a section, or drag the scroll box up or down to move to a specific location.

Figure 2

Keyboard Shortcuts

In many cases, you can use the keyboard instead of the mouse to accomplish a task. To perform tasks using the keyboard, you press one or more keyboard keys, sometimes identified as a **keyboard shortcut**. Some keyboard shortcuts consist of a single key, such as the F1 key. For example, to obtain help in many apps, you can press the F1 key. Other keyboard shortcuts consist of multiple keys, in which case a plus sign separates the key names, such as CTRL+ESC. This notation means to press and hold down the first key listed, press one or more additional keys, and then release all keys. For example, to display the Start menu, press CTRL+ESC, that is, hold down the CTRL key, press the ESC key, and then release both keys.

Starting Windows

It is not unusual for multiple people to use the same computer in a work, educational, recreational, or home setting. Windows enables each user to establish a **user account**, which identifies to Windows the resources, such as apps and storage locations, a user can access when working with the computer.

Each user account has a user name and may have a password and an icon, as well. A **user name** is a unique combination of letters or numbers that identifies a specific user to Windows. A **password** is a private combination of letters, numbers, and special characters associated with the user name that allows access to a user's account resources. An icon is a small image that represents an object; thus, a **user icon** is a picture associated with a user name.

When you turn on a computer, Windows starts and displays a **lock screen** consisting of the time and date (Figure 3). To unlock the screen, swipe up or click the lock screen. Depending on your computer's settings, Windows might display a sign-in screen that shows the user names and user icons for users who have accounts on the computer. This **sign-in screen** enables you to sign in to your user account and makes the computer available for use. Clicking the user icon begins the process of signing in, also called logging on, to your user account.

BTW

Minimize Wrist Injury
Computer users frequently switch between the keyboard and the mouse during an Access session; such switching strains the wrist. To help prevent wrist injury, minimize switching. For instance, if your fingers already are on the keyboard, use keyboard keys to scroll. If your hand already is on the mouse, use the mouse to scroll. If your hand is on the touch screen, use touch gestures to scroll.

Figure 3

At the bottom of the sign-in screen (Figure 4) is the 'Connect to Internet' button, 'Ease of access' button, and a Shut down button. Clicking the 'Connect to Internet' button displays a list of each network connection and its status. You also can connect to or disconnect from a network. Clicking the 'Ease of access' button displays the Ease of access menu, which provides tools to optimize a computer to accommodate the needs of the mobility, hearing, and vision-impaired users. Clicking the Shut down button displays a menu containing commands related to putting the computer or mobile device in a low-power state, shutting it down, and restarting the computer or mobile device. The commands available on your computer or mobile device may differ.

- The Sleep command saves your work, turns off the computer fans and hard drive, and places the computer in a lower-power state. To wake the computer from sleep mode, press the power button or lift a laptop's cover, and sign in to your account.
- The Shut down command exits running apps, shuts down Windows, and then turns off the computer.
- The Restart command exits running apps, shuts down Windows, and then restarts Windows.

To Sign In to an Account

1 SIGN IN | 2 USE WINDOWS | 3 USE APPS | 4 FILE MANAGEMENT | 5 SWITCH APPS
6 SAVE FILES | 7 CHANGE SCREEN RESOLUTION | 8 EXIT APPS | 9 USE HELP

The following steps, which use SCSeries as the user name, sign in to an account based on a typical Windows installation. **Why?** *After starting Windows, you might be required to sign in to an account to access the computer or mobile device's resources.* You may need to ask your instructor how to sign in to your account.

1
- Click the lock screen (shown in Figure 3) to display a sign-in screen.
- Click the user icon (for SCSeries, in this case) on the sign-in screen, which depending on settings, either will display a second sign-in screen that contains a Password text box (Figure 4) or will display the Windows desktop (Figure 5).

Q&A Why do I not see a user icon?
Your computer may require you to type a user name instead of clicking an icon.

What is a text box?
A text box is a rectangular box in which you type text.

Why does my screen not show a Password text box?
Your account does not require a password.

- If Windows displays a sign-in screen with a Password text box, type your password in the text box.

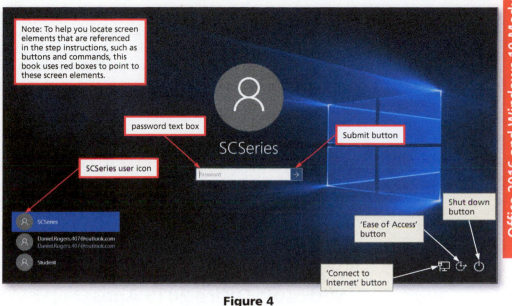

Figure 4

2

- Click the Submit button (shown in Figure 4) to sign in to your account and display the Windows desktop (Figure 5).

Q&A Why does my desktop look different from the one in Figure 5?
The Windows desktop is customizable, and your school or employer may have modified the desktop to meet its needs. Also, your screen resolution, which affects the size of the elements on the screen, may differ from the screen resolution used in this book. Later in this module, you learn how to change screen resolution.

How do I type if my tablet has no keyboard?
You can use your fingers to press keys on a keyboard that appears on the screen, called an on-screen keyboard, or you can purchase a separate physical keyboard that attaches to or wirelessly communicates with the tablet.

The Windows Desktop

The Windows 10 desktop (Figure 5) and the objects on the desktop emulate a work area in an office. Think of the Windows desktop as an electronic version of the top of your desk. You can perform tasks such as placing objects on the desktop, moving the objects around the desktop, and removing items from the desktop.

Figure 5

When you run a program or app in Windows 10, it appears on the desktop. Some icons also may be displayed on the desktop. For instance, the icon for the **Recycle Bin**, the location of files that have been deleted, appears on the desktop by default. A **file** is a named unit of storage. Files can contain text, images, audio, and video. You can customize your desktop so that icons representing programs and files you use often appear on your desktop.

Introduction to Microsoft Office 2016

Microsoft Office 2016 is the newest version of Microsoft Office, offering features that provide users with better functionality and easier ways to work with the various files they create. This version of office also is designed to work more optimally on mobile devices and online.

Microsoft Office 2016 Apps

Microsoft Office 2016 includes a wide variety of apps, such as Word, PowerPoint, Excel, Access, Outlook, Publisher, and OneNote:

- **Microsoft Word 2016**, or Word, is a full-featured word processing app that allows you to create professional-looking documents and revise them easily.
- **Microsoft PowerPoint 2016**, or PowerPoint, is a complete presentation app that enables you to produce professional-looking presentations and then deliver them to an audience.
- **Microsoft Excel 2016**, or Excel, is a powerful spreadsheet app that allows you to organize data, complete calculations, make decisions, graph data, develop professional-looking reports, publish organized data to the web, and access real-time data from websites.
- **Microsoft Access 2016**, or Access, is a database management system that enables you to create a database; add, change, and delete data in the database; ask questions concerning the data in the database; and create forms and reports using the data in the database.
- **Microsoft Outlook 2016**, or Outlook, is a communications and scheduling app that allows you to manage email accounts, calendars, contacts, and access to other Internet content.
- **Microsoft Publisher 2016**, or Publisher, is a desktop publishing app that helps you create professional-quality publications and marketing materials that can be shared easily.
- **Microsoft OneNote 2016**, or OneNote, is a note-taking app that allows you to store and share information in notebooks with other people.

Microsoft Office 2016 Suites

A **suite** is a collection of individual apps available together as a unit. Microsoft offers a variety of Office suites, including a stand-alone desktop app, Microsoft Office 365, and Microsoft Office Online. **Microsoft Office 365**, or Office 365, provides plans that allow organizations to use Office in a mobile setting while also being able to communicate and share files, depending upon the type of plan selected by the organization. **Microsoft Office Online** includes apps that allow you to edit and share files on the web using the familiar Office interface.

During the Office 365 installation, you select a plan, and depending on your plan, you receive different apps and services. Office Online apps do not require a local installation and can be accessed through OneDrive and your browser. **OneDrive** is a cloud storage service that provides storage and other services, such as Office Online, to computer users.

How do you sign up for a OneDrive account?

- Use your browser to navigate to onedrive.live.com.

- Create a Microsoft account by clicking the Sign up button and then entering your information to create the account.

- Sign in to OneDrive using your new account or use it in Office to save your files on OneDrive.

Apps in a suite, such as Microsoft Office, typically use a similar interface and share features. Once you are comfortable working with the elements and the interface and performing tasks in one app, the similarity can help you apply the knowledge and skills you have learned to another app(s) in the suite. For example, the process for saving a file in Word is the same in PowerPoint, Excel, and the other Office apps.

Running and Using An App

To use an app, you must instruct the operating system to run the app. Windows provides many different ways to run an app, one of which is presented in this section (other ways to run an app are presented throughout this module). After an app is running, you can use it to perform a variety of tasks. The following pages use Access to discuss some elements of the Office interface and to perform tasks.

Access

The term **database** describes a collection of data organized in a manner that allows access, retrieval, and use of that data. **Access** is a database management system. A **database management system** is software that allows you to use a computer to create a database; add, change, and delete data in the database; create queries that allow you to ask questions concerning the data in the database; and create forms and reports using the data in the database.

To Run Access Using the Start Menu

1 SIGN IN | 2 USE WINDOWS | 3 USE APPS | 4 FILE MANAGEMENT | 5 SWITCH APPS
6 SAVE FILES | 7 CHANGE SCREEN RESOLUTION | 8 EXIT APPS | 9 USE HELP

Across the bottom of the Windows 10 desktop is the taskbar. The taskbar contains the **Start button**, which you use to access apps, files, folders, and settings. A **folder** is a named location on a storage medium that usually contains related documents.

Clicking the Start button displays the **Start menu**. The Start menu allows you to access programs, folders, and files on the computer or mobile device and contains commands that allow you to start programs, store and search for documents, customize the computer or mobile device, and sign out of a user account or shut down the computer or mobile device. A **menu** is a list of related items, including folders, programs, and commands. Each **command** on a menu performs a specific action, such as saving a file or obtaining help. *Why? When you install an app, for example, tiles are added to the Start menu for the various Office apps included in the suite.*

The following steps, which assume Windows is running, use the Start menu to run Access based on a typical installation. You may need to ask your instructor how to run an Office app on your computer. Although the steps illustrate running the Access app, the steps to run any Office app are similar.

1
- Click the Start button on the Windows 10 taskbar to display the Start menu (Figure 6).

Figure 6

2
- Click All apps at the bottom of the left pane of the Start menu to display a list of apps installed on the computer or mobile device (Figure 7).

Figure 7

3
- If the app you want to run is located in a folder, click or scroll to and then click the folder in the All apps list to display a list of the folder's contents.
- Click, or scroll to and then click, the program name (Microsoft Access 2016, in this case) in the list to run the selected program (Figure 8).

Q&A
What happens when you run an app?

The app appears in a window. A **window** is a rectangular area that displays data and information. The top of a window has a **title bar**, which is a horizontal space that contains the window's name.

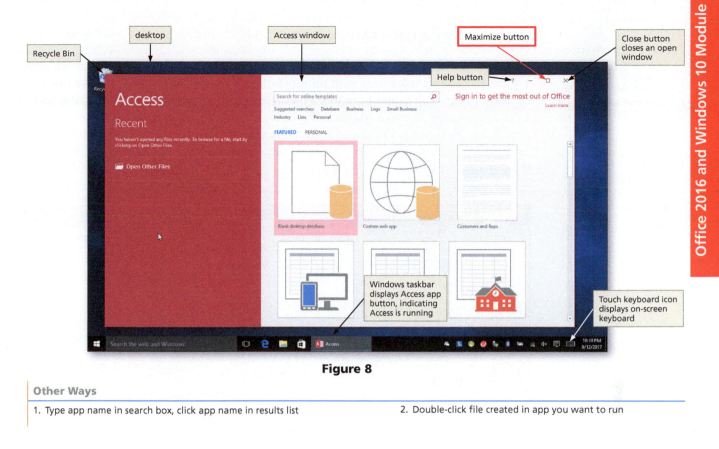

Figure 8

Other Ways

1. Type app name in search box, click app name in results list

2. Double-click file created in app you want to run

To Maximize a Window

1 SIGN IN | **2 USE WINDOWS** | 3 USE APPS | 4 FILE MANAGEMENT | 5 SWITCH APPS
6 SAVE FILES | 7 CHANGE SCREEN RESOLUTION | 8 EXIT APPS | 9 USE HELP

Sometimes content is not visible completely in a window. One method of displaying the entire contents of a window is to **maximize** it, or enlarge the window so that it fills the entire screen. The following step maximizes the Access window; however, any Office app's window can be maximized using this step. *Why? A maximized window provides the most space available for using the app.*

1

- If the app window is not maximized already, click the Maximize button (shown in Figure 8 to the left of the Close button on the window's title bar (the Access window title bar, in this case) to maximize the window (Figure 9).

Q&A

What happened to the Maximize button?
It changed to a Restore Down button, which you can use to return a window to its size and location before you maximized it.

How do I know whether a window is maximized?
A window is maximized if it fills the entire display area and the Restore Down button is displayed on the title bar.

Figure 9

Other Ways

1. Double-click title bar

2. Drag title bar to top of screen

BTW
Touch Keyboard
To display the on-screen touch keyboard, click the Touch Keyboard button on the Windows taskbar (shown in Figure 8). When finished using the touch keyboard, click the X button on the touch keyboard to close the keyboard.

Access Unique Elements

You work on objects such as tables, forms, and reports in the **Access work area**. Figure 10 shows a work area with multiple objects open. **Object tabs** for the open objects appear at the top of the work area. You select an open object by clicking its tab. In the figure, the Account Manager Form is the selected object. To the left of the work area is the Navigation Pane, which contains a list of all the objects in the database. You use this pane to open an object. You also can customize the way objects are displayed in the Navigation Pane.

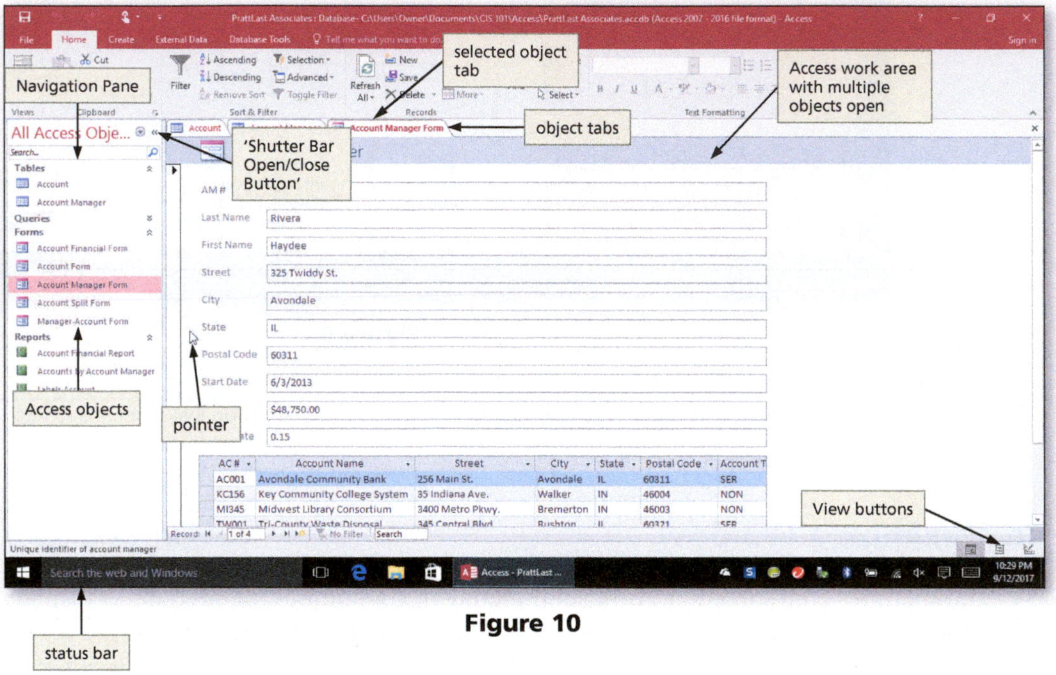

Figure 10

Because the Navigation Pane can take up space in the window, you might not have as much open space for working as you would with Word or Excel. You can use the 'Shutter Bar Open/Close Button' to minimize the Navigation Pane when you are not using it, which allows more space to work with tables, forms, reports, and other database elements.

Saving and Organizing Files

Before starting to work in Access, you must either create a new database or open an existing database. When you create a database, the computer places it on a storage medium such as a hard disk, solid state drive (SSD), USB flash drive, or optical disc. The storage medium can be permanent in your computer, can be portable where you remove it from your computer, or can be on a web server you access through a network or the Internet.

A database or other saved document is referred to as a file. A **file name** is the name assigned to a file when it is saved. When saving files, you should organize them so that you easily can find them later. Windows provides tools to help you organize files.

Organizing Files and Folders

You should organize and store databases and other files in folders to help you find the databases or other files quickly.

If you are taking an introductory computer class (CIS 101, for example), you may want to design a series of folders for the different subjects covered in the class. To accomplish this, you can arrange the folders in a hierarchy for the class, as shown in Figure 11.

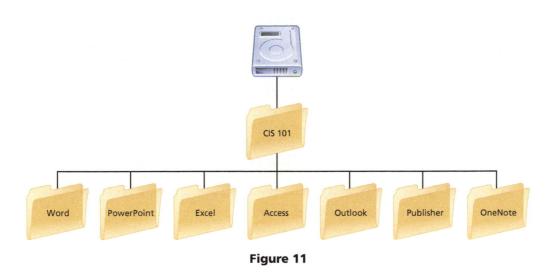

Figure 11

The hierarchy contains three levels. The first level contains the storage medium, such as a hard disk. The second level contains the class folder (CIS 101, in this case), and the third level contains seven folders, one each for a different Office app that will be covered in the class (Word, PowerPoint, Excel, Access, Outlook, Publisher, and OneNote).

When the hierarchy in Figure 11 is created, the storage medium is said to contain the CIS 101 folder, and the CIS 101 folder is said to contain the separate Office folders (i.e., Word, PowerPoint, Excel, etc.). In addition, this hierarchy easily can be expanded to include folders from other classes taken during additional semesters.

The vertical and horizontal lines in Figure 11 form a pathway that allows you to navigate to a drive or folder on a computer or network. A **path** consists of a drive letter (preceded by a drive name when necessary) and colon, to identify the storage device, and one or more folder names. A hard disk typically has a drive letter of C. Each drive or folder in the hierarchy has a corresponding path.

By default, Windows saves documents in the Documents library, music in the Music library, photos in the Pictures library, and videos in the Videos library. A **library** helps you manage multiple folders stored in various locations on a computer and devices. It does not store the folder contents; rather, it keeps track of their locations so that you can access the folders and their contents quickly. For example, you can save pictures from a digital camera in any folder on any storage location on a computer. Normally, this would make organizing the different folders difficult. If you add the folders to a library, however, you can access all the pictures from one location regardless of where they are stored.

The following pages illustrate the steps to organize the folders for this class and create a database in one of those folders:

1. Create the folder identifying your class.
2. Create the Access folder in the folder identifying your class.
3. Create the remaining folders in the folder identifying your class.
4. Create a database in the Access folder.

1 SIGN IN | 2 USE WINDOWS | 3 USE APPS | 4 FILE MANAGEMENT | 5 SWITCH APPS
6 SAVE FILES | 7 CHANGE SCREEN RESOLUTION | 8 EXIT APPS | 9 USE HELP

To Create a Folder

When you create a folder, such as the CIS 101 folder shown in Figure 11, you must name the folder. A folder name should describe the folder and its contents. A folder name can contain spaces and any uppercase or lowercase characters, except a backslash (\), slash (/), colon (:), asterisk (*), question mark (?), quotation marks ("), less than symbol (<), greater than symbol (>), or vertical bar (|). Folder names cannot be CON, AUX, COM1, COM2, COM3, COM4, LPT1, LPT2, LPT3, PRN, or NUL. The same rules for naming folders also apply to naming files.

The following steps create a class folder (CIS 101, in this case) in the Documents folder. *Why? When storing files, you should organize the files so that it will be easier to find them later.*

1

- Click the File Explorer app button on the taskbar to run the File Explorer.
- If necessary, double-click This PC in the navigation pane to expand the contents of your computer.
- Click the Documents folder in the navigation pane to display the contents of the Documents folder in the file list (Figure 12).

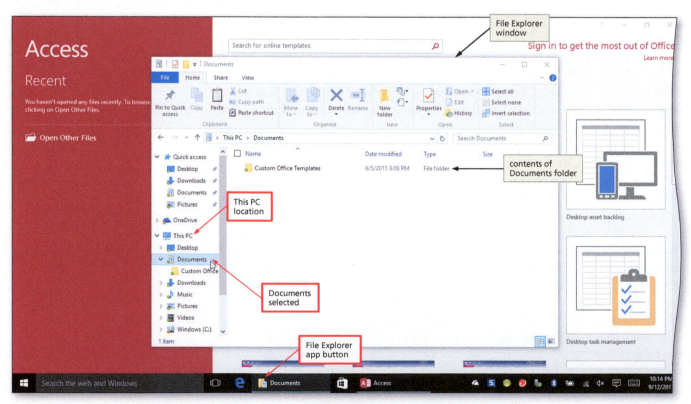

Figure 12

2

- Click the New folder button on the Quick Access Toolbar to create a new folder with the name, New folder, selected in a text box (Figure 13).

Q&A
Why is the folder icon displayed differently on my computer or mobile device?
Windows might be configured to display contents differently on your computer or mobile device.

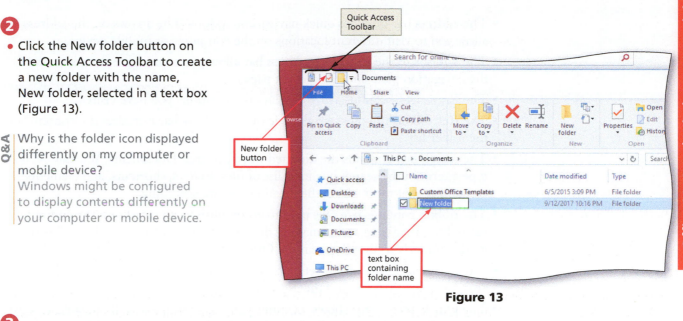

Figure 13

3

- Type **CIS 101** (or your class code) in the text box as the new folder name.

- If requested by your instructor, add your last name to the end of the folder name.

- Press the ENTER key to change the folder name from New folder to a folder name identifying your class (Figure 14).

Q&A
What happens when I press the ENTER key?
The class folder (CIS 101, in this case) is displayed in the file list, which contains the folder name, date modified, type, and size.

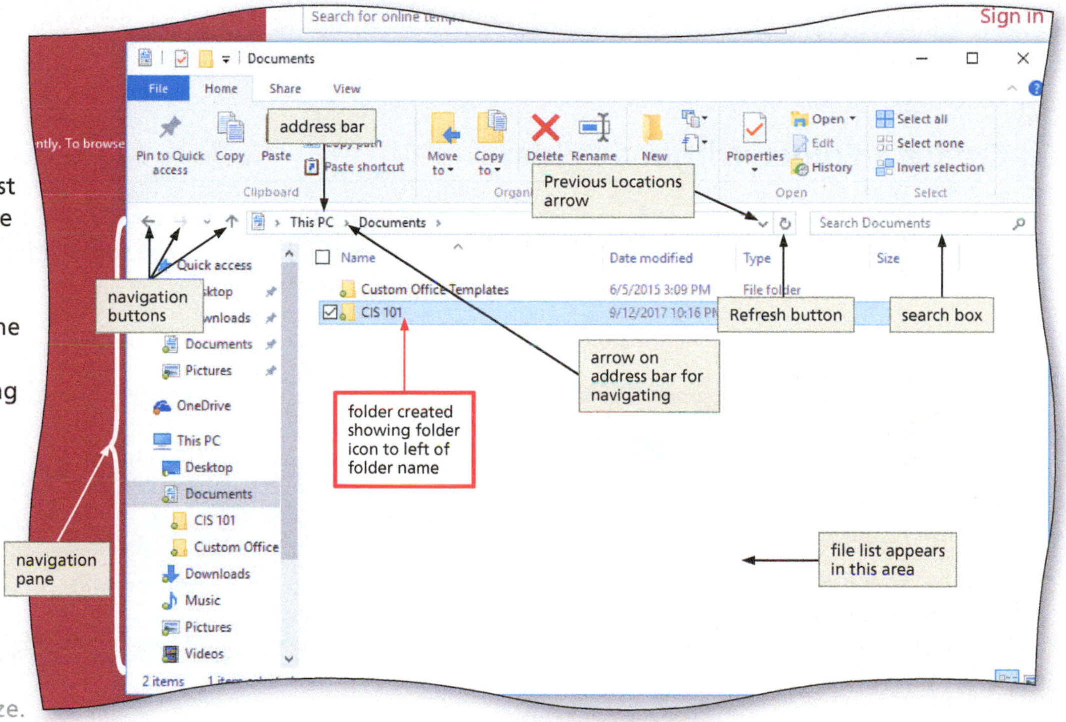

Figure 14

Other Ways

1. Press CTRL+SHIFT+N

2. Click the New folder button (Home tab | New group)

Folder Windows

The File Explorer window (shown in Figure 14) is called a folder window. Recall that a folder is a specific named location on a storage medium that contains related files. Most users rely on **folder windows** for finding, viewing, and managing information on their computers. Folder windows have common design elements, including the following (shown in Figure 14).

- The address bar provides quick navigation options. The arrows on the address bar allow you to visit different locations on the computer or mobile device.
- The buttons to the left of the address bar allow you to navigate the contents of the navigation pane and view recent pages.
- The Previous Locations arrow displays the locations you have visited.
- The Refresh button on the right side of the address bar refreshes the contents of the folder list.
- The search box contains the dimmed words, Search Documents. You can type a term in the search box for a list of files, folders, shortcuts, and elements containing that term within the location you are searching.
- The ribbon contains five tabs used to accomplish various tasks on the computer related to organizing and managing the contents of the open window. This ribbon works similarly to the ribbon in the Office apps.
- The navigation pane on the left contains the Quick access area, the OneDrive area, the This PC area, and the Network area.
- The Quick Access area shows locations you access frequently. By default, this list contains links only to your Desktop, Downloads, Documents, and Pictures.

To Create a Folder within a Folder

1 SIGN IN | 2 USE WINDOWS | 3 USE APPS | 4 FILE MANAGEMENT | 5 SWITCH APPS
6 SAVE FILES | 7 CHANGE SCREEN RESOLUTION | 8 EXIT APPS | 9 USE HELP

With the class folder created, you can create folders that will store the files you create using each Office app. The following step creates an Access folder in the CIS 101 folder (or the folder identifying your class). *Why? To be able to organize your files, you should create a folder structure.*

1

- Double-click the icon or folder name for the CIS 101 folder (or the folder identifying your class) in the file list to open the folder.

- Click the New folder button on the Quick Access Toolbar to create a new folder with the name, New folder, selected in a text box folder.

- Type **Access** in the text box as the new folder name.

- Press the ENTER key to rename the folder (Figure 15).

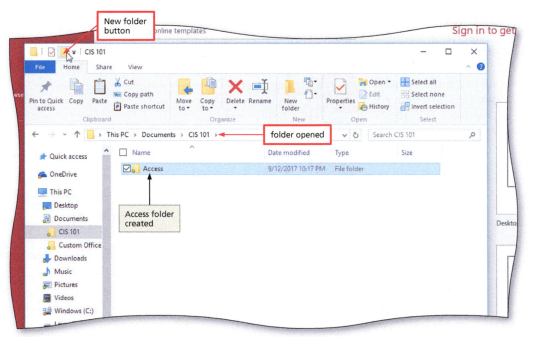

Figure 15

Other Ways

1. Press CTRL+SHIFT+N

2. Click New folder button (Home tab | New group)

To Create the Remaining Folders

The following steps create the remaining folders in the folder identifying your class (in this case, CIS 101).

1 Click the New folder button on the Quick Access Toolbar to create a new folder with the name, New folder, selected in a text box.

2 Type **Excel** in the text box as the new folder name.

3 Press the ENTER key to rename the folder.

4 Repeat Steps 1 through 3 to create each of the remaining folders, using OneNote, Outlook, PowerPoint, Publisher, and Word as the folder names (Figure 16).

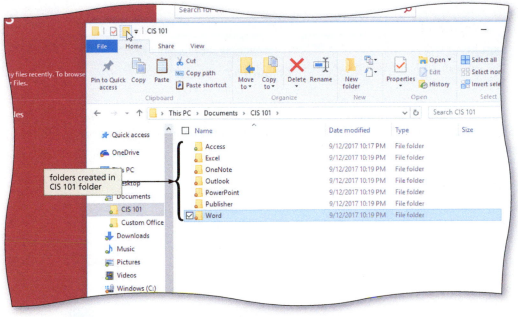

Figure 16

To Expand a Folder, Scroll through Folder Contents, and Collapse a Folder

1 SIGN IN | 2 USE WINDOWS | 3 USE APPS | **4 FILE MANAGEMENT** | **5 SWITCH APPS**
6 SAVE FILES | **7 CHANGE SCREEN RESOLUTION** | **8 EXIT APPS** | **9 USE HELP**

Folder windows display the hierarchy of items and the contents of drives and folders in the file list. You might want to expand a folder in the navigation pane to view its contents, slide or scroll through its contents, and collapse it when you are finished viewing its contents. *Why? When a folder is expanded, you can see all the folders it contains. By contrast, a collapsed folder hides the folders it contains.* The following steps expand, slide or scroll through, and then collapse the folder identifying your class (CIS 101, in this case).

1

- Double-click the Documents folder in the This PC area of the navigation pane, which expands the folder to display its contents and displays a black arrow to the left of the Documents folder icon (Figure 17).

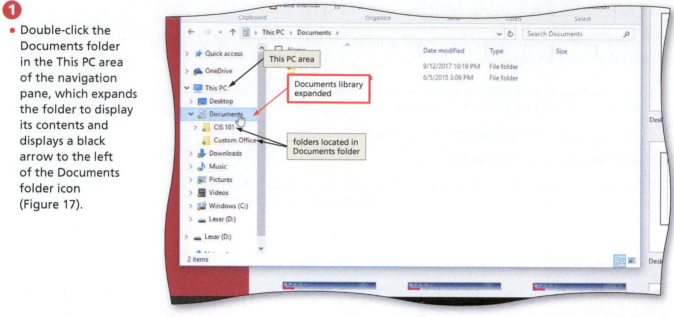

Figure 17

2

- Double-click the CIS 101 folder, which expands the folder to display its contents and displays a black arrow to the left of the folder icon (Figure 18).

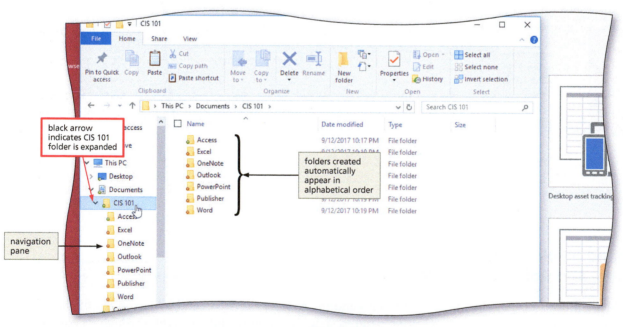

Figure 18

Experiment

- Drag the scroll bar down or click the down scroll arrow on the vertical scroll bar to display additional folders at the bottom of the navigation pane. Drag the scroll bar up or click the scroll bar above the scroll box to move the scroll box to the top of the navigation pane. Drag the scroll box down the scroll bar until the scroll box is halfway down the scroll bar.

3

- Double-click the folder identifying your class (CIS 101, in this case) to collapse the folder (Figure 19).

Q&A Why are some folders indented below others?
A folder contains the indented folders below it.

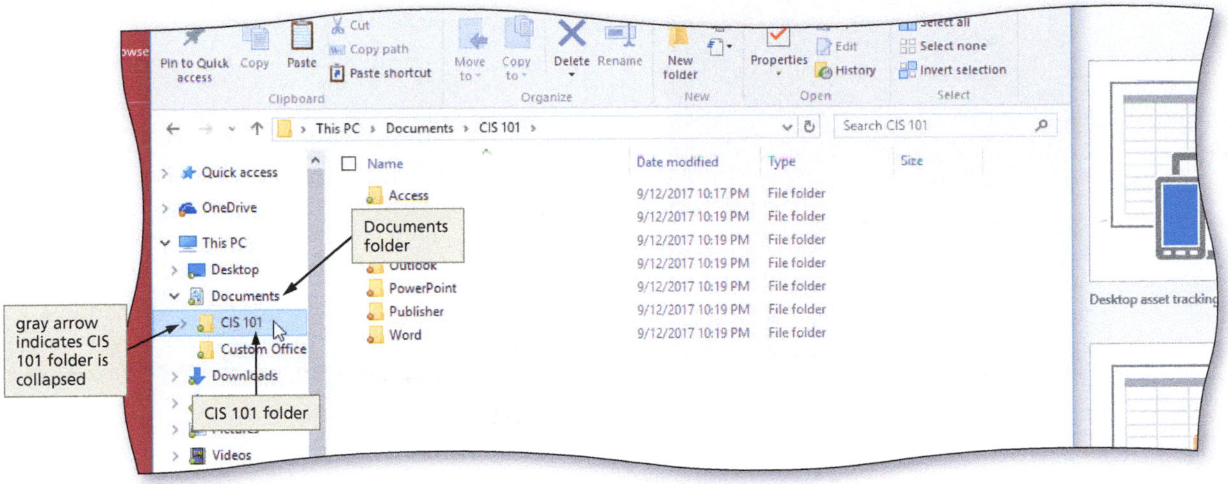

Figure 19

To Switch from One App to Another

1 SIGN IN | 2 USE WINDOWS | 3 USE APPS | 4 FILE MANAGEMENT | **5 SWITCH APPS**
6 SAVE FILES | 7 CHANGE SCREEN RESOLUTION | 8 EXIT APPS | 9 USE HELP

The next step is to create the Access database. Access, however, currently is not the active window. You can use the button on the taskbar and live preview to switch to Access and then use Access to create the database. **Why?** *By clicking the appropriate app button on the taskbar, you can switch to the open app you want to use.* The steps below switch to the Access window; however, the steps are the same for any active Office app currently displayed as a button on the taskbar.

1

- Point to the Access app button on the taskbar (Figure 20).

Q&A What if I am using a touch screen?
If you are using a touch screen and do not have a mouse, proceed to Step 2.

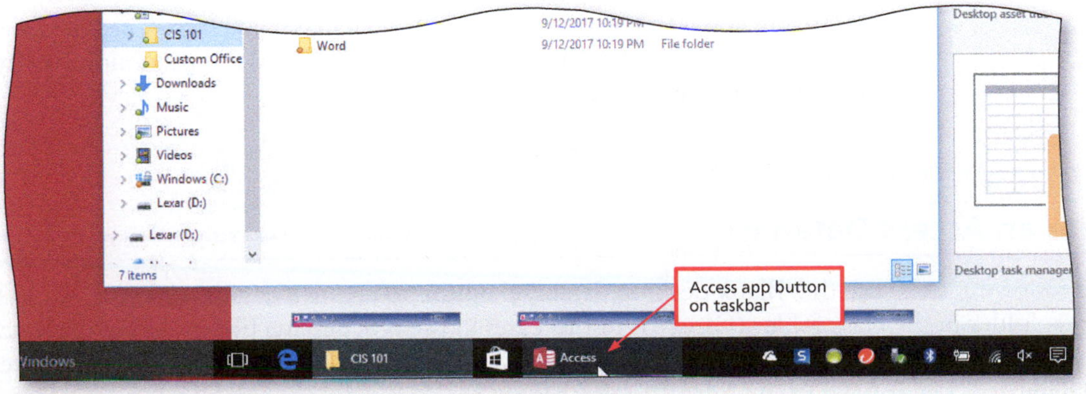

Figure 20

2

- Click the button to make the app associated with the app button the active window (Figure 21).

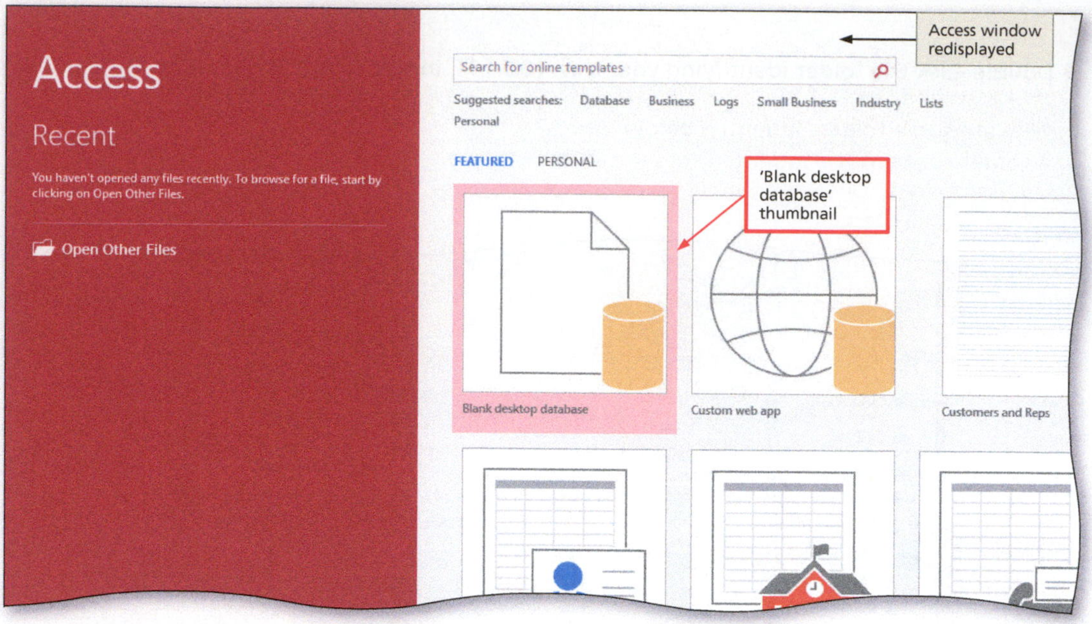

Figure 21

Other Ways

1. Press ALT+TAB until app you want to display is selected

Break Point: If you wish to take a break, this is a good place to do so. To resume at a later time, continue to follow the steps from this location forward.

Creating an Access Database

Unlike the other Office apps, Access saves a database when you first create it. When working in Access, you will add data to an Access database. As you add data to a database, Access automatically saves your changes rather than waiting until you manually save the database or exit Access. In other apps, you first enter data and then save it.

Because Access automatically saves the database as you add and change data, you do not always have to click the Save button on the Quick Access Toolbar. Instead, the Save button in Access is used for saving the objects (including tables, queries, forms, reports, and other database objects that you create) a database contains. You can use either the 'Blank desktop database' option or a template to create a new database. If you already know the organization of your database, you would use the 'Blank desktop database' option. If not, you can use a template. Templates can guide you by suggesting some commonly used database organizations.

To Create an Access Database

1 SIGN IN | 2 USE WINDOWS | 3 USE APPS | 4 FILE MANAGEMENT | 5 SWITCH APPS
6 SAVE FILES | 7 CHANGE SCREEN RESOLUTION | 8 EXIT APPS | 9 USE HELP

The following steps use the 'Blank desktop database' option to create a database named MZL Marketing in the Access folder in the class folder (CIS 101, in this case) in the Documents library. *Why? If you want to maintain data for a company, a database is perfect for the job.* With the folders for storing your files created, you can create the database. The following steps create a database in the Access folder contained in your class folder (CIS 101, in this case) using the file name, MZL Marketing.

1

- Click the 'Blank desktop database' thumbnail (shown in Figure 21) to select the database type (Figure 22).

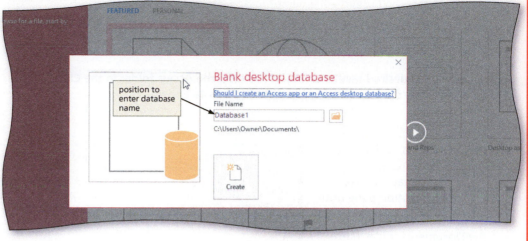

Figure 22

2

- Type **MZL Marketing** in the File Name text box to enter the new file name. Do not press the ENTER key after typing the file name because you do not want to create the database yet (Figure 23).

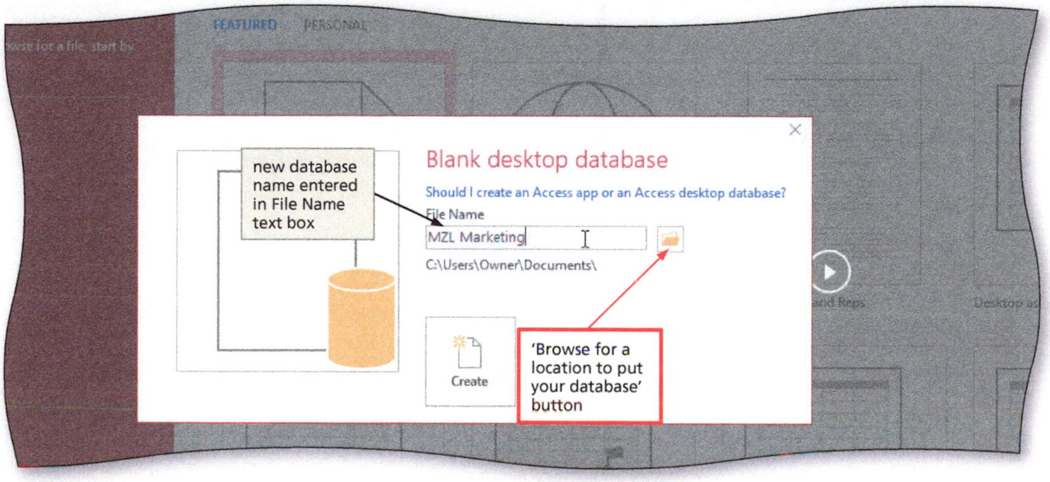

Figure 23

3

- Click the 'Browse for a location to put your database' button to display the File New Database dialog box (Figure 24).

Q&A

How do I close the Backstage view?

Click the Back button in the upper-left corner of the Backstage view to return to the app window.

Why does a file name already appear in the File name box?

You already entered the name of the Access database.

Why does the 'Save as type' box say Microsoft Access 2007–2016 Databases?

Microsoft Access database formats change with some new versions of Microsoft Access. The most recent format is the Microsoft Access 2007–2016 Databases format.

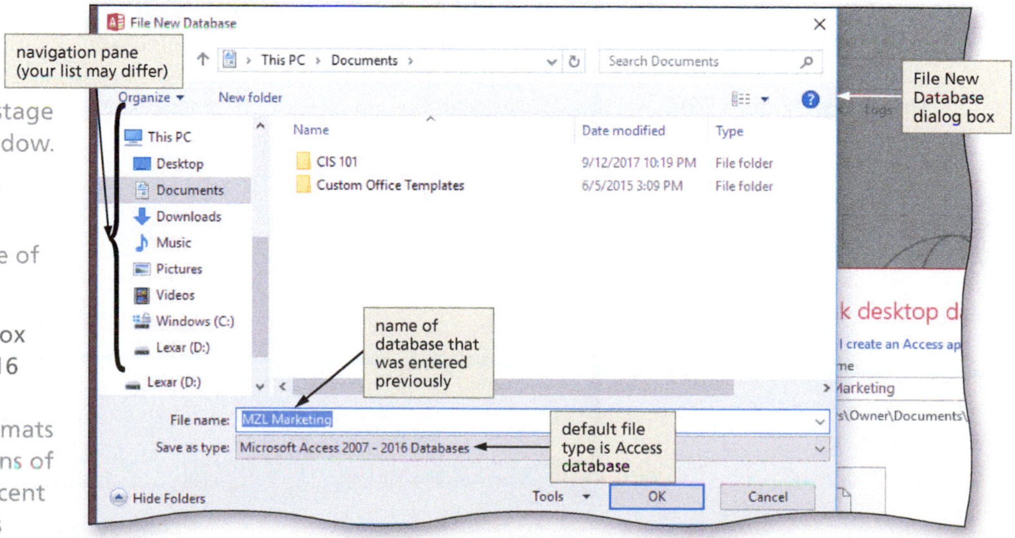

Figure 24

Q&A What characters can I use in a file name?

The only invalid characters are the backslash (\), slash (/), colon (:), asterisk (*), question mark (?), quotation mark ("), less than symbol (<), greater than symbol (>), and vertical bar (|).

4

• Navigate to the desired save location (in this case, the Access folder in the CIS 101 folder [or your class folder] in the Documents folder) by performing the tasks in Steps 4a and 4b.

4a

• If the Documents folder is not displayed in the navigation pane, scroll or drag the scroll bar in the navigation pane until Documents appears.

• If the Documents folder is not expanded in the navigation pane, double-click Documents to display its folders in the navigation pane.

• If your class folder (CIS 101, in this case) is not expanded, double-click the CIS 101 folder to select the folder and display its contents in the navigation pane (Figure 25).

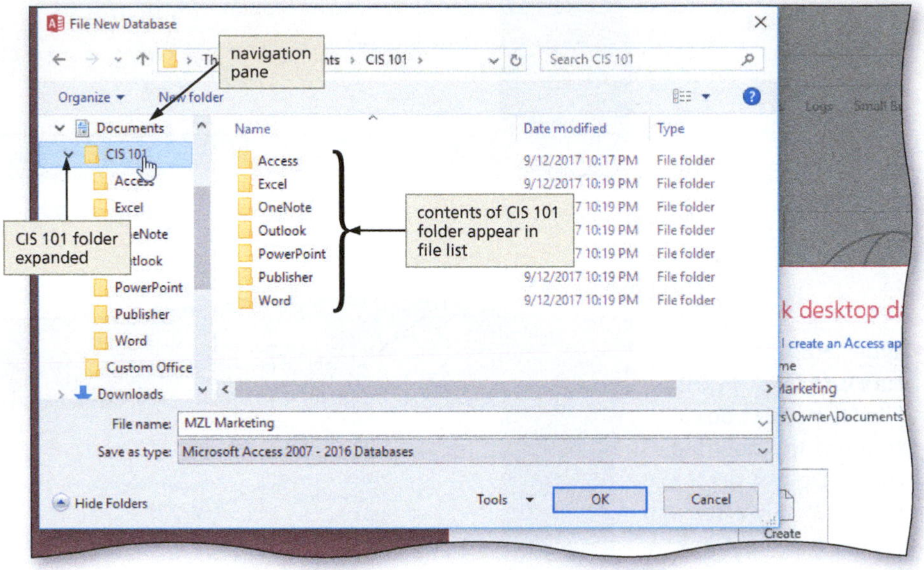

Figure 25

Q&A What if I wanted to save on OneDrive instead?

You would click OneDrive. Saving on OneDrive is discussed in a later section in this module.

What if I do not want to save in a folder?

Although storing files in folders is an effective technique for organizing files, some users prefer not to store files in folders. If you prefer not to save this file in a folder, select the storage device on which you wish to save the file and then proceed to Step 5.

4b

• Click the Access folder in the navigation pane to select it as the new save location and display its contents in the file list (Figure 26).

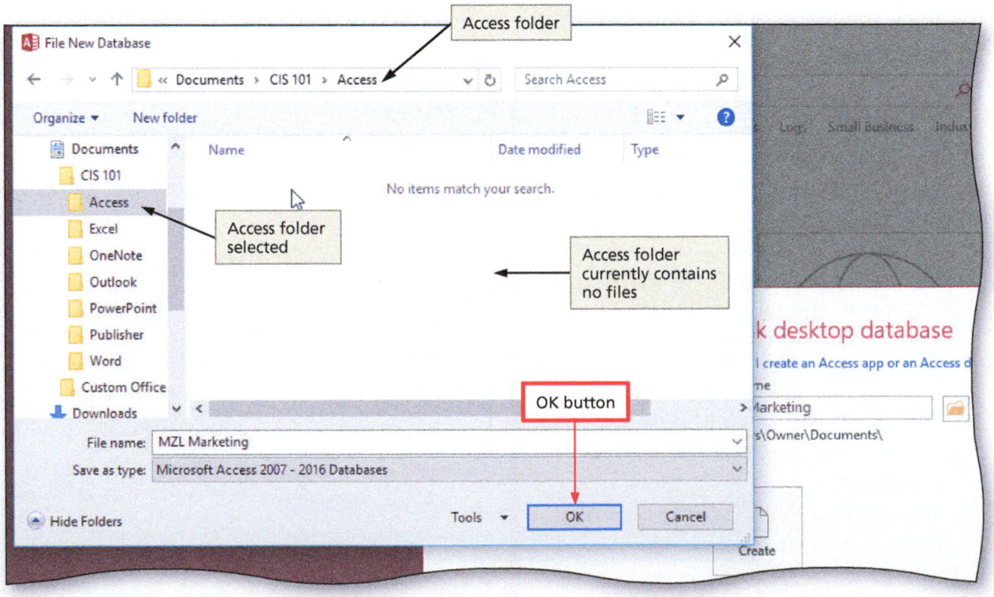

Figure 26

5

- Click the OK button (File New Database dialog box) to select the Access folder as the location for the database and close the dialog box.

- Click the Create button to create the database on the selected drive in the selected folder with the file name, MZL Marketing (Figure 27).

Q&A How do I know that the MZL Marketing database is created?
The file name of the database appears on the title bar.

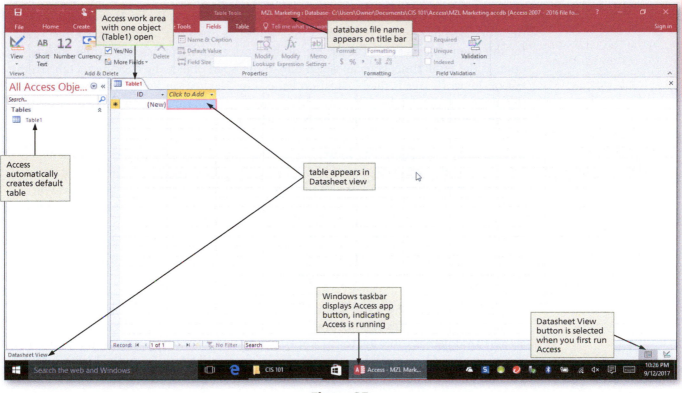

Figure 27

Navigating in Dialog Boxes

Navigating is the process of finding a location on a storage device. While creating the MZL Marketing database, for example, Steps 4a and 4b in the previous set of steps navigated to the Access folder located in the CIS 101 folder in the Documents folder. When performing certain functions in Windows apps, such as saving a file, opening a file, or inserting a picture in a database object, you most likely will have to navigate to the location where you want to save the file or to the folder containing the file you want to open or insert. Most dialog boxes in Windows apps requiring navigation follow a similar procedure; that is, the way you navigate to a folder in one dialog box, such as the Save As dialog box, is similar to how you might navigate in another dialog box, such as the Open dialog box. If you chose to navigate to a specific location in a dialog box, you would follow the instructions in Steps 4a and 4b.

The Access Window

The Access window consists of a variety of components to make your work more efficient. These include the Navigation Pane, Access work area, ribbon, shortcut menus, and Quick Access Toolbar. Some of these components are common to other Office apps; others are unique to Access.

Navigation Pane and Access Work Area

You work on objects such as tables, forms, and reports in the Access work area. In the work area in Figure 27, a single table, Table1, is open in the work area. Object tabs for the open objects appear at the top of the work area. If you have multiple objects open at the same time, you can select one of the open objects by clicking its tab. To the left of the work area is the Navigation Pane. The Navigation Pane contains a list of all the objects in the database. You use this pane to open an object. You also can customize the way objects are displayed in the Navigation Pane.

Status Bar   The status bar, located at the bottom of the Access window, presents information about the database object, the progress of current tasks, and the status of certain commands and keys; it also provides controls for viewing the object. As you enter data or perform certain commands, various indicators may appear on the status bar. The left edge of the status bar in Figure 27 shows that the table object is open in Datasheet view. In Datasheet view, the table is represented as a collection of rows and columns called a datasheet. Toward the right edge are View buttons, which you can use to change the view that currently appears.

Scroll Bars   You use a scroll bar to display different portions of an object. If an object is too long to fit vertically, a vertical scroll bar will appear at the right edge of the work area. If an object is too wide to fit, a horizontal scroll bar also appears at the bottom of the work area. On a scroll bar, the position of the scroll box reflects the location of the portion of the object that is displayed in the work area.

Ribbon   The ribbon, located near the top of the window below the title bar, is the control center in Access and other Office apps (Figure 28). The ribbon provides easy, central access to the tasks you perform while creating a database. The ribbon consists of tabs, groups, and commands. Each tab contains a collection of groups, and each group contains related functions. When you run an Office app, such as Access, it initially displays several main tabs, also called default or top-level tabs. All Office apps have a Home tab, which contains the more frequently used commands.

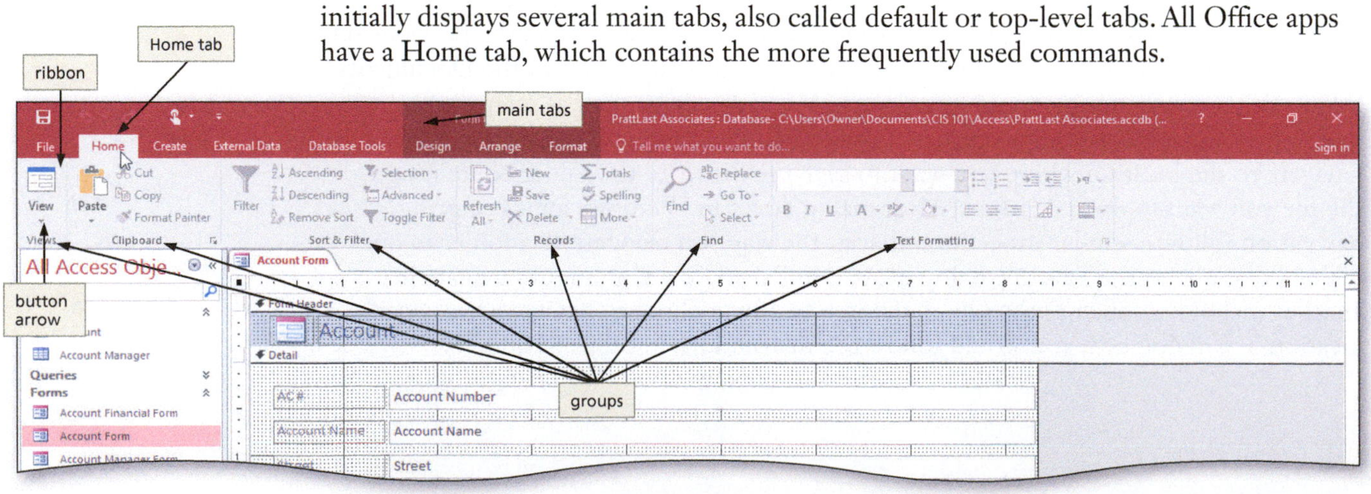

Figure 28

In addition to the main tabs, the Office apps display tool tabs, also called contextual tabs (Figure 29), when you perform certain tasks or work with objects such as pictures or tables. If you modify the design of a form, for example, the Form Design Tools tab and its related subordinate Design tab appear, collectively referred to as the Form Design Tools Design tab. When you are finished working with the form, the Form Design Tools Design tab disappears from the ribbon. Access and other Office apps determine when tool tabs should appear and disappear based on tasks you perform.

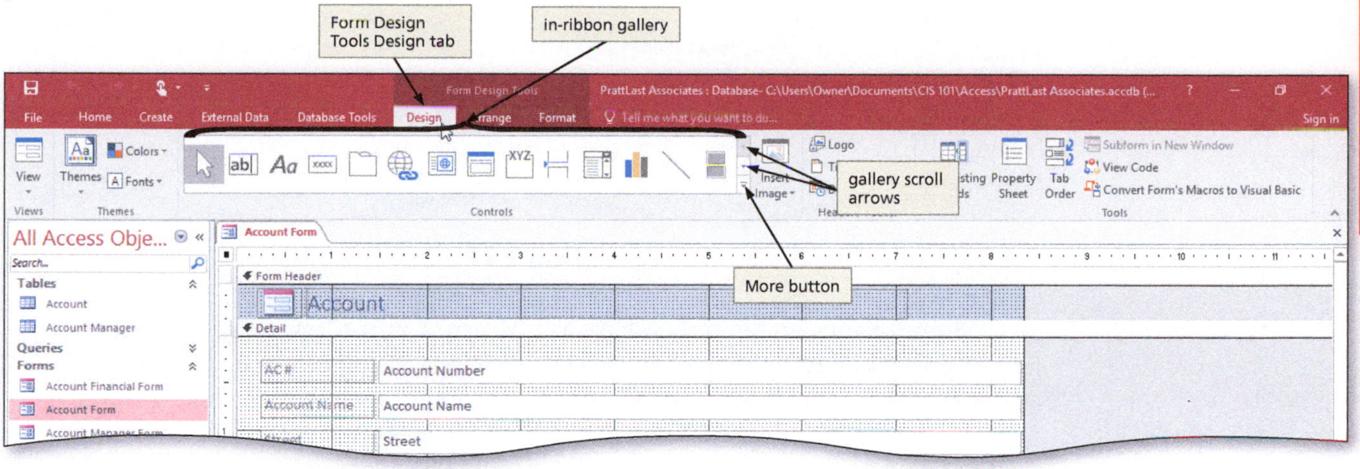

Figure 29

Items on the ribbon include buttons, boxes, and galleries (shown in Figure 29). A **gallery** is a set of choices, often graphical, arranged in a grid or in a list. You can scroll through choices in an in-ribbon gallery by clicking the gallery's scroll arrows. Or, you can click a gallery's More button to view more gallery options on the screen at a time.

Some buttons and boxes have arrows that, when clicked, also display a gallery; others always cause a gallery to be displayed when clicked (Figure 30).

BTW

Touch Mode

The Office and Windows interfaces may vary if you are using touch mode. For this reason, you might notice that the function or appearance of your touch screen differs slightly from this module's presentation.

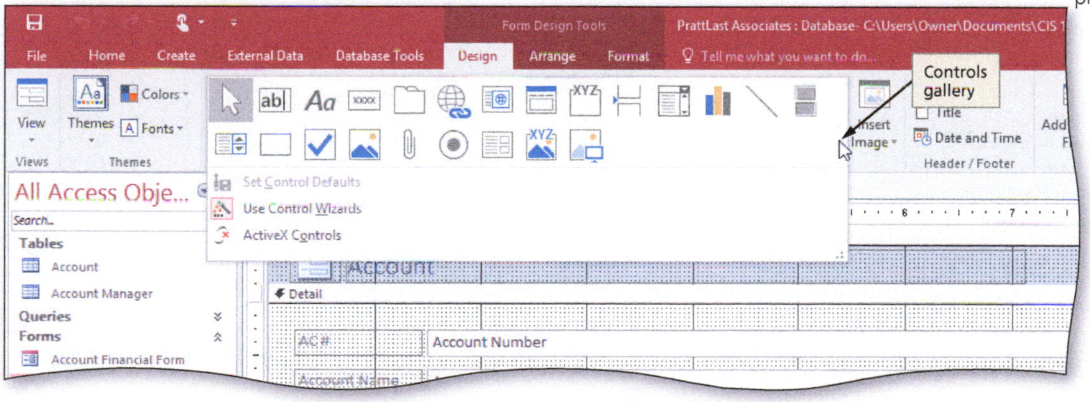

Figure 30

Some commands on the ribbon display an image to help you remember their function. When you point to a command on the ribbon, all or part of the command glows in a shade of blue, and a ScreenTip appears on the screen. A ScreenTip is an on-screen note that provides the name of the command, available keyboard shortcut(s), a description of the command, and sometimes instructions for how to obtain help about the command (Figure 31).

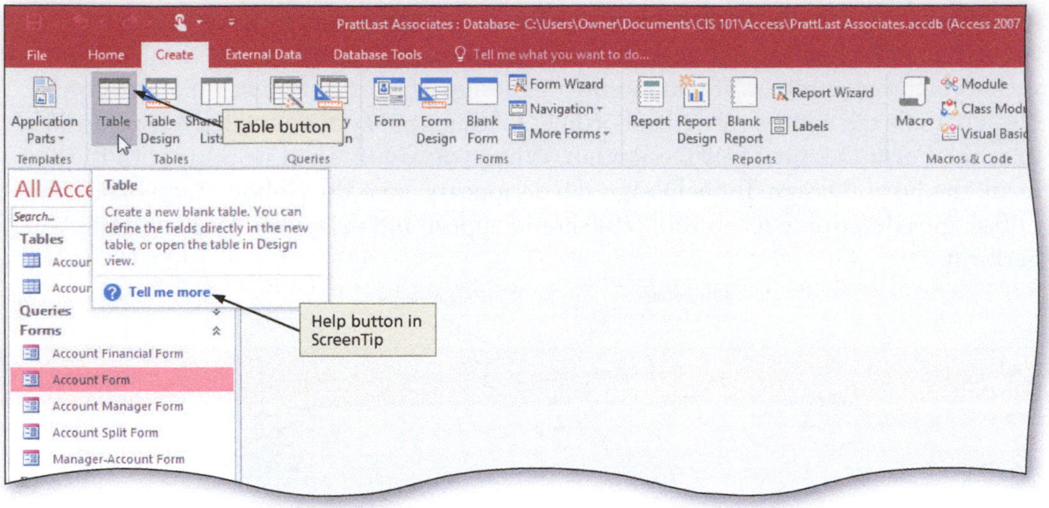

Figure 31

Some groups on the ribbon have a small arrow in the lower-right corner, called a Dialog Box Launcher, that when clicked, displays a dialog box or a task pane with additional options for the group (Figure 32). When presented with a dialog box, you make selections and must close the dialog box before returning to the document. A **task pane**, in contrast to a dialog box, is a window that can remain open and visible while you work in the document.

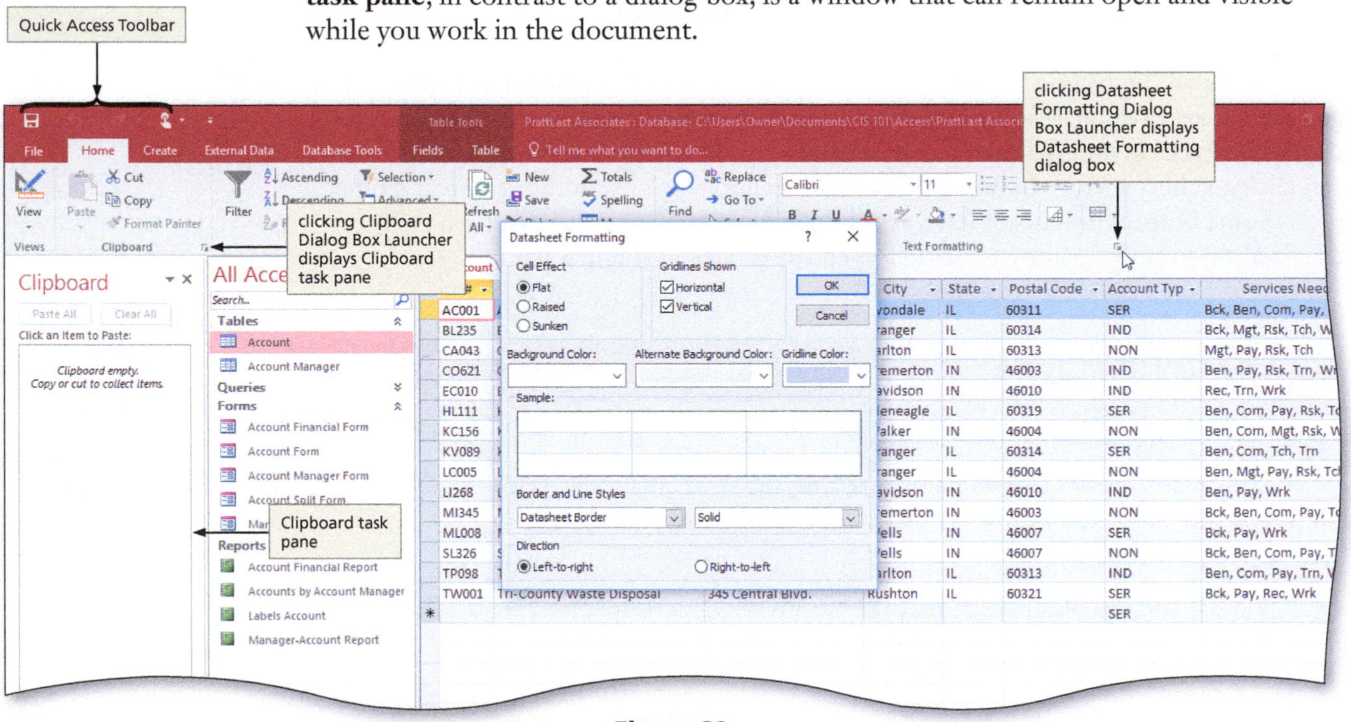

Figure 32

Quick Access Toolbar The Quick Access Toolbar, located initially (by default) above the ribbon at the left edge of the title bar, provides convenient, one-click access to frequently used commands (shown in Figure 32). The commands on the Quick Access Toolbar always are available, regardless of the task you are performing. The Touch/ Mouse Mode button on the Quick Access Toolbar allows you to switch between Touch mode and Mouse mode. If you primarily use touch gestures, Touch mode will add more space between commands on menus and on the ribbon so that they are easier to tap. While touch gestures are convenient ways to interact with Office apps, not all features are supported when you are using Touch mode. If you are using a mouse,

Mouse mode will not add the extra space between buttons and commands. The Quick Access Toolbar is discussed in more depth later in the module.

KeyTips   If you prefer using the keyboard instead of the mouse, you can press the ALT key on the keyboard to display KeyTips, or keyboard code icons, for certain commands (Figure 33). To select a command using the keyboard, press the letter or number displayed in the KeyTip, which may cause additional KeyTips related to the selected command to appear. To remove KeyTips from the screen, press the ALT key or the ESC key until all KeyTips disappear, or click anywhere in the app window.

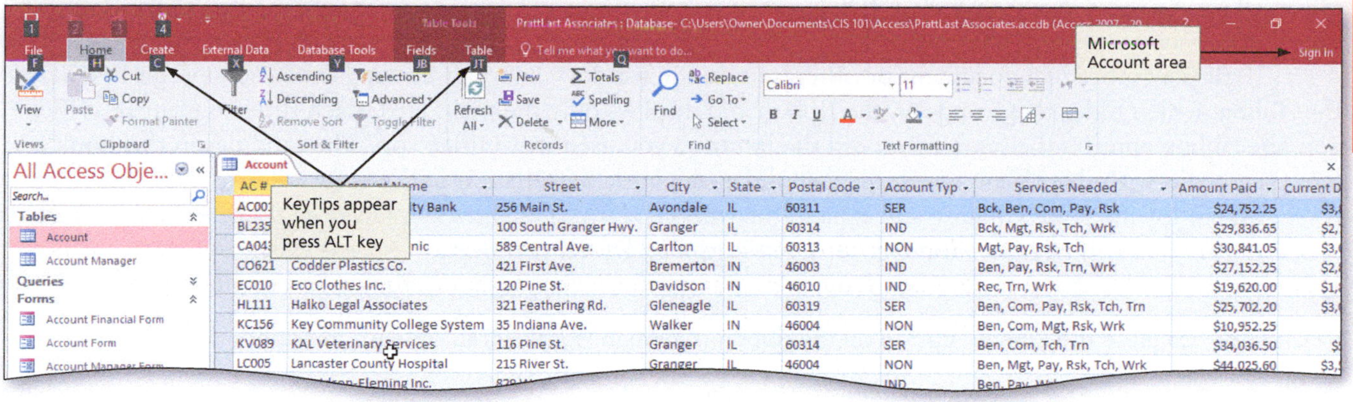

Figure 33

Microsoft Account Area   In this area, you can use the Sign in link to sign in to your Microsoft account. Once signed in, you will see your account information as well as a picture if you have included one in your Microsoft account.

To Display a Different Tab on the Ribbon

1 SIGN IN | 2 USE WINDOWS | 3 USE APPS | 4 FILE MANAGEMENT | 5 SWITCH APPS
6 SAVE FILES | 7 CHANGE SCREEN RESOLUTION | 8 EXIT APPS | 9 USE HELP

When you run Access, the ribbon displays five main tabs: File, Home, Create, External Data, and Database Tools. The tab currently displayed is called the **active tab**.

The following step displays the Create tab, that is, makes it the active tab. *Why? When working with an Office app, you may need to switch tabs to access other options for working with a database.*

1

• Click Create on the ribbon to display the Create tab (Figure 34).

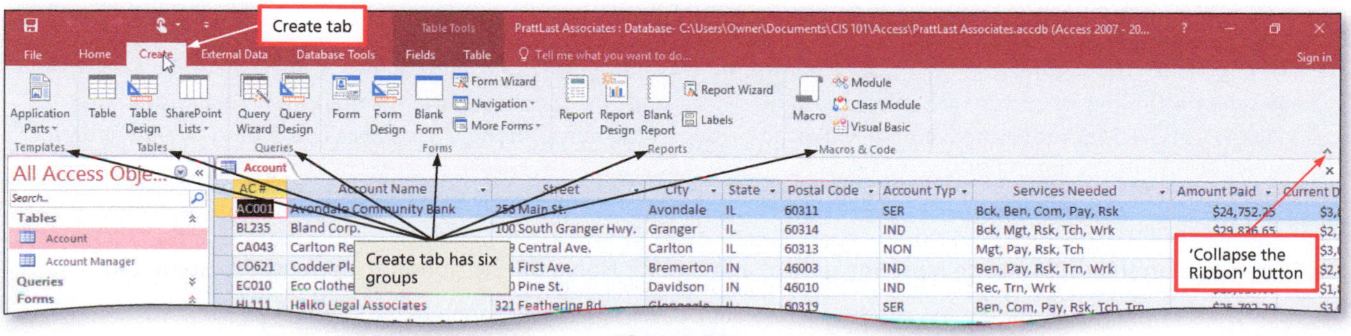

Figure 34

Experiment

• Click the other tabs on the ribbon to view their contents. When you are finished, click Create on the ribbon to redisplay the Create tab.

Q&A If I am working in a different Office app, such as PowerPoint or Word, how do I display a different tab on the ribbon?

Follow this same procedure; that is, click the desired tab on the ribbon.

To Collapse and Expand the Ribbon

1 SIGN IN | 2 USE WINDOWS | 3 USE APPS | 4 FILE MANAGEMENT | 5 SWITCH APPS
6 SAVE FILES | 7 CHANGE SCREEN RESOLUTION | 8 EXIT APPS | 9 USE HELP

To display more of a document or other item in the window of an Office app, some users prefer to collapse the ribbon, which hides the groups on the ribbon and displays only the main tabs. Each time you run an Office app, the ribbon appears the same way it did the last time you used that Office app. The modules in this book, however, begin with the ribbon appearing as it did at the initial installation of the software.

The following steps collapse and expand the ribbon. *Why? If you need more space on the screen to work with your document, you may consider collapsing the ribbon to gain additional workspace.*

1

• Click the 'Collapse the Ribbon' button on the ribbon (shown in Figure 34) to collapse the ribbon (Figure 35).

Q&A What happened to the 'Collapse the Ribbon' button?

The 'Pin the ribbon' button replaces the 'Collapse the Ribbon' button when the ribbon is collapsed. You will see the 'Pin the ribbon' button only when you expand a ribbon by clicking a tab.

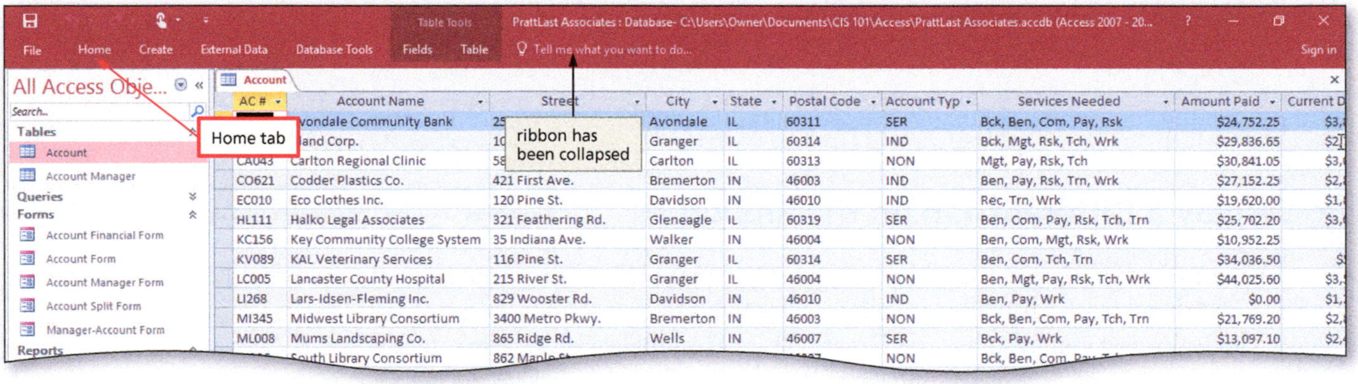

Figure 35

2

• Click Home on the ribbon to expand the Home tab (Figure 36).

Q&A Why would I click the Home tab?

If you want to use a command on a collapsed ribbon, click the main tab to display the groups for that tab. After you select a command on the ribbon and resume working in the document, the groups will be collapsed once again. If you decide not to use a command on the ribbon, you can collapse the groups by clicking the same main tab or clicking in the app window.

Experiment

• Click Home on the ribbon to collapse the groups again. Click Home on the ribbon to expand the Home tab.

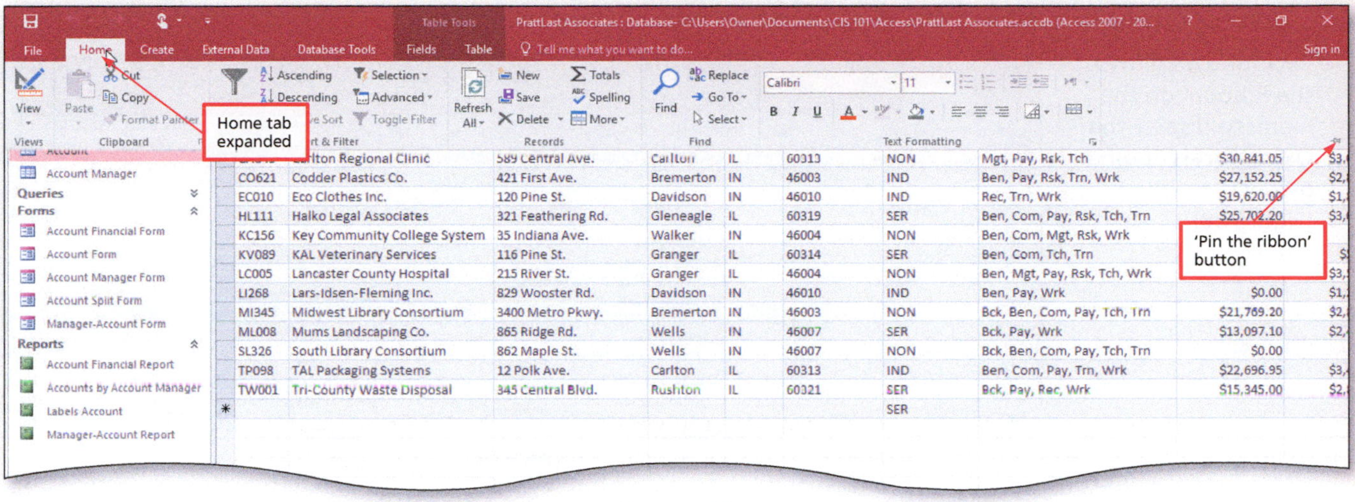

Figure 36

3

- Click the 'Pin the ribbon' button on the expanded Home tab to restore the ribbon (see Figure 34).

Other Ways

1. Double-click a main tab on the ribbon

2. Press CTRL+F1

To Relocate the Quick Access Toolbar

1 SIGN IN | 2 USE WINDOWS | 3 USE APPS | 4 FILE MANAGEMENT | 5 SWITCH APPS
6 SAVE FILES | 7 CHANGE SCREEN RESOLUTION | 8 EXIT APPS | 9 USE HELP

When you click the 'Customize Quick Access Toolbar' button, you will see a list of commands you can use to customize the Quick Access Toolbar. One of the commands allows you to relocate the Quick Access Toolbar below the ribbon. *Why? You might prefer this location.* The following steps use the 'Customize Quick Access Toolbar' button to move the Quick Access Toolbar, which by default is located on the title bar.

1

- Click the 'Customize Quick Access Toolbar' button to display a menu of commands related to the Quick Access Toolbar (Figure 37).

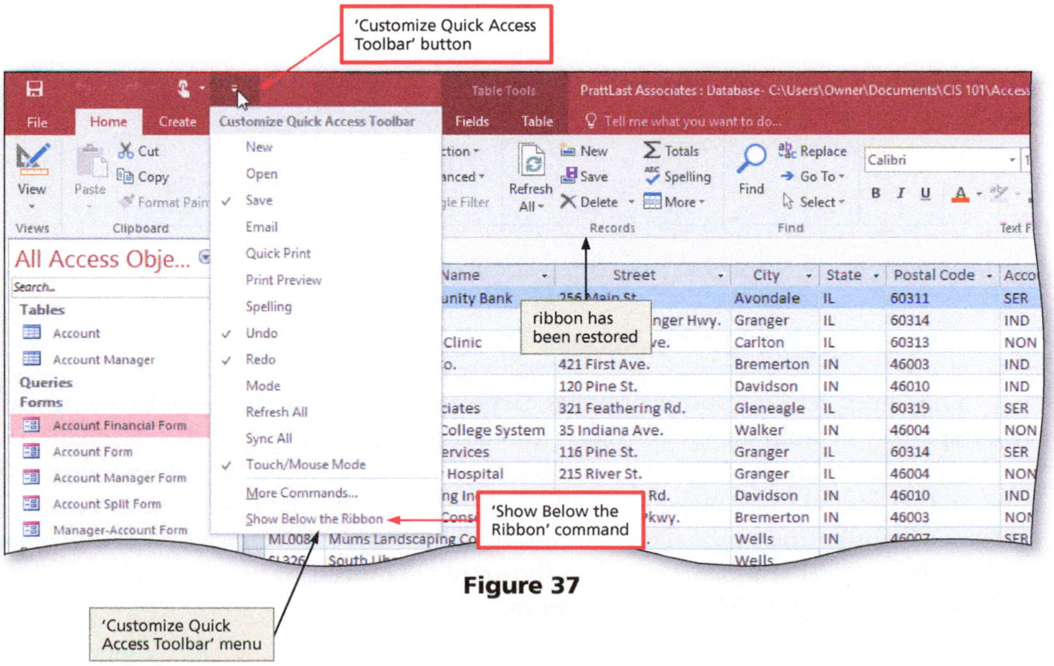

Figure 37

2

- Click 'Show Below the Ribbon' on the menu to display the Quick Access Toolbar below the ribbon (Figure 38).

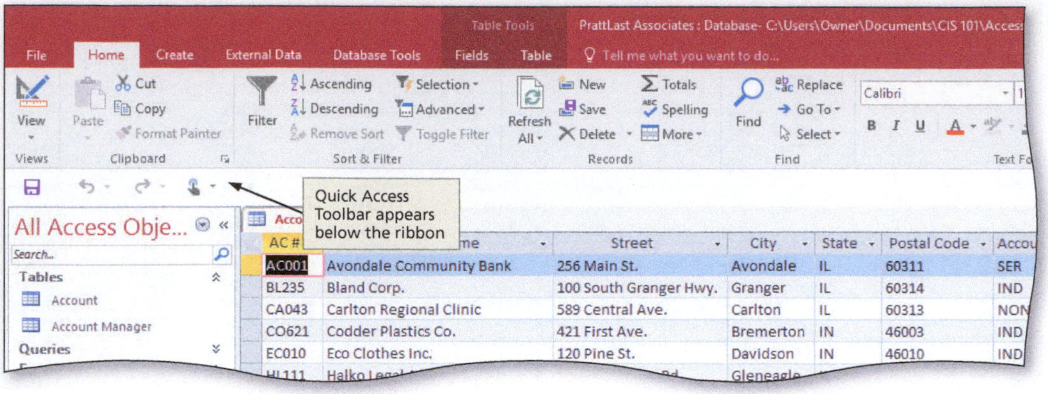

Figure 38

3

- Click the 'Customize Quick Access Toolbar' button, now located below the ribbon, to display a menu of commands related to the Quick Access Toolbar (Figure 39).

4

- Click 'Show Above the Ribbon' on the menu to once again display the Quick Access Toolbar above the ribbon.

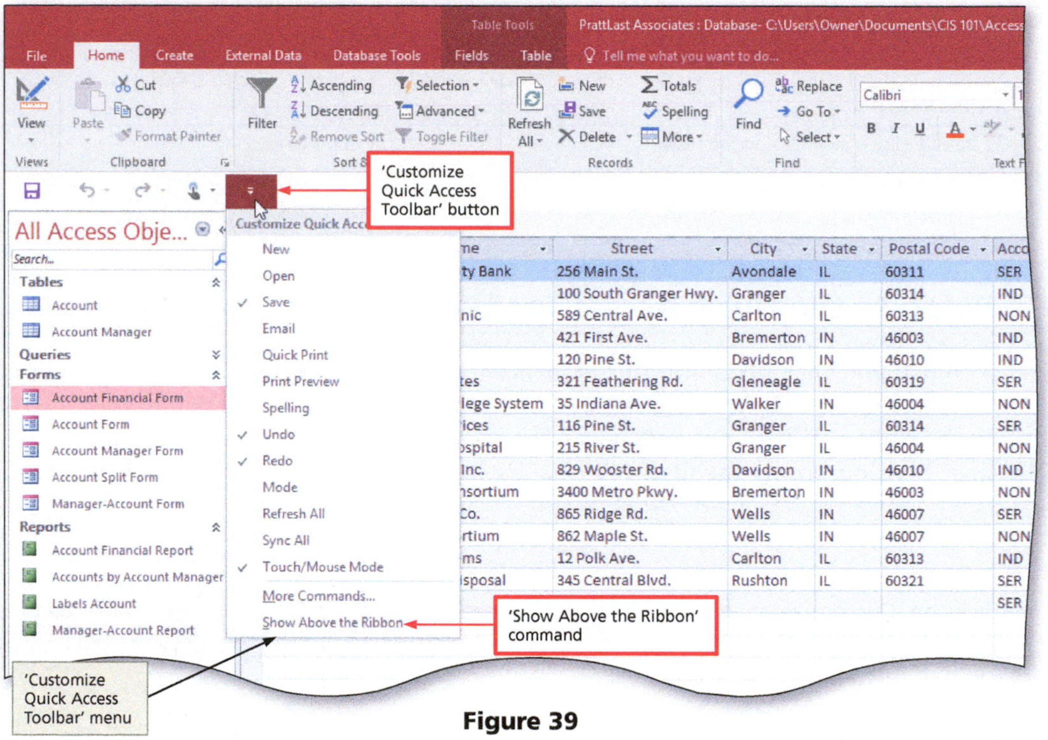

Figure 39

To Customize the Quick Access Toolbar

1 SIGN IN | 2 USE WINDOWS | 3 USE APPS | 4 FILE MANAGEMENT | 5 SWITCH APPS
6 SAVE FILES | 7 CHANGE SCREEN RESOLUTION | 8 EXIT APPS | 9 USE HELP

The Quick Access Toolbar provides easy access to some of the more frequently used commands in the Office apps. By default, the Quick Access Toolbar contains buttons for the Save, Undo, and Redo commands. You can customize the Quick Access Toolbar by changing its location in the window, as shown in the previous steps, and by adding more buttons to reflect commands you would like to access easily. The following steps add the Quick Print button to the Quick Access Toolbar. *Why? Adding the Quick Print button to the Quick Access Toolbar speeds up the process of printing.* They then Illustrate the process of removing a button from the Quick Access Toolbar by removing the Quick Print button.

1

- Click the 'Customize Quick Access Toolbar' button to display the Customize Quick Access Toolbar menu (Figure 40).

Q&A
Which commands are listed on the Customize Quick Access Toolbar menu?
It lists commands that commonly are added to the Quick Access Toolbar.

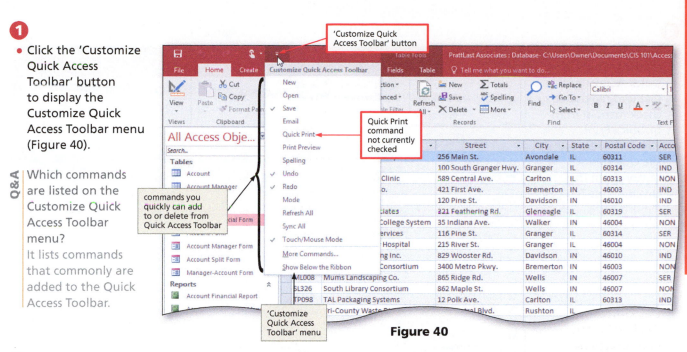

Figure 40

2

- Click Quick Print on the Customize Quick Access Toolbar menu to add the Quick Print button to the Quick Access Toolbar (Figure 41).

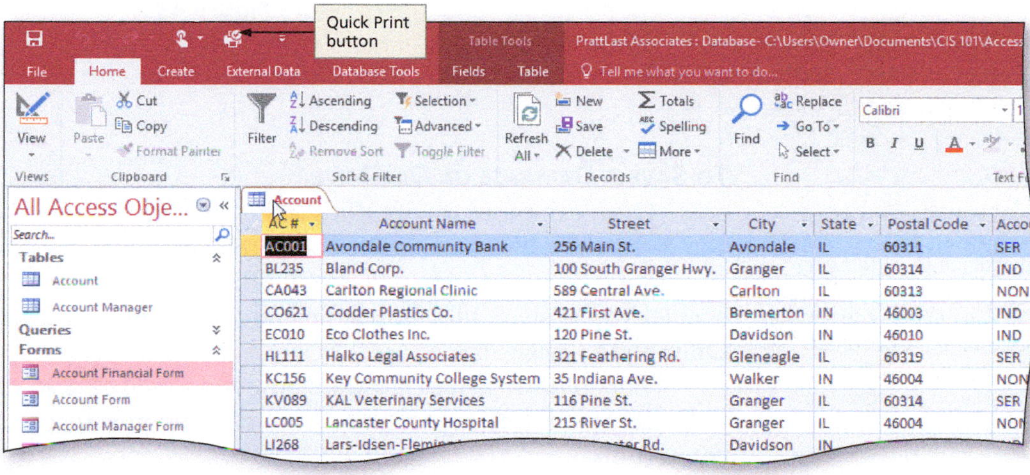

Figure 41

3

- Click the 'Customize Quick Access Toolbar' button to display the Customize Quick Access Toolbar menu (Figure 42).

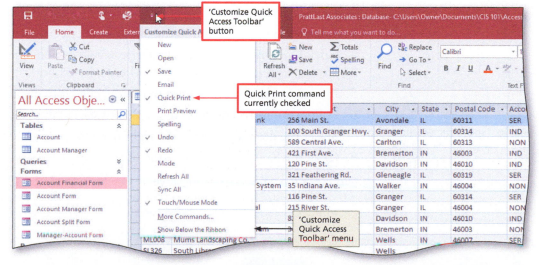

Figure 42

4

- Click Quick Print on the Customize Quick Access Toolbar menu to remove check mark in front of Quick Print, which will remove the Quick Print button from the Quick Access Toolbar (Figure 43).

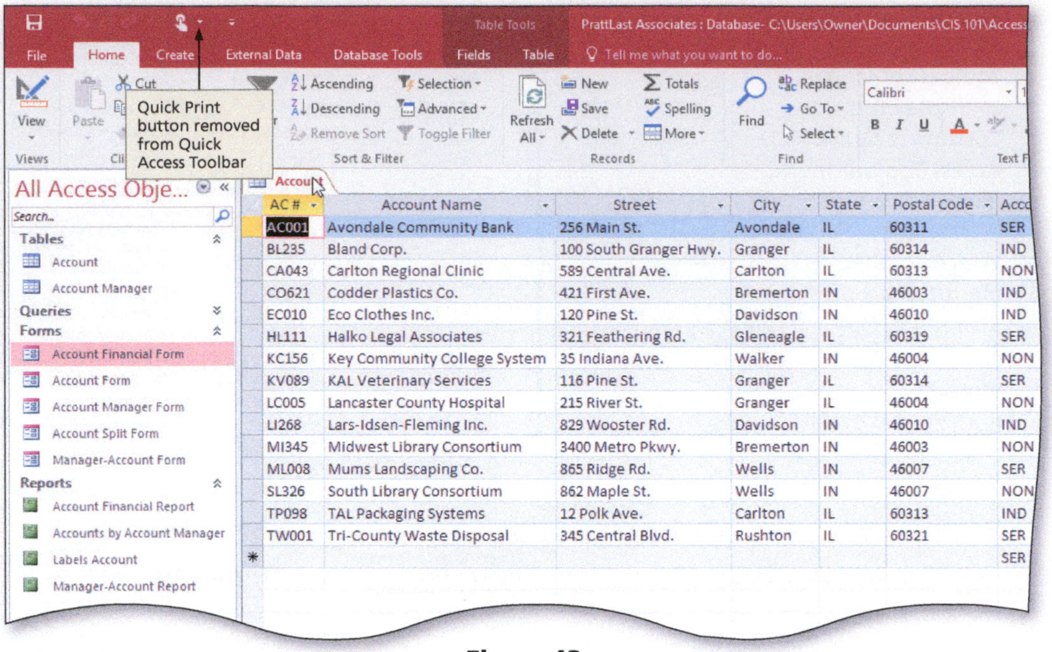

Figure 43

BTW

Customizing the Ribbon

In addition to customizing the Quick Access Toolbar, you can add items to and remove items from the ribbon. To customize the ribbon, click File on the ribbon to open the Backstage view, click the Options tab in the Backstage view, and then click Customize Ribbon in the left pane of the Options dialog box.

TO SAVE A DATABASE ON ONEDRIVE

One of the features of Office is the capability to save files on OneDrive so that you can use the files on multiple computers or mobile devices without having to use an external storage device, such as a USB flash drive. Storing files on OneDrive also enables you to share files more efficiently with others, such as when using Office Online and Office 365.

The following steps illustrate how you would save an existing Access database to OneDrive. These steps require you have a Microsoft account and an Internet connection.

1. With the database to be saved open, click File on the ribbon to open the Backstage view.
2. Click the Save As tab in the Backstage view to display the Save As gallery.
3. Click the Save As button in the Save As gallery.
4. Click OneDrive to display OneDrive saving options or a Sign In button, if you are not signed in already to your Microsoft account.
5. If your screen displays a Sign In button, click it to display the Sign in dialog box.
6. Follow the instructions on the screen to sign in to your Microsoft account.
7. Select the desired folder in the right pane to specify the save location
8. Click the Save button to save the file on OneDrive.

BTW

File Type

Depending on your Windows settings, the file type .accdb may be displayed immediately to the right of the file name after you save the file. The file type .accdb is an Access 2016 database.

Q&A Can I create a database on OneDrive?

Yes. After "browsing for a location to put your database," select OneDrive for the location. You can then select the desired folder within OneDrive.

To Copy a Folder to OneDrive

To back up your files or easily make them available on another computer or mobile device, you can copy them to OneDrive. To do so, you would use the following steps.

1. Click the File Explorer button on the taskbar to make the folder window the active window.

2. Navigate to the folder to be copied. For example, to navigate to the folder called CIS 101, you could click Documents in the This PC area of the navigation pane to display the CIS 101 folder in the file list, and then click the CIS 101 folder in the file list to select it.

3. Click Home on the ribbon to display the Home tab.

4. Click the Copy to button (Home tab | Organize group) to display the Copy to menu.

5. Click Choose location on the Copy to menu to display the Copy Items dialog box.

6. Click OneDrive (Copy Items dialog box) to select it.

7. Click the Copy button (Copy Items dialog box) to copy the selected folder to OneDrive.

8. Click OneDrive in the navigation pane to verify the CIS 101 folder is displayed in the file list.

To Unlink a OneDrive Account

If you are using a public computer and are not signed in to Windows with a Microsoft account, you should unlink your OneDrive account so that other users cannot access it. To do so, you would use the following steps, which begin with clicking the 'Show hidden icons' button on the Windows taskbar to show a menu of hidden icons, including the OneDrive icon (Figure 44).

Figure 44

1. Click the 'Show hidden icons' button on the Windows taskbar to display a menu of hidden icons.

2. Right-click the OneDrive icon to display a shortcut menu, and then click Settings on the shortcut menu to display the Microsoft OneDrive dialog box.

3. Click the Unlink OneDrive button (Microsoft OneDrive dialog box) to unlink the OneDrive account.

4. When the Microsoft OneDrive dialog box appears with a Welcome to OneDrive message, click the Close button.

To Sign Out of a Microsoft Account

If you are using a public computer or otherwise wish to sign out of your Microsoft account, you should sign out of the account from the Account gallery in the Backstage view. Signing out of the account is the safest way to make sure that nobody else can access online files or settings stored in your Microsoft account.

To sign out of a Microsoft account from Access, you would use the following steps.

1. Click File on the ribbon to open the Backstage view.

2 Click the Account tab to display the Account gallery.

3. Click the Sign out link, which displays the Remove Account dialog box. If a Can't remove Windows accounts dialog box appears instead of the Remove Account dialog box, click the OK button and skip the remaining steps.

Q&A | Why does a Can't remove Windows accounts dialog box appear?
If you signed in to Windows using your Microsoft account, then you also must sign out from Windows, rather than signing out from within Access. When you are finished using Windows, be sure to sign out at that time.

4. Click the Yes button (Remove Account dialog box) to sign out of your Microsoft account on this computer.

Q&A | Should I sign out of Windows after removing my Microsoft account?
When you are finished using the computer, you should sign out of Windows for maximum security.

5. Click the Back button in the upper-left corner of the Backstage view to return to the document.

Screen Resolution

Screen resolution indicates the number of pixels (dots) that the computer uses to display the letters, numbers, graphics, and background you see on the screen. When you increase the screen resolution, Windows displays more information on the screen, but the information decreases in size. The reverse also is true: as you decrease the screen resolution, Windows displays less information on the screen, but the information increases in size.

Screen resolution usually is stated as the product of two numbers, such as 1366 × 768 (pronounced "thirteen sixty-six by seven sixty-eight"). A 1366 × 768 screen resolution results in a display of 1366 distinct pixels on each of 768 lines, or about 1,050,624 pixels. Changing the screen resolution affects how the ribbon appears in Office apps and some Windows dialog boxes. Figure 45 shows the Access ribbon at screen resolutions of 1366 × 768 and 1024 × 768. All of the same commands are available regardless of screen resolution. The app (Access, in this case), however, makes changes to the groups and the buttons within the groups to accommodate the various screen resolutions. The result is that certain commands may need to be accessed differently depending on the resolution chosen. A command that is visible on the ribbon and available by clicking a button at one resolution may not be visible and may need to be accessed using its Dialog Box Launcher at a different resolution.

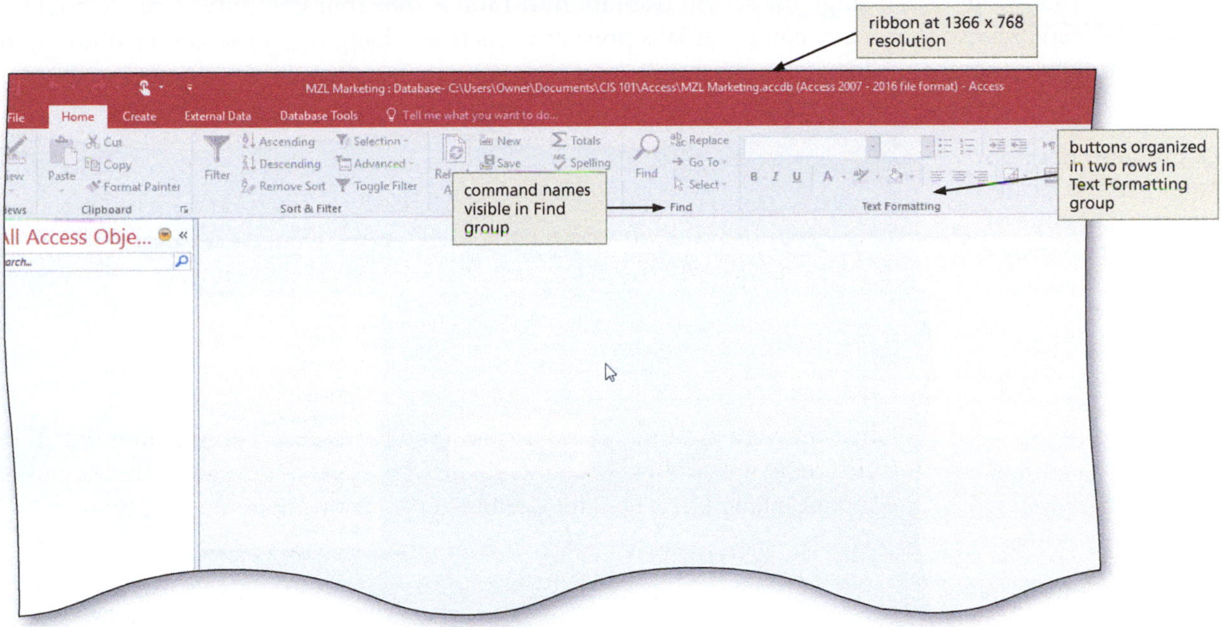

Figure 45a

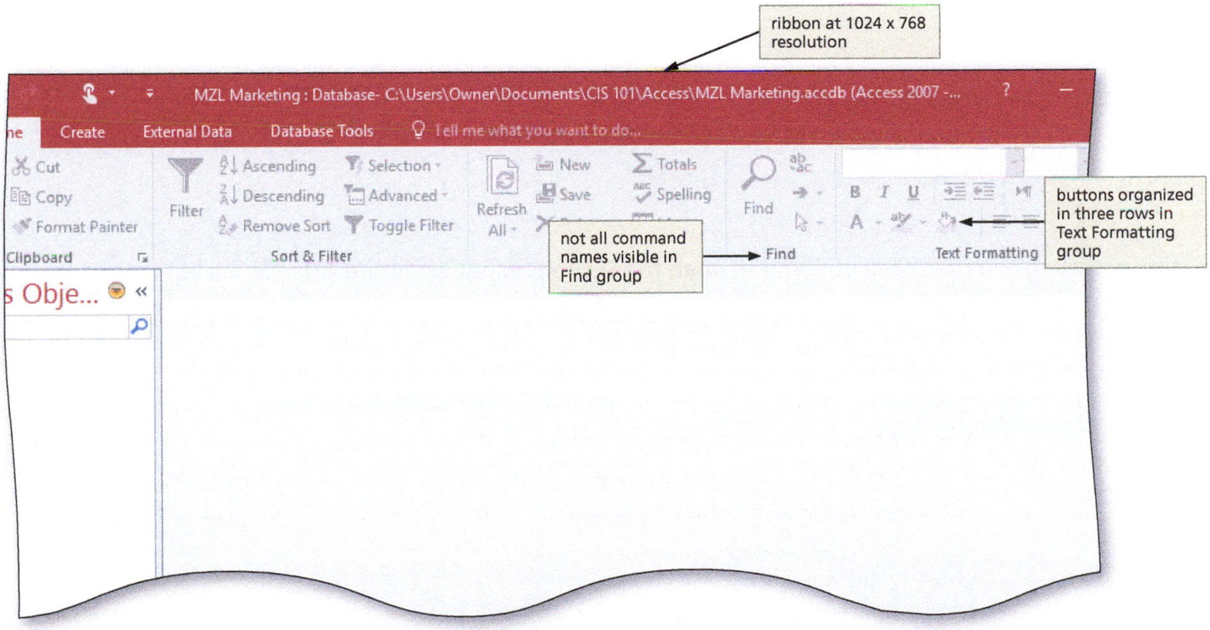

Figure 45b

Comparing the two ribbons in Figure 45, notice the changes in content and layout of the groups and galleries. In some cases, the content of a group is the same in each resolution, but the layout of the group differs. For example, the same gallery and buttons appear in the Text Formatting groups in the two resolutions, but the layouts differ. In other cases, the content and layout are the same across the resolution, but the level of detail differs with the resolution.

OFF 36   **Office 2016 and Windows 10 Module**   Essential Concepts and Skills

1 SIGN IN | 2 USE WINDOWS | 3 USE APPS | 4 FILE MANAGEMENT | 5 SWITCH APPS
6 SAVE FILES | 7 CHANGE SCREEN RESOLUTION | 8 EXIT APPS | 9 USE HELP

To Change the Screen Resolution

If you are using a computer to step through the modules in this book and you want your screen to match the figures, you may need to change your screen's resolution. *Why? The figures in this book use a screen resolution of 1366 × 768.* The following steps change the screen resolution to 1366 × 768. Your computer already might be set to 1366 × 768. Keep in mind that many computer labs prevent users from changing the screen resolution; in that case, read the following steps for illustration purposes.

1

- Click the Show desktop button, which is located at the far-right edge of the taskbar, to display the Windows desktop.

Q&A I cannot see the Show desktop button. Why not? When you point to the far-right edge of the taskbar, a small outline appears to mark the Show desktop button.

- Right-click an empty area on the Windows desktop to display a shortcut menu that contains a list of commands related to the desktop (Figure 46).

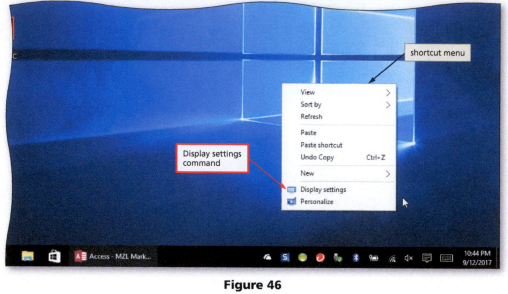

Figure 46

Q&A Why does my shortcut menu display different commands?
Depending on your computer's hardware and configuration, different commands might appear on the shortcut menu.

2

- Click Display settings on the shortcut menu to open the Settings window (Figure 47).

Figure 47

3

- Scroll down, if necessary, so that 'Advanced display settings' appears, and then click 'Advanced display settings' in the Settings window to display the advanced display settings.

- If necessary, scroll to display the Resolution box (Figure 48).

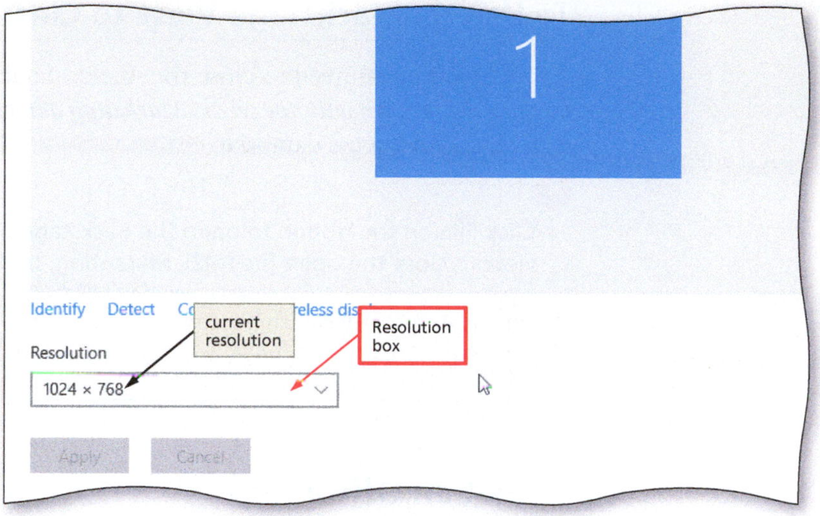

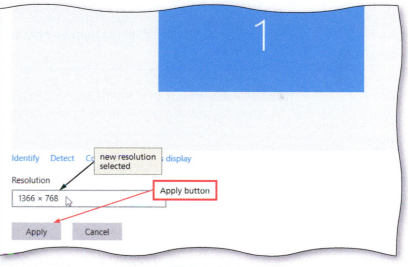

Figure 48

4

- Click the Resolution box to display a list of available screen resolutions (Figure 49).

- If necessary, scroll to and then click 1366 × 768 to select the screen resolution.

Q&A

What if my computer does not support the 1366 × 768 resolution?
Some computers do not support the 1366 × 768 resolution. In this case, select a resolution that is close to the 1366 × 768 resolution.

Figure 49

5

- Click the Apply button (Advanced Display Settings window) to change the screen resolution and display a confirmation message (Figure 50).

- Click the Keep changes button to accept the new screen resolution.

- Click the Close button to close the Settings window.

Figure 50

Other Ways

1. Click Start button, click Settings, click System, click Display, click 'Advanced display settings,' select desired resolution in Resolution box, click Apply button, click Keep changes button

2. Type `screen resolution` in search box, click 'Change the screen resolution,' select desired resolution in Resolution box, click Apply, click Keep changes

To Use the Backstage View to Close a Database

Assume you need to close the Access database and return to it later. *Why? You no longer need to work with the MZL Marketing database, so you may close it.* The following step closes an Access database.

1
- Click File on the ribbon to open the Backstage view and then click Close in the Backstage view to close the open file (MZL Marketing, in this case) without exiting Access.

Q&A   Why is Access still on the screen?
When you close a database, the app remains running.

To Exit an Office App

You are finished using Access. The following step exits Access. *Why? It is good practice to exit an app when you are finished using it.*

1
- Click the Close button on the right side of the title bar to close the file and exit the Office app.

Break Point: If you wish to take a break, this is a good place to do so. To resume at a later time, continue to follow the steps from this location forward.

To Run Access Using the Search Box

The following steps, which assume Windows is running, use the search box to run the Access app based on a typical installation. You may need to ask your instructor how to run apps for your computer.

1   Type `Access 2016` as the search text in the Search box and watch the search results appear in the search results.

Q&A   Do I need to type the complete app name or use correct capitalization?
No, you need to type just enough characters of the app name for it to appear in the Apps list. For example, you may be able to type Access or access, instead of Access 2016.

2   Click the app name, Access 2016 in this case, in the search results to run Access.

3   If the app window is not maximized, click the Maximize button on its title bar to maximize the window (Figure 51).

Q&A   Do I have to run Access using these steps?
No. You can use whichever method you prefer to run Access.

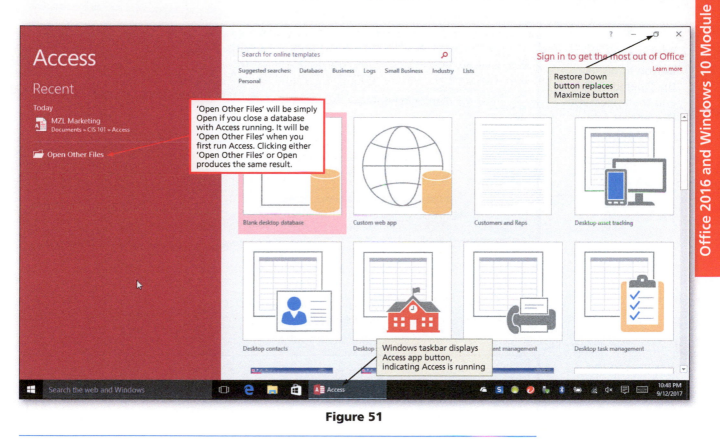

Figure 51

To Open an Existing Database

1 SIGN IN | 2 USE WINDOWS | 3 USE APPS | 4 FILE MANAGEMENT | 5 SWITCH APPS
6 SAVE FILES | 7 CHANGE SCREEN RESOLUTION | 8 EXIT APPS | 9 USE HELP

To work on an existing database, that is, a database you previously created, you must open the database. To do so, you will use the Backstage view. The following step opens an existing database, specifically the MZL Marketing database. **Why?** *Because the database has been created already, you just need to open it.*

1

- If you have just run Access, click 'Open Other Files' to display the Open gallery in the Backstage view. If not, click File on the ribbon to open the Backstage view and then click Open in the Backstage view to display the Open gallery (Figure 52).

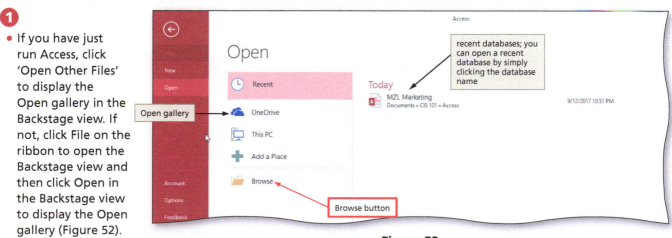

Figure 52

I see the name of the database I want to open in the Recent list in Backstage view. Can I just click the name to open the file?

Yes. That is an alternative way to open a database, provided the name of the database is included in the Recent list.

2

● Click the Browse button to display the Open dialog box and then select the Documents folder (Figure 53).

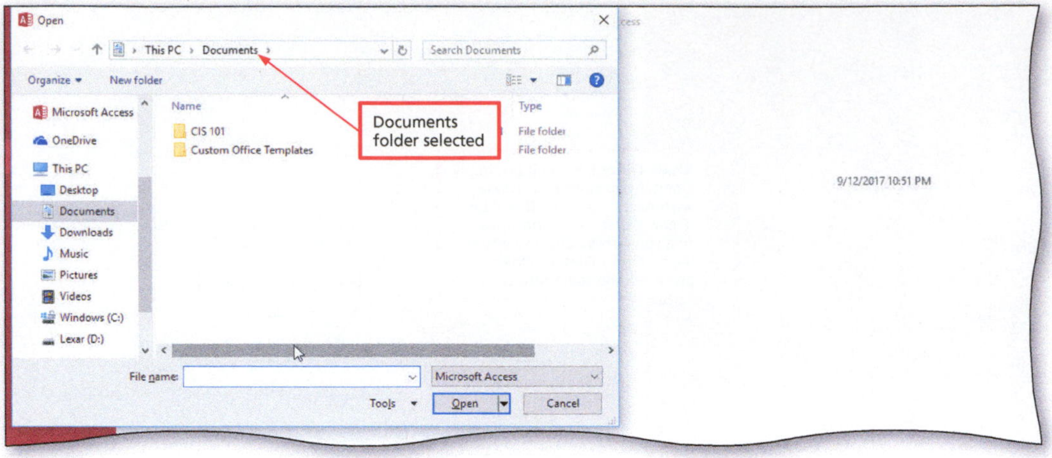

Documents folder selected

Figure 53

3

Open dialog box

● Navigate to the folder containing the file to open (for example, the Access folder) in the CIS 101 folder (Figure 54).

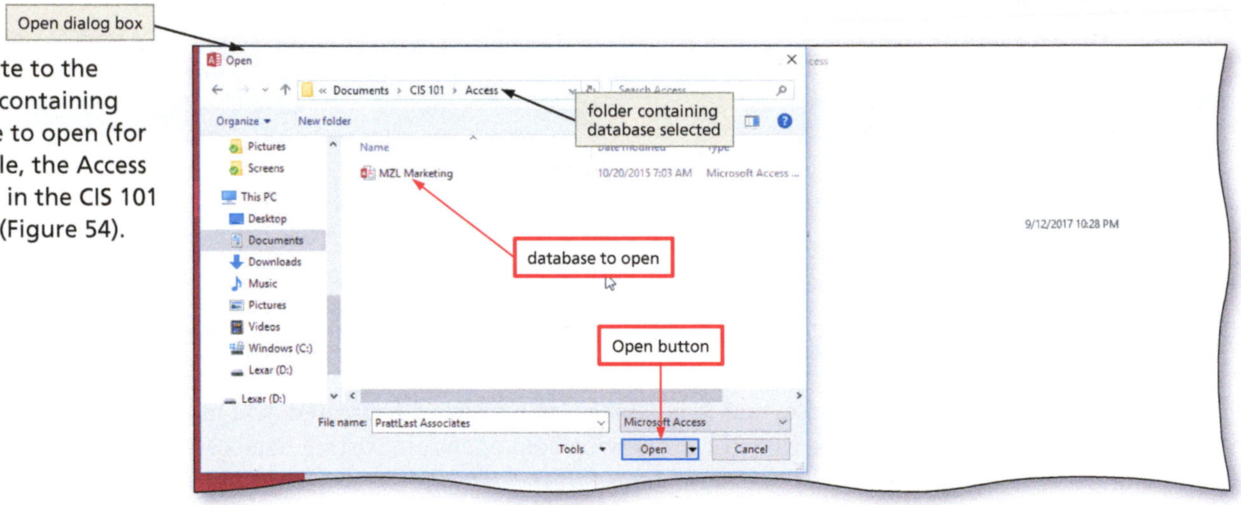

folder containing database selected

database to open

Open button

Figure 54

4

● Click the file to open, MZL Marketing in this case, to select the file.

MZL Marketing database open

● Click the Open button (Open dialog box) to open the database (Figure 55). If a security warning appears, click the Enable Content button.

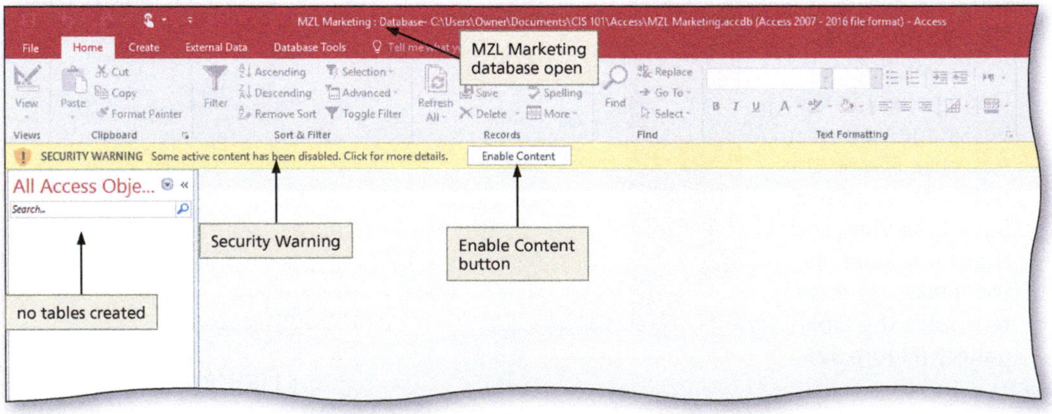

Security Warning

Enable Content button

no tables created

Figure 55

◄ Q&A | Why might a Security Warning appear?

A Security Warning appears when you open a database that might contain harmful content. The files you create in this chapter are not harmful, but you should be cautious when opening files from other people.

Other Ways

1. Press CTRL+O

2. Navigate to File Explorer window, double-click file

To Exit Access

You are finished using Access. The following step exits Access.

1 Click the Close button on the right side of the title bar to close the file and exit Access.

To Create a New Access Database from File Explorer

File Explorer provides a means to create an Access database without running an Office app. To do so, you would use the following steps.

1. Double-click the File Explorer app button on the taskbar to make the folder window the active window, and then navigate to the folder in which you want to create the database.

2. Double-click the folder in which you wish to create the database.

3. Right-click an open area in the file list to display a shortcut menu, and then point to New on the shortcut menu to display the New submenu.

4. Click 'Microsoft Access Database' on the New submenu to display an icon and text box for a new file in the current folder window with the file name, New Microsoft Access Database, selected.

5. Type the desired name in the text box and then press the ENTER key to create the database in the desired folder.

To Run Access from File Explorer and Open a Database

Previously, you learned how to run Access using the Start screen and the Search bar. You can also run it from File Explorer. To do so, you would use the following steps.

1. If necessary, display the database to open in the folder window in File Explorer.

2. Right-click the file icon or database name to display a shortcut menu, and then click Open on the shortcut menu to open the selected database in Access. If a security warning appears, click the Enable Content button.

Renaming, Moving, and Deleting Files

Earlier in this module, you learned how to organize files in folders, which is part of a process known as **file management**. The following sections cover additional file management topics including renaming, moving, and deleting files.

TO RENAME A FILE

In some circumstances, you may want to change the name of, or rename, a file or a folder. To do so, you would use the following steps.

1. If necessary, click the File Explorer button on the taskbar to make the folder window the active window, and then navigate to the location of the file to be renamed.

2. Right-click the icon or file name of the file to be renamed to display a shortcut menu that presents a list of commands related to files.

3. Click Rename on the shortcut menu to place the current file name in a text box, type the new name, and then press the ENTER key.

Q&A Are any risks involved in renaming files that are located on a hard drive?
If you inadvertently rename a file that is associated with certain apps, the apps might not be able to find the file and, therefore, might not run properly. Always use caution when renaming files.

Can I rename a file when it is open?
No, a file must be closed to change its name.

TO MOVE A FILE

When you move a file, it no longer appears in the original folder. If the destination and the source folders are on the same media, you can move a file by dragging it. If the folders are on different media, then you will need to right-click the file, and then click Cut on the shortcut menu. In the destination folder, you will need to right-click and then click Paste on the shortcut menu. To do so, you would use the following steps.

1. If necessary, click the File Explorer button on the taskbar to make the folder window the active window, and then navigate to the location of the file to be moved.

2. Right-click the icon or file name of the file to be moved to display a shortcut menu that presents a list of commands related to files.

3. Click Cut on the shortcut menu to cut the current file to the clipboard, and then navigate to the folder to which you wish to move the file.

4. Click any open area in the folder, and then click Paste on the shortcut menu to paste the file.

TO DELETE A FILE

A final task you may want to perform is to delete a file. Exercise extreme caution when deleting a file or files. When you delete a file from a hard drive, the deleted file is stored in the Recycle Bin where you can recover it until you empty the Recycle Bin. If you delete a file from removable media, such as a USB flash drive, the file is deleted permanently. To delete a file, you would use the following steps.

1. If necessary, click the File Explorer button on the taskbar to make the folder window the active window, and then navigate to the location of the file to be deleted.

2. Right-click the icon or file name of the file to be deleted to display a shortcut menu that presents a list of commands related to files.

3. Click Delete on the shortcut menu to delete the file, and then click the Yes button to confirm the deletion.

Q&A

Can I use this same technique to delete a folder?

Yes. Right-click the folder and then click Delete on the shortcut menu. When you delete a folder, all of the files and folders contained in the folder you are deleting, together with any files and folders on lower hierarchical levels, are deleted as well. For example, if you delete the CIS 101 folder, you will delete all folders and files inside the CIS 101 folder.

Microsoft Office and Windows Help

At any time while you are using one of the Office apps, you can use Office Help to display information about all topics associated with the app. To illustrate the use of Office Help, this section uses Access. Help in other Office apps operates in a similar fashion.

In Office, Help is presented in a window that has browser-style navigation buttons. Each Office app has its own Help home page, which is the starting Help page that is displayed in the Help window. If your computer is connected to the Internet, the contents of the Help page reflect both the local help files installed on the computer and material from Microsoft's website.

To Open the Help Window in an Office App

1 SIGN IN | 2 USE WINDOWS | 3 USE APPS | 4 FILE MANAGEMENT | 5 SWITCH APPS
6 SAVE FILES | 7 CHANGE SCREEN RESOLUTION | 8 EXIT APPS | 9 USE HELP

The following step opens the Access Help window. *Why? You might not understand how certain commands or operations work in Access, so you can obtain the necessary information using help.*

1

• Run an Office app, in this case Access.

• Click the MZL Marketing database in the Recent list to open the MZL Marketing database.

• Press F1 to open the app's Help window (Figure 56).

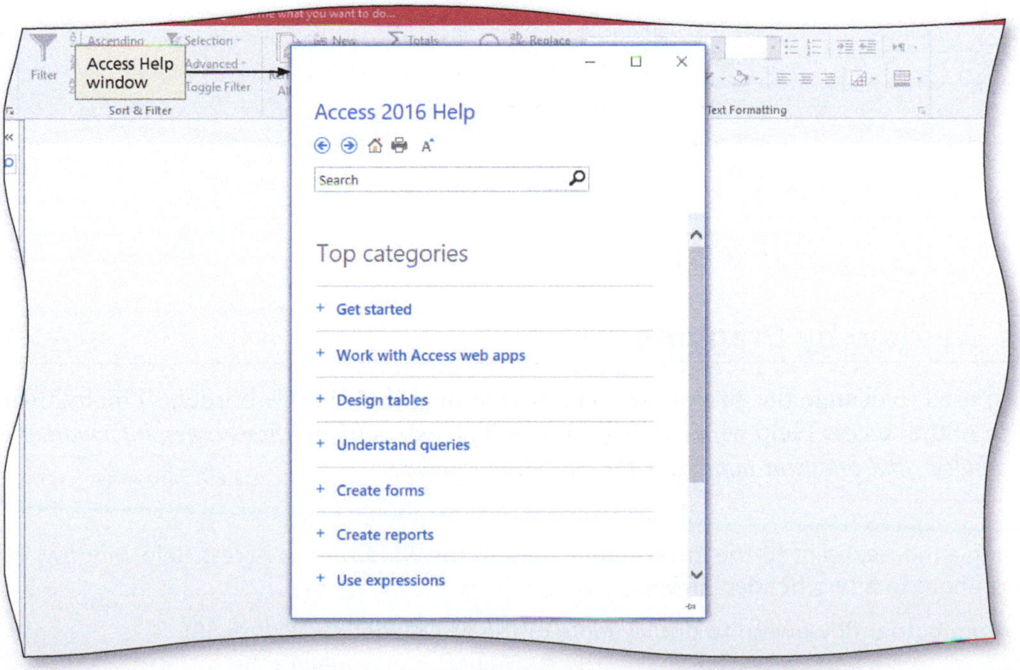

Figure 56

Moving and Resizing Windows

At times, it is useful, or even necessary, to have more than one window open and visible on the screen at the same time. You can resize and move these open windows so that you can view different areas of and elements in the window. In the case of the Help window, for example, it could be covering database objects in the Access window that you need to see.

To Move a Window by Dragging

1 SIGN IN | 2 USE WINDOWS | 3 USE APPS | 4 FILE MANAGEMENT | 5 SWITCH APPS
6 SAVE FILES | 7 CHANGE SCREEN RESOLUTION | 8 EXIT APPS | 9 USE HELP

You can move any open window that is not maximized to another location on the desktop by dragging the title bar of the window. **Why?** *You might want to have a better view of what is behind the window or just want to move the window so that you can see it better.* The following step drags the Access Help window to the upper-left corner of the desktop.

1

• Drag the window title bar (the Access Help window title bar, in this case) so that the window moves to the upper-left corner of the desktop, as shown in Figure 57.

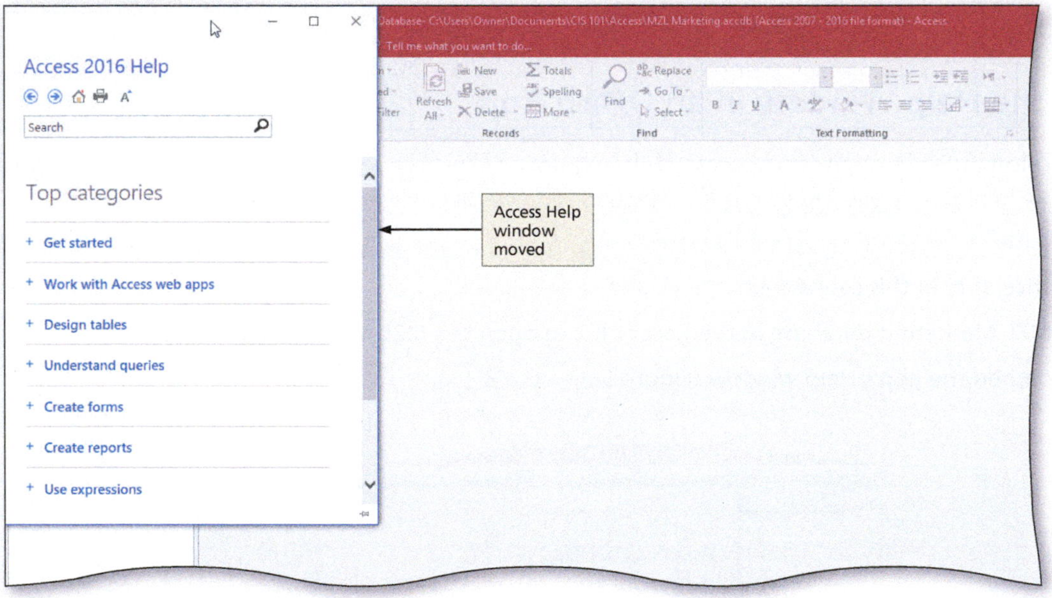

Figure 57

To Resize a Window by Dragging

1 SIGN IN | 2 USE WINDOWS | 3 USE APPS | 4 FILE MANAGEMENT | 5 SWITCH APPS
6 SAVE FILES | 7 CHANGE SCREEN RESOLUTION | 8 EXIT APPS | 9 USE HELP

A method used to change the size of the window is to drag the window borders. The following step changes the size of the Access Help window by dragging its borders. **Why?** *Sometimes, information is not visible completely in a window, and you want to increase the size of the window.*

1

• If you are using a mouse, point to the lower-right corner of the window (the Access Help window, in this case) until the pointer changes to a two-headed arrow.

• Drag the bottom border downward to display more of the active window (Figure 58).

Q&A

Can I drag other borders on the window to enlarge or shrink the window?
Yes, you can drag the left, right, and top borders and any window corner to resize a window.

Will Windows remember the new size of the window after I close it?
Yes. When you reopen the window, Windows will display it at the same size it was when you closed it.

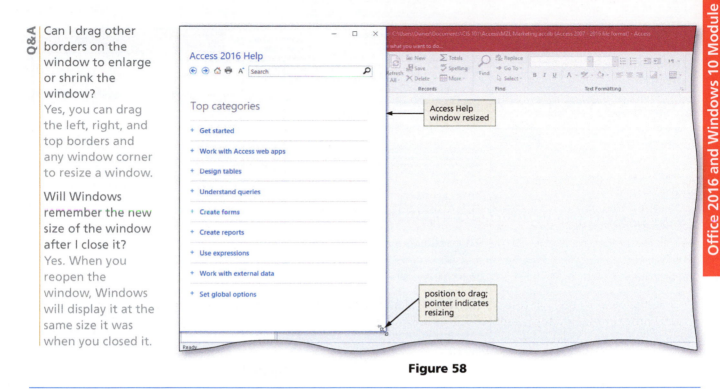

Figure 58

Using Office Help

Once an Office app's Help window is open, several methods exist for navigating Help. You can search for help by using any of the three following methods from the Help window:

1. Enter search text in the Search text box.
2. Click the links in the Help window.
3. Use the Table of Contents.

To Obtain Help Using the Search Text Box

1 SIGN IN | 2 USE WINDOWS | 3 USE APPS | 4 FILE MANAGEMENT | 5 SWITCH APPS
6 SAVE FILES | 7 CHANGE SCREEN RESOLUTION | 8 EXIT APPS | 9 USE HELP

Assume for the following example that you want to know more about forms. The following steps use the 'Search online help' text box to obtain useful information about forms by entering the word, forms, as search text. *Why? You may not know the exact help topic you are looking to find, so using keywords can help narrow your search.*

1

- Type `forms` in the Search text box at the top of the Access Help window to enter the search text.
- Press the ENTER key to display the search results (Figure 59).

Q&A

Why do my search results differ?
If you do not have an Internet connection, your results will reflect only the content of the Help files on your computer. When searching for help online, results also can change as material is added, deleted, and updated on the online Help webpages maintained by Microsoft.

Q&A

Why were my search results not very helpful?
When initiating a search, be sure to check the spelling of the search text; also, keep your search specific to return the most accurate results.

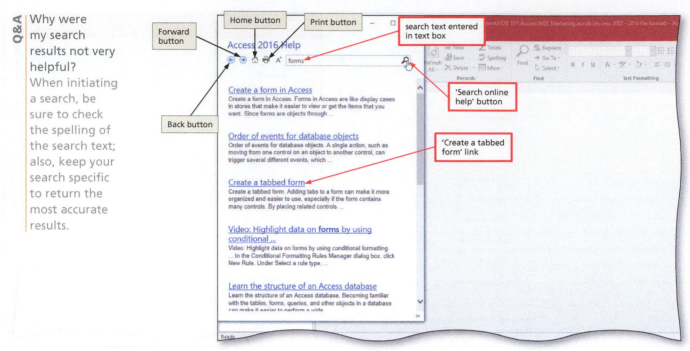

Figure 59

• Click the 'Create a tabbed form' link to display the Help information associated with the selected topic (Figure 60).

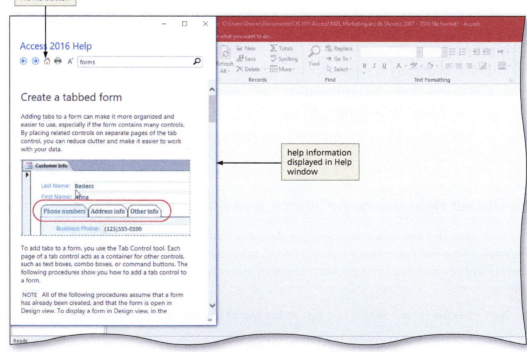

Figure 60

3

- Click the Home button in the Help window to clear the search results and redisplay the Help home page (Figure 61).

- Click the Close button in the Access 2016 Help window to close the window.

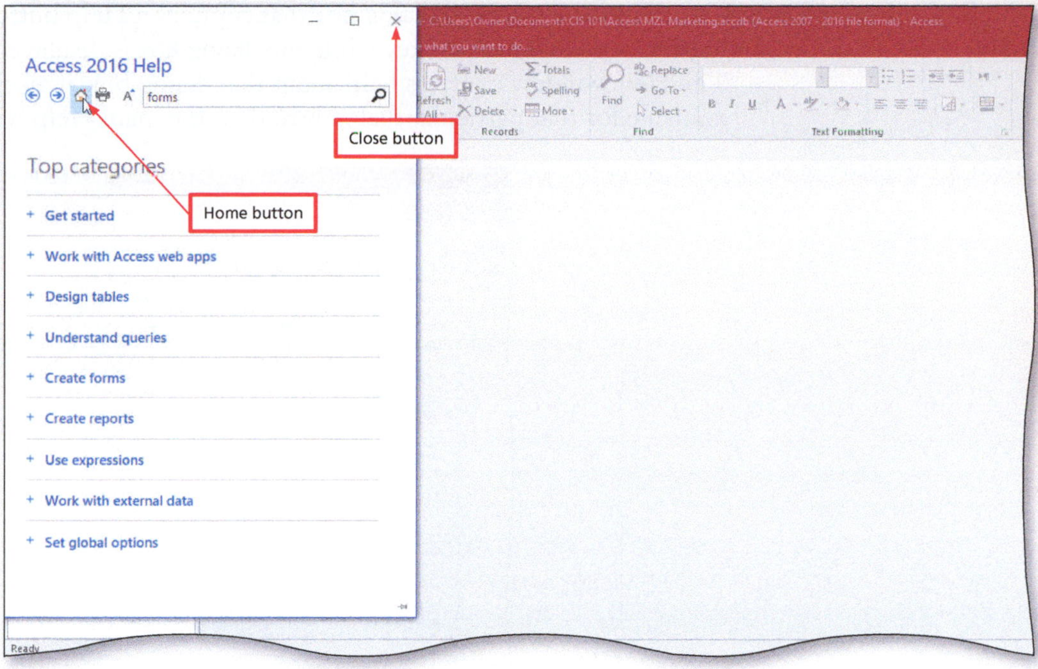

Figure 61

Obtaining Help while Working in an Office App

Help in the Office apps provides you with the ability to obtain help directly, without opening the Help window and initiating a search. For example, you may be unsure about how a particular command works, or you may be presented with a dialog box that you are not sure how to use.

Figure 62 shows one option for obtaining help while working in an Office app. If you want to learn more about a command, point to its button and wait for the ScreenTip to appear. If the Help icon and 'Tell me more' link appear in the ScreenTip, click the 'Tell me more' link or press the F1 key while pointing to the button to open the Help window associated with that command.

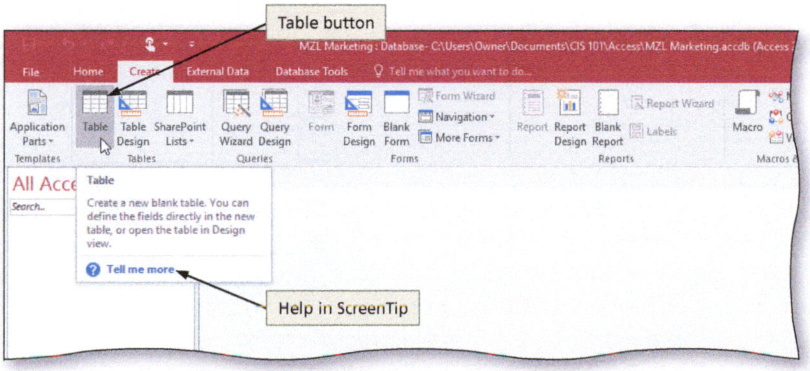

Figure 62

Figure 63 shows a dialog box that contains a Help button. Clicking the Help button or pressing the F1 key while the dialog box is displayed opens a Help window. The Help window contains help about that dialog box, if available. If no help file is available for that particular dialog box, then the main Help window opens.

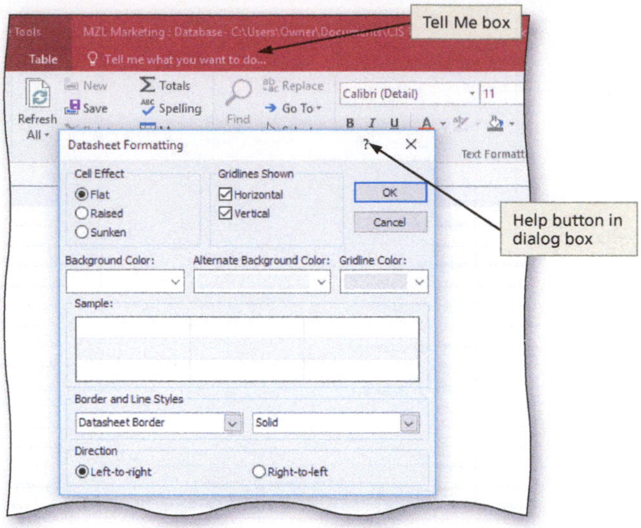

Figure 63

The Tell Me box is available in most Office apps and can perform a variety of functions. One of these functions is to provide easy access to commands by typing a description of the command.

To Obtain Help Using the Tell Me Box

1 SIGN IN | 2 USE WINDOWS | 3 USE APPS | 4 FILE MANAGEMENT | 5 SWITCH APPS
6 SAVE FILES | 7 CHANGE SCREEN RESOLUTION | 8 EXIT APPS | 9 USE HELP

If you are having trouble finding a command in an Office app, you can use the Tell Me box to search for the function you are trying to perform. As you type, the Tell Me box will suggest commands that match the search text you are entering. *Why? You can use the Tell Me box to quickly access commands you otherwise may be unable to find on the ribbon.* The following step finds information about forms.

1

- Type **forms** in the Tell Me box and watch the search results appear.

- Point to Client Forms to display a submenu displaying the various types of forms (Figure 64).

- Click an empty area of the document window to close the search results.

2

- Exit Microsoft Access.

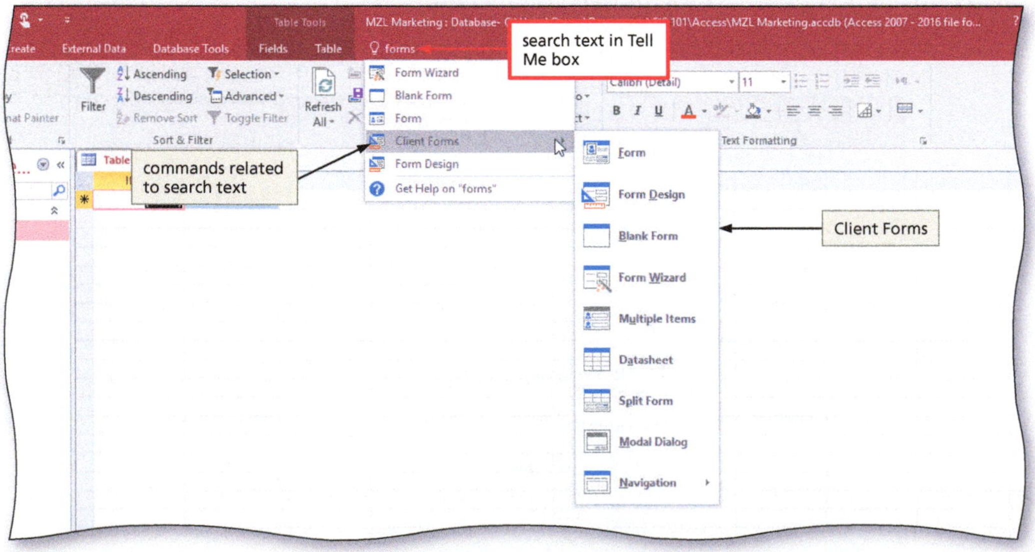

Figure 64

Using the Windows Search Box

One of the more powerful Windows features is the Windows search box. The search box is a central location from where you can type search text and quickly access related Windows commands or web search results. In addition, **Cortana** is a new search tool in Windows that you can access using the search box. It can act as a personal assistant by performing functions such as providing ideas; searching for apps, files, and folders; and setting reminders. In addition to typing search text in the search box, you also can use your computer or mobile device's microphone to give verbal commands.

To Use the Windows Search Box

1 SIGN IN | 2 USE WINDOWS | 3 USE APPS | 4 FILE MANAGEMENT | 5 SWITCH APPS
6 SAVE FILES | 7 CHANGE SCREEN RESOLUTION | 8 EXIT APPS | 9 USE HELP

The following step uses the Windows search box to search for a Windows command. *Why? Using the search box to locate apps, settings, folders, and files can be faster than navigating windows and dialog boxes to search for the desired content.*

1

- Type **notification** in the search box to display the search results. The search results include related Windows settings, Windows Store apps, and web search results (Figure 65).

- Click an empty area of the desktop to close the search results.

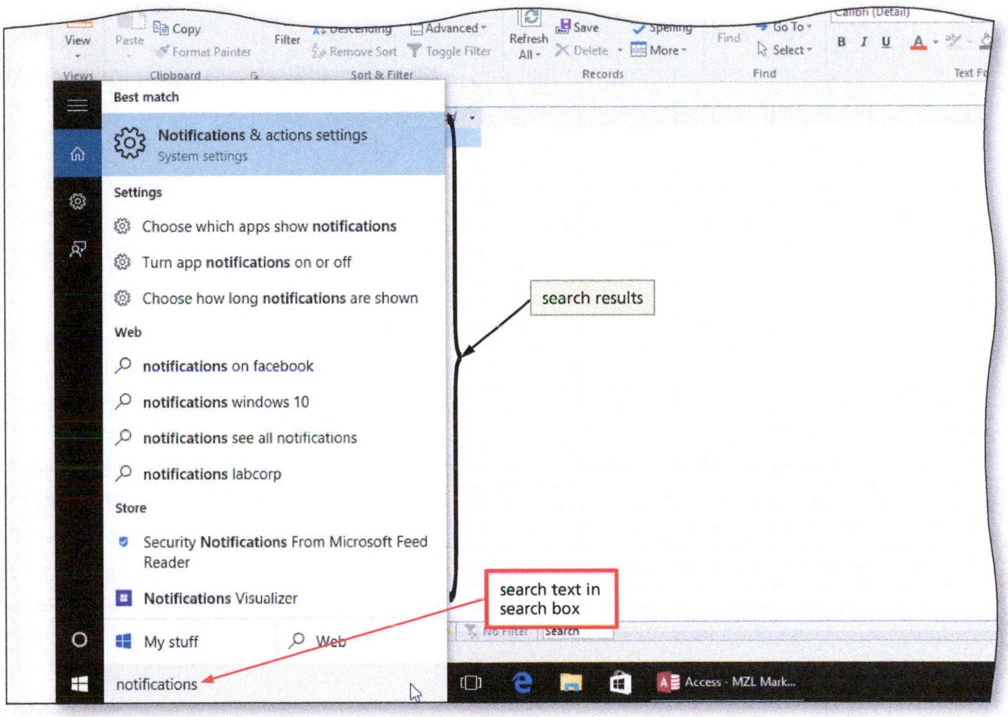

Figure 65

Summary

In this module, you learned how to use the Windows interface, several touch screen and mouse operations, file and folder management, some basic features of Microsoft Access, and discovered the common elements that exist among the different Office apps. Topics covered included signing in, using Windows, using apps, file management, switching between apps, saving files, changing screen resolution, exiting apps, and using help.

What guidelines should you follow to plan your projects?

The process of communicating specific information is a learned, rational skill. Computers and software, especially Microsoft Office 2016, can help you develop ideas and present detailed information to a particular audience and minimize much of the laborious work of drafting and revising projects. No matter what method you use to plan a project, it is beneficial to follow some specific guidelines from the onset to arrive at a final product that is informative, relevant, and effective. Use some aspects of these guidelines every time you undertake a project, and others as needed in specific instances.

1. Determine the project's purpose.

   a) Clearly define why you are undertaking this assignment.

   b) Begin to draft ideas of how best to communicate information by handwriting ideas on paper; composing directly on a laptop, tablet, or mobile device; or developing a strategy that fits your particular thinking and writing style.

2. Analyze your audience.

   a) Learn about the people who will read, analyze, or view your work.

   b) Determine their interests and needs so that you can present the information they need to know and omit the information they already possess.

   c) Form a mental picture of these people or find photos of people who fit this profile so that you can develop a project with the audience in mind.

3. Gather possible content.

   a) Locate existing information that may reside in spreadsheets, databases, or other files.

   b) Conduct a web search to find relevant websites.

   c) Read pamphlets, magazine and newspaper articles, and books to gain insights of how others have approached your topic.

   d) Conduct personal interviews to obtain perspectives not available by any other means.

   e) Consider video and audio clips as potential sources for material that might complement or support the factual data you uncover.

4. Determine what content to present to your audience.

   a) Write three or four major ideas you want an audience member to remember after reading or viewing your project.

   b) Envision your project's endpoint, the key fact you wish to emphasize, so that all project elements lead to this final element.

   c) Determine relevant time factors, such as the length of time to develop the project, how long readers will spend reviewing your project, or the amount of time allocated for your speaking engagement.

   d) Decide whether a graph, photo, or artistic element can express or enhance a particular concept.

   e) Be mindful of the order in which you plan to present the content, and place the most important material at the top or bottom of the page, because readers and audience members generally remember the first and last pieces of information they see and hear.

How should you submit solutions to questions in the assignments identified with a ✳ symbol?

Every assignment in this book contains one or more questions with a ✳ symbol. These questions require you to think beyond the assigned file. Present your solutions to the question in the format required by your instructor. Possible formats may include one or more of these options: write the answer; create a document that contains the answer; present your answer to the class; discuss your answer in a group; record the answer as audio or video using a webcam, smartphone, or portable media player; or post answers on a blog, wiki, or website.

Apply Your Knowledge

Reinforce the skills and apply the concepts you learned in this module.

Creating a Folder and a Database

Instructions: You will create an Access Assignments folder and then create an Access database and save it in the folder.

Perform the following tasks:
1. Open the File Explorer window and then double-click to open the Documents folder.
2. Click the New folder button on the Quick Access Toolbar to display a new folder icon and text box for the folder name.
3. Type **Access Assignments** in the text box to name the folder. Press the ENTER key to create the folder in the Documents folder.
4. Run Access.
5. Use the 'Blank desktop database' option to create a database with the name AYK 1. Do not press the ENTER key after typing the file name.
6. If requested by your instructor, name the database AYK 1 Lastname where Lastname is your last name.
7. Click the 'Browse for a location to put your database' button and navigate to the Access Assignments folder in the Documents library. Click the OK button to select the Access Assignments folder as the location for the database and close the dialog box. Click the Create button to create the database.
8. If your Quick Access Toolbar does not show the Quick Print button, add the Quick Print button to the Quick Access Toolbar.
9. Exit Access.
10. Open the File Explorer window, open the Documents library, and then open the Access Assignments folder you created.
11. Double-click the AYK 1 database to run Access and open the AYK 1 database.
12. Remove the Quick Print button from the Quick Access Toolbar.
13. Submit the database in the format specified by your instructor.
14. ✳ What other commands might you find useful to include on the Quick Access Toolbar?

Extend Your Knowledge

Extend the skills you learned in this module and experiment with new skills. You will use Help to complete the assignment.

Using Help

Instructions: Use Access Help to perform the following tasks.

Perform the following tasks:
1. Run Access.
2. Click the Microsoft Access Help button to open the Access Help window (see Figure 56).
3. Search Access Help to answer the following questions.

    a. What shortcut keys are available for entering data in Datasheet or Form view?
    b. What is the AutoCorrect feature?

Continued >

Extend Your Knowledge *continued*

 c. What is the purpose of the Navigation Pane?

 d. How do you back up a database?

 e. What are data types?

 f. What is a query?

 g. What is a template?

 h. What is the purpose of compacting and repairing a database?

4. Exit Access.

5. Type the answers from your searches in a new blank Word document.

6. If requested to do so by your instructor, enter your name in the Word document.

7. Save the document with a new file name and then submit it in the format specified by your instructor.

8. Exit Word.

9. ✺ What search text did you use to perform the searches above? Did it take multiple attempts to search and locate the exact information for which you were searching?

Expand Your World

Create a solution that uses cloud or web technologies by learning and investigating on your own from general guidance.

Instructions: Create the folders shown in Figure 66. Then, using the respective Office Online app, create a small file to save in each folder (i.e., create a Word document to save in the Word folder, a PowerPoint presentation to save in the PowerPoint folder, and so on).

Perform the following tasks:

1. Sign in to OneDrive in your browser.

2. Use the New button to create the folder structure shown in Figure 66.

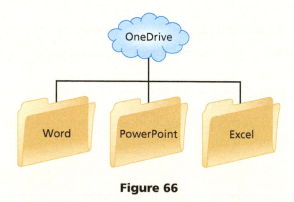

Figure 66

3. In the Word folder, use the New button to create a Word document with the file name, Reminders, and containing the text, Lunch with Laura on Tuesday.

4. Save the document and then exit the app.

5. Navigate to the PowerPoint folder.

6. Create a PowerPoint presentation called Database Sales with one slide containing the title text, Online Presentation, and then exit the app.

7. Navigate to the Excel folder.

8. Create an Excel spreadsheet called Database Sales Analysis containing the text, Sales Cost Analysis, in cell A1, and then exit the app.

9. Submit the assignment in the format specified by your instructor.

10. ✳ Based on your current knowledge of OneDrive, do you think you will use it? What about the Office Online apps?

In the Labs

Design, create, modify, and/or use files following the guidelines, concepts, and skills presented in this module. Labs 1 and 2, which increase in difficulty, require you to create solutions based on what you learned in the module; Lab 3 requires you to apply your creative thinking and problem-solving skills to design and implement a solution.

Lab 1: Creating Folders for a Bookstore

Problem: Your friend works for a local bookstore. He would like to organize his files in relation to the types of books available in the store. He has seven main categories: fiction, biography, children, humor, social science, nonfiction, and medical. You are to create a folder structure similar to the one in Figure 67.

Perform the following tasks:

1. Click the File Explorer button on the taskbar and display the contents of the Documents folder.

2. In the Documents folder, create the main folder and name it Book Categories.

3. Navigate to the Book Categories folder.

4. Within the Book Categories folder, create a folder for each of the following: Fiction, Biography, Children, Humor, Social Science, Nonfiction, and Medical.

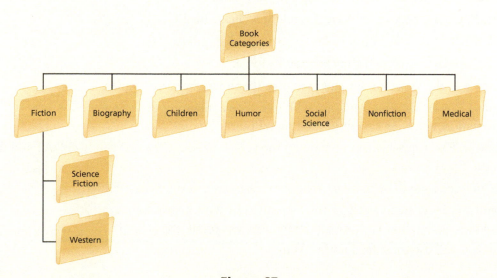

Figure 67

Continued >

In the Labs *continued*

5. Within the Fiction folder, create two additional folders, one for Science Fiction and the second for Western.

6. Submit the assignment in the format specified by your instructor.

7. Think about how you use your computer for various tasks (consider personal, professional, and academic reasons). What folders do you think will be required on your computer to store the files you save?

Lab 2: **Saving Files in Folders**

Problem: You are taking a class that requires you to create Word, PowerPoint, Excel, and Access files. You will save these files to folders named for four different Office apps (Figure 68).

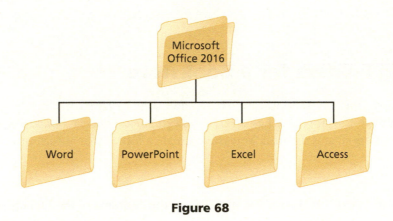

Figure 68

Perform the following tasks:

1. Create the folders shown in Figure 68.

2. Create a Word document containing the text, Week 1 Notes.

3. In the Backstage view, click Save As and then click This PC.

4. Click the Browse button to display the Save As dialog box.

5. Click Documents to open the Documents folder.

6. Navigate to the Word folder and then save the file in the Word folder.

7. Create a PowerPoint presentation with one slide containing the title text, In-Class Presentation, and then save it in the PowerPoint folder.

8. Create an Excel spreadsheet containing the text, Financial Spreadsheet, in cell A1 and then save it in the Excel folder.

9. Save an Access database named, My Movie Database, in the Access folder.

10. Submit the assignment in the format specified by your instructor.

11. Based on your current knowledge of Word, PowerPoint, Excel, and Access, which app do you think you will use most frequently? Why?

Lab 3: **Consider This: Your Turn**

Performing Research about Malware

Problem: You have just installed a new computer with the Windows operating system. Because you want to be sure that it is protected from the threat of malware, you decide to research malware, malware protection, and removing malware.

Part 1: Research the following three topics: malware, malware protection, and removing malware. Use the concepts and techniques presented in this module to use the search box to find information regarding these topics. Create a Word or OneNote document that contains steps to properly safeguard a computer from malware, ways to prevent malware, as well as the different ways to remove malware or a virus should your computer become infected. Submit your assignment in the format specified by your instructor.

Part 2: You made several decisions while searching for this assignment. What decisions did you make? What was the rationale behind these decisions? How did you locate the required information about malware?

1 | Databases and Database Objects: An Introduction

Objectives

You will have mastered the material in this module when you can:

- Describe the features of the Access window
- Create a database
- Create tables in Datasheet and Design views
- Add records to a table
- Close a database
- Open a database
- Print the contents of a table
- Import data
- Create and use a query
- Create and use a form
- Create and print custom reports
- Modify a report in Layout view
- Perform special database operations
- Design a database to satisfy a collection of requirements

Introduction

The term **database** describes a collection of data organized in a manner that allows access, retrieval, and use of that data. Microsoft Access 2016, usually referred to as simply Access, is a database management system. A **database management system** is software that allows you to use a computer to create a database; add, change, and delete data in the database; ask and answer questions concerning the data; and create forms and reports using the data.

Project — Database Creation

PrattLast Associates is a human resources outsourcing company that provides HR services, such as payroll, hiring, training, and employee benefits management to small and medium-size businesses in the Midwest. Organizations might outsource only one function, such as payroll, or might outsource several functions. While there are many different ways to charge customers, PrattLast charges a set amount per employee per month. The amount varies based on number and type of functions outsourced.

Microsoft Access 2016

File Home Create External Data Database Tools Tell me what you want to do...

PrattLast Associates : Database- C:\Users\Owner\Documents\Cl

Account managers serve their respective client companies by providing HR solutions and understanding the businesses for which they are responsible. The PrattLast account managers can earn bonuses if their client companies elect to outsource additional HR functions. For example, if the business currently outsources only payroll but is convinced by the account manager to add hiring to the outsourced functions, the account manager receives a bonus.

To ensure that operations run smoothly, PrattLast organizes data on its accounts and account managers in a database managed by Access. In this way, PrattLast keeps its data current and accurate and can analyze it for trends; PrattLast can also create a variety of useful reports.

In a **relational database** such as those maintained by Access, a database consists of a collection of tables, each of which contains information on a specific subject. Figure 1–1 shows the database for PrattLast Associates. It consists of two tables: the Account table (Figure 1–1a) contains information about PrattLast accounts, and the Account Manager table (Figure 1–1b) contains information about the account managers to whom these accounts are assigned.

caption for Account Number field | fields

records

AC #	Account Name	Street	City	State	Postal Code	Amount Paid	Current Due	AM #
AC001	Avondale Community Bank	256 Main St.	Avondale	IL	60311	$24,752.25	$3,875.25	31
BL235	Bland Corp.	100 Granger Hwy.	Granger	IL	60314	$29,836.65	$2,765.30	35
CA043	Carlton Regional Clinic	589 Central Ave.	Carlton	IL	60313	$30,841.05	$3,074.30	58
CO621	Codder Plastics Co.	421 First Ave.	Bremerton	IN	46003	$27,152.25	$2,875.00	35
EC010	Eco Clothes Inc.	120 Pine St.	Davidson	IN	46010	$19,620.00	$1,875.00	58
HL111	Halko Legal Associates	321 Feathering Rd.	Gleneagle	IL	60319	$25,702.20	$3,016.75	58
JM323	JSP Manufacturing Inc.	1200 Franklin Blvd.	Wells	IN	46007	$19,739.70	$2,015.00	31
KC156	Key Community College System	35 Indiana Ave.	Walker	IN	46004	$10,952.25	$0.00	31
KV089	KAL Veterinary Services	116 Pine St.	Granger	IL	60314	$34,036.50	$580.00	35
LC005	Lancaster County Hospital	215 River St.	Granger	IL	46004	$44,025.60	$6,590.83	58
LI268	Lars-Idsen Inc.	829 Wooster Rd.	Davidson	IN	46010	$0.00	$1,280.75	35
MI345	Midwest Library Consortium	3400 Metro Pkwy.	Bremerton	IN	46003	$21,769.20	$2,890.60	31
ML008	Mums Landscaping Co.	865 Ridge Rd.	Wells	IN	46007	$13,097.10	$2,450.00	35
TP098	TAL Packaging Systems	12 Polk Ave.	Carlton	IL	60313	$22,696.95	$3,480.45	58
TW001	Tri-County Waste Disposal	345 Central Blvd.	Rushton	IL	60321	$15,345.00	$2,875.50	31

Figure 1–1a Account Table

AM # (Account Manager Number) is 35

AM #	Last Name	First Name	Street	City	State	Postal Code	Start Date	Salary	Bonus Rate
31	Rivera	Haydee	325 Twiddy St.	Avondale	IL	60311	6/3/2013	$48,750.00	0.15
35	Simson	Mark	1467 Hartwell St.	Walker	IN	46004	5/19/2014	$40,500.00	0.12
42	Lu	Peter	5624 Murray Ave.	Davidson	IN	46007	8/3/2015	$36,750.00	0.09
58	Murowski	Karen	168 Truesdale Dr.	Carlton	IL	60313	11/9/2016	$24,000.00	0.08

Figure 1–1b Account Manager Table

AM # (Account Manager Number) for Mark Simson is 35

The rows in the tables are called **records**. A record contains information about a given person, product, or event. A row in the Account table, for example, contains information about a specific account, such as the account's name, address information, and other data.

The columns in the tables are called fields. A **field** contains a specific piece of information within a record. In the Account table, for example, the fourth field, City, contains the name of the city where the account is located.

The first field in the Account table is AC #, which is an abbreviation for Account Number. PrattLast Associates assigns each account a number; the PrattLast account numbers consist of two uppercase letters followed by a three-digit number.

The account numbers are unique; that is, no two accounts have the same number. Such a field is a **unique identifier**. A unique identifier, as its name suggests, is a way of uniquely identifying each record in the database. A given account number will appear only in a single record in the table. Only one record exists, for example, in which the account number is JM323. A unique identifier is also called a **primary key**. Thus, the Account Number field is the primary key for the Account table. This means the Account Number field can be used to uniquely identify a record in the table. No two records can have the same value in the Account Number field.

The next seven fields in the Account table are Account Name, Street, City, State, Postal Code, Amount Paid, and Current Due. The Amount Paid column contains the amount that the account has paid PrattLast Associates year to date (YTD) prior to the current period. The Current Due column contains the amount due to PrattLast for the current period. For example, account JM323 is JSP Manufacturing Inc. The address is 1200 Franklin Blvd., in Wells, Indiana. The postal code is 46007. The amount paid is $19,739.70 and the current due amount is $2,095.00.

PrattLast assigns a single account manager to work with each account. The last column in the Account table, AM # (an abbreviation for Account Manager Number) gives the number of the account's account manager. The account manager number for JSP Manufacturing is 31.

The first field in the Account Manager table is also AM #, for Account Manager Number. The account manager numbers are unique, so the Account Manager Number field is the primary key of the Account Manager table.

The other fields in the Account Manager table are Last Name, First Name, Street, City, State, Postal Code, Start Date, Salary, and Bonus Rate. The Start Date field gives the date the account manager began working for PrattLast. The Salary field gives the salary paid to the account manager thus far this year. The Bonus Rate gives the potential bonus percentage based on personal performance. The bonus rate applies when the account manager either brings in new business or recommends productivity improvements. For example, account manager 31 is Haydee Rivera. Her address is 325 Twiddy St., in Avondale, Illinois. Her postal code is 60311. Haydee started working for PrattLast on June 3, 2013. So far this year, she has been paid $48,750.00 in salary. Her bonus rate is 0.15 (15%).

The account manager number appears in both the Account table and the Account Manager table, and relates accounts and account managers. Account manager 42, Peter Lu, was recently promoted to account manager and has not yet been assigned any accounts. His account manager number, therefore, does not appear on any row in the Account table.

BTW
Naming Fields
Access 2016 has a number of reserved words, words that have a special meaning to Access. You cannot use these reserved words as field names. For example, Name is a reserved word and could not be used in the Account table to describe an account's name. For a complete list of reserved words in Access 2016, consult Access Help.

How would you find the name of the account manager for Midwest Library Consortium?
In the Account table, you see that the account manager number for account Midwest Library Consortium is 31. To find the name of this account manager, look for the row in the Account Manager table that contains 31 in the AM # column. After you have found it, you know that the account manager for Midwest Library Consortium is Haydee Rivera.

CONSIDER THIS

How would you find all the accounts assigned to Haydee Rivera?
First, look in the Account Manager table to find that her number is 31. You would then look through the Account table for all the accounts that contain 31 in the AM # column. Haydee's accounts are AC001 (Avondale Community Bank), JM323 (JSP Manufacturing Inc.), KC156 (Key Community College System), MI345 (Midwest Library Consortium), and TW001 (Tri-County Waste Disposal).

In this module, you will learn how to create and use the database shown in Figure 1–1. The following roadmap identifies general activities you will perform as you progress through this module:

> For an introduction to Windows and instructions about how to perform basic Windows tasks, read the Office and Windows module at the beginning of this book, where you can learn how to resize windows, change screen resolution, create folders, move and rename files, use Windows Help, and much more.

1. **CREATE** the **FIRST TABLE**, Account Manager, using Datasheet view.
2. **ADD RECORDS** to the Account Manager table.
3. **PRINT** the **CONTENTS** of the Account Manager table.
4. **IMPORT RECORDS** into the second table, Account.
5. **MODIFY** the **SECOND TABLE** using Design view.
6. **CREATE** a **QUERY** for the Account table.
7. **CREATE** a **FORM** for the Account table.
8. **CREATE** a **REPORT** for the Account table.

Creating a Database

> For an introduction to Office and instructions about how to perform basic tasks in Office apps, read the Office and Windows module at the beginning of this book, where you can learn how to run an application, use the ribbon, save a file, open a file, print a file, exit an application, use Help, and much more.

In Access, all the tables, reports, forms, and queries that you create are stored in a single file called a database. A database is a structure that can store information about multiple types of objects, the properties of those objects, and the relationships among the objects. The first step is to create the database that will hold your tables, reports, forms, and queries. You can use either the Blank desktop database option or a template to create a new database. If you already know the tables and fields you want in your database, you would use the Blank desktop database option. If not, you can use a template. Templates can guide you by suggesting some commonly used databases.

To Create a Database

Because you already know the tables and fields you want in the PrattLast Associates database, you would use the Blank desktop database option rather than using a template. The following steps create the database.

1 Run Access.

2 Using the steps in the "To Create an Access Database" section in the Office and Windows module, create the database on your hard disk, OneDrive, or other storage location using PrattLast Associates as the file name (Figure 1–2).

Q&A The title bar for my Navigation Pane contains All Tables rather than All Access Objects, as in the figure. Is that a problem?
It is not a problem. The title bar indicates how the Navigation Pane is organized. You can carry out the steps in the text with either organization. To make your screens match the ones in the text, click the Navigation Pane arrow and then click Object Type.

I do not have the Search bar that appears in the figure. Is that a problem?
It is not a problem. If your Navigation Pane does not display a Search bar and you want your screens to match the ones in the text, right-click the Navigation Pane title bar arrow to display a shortcut menu, and then click Search Bar.

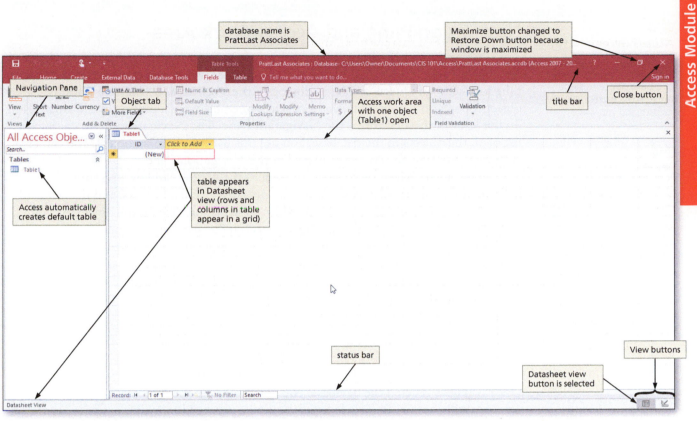

Figure 1–2

To Create a Database Using a Template

Ideally, you will design your own database, create a blank database, and then create the tables you have determined that your database should contain. If you are not sure what database design you will need, you could use a template. Templates can guide you by suggesting some commonly used databases. To create a database using a template, you would use the following steps.

1. If you have another database open, close it without exiting Access by clicking File on the ribbon to open the Backstage view and then clicking Close.

2. If you do not see a template that you want, you can search Microsoft Office online for additional templates.

3. Click the template you want to use. Be sure you have selected one that indicates it is for a desktop database.

4. Enter a file name and select a location for the database.

5. Click the Create button to create the database.

The Access Window

The Access window consists of a variety of components to make your work more efficient. These include the Navigation Pane, Access work area, ribbon, shortcut menus, and Quick Access Toolbar. Some of these components are common to other Microsoft Office apps; others are unique to Access.

BTW

Available Templates
The templates gallery includes both desktop and web-based templates. If you are creating an Access database for your own use, select a desktop template. Web-based templates allow you to create databases that you can publish to a SharePoint server.

BTW

Organizing Files and Folders
You should organize and store files in folders so that you easily can find the files later. For example, if you are taking an introductory computer class called CIS 101, a good practice would be to save all Access files in an Access folder in a CIS 101 folder. For a discussion of folders and detailed examples of creating folders, refer to the Office and Windows module at the beginning of this book.

Navigation Pane and Access Work Area

You work on objects such as tables, forms, and reports in the **Access work area**. In the work area in Figure 1–2, a single table, Table1, is open in the work area. **Object tabs** for the open objects appear at the top of the work area. If you have multiple objects open at the same time, you can select one of the open objects by clicking its tab. To the left of the work area is the Navigation Pane. The **Navigation Pane** contains a list of all the objects in the database. You use this pane to open an object. You can also customize the way objects are displayed in the Navigation Pane.

The **status bar**, located at the bottom of the Access window, presents information about the database object, the progress of current tasks, and the status of certain commands and keys; it also provides controls for viewing the object. As you type text or perform certain commands, various indicators might appear on the status bar. The left edge of the status bar in Figure 1–2 shows that the table object is open in **Datasheet view**. In Datasheet view, the table is represented as a collection of rows and columns called a **datasheet**. Toward the right edge are View buttons, which you can use to change the view that currently appears.

Determining Tables and Fields

Once you have created the database, you need to create the tables and fields that your database will contain. Before doing so, however, you need to make some decisions regarding the tables and fields.

Naming Tables and Fields

In creating your database, you must name tables, fields, and other objects. Before beginning the design process, you must understand the rules Access applies to table and field names. These rules are:

1. Names can be up to 64 characters in length.
2. Names can contain letters, digits, and spaces, as well as most of the punctuation symbols.
3. Names cannot contain periods (.), exclamation points (!), accent graves (`), or square brackets ([ ]).
4. Each field in a table must have a unique name.

The approach to naming tables and fields used in this text is to begin the names with an uppercase letter and to use lowercase for the other letters. In multiple-word names, each word begins with an uppercase letter, and there is a space between words (for example, Account Number).

Determining the Primary Key

For each table, you need to determine the primary key, the unique identifier. In many cases, you will have obvious choices, such as Account Number or Account Manager Number. If you do not have an obvious choice, you can use the primary key that Access creates automatically. It is a field called ID. It is an **autonumber field**, which means that Access will assign the value 1 to the first record, 2 to the second record, and so on.

Determining Data Types for the Fields

For each field in your database, you must determine the field's **data type**, that is, the type of data that can be stored in the field. Four of the most commonly used data types in Access are:

1. **Short Text** — The field can contain any characters. A maximum number of 255 characters is allowed in a field whose data type is Short Text.

2. **Number** — The field can contain only numbers. The numbers can be either positive or negative. Fields assigned this type can be used in arithmetic operations. You usually assign fields that contain numbers but will not be used for arithmetic operations (such as postal codes) a data type of Short Text.

3. **Currency** — The field can contain only monetary data. The values will appear with currency symbols, such as dollar signs, commas, and decimal points, and with two digits following the decimal point. Like numeric fields, you can use currency fields in arithmetic operations. Access assigns a size to currency fields automatically.

4. **Date & Time** — The field can contain dates and/or times.

Table 1–1 shows the other data types that are available in Access.

Table 1-1 Additional Data Types	
Data Type	**Description**
Long Text	Field can store a variable amount of text or combinations of text and numbers where the total number of characters may exceed 255.
AutoNumber	Field can store a unique sequential number that Access assigns to a record. Access will increment the number by 1 as each new record is added.
Yes/No	Field can store only one of two values. The choices are Yes/No, True/False, or On/Off.
OLE Object	Field can store an OLE object, which is an object linked to or embedded in the table.
Hyperlink	Field can store text that can be used as a hyperlink address.
Attachment	Field can contain an attached file. Images, spreadsheets, documents, charts, and other elements can be attached to this field in a record in the database. You can view and edit the attached file.
Calculated	Field specified as a calculation based on other fields. The value is not actually stored.

In the Account table, because the Account Number, Account Name, Street, City, and State can all contain letters, their data types should be Short Text. The data type for Postal Code is Short Text instead of Number because you typically do not use postal codes in arithmetic operations; you do not add postal codes or find an average postal code, for example. The Amount Paid and Current Due fields contain monetary data, so their data types should be Currency. The Account Manager Number field contains numbers, but you will not use these numbers in arithmetic operations, so its data type should be Short Text.

Similarly, in the Account Manager table, the data type for the Account Manager Number, Last Name, First Name, Street, City, State, and Postal Code fields should all be Short Text. The Start Date field should have a data type of Date & Time. The Salary field contains monetary amounts, so its data type should be Currency. The Bonus Rate field contains numbers that are not dollar amounts, so its data type should be Number.

For fields whose data type is Short Text, you can change the field size, that is, the maximum number of characters that can be entered in the field. If you set the field size

BTW

Data Types
Different database management systems have different available data types. Even data types that are essentially the same can have different names. The Currency data type in Access, for example, is referred to as Money in SQL Server.

BTW

AutoNumber Fields
AutoNumber fields also are called AutoIncrement fields. In Design view, the New Values field property allows you to increment the field sequentially (Sequential) or randomly (Random). The default is sequential.

BTW

Currency Symbols
To show the symbol for the Euro (€) instead of the dollar sign, change the Format property for the field whose data type is currency. To change the default symbols for currency, change the settings in Windows.

for the State field to 2, for example, Access will not allow the user to enter more than two characters in the field. On the other hand, fields whose data type is Number often require you to change the field size, which is the storage space assigned to the field by Access. Table 1–2 shows the possible field sizes for Number fields.

Table 1-2 Field Sizes for Number Fields	
Field Size	**Description**
Byte	Integer value in the range of 0 to 255
Integer	Integer value in the range of -32,768 to 32,767
Long Integer	Integer value in the range of -2,147,483,648 to 2,147,483,647
Single	Numeric values with decimal places to seven significant digits—requires 4 bytes of storage
Double	Numeric values with decimal places to more accuracy than Single—requires 8 bytes of storage
Replication ID	Special identifier required for replication
Decimal	Numeric values with decimal places to more accuracy than Single or Double—requires 12 bytes of storage.

CONSIDER THIS

What is the appropriate size for the Bonus Rate field?

If the size were Byte, Integer, or Long Integer, only integers could be stored. If you try to store a value that has decimal places, such as 0.18, in fields of these sizes, the portion to the right of the decimal point would be removed, giving a result of 0. To address this problem, the bonus rate should have a size of Single, Double, or Decimal. With such small numbers involved, Single, which requires the least storage of the three, is the appropriate choice.

BTW

Naming Files
The following characters cannot be used in a file name: question mark (?), quotation mark ("), slash (/), backslash (\ ), colon (:), asterisk (*), vertical bar (|), greater than symbol (>), and less than symbol (<).

Creating a Table

To create a table in Access, you must define its structure. That is, you must define all the fields that make up the table and their characteristics. You must also indicate the primary key.

In Access, you can use two different views to create a table: Datasheet view and Design view. In **Datasheet view**, the data in the table is presented in rows and columns, similar to a spreadsheet. Although the main reason to use Datasheet view is to add or update records in a table, you can also use it to create a table or to later modify its structure. The other view, **Design view**, is only used to create a table or to modify the structure of a table.

As you might expect, Design view has more functionality for creating a table than Datasheet view. That is, there are certain actions that can only be performed in Design view. One such action is assigning Single as the field size for the Bonus Rate field. In this module, you will create the first table, the Account Manager table, in Datasheet view. Once you have created the table in Datasheet view, you will use Design view to change the field size.

Whichever view you choose to use, before creating the table, you need to know the names and data types of the fields that will make up the table. You can also decide to enter a description for a particular field to explain important details about the field. When you select this field, this description will appear on the status bar. You might also choose to assign a **caption** to a particular field. If you assign a caption, Access will display the value you assign, rather than the field name, in datasheets and in forms. If you do not assign a caption, Access will display the field name.

When would you want to use a caption?
You would use a caption whenever you want something other than the field name displayed. One common example is when the field name is relatively long and the data in the field is relatively short. In the Account Manager table, the name of the first field is Account Manager Number, but the field contains data that is only two characters long. You will change the caption for this field to AM #, which is much shorter than Account Manager Number yet still describes the field. Doing so will enable you to greatly reduce the width of the column.

The results of these decisions for the fields in the Account Manager table are shown in Table 1–3. The table also shows the data types and field sizes of the fields as well as any special properties that need to be changed. The Account Manager Number field has a caption of AM #, enabling the width of the Account Manager Number column to be reduced in the datasheet.

Table 1-3 Structure of Account Manager Table			
Field Name	**Data Type**	**Field Size**	**Description**
Account Manager Number	Short Text	2	Primary Key **Description:** Unique identifier of account manager **Caption:** AM #
Last Name	Short Text	15	
First Name	Short Text	15	
Street	Short Text	20	
City	Short Text	20	
State	Short Text	2	
Postal Code	Short Text	5	
Start Date	Date/Time	(This appears as Date & Time on the menu of available data types)	
Salary	Currency		
Bonus Rate	Number	Single	Format: Fixed Decimal Places: 2

How do you determine the field size?
You need to determine the maximum number of characters that can be entered in the field. In some cases, it is obvious. Field sizes of 2 for the State field and 5 for the Postal Code field are certainly the appropriate choices. In other cases, you need to determine how many characters you want to allow. In the list shown in Table 1–3, PrattLast decided allowing 15 characters was sufficient for last names. This field size can be changed later if it proves to be insufficient.

What is the purpose of the Format and Decimal Places properties?
The format guarantees that bonus rates will be displayed with a fixed number of decimal places. Setting the decimal places property to 2 guarantees that the rates will be displayed with precisely two decimal places. Thus, a bonus rate of 0.2 will be displayed as 0.20.

To Modify the Primary Key

1 CREATE FIRST TABLE | 2 ADD RECORDS | 3 PRINT CONTENTS | 4 IMPORT RECORDS
5 MODIFY SECOND TABLE | 6 CREATE QUERY | 7 CREATE FORM | 8 CREATE REPORT

When you first create your database, Access automatically creates a table for you. You can immediately begin defining the fields. If, for any reason, you do not have this table or inadvertently delete it, you can create the table by clicking Create on the ribbon and then clicking the Table button (Create tab | Tables group). In either case, you are ready to define the fields.

The following steps change the name, data type, and other properties of the first field to match the Account Manager Number field in Table 1–3, which is the primary key. **Why?** *Access has already created the first field as the primary key field, which it has named ID. Account Manager Number is a more appropriate choice.*

1

- Right-click the column heading for the ID field to display a shortcut menu (Figure 1–3).

Q&A

Why does my shortcut menu look different?
You displayed a shortcut menu for the column instead of the column heading. Be sure you right-click the column heading.

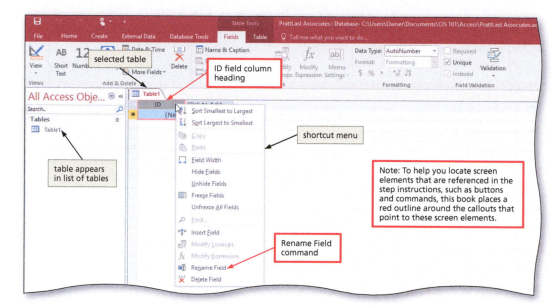

Figure 1–3

2

- Click Rename Field on the shortcut menu to highlight the current name.

- Type `Account Manager Number` to assign a name to the new field.

- Click the white space immediately below the field name to complete the addition of the field (Figure 1–4).

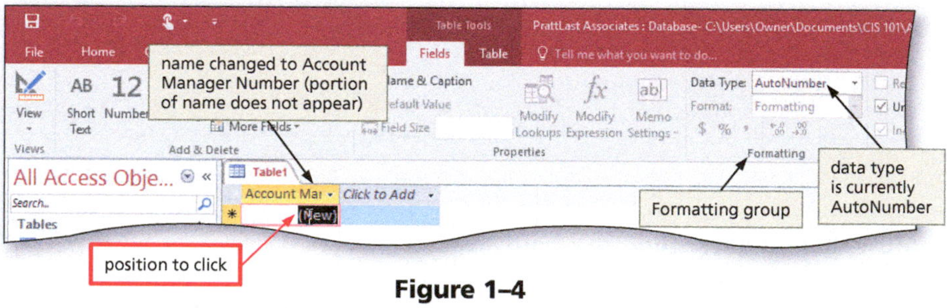

Figure 1–4

Q&A

Why does the full name of the field not appear?
The default column size is not large enough for Account Manager Number to be displayed in its entirety. You will address this issue in later steps.

3

- Because the data type needs to be changed from AutoNumber to Short Text, click the Data Type arrow (Table Tools Fields tab | Formatting group) to display a menu of available data types (Figure 1–5).

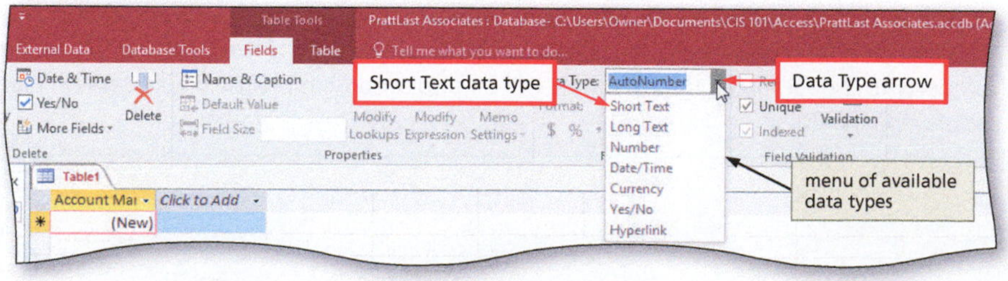

Figure 1–5

4

- Click Short Text to select the data type for the field (Figure 1–6).

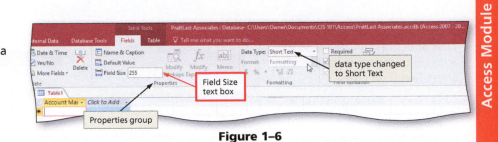

Figure 1–6

5

- Click the Field Size text box (Table Tools Fields tab | Properties group) to select the current field size, use either the DELETE or BACKSPACE keys to erase the current field size, if necessary, and then type 2 as the new field size.

- Click the Name & Caption button (Table Tools Fields tab | Properties group) to display the Enter Field Properties dialog box.

- Click the Caption text box (Enter Field Properties dialog box), and then type AM # as the caption.

- Click the Description text box, and then type **Unique identifier of account manager** as the description (Figure 1–7).

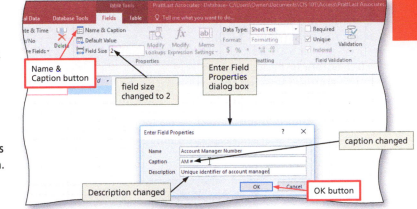

Figure 1–7

6

- Click the OK button (Enter Field Properties dialog box) to change the caption and description (Figure 1–8).

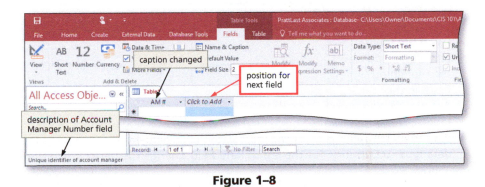

Figure 1–8

To Define the Remaining Fields in a Table

1 CREATE FIRST TABLE | 2 ADD RECORDS | 3 PRINT CONTENTS | 4 IMPORT RECORDS
5 MODIFY SECOND TABLE | 6 CREATE QUERY | 7 CREATE FORM | 8 CREATE REPORT

To define an additional field, you click the 'Click to Add' column heading, select the data type, and then type the field name. This is different from the process you used to modify the ID field. The following steps define the remaining fields shown in Table 1–3. These steps do not change the field size of the Bonus Rate field, however. ***Why?*** *You can only change the field size of a Number field in Design view. Later, you will use Design view to change this field size and change the format and number of decimal places.*

1

- Click the 'Click to Add' column heading to display a menu of available data types (Figure 1–9).

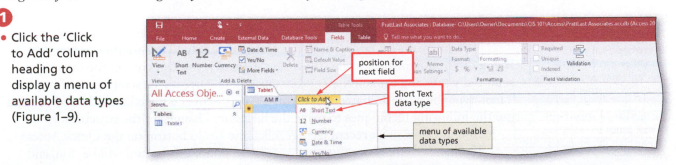

Figure 1–9

2

- Click Short Text in the menu of available data types to select the Short Text data type.

- Type **Last Name** to enter a field name.

- Click the blank space below the field name to complete the change of the name. Click the blank space a second time to select the field (Figure 1–10).

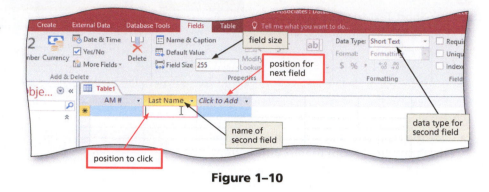

Figure 1–10

Q&A After entering the field name, I realized that I selected the wrong data type. How can I correct it?
Click the Data Type arrow, and then select the correct type.

I inadvertently clicked the blank space before entering the field name. How can I correct the name?
Right-click the field name, click Rename Field on the shortcut menu, and then type the new name.

3

- Change the field size to 15 just as you changed the field size of the Account Manager Number field.

- Using the same technique, add the remaining fields in the Account Manager

Figure 1–11

table. For the First Name, Street, City, State, and Postal Code fields, use the Short Text data type, but change the field sizes to match Table 1–3. For the Start Date field, change the data type to Date/Time. For the Salary field, change the data type to Currency. For the Bonus Rate field, change the data type to Number (Figure 1–11).

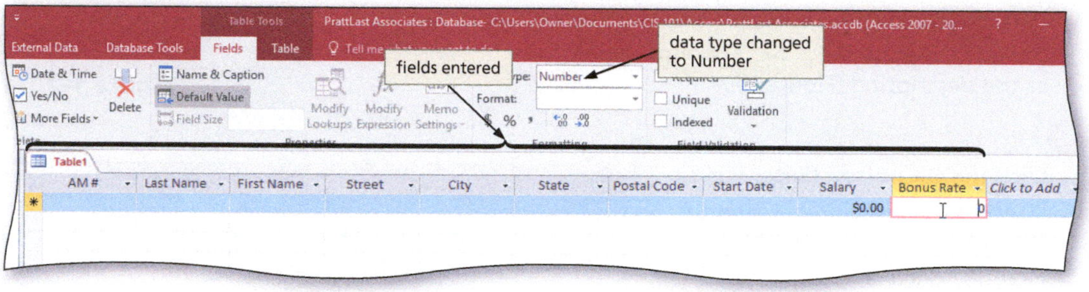

Q&A I have an extra row between the row containing the field names and the row that begins with the asterisk. What happened? Is this a problem? If so, how do I fix it?
You inadvertently added a record to the table by pressing a key. Even pressing the SPACEBAR would add a record. You now have an unwanted record. To fix it, press the ESC key or click the Undo button to undo the action. You may need to do this more than once.

When I try to move on to specify another field, I get an error message indicating that the primary key cannot contain a null value. How do I correct this?
First, click the OK button to remove the error message. Next, press the ESC key or click the Undo button to undo the action. You may need to do this more than once.

BTW
Touch Screen Differences
The Office and Windows interfaces may vary if you are using a touch screen. For this reason, you might notice that the function or appearance of your touch screen differs slightly from this module's presentation.

Making Changes to the Structure

When creating a table, check the entries carefully to ensure they are correct. If you discover a mistake while still typing the entry, you can correct the error by repeatedly pressing the BACKSPACE key until the incorrect characters are removed. Then, type the correct characters. If you do not discover a mistake until later, you can use the following techniques to make the necessary changes to the structure:

- To undo your most recent change, click the Undo button on the Quick Access Toolbar. If there is nothing that Access can undo, this button will be dim, and clicking it will have no effect.

- To delete a field, right-click the column heading for the field (the position containing the field name), and then click Delete Field on the shortcut menu.

- To change the name of a field, right-click the column heading for the field, click Rename Field on the shortcut menu, and then type the desired field name.

- To insert a field as the last field, click the 'Click to Add' column heading, click the appropriate data type on the menu of available data types, type the desired field name, and, if necessary, change the field size.

- To insert a field between existing fields, right-click the column heading for the field that will follow the new field, and then click Insert Field on the shortcut menu. Right-click the column heading for the field, click Rename Field on the shortcut menu, and then type the desired field name.

- To move a field, click the column heading for the field to be moved to select the field, and then drag the field to the desired position.

As an alternative to these steps, you might want to start over. To do so, click the Close button for the table, and then click the No button in the Microsoft Access dialog box. Click Create on the ribbon, and then click the Table button to create a table. You then can repeat the process you used earlier to define the fields in the table.

To Save a Table

1 CREATE FIRST TABLE | 2 ADD RECORDS | 3 PRINT CONTENTS | 4 IMPORT RECORDS
5 MODIFY SECOND TABLE | 6 CREATE QUERY | 7 CREATE FORM | 8 CREATE REPORT

The Account Manager table structure is complete. The final step is to save the table within the database. As part of the process, you will give the table a name. The following steps save the table, giving it the name Account Manager. **Why?** *PrattLast has decided that Account Manager is an appropriate name for the table.*

1

- Click the **Save** button on the Quick Access Toolbar to display the Save As dialog box (Figure 1–12).

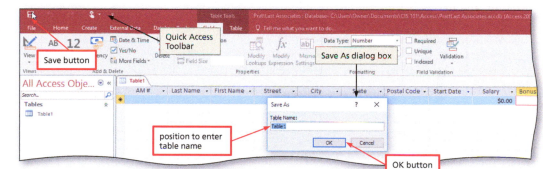

Figure 1–12

2

- Type **Account Manager** to change the name assigned to the table.

- Click the OK button (Save As dialog box) to save the table (Figure 1–13).

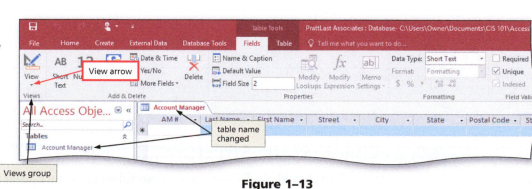

Figure 1–13

Other Ways

1. Click File on the ribbon, click Save in the Backstage view
2. Right-click tab for table, click Save on shortcut menu
3. Press **CTRL+S**

1 CREATE FIRST TABLE | 2 ADD RECORDS | 3 PRINT CONTENTS | 4 IMPORT RECORDS

5 MODIFY SECOND TABLE | 6 CREATE QUERY | 7 CREATE FORM | 8 CREATE REPORT

To View the Table in Design View

Even when creating a table in Datasheet view, Design view can be helpful. *Why? You easily can view the fields, data types, and properties to ensure you have entered them correctly. It is also easier to determine the primary key in Design view.* The following steps display the structure of the Account Manager table in Design view so that you can verify the design is correct.

1
- Click the View arrow (Table Tools Fields tab | Views group) to display the View menu (Figure 1–14).

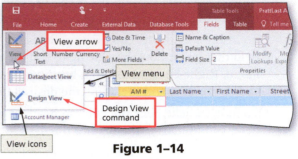

Q&A
Could I just click the View button rather than the arrow?
Yes. Clicking the button is equivalent to clicking the command represented by the icon currently appearing on the button. Because the icon on the button in Figure 1–14 is for Design view, clicking the button would display the table in Design view. If you are uncertain, you can always click the arrow and select from the menu.

Figure 1–14

2
- Click Design View on the View menu to view the table in Design view (Figure 1–15).

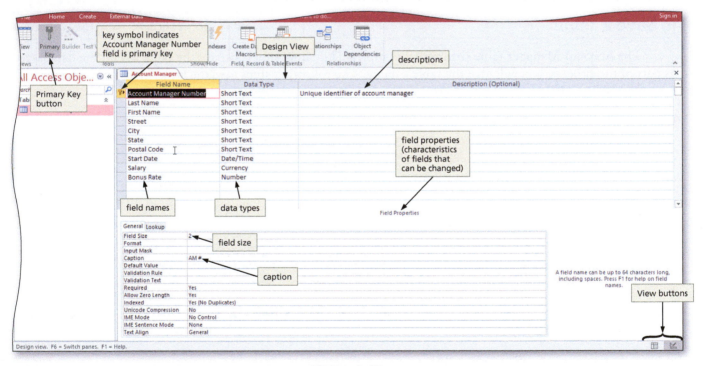

Figure 1–15

Other Ways

1. Click Design View button on status bar

Checking the Structure in Design View

You should use Design view to carefully check the entries you have made. In Figure 1–15, for example, you can see that the Account Manager Number field is the primary key of the Account Manager table by the key symbol in front of the field name. If your table does not have a key symbol, you can click the Primary Key button (Table Tools Design tab | Tools group) to designate a field as the primary key. You can also check that the data type, description, field size, and caption are all correct.

For the other fields, you can see the field name, data type, and description without taking any special action. To see the field size and/or caption for a field, click the field's **row selector**, the small box to the left of the field. Clicking the row selector for the Last Name field, for example, displays the properties for that field. You then can check to see that the field size is correct. In addition, if the field has a caption, you can check to see if that is correct. If you find any mistakes, you can make the necessary corrections on this screen. When you have finished, click the Save button to save your changes.

To Change a Field Size in Design View

1 CREATE FIRST TABLE | 2 ADD RECORDS | 3 PRINT CONTENTS | 4 IMPORT RECORDS
5 MODIFY SECOND TABLE | 6 CREATE QUERY | 7 CREATE FORM | 8 CREATE REPORT

Most field size changes can be made in either Datasheet view or Design view. However, changing the field size for Number fields, such as the Bonus Rate field, can only be done in Design view. Because the values in the Bonus Rate field have decimal places, only Single, Double, or Decimal are possible choices for the field size. The difference between these choices concerns the amount of accuracy, that is, the number of decimal places to which the number is accurate. Double is more accurate than Single, for example, but requires more storage space. Because the rates are only two decimal places, Single is an acceptable choice.

The following steps change the field size of the Bonus Rate field to Single, the format to Fixed, and the number of decimal places to 2. *Why change the format and number of decimal places? Changing the format and number ensures that each value will appear with precisely two decimal places.*

1
- If necessary, click the vertical scroll bar to display the Bonus Rate field. Click the row selector for the Bonus Rate field to select the field (Figure 1–16).

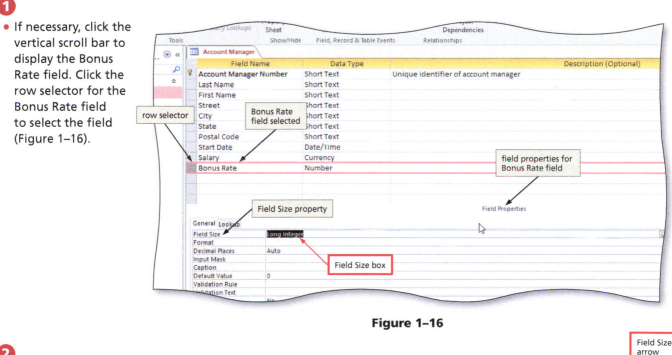

Figure 1–16

2
- Click the Field Size box to display the Field Size arrow.
- Click the Field Size arrow to display the Field Size menu (Figure 1–17).

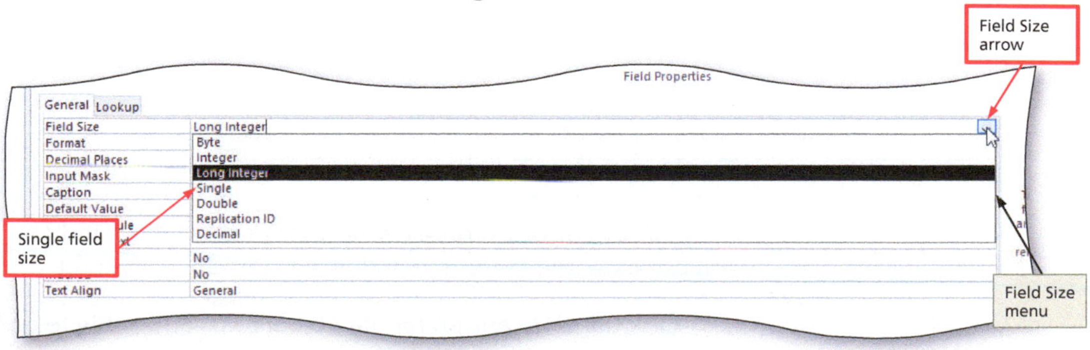

Q&A
What would happen if I left the field size set to Long Integer?
If the field size is Long Integer, Integer, or Byte, no decimal places can be stored. For example, a value of .10 would be stored as 0. If you enter rates and the values all appear as 0, chances are you did not change the field size property.

Figure 1–17

3

- Click Single to select single precision as the field size.

- Click the Format box to display the Format arrow (Figure 1-18).

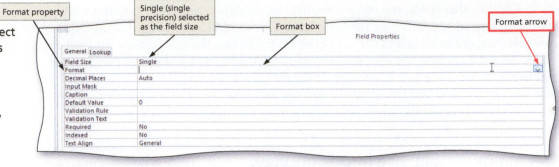

Figure 1–18

4

- Click the Format arrow to display the Format menu.

- Click Fixed to select fixed as the format.

- Click the Decimal Places box to display the Decimal Places arrow.

- Click the Decimal Places arrow to enter the number of decimal places.

- Click 2 to assign the number of decimal places.

- Click the Save button to save your changes (Figure 1–19).

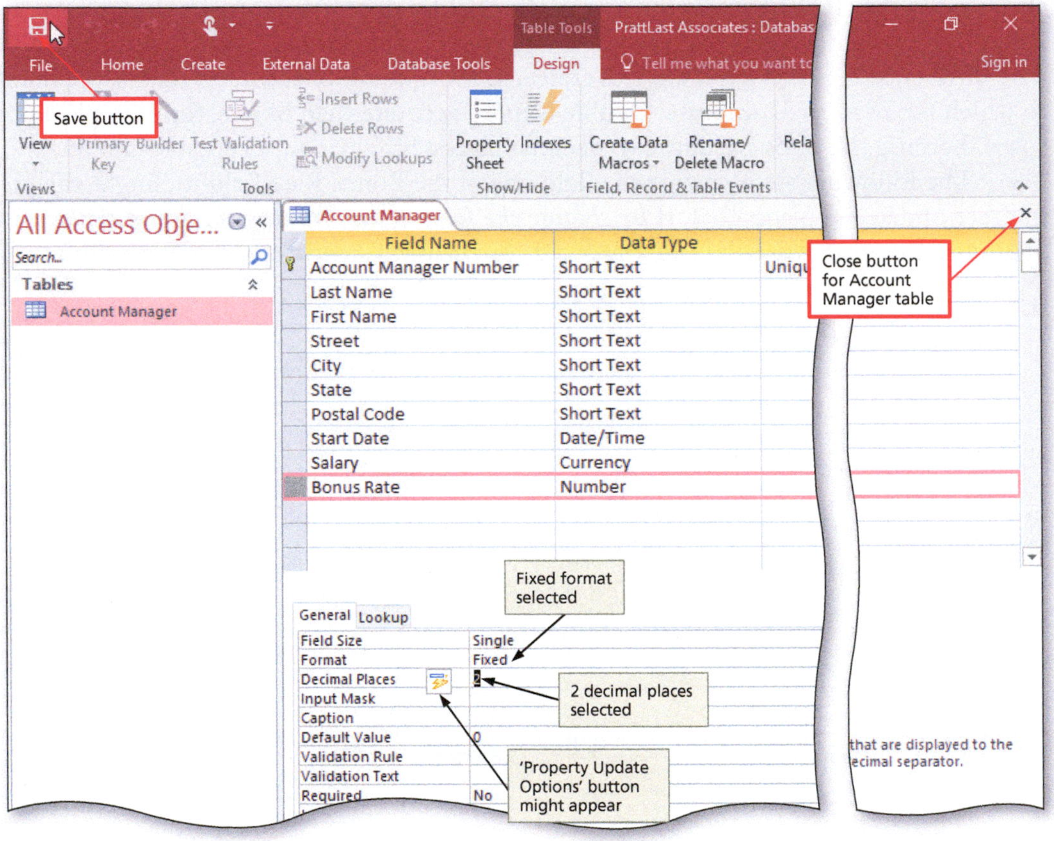

Q&A

Why did the 'Property Update Options' button appear?

You changed the number of decimal places. The 'Property Update Options' button offers a quick way of making the same change everywhere Bonus Rate appears. So far, you have not added any data or created any forms or reports that use the Bonus Rate field, so no such changes are necessary.

Figure 1–19

To Close the Table

Once you are sure that your entries are correct and you have saved your changes, you can close the table. The following step closes the table.

1 Click the Close button for the Account Manager table to close the table.

Other Ways

1. Right-click tab for table, click Close on shortcut menu

To Add Records to a Table

Creating a table by building the structure and saving the table is the first step in the two-step process of using a table in a database. The second step is to add records to the table. To add records to a table, the table must be open. When making changes to tables, you work in Datasheet view.

You often add records in phases. *Why? You might not have enough time to add all the records in one session, or you might not have all the records currently available.* The following steps open the Account Manager table in Datasheet view and then add the first two records in the Account Manager table (Figure 1–20).

AM #	Last Name	First Name	Street	City	State	Postal Code	Start Date	Salary	Bonus Rate
42	Lu	Peter	5624 Murray Ave.	Davidson	IN	46007	8/3/2015	$36,750.00	0.09
31	Rivera	Haydee	325 Twiddy St.	Avondale	IL	60311	6/3/2013	$48,750.00	0.15

Figure 1–20

1

- Right-click the Account Manager table in the Navigation Pane to display the shortcut menu (Figure 1–21).

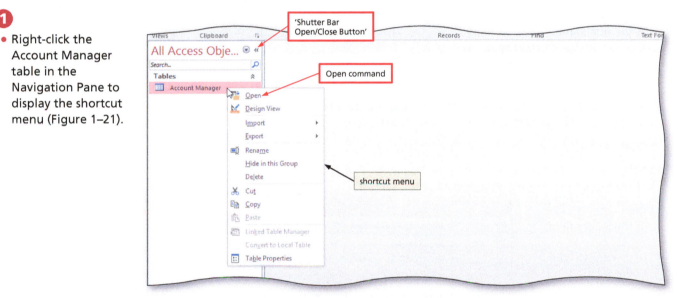

Figure 1–21

2

- Click Open on the shortcut menu to open the table in Datasheet view.

- Click the 'Shutter Bar Open/Close Button' to close the Navigation Pane (Figure 1–22).

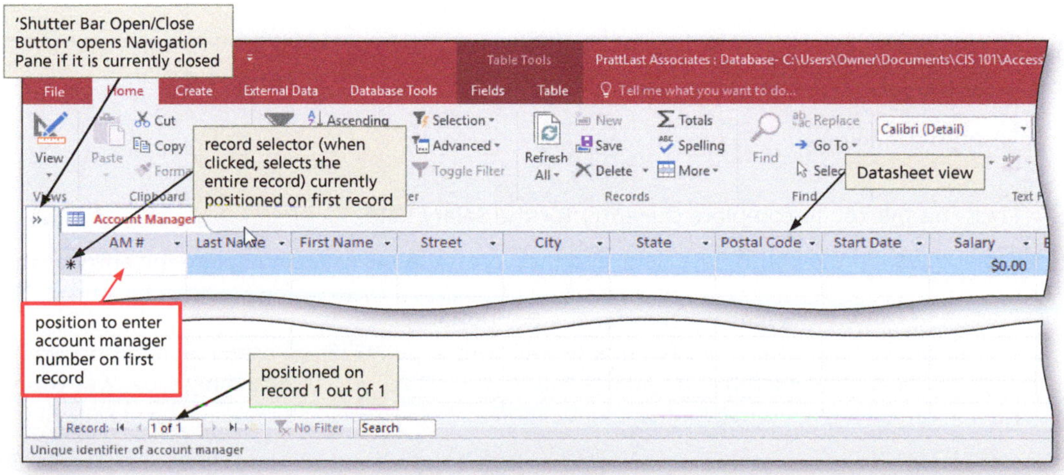

Figure 1–22

3

- Click the first row in the AM # field if necessary to display an insertion point, and type `42` to enter the first account manager number (Figure 1–23).

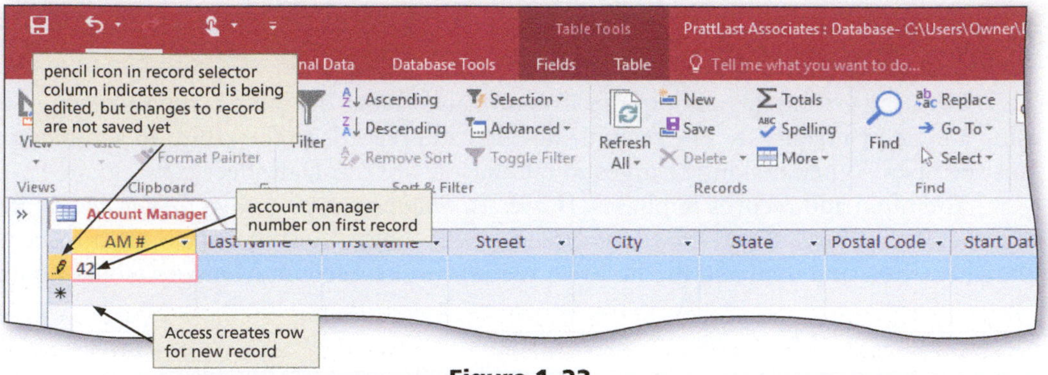

Figure 1–23

4

- Press the TAB key to move to the next field.

- Enter the last name, first name, street, city, state, and postal code by typing the following entries, pressing the TAB key after each one: `Lu` as the last name, `Peter` as the first name, `5624 Murray Ave.` as the street, `Davidson` as the city, `IN` as the state, and `46007` as the postal code.

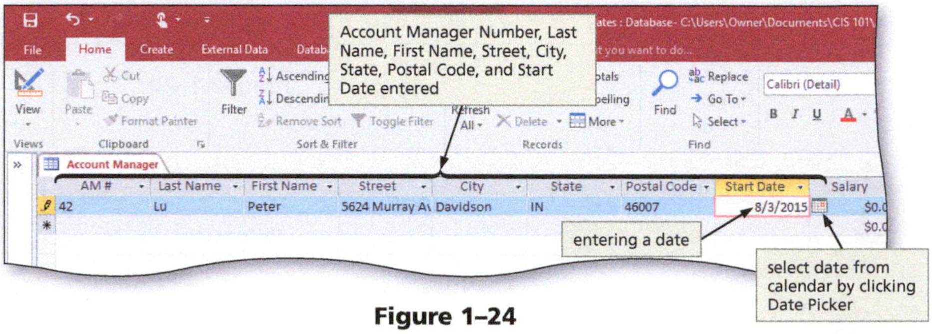

Figure 1–24

- If requested by your instructor, enter your address instead of `5624 Murray Ave.` as the street. If your address is longer than 20 characters, enter the first 20 characters.

- Type `8/3/2015` in the Start Date field (Figure 1–24).

5

- Press the TAB key and then type `36750` in the Salary field.

Q&A | Do I need to type a dollar sign?
You do not need to type dollar signs or commas. In addition, because the digits to the right of the decimal point are both zeros, you do not need to type either the decimal point or the zeros.

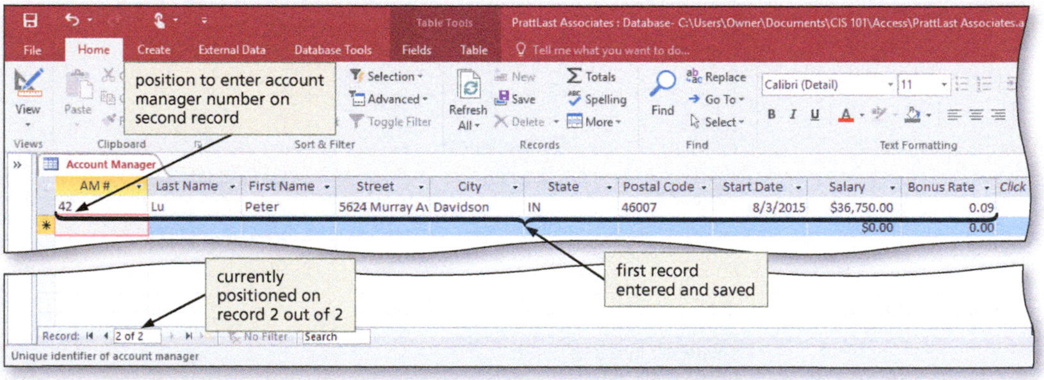

Figure 1–25

- Press the TAB key to complete the entry for the Salary field.

- Type `0.09` in the Bonus Rate field, and then press the TAB key to complete the entry of the first record (Figure 1–25).

Q&A | Do I need to type the leading zero for the Bonus Rate?
Typing the leading zero is not necessary. You could type .09 if you prefer. In addition, you would not have to type any final zeros. For example, if you needed to enter 0.20, you could simply type .2 as your entry.

How and when do I save the record?
As soon as you have entered or modified a record and moved to another record, Access saves the original record. This is different from other applications. The rows entered in an Excel worksheet, for example, are not saved until the entire worksheet is saved.

6

• Use the techniques shown in Steps 3 through 5 to enter the data for the second record (Figure 1–26).

Q&A
Does it matter that I entered account manager 31 after I entered account manager 42? Should the account manager numbers be in order?

The order in which you enter the records is not important. When you close and later reopen the table, the records will be in account manager number order, because the Account Manager Number field is the primary key.

Experiment

• Click the Salary field on either of the records. Be sure the Table Tools Fields tab is selected. Click the Format arrow, and then click each of the formats in the Format box menu to see the effect on the values in the Salary field. When finished, click Currency in the Format box menu.

Q&A
I made a mistake in entering the data. When should I fix it?

It is a good idea to fix it now, although you can fix it later as well. In any case, the following section gives you the techniques you can use to make any necessary corrections. If you want to fix it now, read that section and make your corrections before proceeding to the next step.

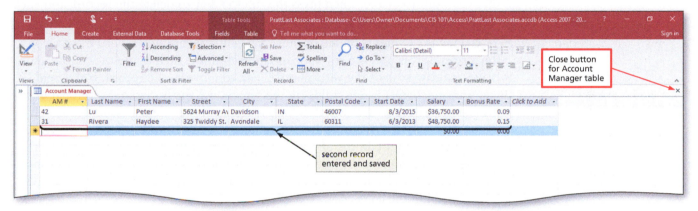

Figure 1–26

7

• Click the Close button for the Account Manager table, shown in Figure 1–26, to close the table (Figure 1–27).

• Exit Access.

Q&A
Is it necessary for me to exit Access at this point?

No. The step is here for two reasons.

First, you will
often not be able to add all the records you need to add in one sitting. In such a case, you will add some records, and then exit Access. When you are ready to resume adding the records, you will run Access, open the table, and then continue the addition process. Second, there is a break point coming up in the module. If you want to take advantage of that break, you need to first exit Access.

Figure 1–27

Making Changes to the Data

As you enter data, check your entries carefully to ensure they are correct. If you make a mistake and discover it before you press the TAB key, correct it by pressing the BACKSPACE key until the incorrect characters are removed, and then type the correct characters. If you do not discover a mistake until later, you can use the following techniques to make the necessary corrections to the data:

BTW

AutoCorrect Feature
The AutoCorrect feature of Access corrects common data entry errors. AutoCorrect corrects two capital letters by changing the second letter to lowercase and capitalizes the first letter in the names of days. It also corrects more than 400 commonly misspelled words.

- To undo your most recent change, click the Undo button on the Quick Access Toolbar. If there is nothing that Access can undo, this button will be dimmed, and clicking it will have no effect.

- To add a record, click the 'New (blank) record' button, click the position for the Account Manager Number field on the first open record, and then add the record. Do not worry about it being in the correct position in the table. Access will reposition the record based on the primary key, in this case, the Account Manager Number.

- To delete a record, click the record selector, shown in Figure 1–22, for the record that you want to delete. Then press the DELETE key to delete the record, and click the Yes button when Access asks you to verify that you want to delete the record.

BTW

Other AutoCorrect Options
Using the Office AutoCorrect feature, you can create entries that will replace abbreviations with spelled-out names and phrases automatically. To specify AutoCorrect rules, click File on the ribbon to open the Backstage view, click Options, and then click Proofing in the Access Options dialog box.

- To change the contents of one or more fields in a record, the record must be on the screen. If it is not, use any appropriate technique, such as the UP ARROW and DOWN ARROW keys or the vertical scroll bar, to move to the record. If the field you want to correct is not visible on the screen, use the horizontal scroll bar along the bottom of the screen to shift all the fields until the one you want appears. If the value in the field is currently highlighted, you can simply type the new value. If you would rather edit the existing value, you must have an insertion point in the field. You can place the insertion point by clicking in the field or by pressing the F2 key. You then can use the arrow keys, the DELETE key, and the BACKSPACE key for making the correction. You can also use the INSERT key to switch between Insert and Overtype mode. When you have made the change, press the TAB key to move to the next field.

If you cannot determine how to correct the data, you may find that you are "stuck" on the record, in which case Access neither allows you to move to another record nor allows you to close the table until you have made the correction. If you encounter this situation, simply press the ESC key. Pressing the ESC key will remove from the screen the record you are trying to add. You then can move to any other record, close the table, or take any other action you desire.

Break Point: If you wish to take a break, this is a good place to do so. You can exit Access now. To resume at a later time, run Access, open the database called PrattLast Associates, and continue following the steps from this location forward.

To Add Records to a Table that Contains Data

1 CREATE FIRST TABLE | 2 ADD RECORDS | 3 PRINT CONTENTS | 4 IMPORT RECORDS
5 MODIFY SECOND TABLE | 6 CREATE QUERY | 7 CREATE FORM | 8 CREATE REPORT

You can add records to a table that already contains data using a process almost identical to that used to add records to an empty table. The only difference is that you place the insertion point after the last record before you enter the additional data. To position the insertion point after the last record, you can use the **Navigation buttons**, which are buttons used to move within a table, found near the lower-left corner of the screen when a table is open. *Why not just click the Account Manager Number (AM #) on the first open record? You could click the first open record, but it is a good habit to use the 'New (blank) record' button. Once a table contains more records than will fit on the screen, it is easier to click the 'New (blank) record' button.* The purpose of each Navigation button is described in Table 1–4.

Table 1–4 Navigation Buttons in Datasheet View	
Button	**Purpose**
First record	Moves to the first record in the table
Previous record	Moves to the previous record
Next record	Moves to the next record
Last record	Moves to the last record in the table
New (blank) record	Moves to the end of the table to a position for entering a new record

BTW

Enabling Content
If the database is one that you created, or if it comes from a trusted source, you can enable the content. You should disable the content of a database if you suspect that your database might contain harmful content or damaging macros.

The following steps add the remaining records (Figure 1–28) to the Account Manager table.

AM #	Last Name	First Name	Street	City	State	Postal Code	Start Date	Salary	Bonus Rate
58	Murowski	Karen	168 Truesdale Dr.	Carlton	IL	60313	11/9/2016	$24,000.00	0.08
35	Simson	Mark	1467 Hartwell St.	Walker	IN	46004	5/19/2014	$40,500.00	0.12

Figure 1–28

1

- Run Access, unless it is already running.
- Open the PrattLast Associates database from your hard disk, OneDrive, or other storage location (Figure 1-29).
- If a Security Warning appears, click the Enable Content button.

Figure 1–29

2

- If the Navigation Pane is closed, click the 'Shutter Bar Open/Close Button', shown in Figure 1–27, to open the Navigation Pane (Figure 1–30).

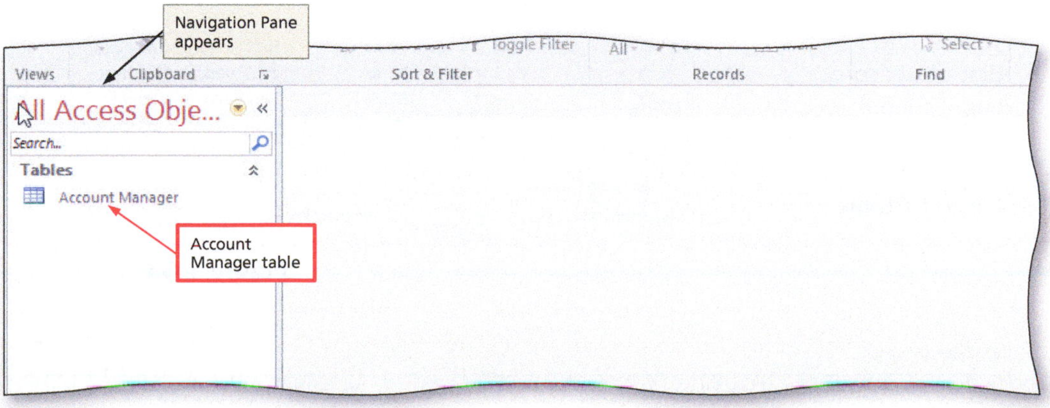

Figure 1–30

3

- Right-click the Account Manager table in the Navigation Pane to display a shortcut menu.

- Click Open on the shortcut menu to open the table in Datasheet view.

Why do the records appear in a different order than the order in which I entered them?
When you open the table, they are sorted in the order of the primary key. In this case, that means they will appear in Account Manager Number order.

- Close the Navigation Pane by clicking the 'Shutter Bar Open/ Close Button' (Figure 1–31).

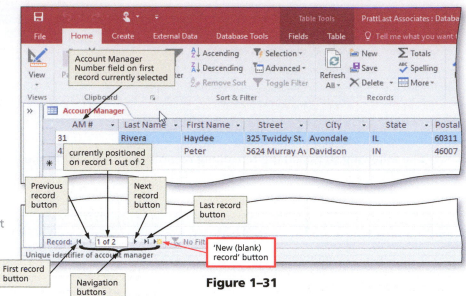

Figure 1–31

4

- Click the 'New (blank) record' button to move to a position to enter a new record (Figure 1–32).

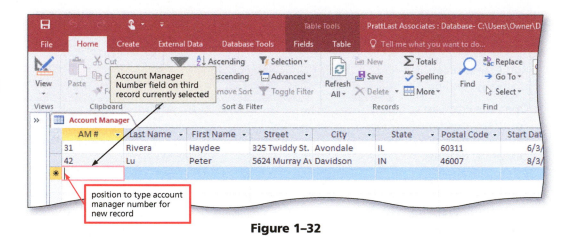

Figure 1–32

5

- Add the records shown in Figure 1–28 using the same techniques you used to add the first two records (Figure 1–33).

6

- Close the table.

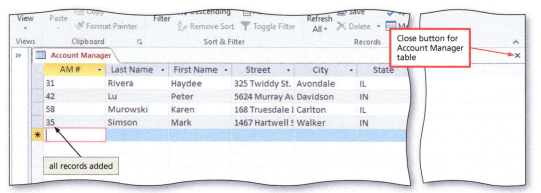

Figure 1–33

Other Ways

1. Click New button (Home tab | Records group)   2. Press CTRL+PLUS SIGN (+)

1 CREATE FIRST TABLE | **2 ADD RECORDS** | 3 PRINT CONTENTS | 4 IMPORT RECORDS
5 MODIFY SECOND TABLE | 6 CREATE QUERY | 7 CREATE FORM | 8 CREATE REPORT

To Resize Columns in a Datasheet

Access assigns default column sizes, which do not always provide space to display all the data in the field. In some cases, the data might appear but the entire field name will not. You can correct this problem by resizing the column (changing its size) in the datasheet. In some instances, you may want to reduce the size of a column. *Why? Some fields, such as the State field, are short enough that they do not require all the space on the screen that is allotted to them.* Changing a column width changes the layout, or design, of a table. The following steps resize the columns in the Account Manager table and save the changes to the layout.

1

- Open the Navigation Pane if it is not already open.

- Open the Account Manager table and then close the Navigation Pane.

- Point to the right boundary of the field selector for the Account Manager Number (AM #) field (Figure 1–34) so that the pointer becomes a two-headed arrow.

Q&A I am using touch and I cannot see the pointer. Is this a problem?
It is not a problem. Remember that if you are using your finger on a touch screen, you will not see the pointer.

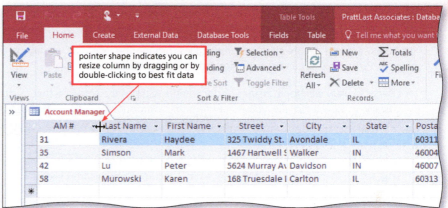

Figure 1–34

2

- Double-click the right boundary of the field selector to resize the field so that it best fits the data.

- Use the same technique to resize all the other fields to best fit the data.

- Save the changes to the layout by clicking the Save button on the Quick Access Toolbar (Figure 1–35).

Figure 1–35

3

- Click the table's Close button (shown in Figure 1–33) to close the table.

Q&A What if I closed the table without saving the layout changes?
You would be asked if you want to save the changes.

Other Ways

1. Right-click field name, click Field Width

What is the best method for distributing database objects?

The traditional method of distributing database objects such as tables, reports, and forms uses a printer to produce a hard copy. A hard copy or printout is information that exists on a physical medium such as paper. Hard copies can be useful for the following reasons:

- Some people prefer proofreading a hard copy of a document rather than viewing it on the screen to check for errors and readability.

- Hard copies can serve as a backup reference if your storage medium is lost or becomes corrupted and you need to recreate the document. Instead of distributing a hard copy, users can distribute the document as an electronic image that mirrors the original document's appearance. The electronic image of the document can be emailed, posted on a website, or copied to a portable storage medium such as a USB flash drive. Two popular electronic image formats, sometimes called fixed formats, are PDF by Adobe Systems and XPS by Microsoft.

In Access, you can create electronic image files through the External Data tab on the ribbon. Electronic images of documents, such as PDF and XPS, can be useful for the following reasons:

- Users can view electronic images of documents without the software that created the original document (e.g., Access). Specifically, to view a PDF file, you use a program called Adobe Reader, which can be downloaded free from Adobe's website. Similarly, to view an XPS file, you use a program called XPS Viewer, which is included in the latest versions of Windows and Edge.

- Sending electronic documents saves paper and printer supplies. Society encourages users to contribute to **green computing**, which involves reducing the electricity consumed and environmental waste generated when using computers, mobile devices, and related technologies.

BTW

Changing Printers
To change the default printer that appears in the Print dialog box, click File on the ribbon, click the Print tab in the Backstage view, click Print in the Print gallery, then click the Name arrow and select the desired printer.

Previewing and Printing the Contents of a Table

When working with a database, you will often need to print a copy of the table contents. Figure 1–36 shows a printed copy of the contents of the Account Manager table. (Yours might look slightly different, depending on your printer.) Because the Account Manager table is substantially wider than the screen, it will also be wider than the normal printed page in portrait orientation. **Portrait orientation** means the printout is across the width of the page. **Landscape orientation** means the printout is across the height of the page. To print the wide database table, you might prefer to use landscape orientation. A convenient way to change to landscape orientation is to preview what the printed copy will look like by using Print Preview. This allows you to determine whether landscape orientation is necessary and, if it is, to change the orientation easily to landscape. In addition, you can also use Print Preview to determine whether any adjustments are necessary to the page margins.

Account Manager									9/12/2017
AM #	**Last Name**	**First Name**	**Street**	**City**	**State**	**Postal Code**	**Start Date**	**Salary**	**Bonus Rate**
31	Rivera	Haydee	325 Twiddy St.	Avondale	IL	60311	6/3/2013	$48,750.00	0.15
35	Simson	Mark	1467 Hartwell St.	Walker	IN	46004	5/19/2014	$40,500.00	0.12
42	Lu	Peter	5624 Murray Ave.	Davidson	IN	46007	8/3/2015	$36,750.00	0.09
58	Murowski	Karen	168 Truesdale Dr.	Carlton	IL	60313	11/9/2016	$24,000.00	0.08

Figure 1–36

To Preview and Print the Contents of a Table

1 CREATE FIRST TABLE | 2 ADD RECORDS | 3 PRINT CONTENTS | 4 IMPORT RECORDS
5 MODIFY SECOND TABLE | 6 CREATE QUERY | 7 CREATE FORM | 8 CREATE REPORT

The following steps use Print Preview to preview and then print the contents of the Account Manager table. *Why? By previewing the contents of the table in Print Preview, you can make any necessary adjustments to the orientation or to the margins before printing the contents.*

1

- If the Navigation Pane is closed, open the Navigation Pane by clicking the 'Shutter Bar Open/ Close Button'.

- Be sure the Account Manager table is selected.

Q&A Why do I have to be sure the Account Manager table is selected? It is the only object in the database.

When the database contains only one object, you do not have to worry about selecting the object. Ensuring that the correct object is selected is a good habit to form, however, to make sure that the object you print is the one you want.

- Click File on the ribbon to open the Backstage view.

- Click the Print tab in the Backstage view to display the Print gallery (Figure 1–37).

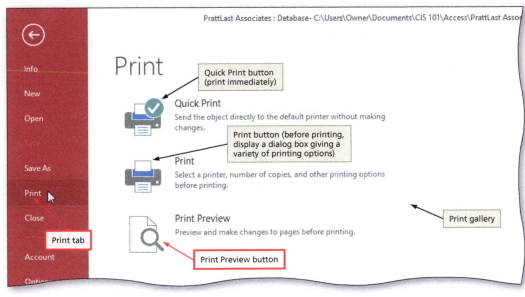

Figure 1–37

2

- Click the Print Preview button in the Print gallery to display a preview of what the table will look like when printed (Figure 1–38).

Q&A I cannot read the table. Can I magnify a portion of the table?

Yes. Point the pointer, whose shape will change to a magnifying glass, at the portion of the table that you want to magnify, and then click. You can return to the original view of the table by clicking a second time.

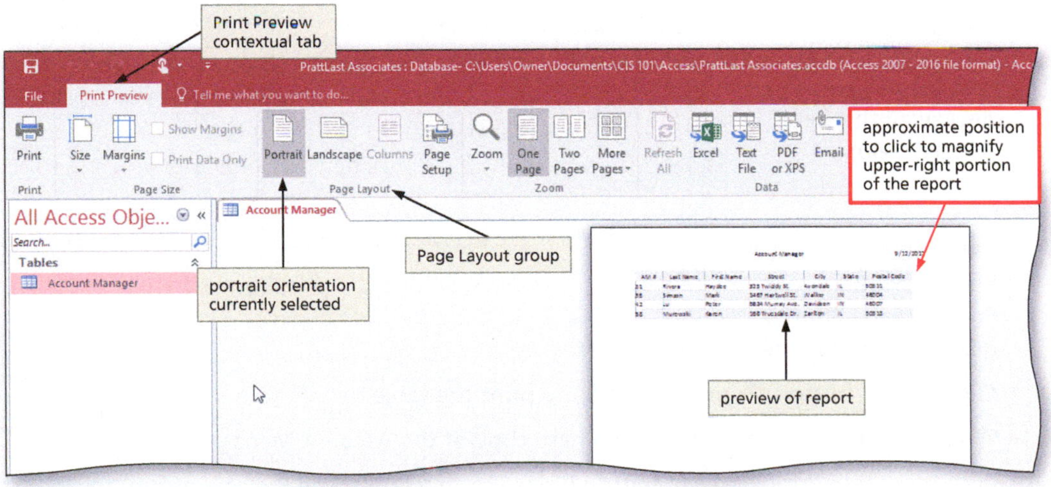

Figure 1–38

3

- Click the pointer in the position shown in Figure 1–38 to magnify the upper-right section of the table (Figure 1–39).

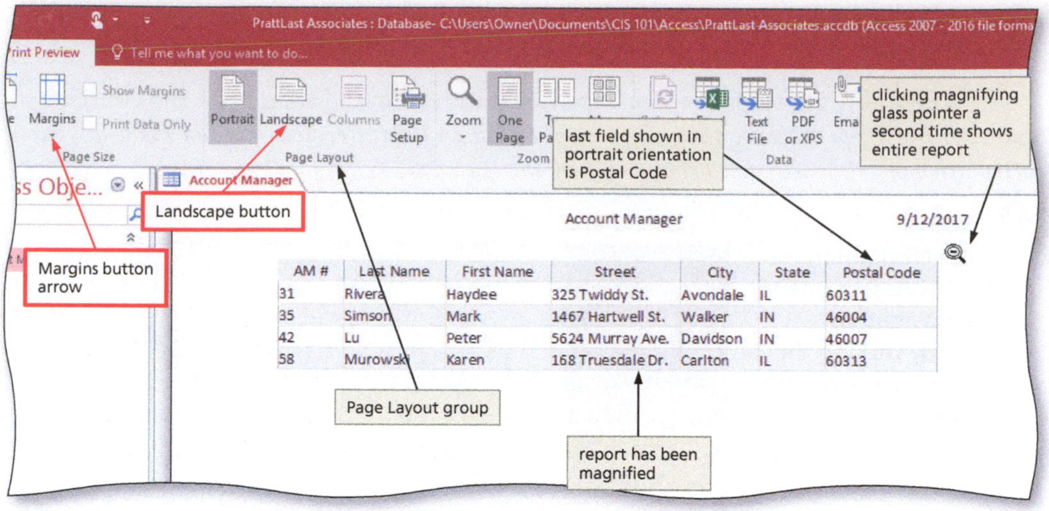

Q&A

My table was already magnified in a different area. How can I see the area shown in the figure? One way is to use the scroll bars to move to the desired portion of the table. You can also click the pointer anywhere in the table to produce a screen like the one shown in Figure 1–38, and then click in the location shown in the figure.

When I magnify the upper-right section, my table moves to the right of the screen and there is a lot of white space. Is that a problem?

No, use the horizontal scroll bar to move the table to the left and reduce the size of the white space.

Figure 1–39 labels:
- Landscape button
- Margins button arrow
- clicking magnifying glass pointer a second time shows entire report
- last field shown in portrait orientation is Postal Code
- Account Manager   9/12/2017

AM #	Last Name	First Name	Street	City	State	Postal Code
31	Rivera	Haydee	325 Twiddy St.	Avondale	IL	60311
35	Simson	Mark	1467 Hartwell St.	Walker	IN	46004
42	Lu	Peter	5624 Murray Ave.	Davidson	IN	46007
58	Murowski	Karen	168 Truesdale Dr.	Carlton	IL	60313

- Page Layout group
- report has been magnified

Figure 1–39

4

- Click the Landscape button (Print Preview tab | Page Layout group) to change to landscape orientation.

- Click the Margins button arrow (Print Preview tab | Page Size group) and then click Normal, if necessary, to display all the fields (Figure 1–40).

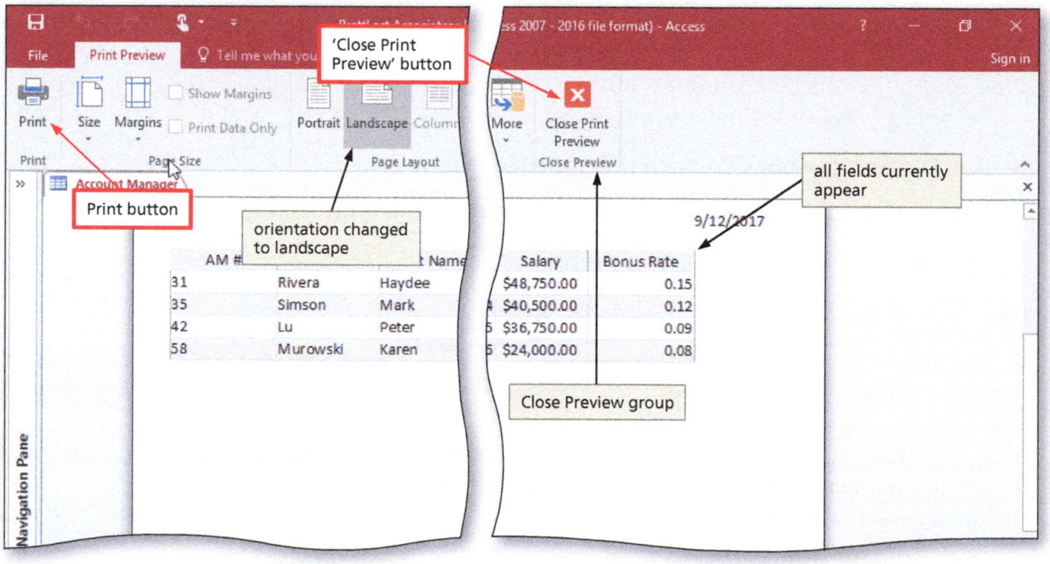

5

- Click the Print button (Print Preview tab | Print group) to display the Print dialog box.

Figure 1–40 labels:
- 'Close Print Preview' button
- Print button
- orientation changed to landscape
- all fields currently appear
- 9/12/2017

AM #		Name	Salary	Bonus Rate
31	Rivera	Haydee	$48,750.00	0.15
35	Simson	Mark	$40,500.00	0.12
42	Lu	Peter	$36,750.00	0.09
58	Murowski	Karen	$24,000.00	0.08

- Close Preview group

Figure 1–40

- Click the OK button (Print dialog box) to print the table.

- When the printer stops, retrieve the hard copy of the Account Manager table.

- Click the 'Close Print Preview' button (Print Preview tab | Close Preview group) to close the Print Preview window.

Q&A

Do I have to select Print Preview before printing the table?

No. If you want to print without previewing, you would select either Print or Quick Print rather than Print Preview.

Other Ways

1. Press CTRL+P, click OK button in Print dialog box

Importing or Linking Data From Other Applications to Access

If your data for a table is stored in an Excel worksheet, you can **import** the data, which means to make a copy of the data as a table in the Access database. In this case, any changes to the data made in Access would not be reflected in the Excel worksheet.

Figure 1–41, which contains the Account data, is an example of the type of worksheet that can be imported. In this type of worksheet, the data is stored as a **list**, that is, a collection of rows and columns in which all the entries in a column represent the same type of data. In this type of list, the first row contains **column headings**, that is, descriptions of the contents of the column, rather than data. In the worksheet in Figure 1–41, for example, the entry in the first column of the first row is Account Number. This indicates that all the other values in this column are account numbers. The fact that the entry in the second column of the first row is Account Name indicates that all the other values in the second column are account names.

BTW

Linking Versus Importing

When you link to the data in the worksheet, the data appears as a table in the Access database but it is maintained in its original form in Excel. Any changes to the Excel data are reflected when the linked table is viewed in Access. In this arrangement, Access would typically be used as a vehicle for querying and presenting the data, with actual updates being made in Excel.

BTW

Importing Data in Other Formats

You can import data into a table from Excel workbooks, Access databases, XML files, ODBC databases such as SQL Server, text files, HTML documents, Outlook folders, and SharePoint lists.

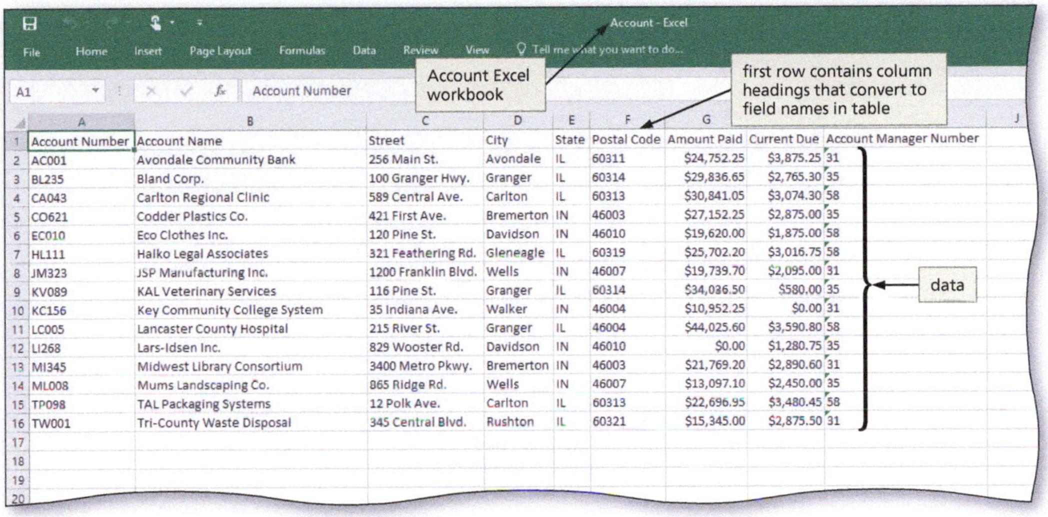

	A	B	C	D	E	F	G	H	I	J
1	Account Number	Account Name	Street	City	State	Postal Code	Amount Paid	Current Due	Account Manager Number	
2	AC001	Avondale Community Bank	256 Main St.	Avondale	IL	60311	$24,752.25	$3,875.25	31	
3	BL235	Bland Corp.	100 Granger Hwy.	Granger	IL	60314	$29,836.65	$2,765.30	35	
4	CA043	Carlton Regional Clinic	589 Central Ave.	Carlton	IL	60313	$30,841.05	$3,074.30	58	
5	CO621	Codder Plastics Co.	421 First Ave.	Bremerton	IN	46003	$27,152.25	$2,875.00	35	
6	EC010	Eco Clothes Inc.	120 Pine St.	Davidson	IN	46010	$19,620.00	$1,875.00	58	
7	HL111	Halko Legal Associates	321 Feathering Rd.	Gleneagle	IL	60319	$25,702.20	$3,016.75	58	
8	JM323	JSP Manufacturing Inc.	1200 Franklin Blvd.	Wells	IN	46007	$19,739.70	$2,095.00	31	
9	KV089	KAL Veterinary Services	116 Pine St.	Granger	IL	60314	$34,036.50	$580.00	35	
10	KC156	Key Community College System	35 Indiana Ave.	Walker	IN	46004	$10,952.25	$0.00	31	
11	LC005	Lancaster County Hospital	215 River St.	Granger	IL	46004	$44,025.60	$3,590.80	58	
12	LI268	Lars-Idsen Inc.	829 Wooster Rd.	Davidson	IN	46010	$0.00	$1,280.75	35	
13	MI345	Midwest Library Consortium	3400 Metro Pkwy.	Bremerton	IN	46003	$21,769.20	$2,890.60	31	
14	ML008	Mums Landscaping Co.	865 Ridge Rd.	Wells	IN	46007	$13,097.10	$2,450.00	35	
15	TP098	TAL Packaging Systems	12 Polk Ave.	Carlton	IL	60313	$22,696.95	$3,480.45	58	
16	TW001	Tri-County Waste Disposal	345 Central Blvd.	Rushton	IL	60321	$15,345.00	$2,875.50	31	
17										
18										
19										
20										

Figure 1–41

CONSIDER THIS

Does it matter how the data in the Excel workbook is formatted? If so, how can you be sure the Excel data is formatted in such a way that you can import it?

The format of data in an Excel workbook is important when you want to import it into Access. To ensure the data is in an appropriate format:

1. Make sure the data is in the form of a list; a collection of rows and columns in which all the entries in a column represent the same type of data.
2. Make sure there are no blank rows within the list. If there are, remove them prior to importing or linking.
3. Make sure there are no blank columns within the list. If there are, remove them prior to importing or linking.
4. Determine whether the first row contains column headings that will make appropriate field names in the resulting table. If not, you should consider adding such a row. In general, the process is simpler if the first row in the worksheet contains appropriate column headings.

The Import process will create a table. In this table, the column headings in the first row of the worksheet become the field names. The rows of the worksheet, other than the first row, become the records in the table. In the process, each field will be assigned the data type that seems the most reasonable, given the data currently in the worksheet. When the Import process is finished, you can use Datasheet view or Design view to modify these data types or to make any other changes to the structure you feel are necessary.

To Import an Excel Worksheet

1 CREATE FIRST TABLE | 2 ADD RECORDS | 3 PRINT CONTENTS | **4 IMPORT RECORDS**
5 MODIFY SECOND TABLE | 6 CREATE QUERY | 7 CREATE FORM | 8 CREATE REPORT

You import a worksheet by using the Import Spreadsheet Wizard. In the process, you will indicate that the first row in the worksheet contains the column headings. *Why? You are indicating that Access is to use those column headings as the field names in the Access table.* In addition, you will indicate the primary key for the table. As part of the process, you could, if appropriate, choose not to include all the fields from the worksheet in the resulting table.

The following steps import the Account worksheet.

1

• Click External Data on the ribbon to display the External Data tab (Figure 1–42).

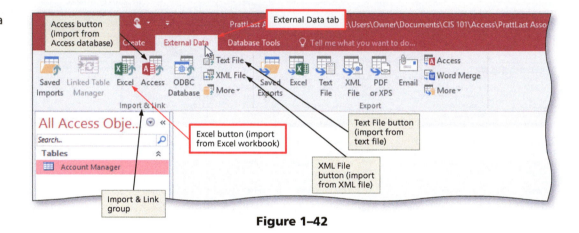

Figure 1–42

2

• Click the Excel button (External Data tab | Import & Link group) to display the Get External Data - Excel Spreadsheet dialog box.

• Click the Browse button in the Get External Data - Excel Spreadsheet dialog box.

• Navigate to the location containing the workbook (for example, the Access folder in the CIS 101 folder). For a detailed example of this procedure, refer to the Office and Windows module at the beginning of this book.

• Click the Account workbook, and then click the Open button to select the workbook (Figure 1–43).

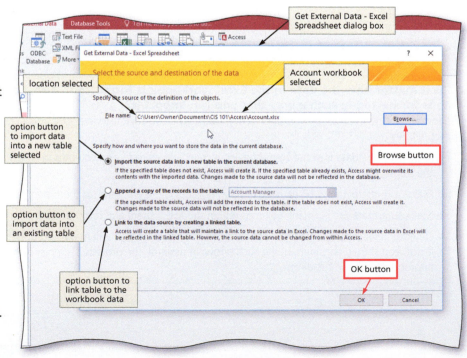

Figure 1–43

3

- With the option button to import the source data to a new table selected, click the OK button to display the Import Spreadsheet Wizard dialog box (Figure 1–44).

Q&A What happens if I select the option button to append records to an existing table?
Instead of the records being placed in a new table, they will be added to an existing table that you specify, provided the value in the primary key field does not duplicate that of an existing record.

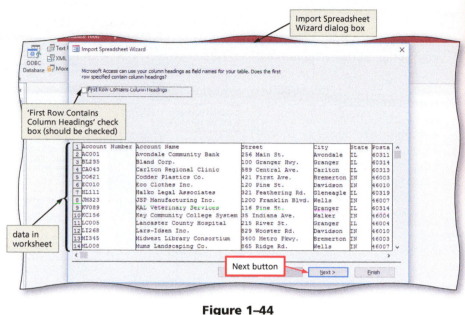

Figure 1–44

4

- Be sure the 'First Row Contains Column Headings' check box is selected. If it is not, click the 'First Row Contains Column Headings' check box to select it.

- Click the Next button (Figure 1–45).

Q&A When would I use the Field Options on the Import Spreadsheet Wizard?
You would use these options if you wanted to change properties for one or more fields. You can change the name, the data type, and whether the field is indexed. You can also indicate that some fields should not be imported.

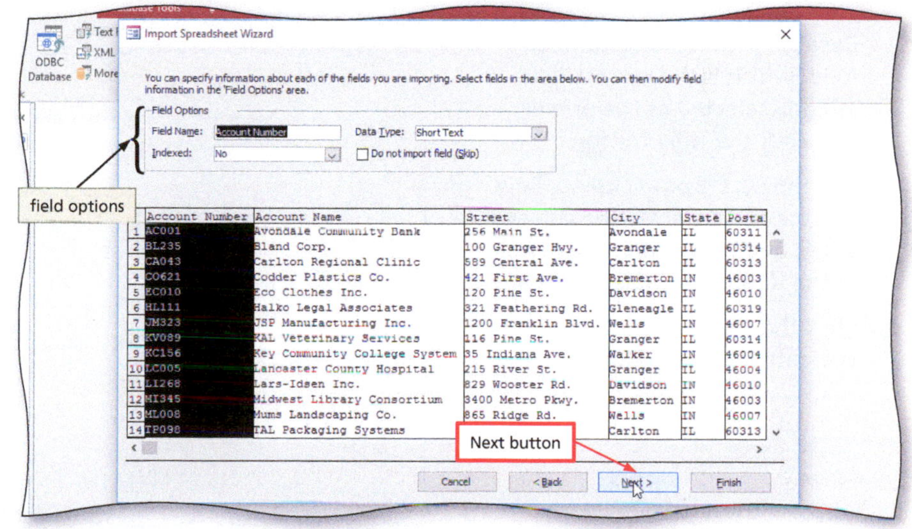

Figure 1–45

5

- Because the Field Options need not be specified, click the Next button (Figure 1–46).

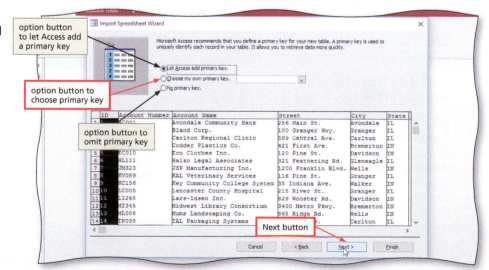

Figure 1–46

6

- Click the 'Choose my own primary key' option button (Figure 1–47).

Q&A How do I decide which option button to select?
If one of the fields is an appropriate primary key, choose your own primary key from the list of fields. If you are sure you do not want a primary key, choose 'No primary key'. Otherwise, let Access add the primary key.

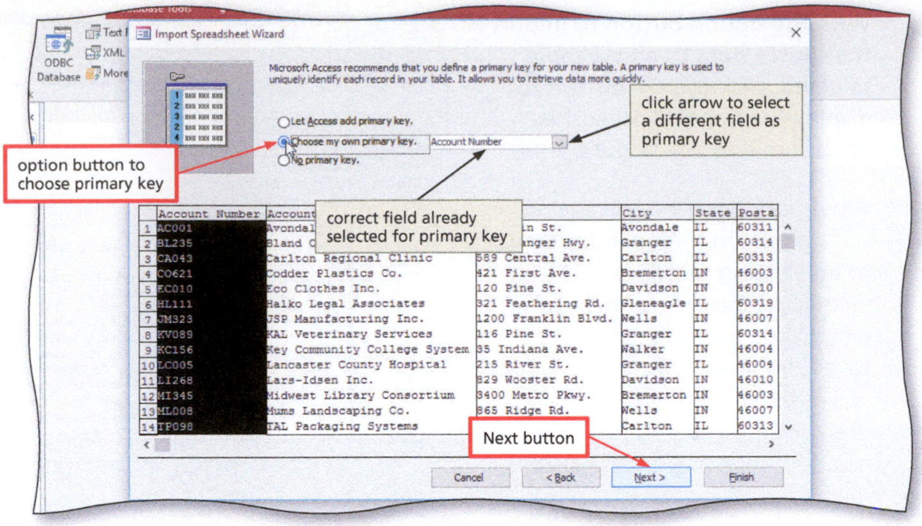

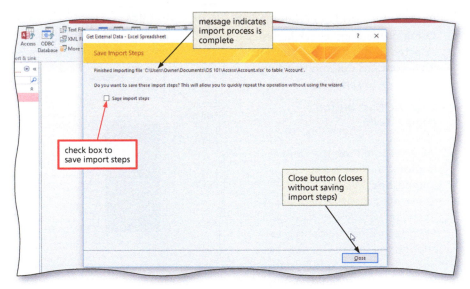

Figure 1–47

7

- Because the Account Number field, which is the correct field, is already selected as the primary key, click the Next button.

- Use the DELETE or BACKSPACE keys as necessary to erase the current entry, and then type **Account** in the Import to Table text box.

- Click the Finish button to import the data (Figure 1–48).

Figure 1–48

8

- Click the 'Save import steps' check box to display the Save import steps options.

- If necessary, type **Import-Account** in the Save as text box.

- Type **Import data from Account workbook into Account table** in the Description text box (Figure 1–49).

Q&A When would I create an Outlook task?
If the import operation is one you will repeat on a regular basis, you can create and schedule the import process just as you can schedule any other Outlook task.

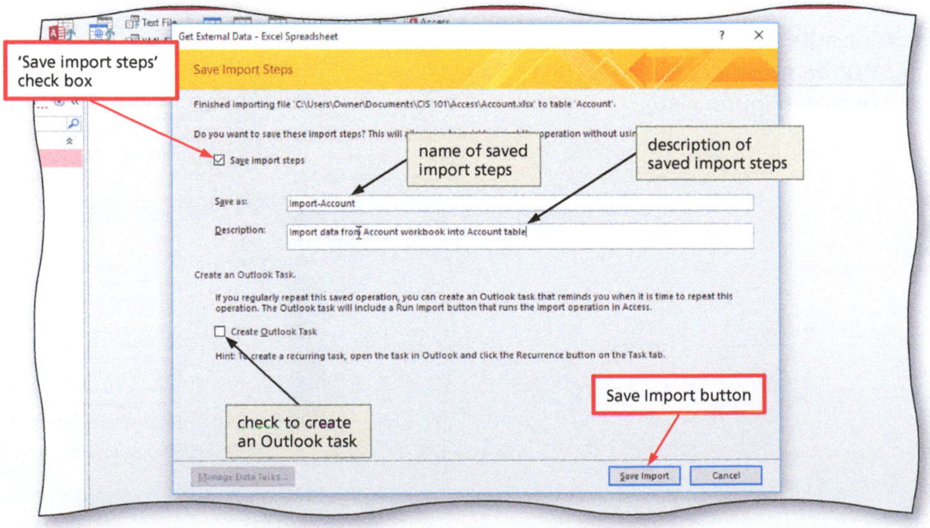

Figure 1–49

9

- Click the Save Import button to save the import steps (Figure 1–50).

Q&A

I saved the table as Account Data. How can I change the name?
Right-click the table name in the Navigation Pane. Click Rename on the shortcut menu and change the table name to Account.

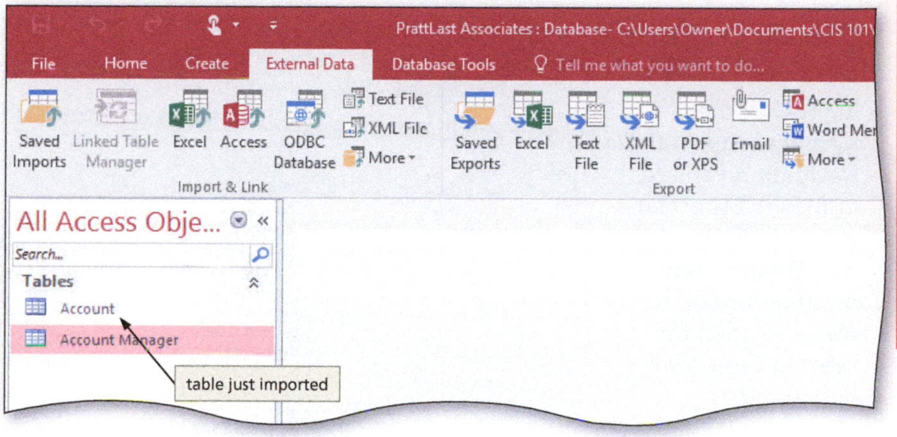

Figure 1–50

Modifying the Table

The import process has created the Account table. The table has the correct fields and records. There are some details the process cannot handle, however. These include field sizes, descriptions, and captions. You will use Design view to make the necessary changes. The information you need is shown in Table 1–5.

BTW

Creating a Table in Design View
To create a table in Design view, display the Create tab, and then click the Table Design button (Create tab | Tables group). You will then see the same screen as in Figure 1–51, except that there will be no entries. Make all the necessary entries for the fields in your table, save the table, and assign the table a name.

Table 1–5 Structure of Account Table			
Field Name	**Data Type**	**Field Size**	**Notes**
Account Number	Short Text	5	Primary Key **Description:** Account Number (two uppercase letters followed by 3-digit number) **Caption:** AC #
Account Name	Short Text	30	
Street	Short Text	20	
City	Short Text	20	
State	Short Text	2	
Postal Code	Short Text	5	
Amount Paid	Currency		
Current Due	Currency		
Account Manager Number	Short Text	2	**Description:** Account Manager Number (number of account manager for account) **Caption:** AM #

To Modify a Table in Design View

1 CREATE FIRST TABLE | 2 ADD RECORDS | 3 PRINT CONTENTS | 4 IMPORT RECORDS
5 MODIFY SECOND TABLE | 6 CREATE QUERY | 7 CREATE FORM | 8 CREATE REPORT

You will usually need to modify the design of a table created during the import process. *Why? Some properties of a table are not specified during the import process, such as descriptions, captions, and field sizes. You might also need to change a data type.* The following steps make the necessary modifications to the design of the Account table.

1

- Open the Navigation Pane, if necessary.

- Right-click the Account table in the Navigation Pane to display the shortcut menu, and then click Design View on the shortcut menu to open the table in Design view (Figure 1–51).

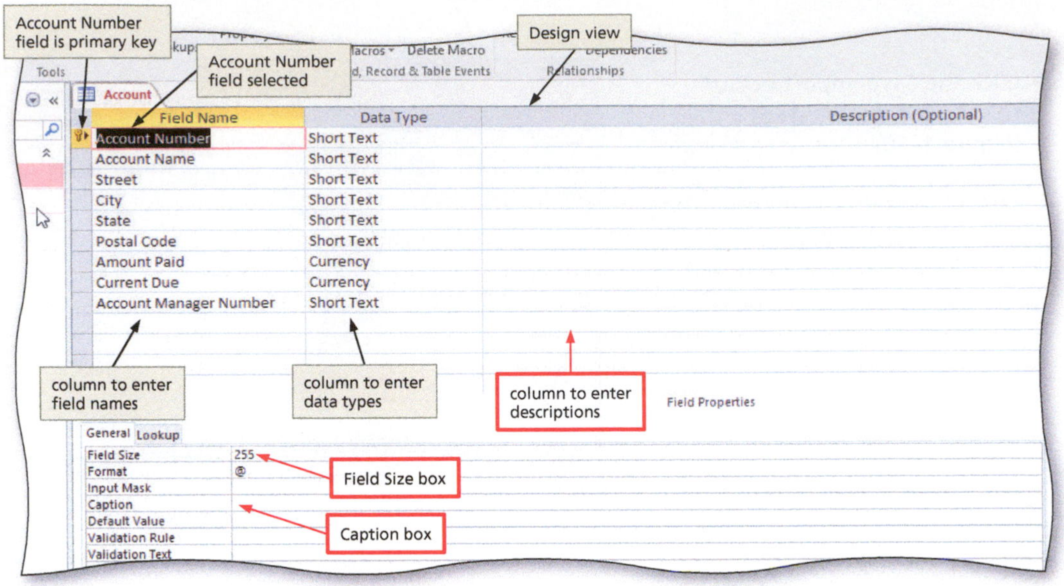

Figure 1–51

2

- Click the Description (Optional) box for the Account Number field, and then type **Account Number (two uppercase letters followed by a 3-digit number)** as the description.

- With the Account Number field selected, click the Field Size box, erase the current field size, and type **5** as the new field size.

Figure 1–52

- Click the Caption box, and type **AC #** as the caption (Figure 1–52).

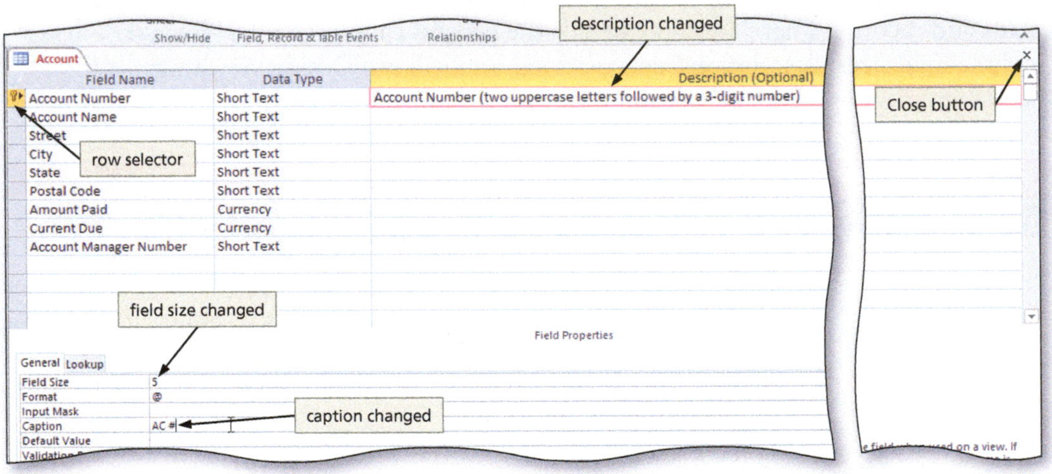

Q&A | What does the @ symbol represent in the Format box?
The @ symbol is a default format added by Access when the table was imported from Excel.

3

- Make the other changes shown in Table 1–5. To select a field to be changed, click the field's row selector. For most fields, you only need to change the field size. For the Account Manager Number field, you also need to change the description and caption.

- Click the Save button on the Quick Access Toolbar to save your changes.

- Because you know the data will satisfy the new field sizes, click the Yes button when given a message about the possibility of data loss.

Other Ways

1. Press F6 to move between upper and lower panes in Table Design window

Correcting Errors in the Structure

Whenever you create or modify a table in Design view, you should check the entries carefully to ensure they are correct. If you make a mistake and discover it before you press the TAB key, you can correct the error by repeatedly pressing the BACKSPACE key until the incorrect characters are removed. Then, type the correct characters. If you do not discover a mistake until later, you can click the entry, type the correct value, and then press the ENTER key. You can use the following techniques to make changes to the structure:

- If you accidentally add an extra field to the structure, select the field by clicking the row selector (the leftmost column on the row that contains the field to be deleted). Once you have selected the field, press the DELETE key. This will remove the field from the structure.

- If you forget to include a field, select the field that will follow the one you want to add by clicking the row selector, and then press the INSERT key. The remaining fields move down one row, making room for the missing field. Make the entries for the new field in the usual manner.

- If you made the wrong field a primary key field, click the correct primary key entry for the field and then click the Primary Key button (Table Tools Design tab | Tools group).

- To move a field, click the row selector for the field to be moved to select the field, and then drag the field to the desired position.

As an alternative to these steps, you might want to start over. To do so, click the Close button for the window containing the table, and then click the No button in the Microsoft Access dialog box. You then can repeat the process you used earlier to define the fields in the table.

BTW

Importing Data to an Existing Table

When you create a new table in Design view, you can import data from other sources into the table using the External Data tab.

To Close the Table

Now that you have completed and saved the Account table, you can close it. The following step closes the table.

1 Click the Close button for the Account table (see Figure 1–52) to close the table.

To Resize Columns in a Datasheet

You can resize the columns in the datasheet for the Account table just as you resized the columns in the datasheet for the Account Manager table. The following steps resize the columns in the Account table to best fit the data.

1 Open the Account table in Datasheet view.

2 Double-click the right boundary of the field selectors of each of the fields to resize the columns so that they best fit the data.

3 Save the changes to the layout by clicking the Save button on the Quick Access Toolbar.

4 Close the table.

BTW

Resizing Columns

To resize all columns in a datasheet to best fit simultaneously, select the column heading for the first column, hold down the SHIFT key and select the last column in the datasheet. Then, double-click the right boundary of any field selector.

Break Point: If you wish to take a break, this is a good place to do so. You can exit Access now. To resume at a later time, run Access, open the database called PrattLast Associates, and continue following the steps from this location forward.

Additional Database Objects

A database contains many types of objects. Tables are the objects you use to store and manipulate data. Access supports other important types of objects as well; each object has a specific purpose that helps maximize the benefits of a database. Through queries (questions), Access makes it possible to ask complex questions concerning the data in the database and then receive instant answers. Access also allows the user to produce attractive and useful forms for viewing and updating data. Additionally, Access includes report creation tools that make it easy to produce sophisticated reports for presenting data.

BTW
Creating Queries
Although the Simple Query Wizard is a convenient way to create straightforward queries, you will find that many of the queries you create require more control than the wizard provides. In Module 2, you will use Design view to create customized queries.

Creating Queries

Queries are simply questions, the answers to which are in the database. Access contains a powerful query feature that helps you find the answers to a wide variety of questions. Once you have examined the question you want to ask to determine the fields involved in the question, you can begin creating the query. If the query involves no special sort order, restrictions, or calculations, you can use the Simple Query Wizard.

To Use the Simple Query Wizard to Create a Query

1 CREATE FIRST TABLE | 2 ADD RECORDS | 3 PRINT CONTENTS | 4 IMPORT RECORDS
5 MODIFY SECOND TABLE | 6 CREATE QUERY | 7 CREATE FORM | 8 CREATE REPORT

The following steps use the Simple Query Wizard to create a query that PrattLast Associates might use to obtain financial information on its accounts. *Why? The Simple Query Wizard is the quickest and easiest way to create a query.* This query displays the number, name, amount paid, current due, and account manager number of all accounts.

1

- If the Navigation Pane is closed, click the 'Shutter Bar Open/Close Button' to open the Navigation Pane.

- Be sure the Account table is selected.

- Click Create on the ribbon to display the Create tab.

- Click the Query Wizard button (Create tab | Queries group) to display the New Query dialog box (Figure 1–53).

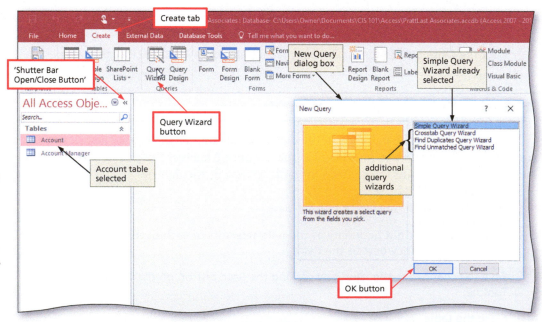

Figure 1–53

2

- Be sure Simple Query Wizard is selected, and then click the OK button (New Query dialog box) to display the Simple Query Wizard dialog box (Figure 1–54).

Q&A What would happen if the Account Manager table were selected instead of the Account table?
The list of available fields would contain fields from the Account Manager table rather than the Account table.

If the list contained Account Manager table fields, how could I make it contain Account table fields?
Click the arrow in the Tables/Queries box, and then click the Account table in the list that appears.

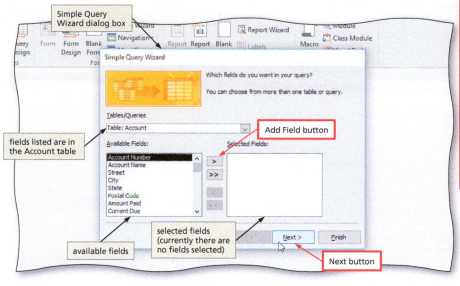

Figure 1–54

3

- With the Account Number field selected, click the Add Field button to add the field to the query.

- With the Account Name field selected, click the Add Field button a second time to add the field.

- Click the Amount Paid field, and then click the Add Field button to add the field.

- In a similar fashion, add the Current Due and Account Manager Number fields (Figure 1–55).

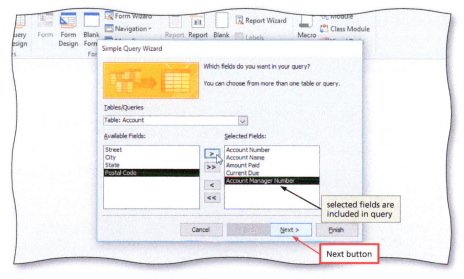

Figure 1–55

4

- Click the Next button to move to the next screen.

- Ensure that the 'Detail (shows every field of every record)' option button is selected (Figure 1–56).

Q&A What is the difference between Detail and Summary?
Detail shows all the records and fields. Summary only shows computations (for example, the total amount paid).

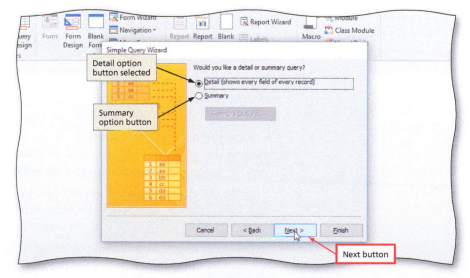

Figure 1–56

5

- Click the Next button to move to the next screen.

- Confirm that the title of the query is Account Query (Figure 1–57).

Q&A
What should I do if the title is incorrect?
Click the box containing the title to produce an insertion point. Erase the current title and then type Account Query.

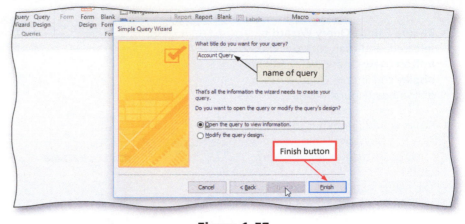

Figure 1–57

6

- Click the Finish button to create the query (Figure 1–58).

- Click the Close button for the Account Query to remove the query results from the screen.

Q&A
If I want to use this query in the future, do I need to save the query?
Normally you would. The one exception is a query created by the wizard. The wizard automatically saves the query it creates.

Figure 1–58

Using Queries

After you have created and saved a query, Access stores it as a database object and makes it available for use in a variety of ways:

- If you want to change the design of the query, right-click the query in the Navigation Pane and then click Design View on the shortcut menu to open the query in Design view.

- To view the results of the query from Design view, click the Run button to instruct Access to **run** the query, that is, to perform the necessary actions to produce and display the results in Datasheet view.

- To view the results of the query from the Navigation Pane, open it by right-clicking the query and clicking Open on the shortcut menu. Access automatically runs the query and displays the results in Datasheet view.

- To print the results with the query open in either Design view or Datasheet view, click File on the ribbon, click the Print tab, and then click either Print or Quick Print.

- To print the query without first opening it, be sure the query is selected in the Navigation Pane and click File on the ribbon, click the Print tab, and then click either Print or Quick Print.

You can switch between views of a query using the View button (Home tab | Views group). Clicking the arrow in the bottom of the button produces the View button menu. You then click the desired view in the menu. The two query views you will use in this module are Datasheet view (which displays the query results) and Design view (for changing the query design). You can also click the top part of the View button, in which case you will switch to the view identified by the icon on the button. For the most part, the icon on the button represents the view you want, so you can usually simply click the button.

To Use a Criterion in a Query

1 CREATE FIRST TABLE | 2 ADD RECORDS | 3 PRINT CONTENTS | 4 IMPORT RECORDS
5 MODIFY SECOND TABLE | 6 CREATE QUERY | 7 CREATE FORM | 8 CREATE REPORT

After you have determined the fields to be included in a query, you will determine whether you need to further restrict the results of the query. For example, you might want to include only those accounts managed by account manager 35, Mark Simson. In such a case, you need to enter the number 35 as a criterion for the account manager field. *Why? A criterion is a condition that the records must satisfy in order to be included in the query results.* To do so, you will open the query in Design view, enter the criterion below the appropriate field, and then view the results of the query. The following steps enter a criterion to include only the accounts of account manager 35 and then view the query results.

1
- Right-click the Account Query in the Navigation Pane to produce a shortcut menu (Figure 1–59).

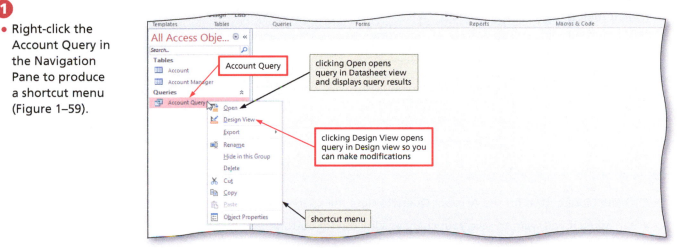

Figure 1–59

2
- Click Design View on the shortcut menu to open the query in Design view (Figure 1–60).

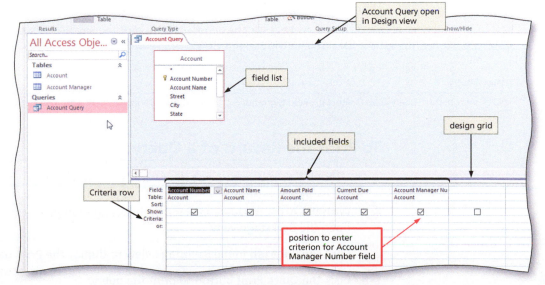

Figure 1–60

3

- Click the Criteria row in the Account Manager Number column of the grid, and then type 35 as the criterion (Figure 1–61).

Q&A The Account Manager Number field is a text field. Do I need to enclose the value for a text field in quotation marks?
You could, but it is not necessary because Access inserts the quotation marks for you automatically.

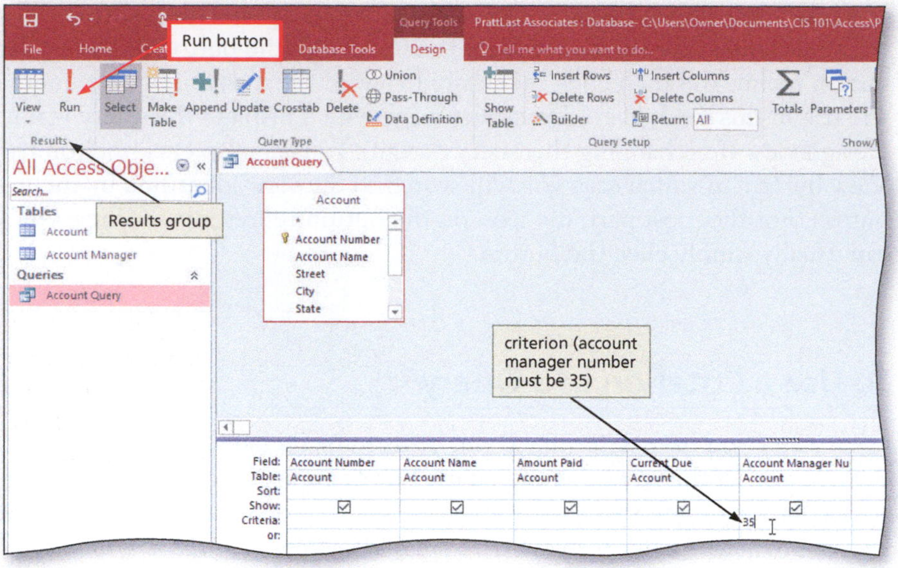
Run button
Results group
criterion (account manager number must be 35)
Account Query
Account
Account Number
Account Name
Street
City
State
Field: Account Number | Account Name | Amount Paid | Current Due | Account Manager Nu
Table: Account
Criteria: 35

Figure 1–61

4

- Click the Run button (Query Tools Design tab | Results group) to run the query and display the results in Datasheet view (Figure 1–62).

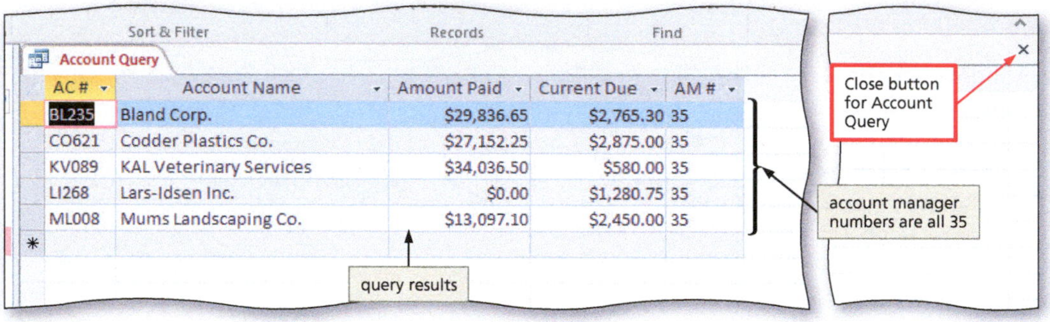
Account Query
AC # | Account Name | Amount Paid | Current Due | AM #
BL235 | Bland Corp. | $29,836.65 | $2,765.30 | 35
CO621 | Codder Plastics Co. | $27,152.25 | $2,875.00 | 35
KV089 | KAL Veterinary Services | $34,036.50 | $580.00 | 35
LI268 | Lars-Idsen Inc. | $0.00 | $1,280.75 | 35
ML008 | Mums Landscaping Co. | $13,097.10 | $2,450.00 | 35
query results
Close button for Account Query
account manager numbers are all 35

Figure 1–62

5

- Click the Close button for the Account Query to close the query.
- When asked if you want to save your changes, click the No button.

Q&A If I saved the query, what would happen the next time I ran the query?
You would see only accounts of account manager 35.

Could I save a query with another name?
Yes. To save a query with a different name, click File on the ribbon, click the Save As tab, click Save Object As, click the Save As button, enter a new file name in the Save As dialog box, and then click the OK button (Save As dialog box).

Other Ways

1. Click View button (Query Tools Design tab | Results group)
2. Click Datasheet View button on status bar

To Print the Results of a Query

The following steps print the results of a saved query.

1. With the Account Query selected in the Navigation Pane, click File on the ribbon to open the Backstage view.
2. Click the Print tab in the Backstage view to display the Print gallery.
3. Click the Quick Print button to print the query.

Creating Forms

In Datasheet view, you can view many records at once. If there are many fields, however, only some of the fields in each record might be visible at a time. In **Form view**, where data is displayed in a form on the screen, you can usually see all the fields, but only for one record.

To Create a Form

1 CREATE FIRST TABLE | 2 ADD RECORDS | 3 PRINT CONTENTS | 4 IMPORT RECORDS
5 MODIFY SECOND TABLE | 6 CREATE QUERY | 7 CREATE FORM | 8 CREATE REPORT

Like a paper form, a **form** in a database is a formatted document with fields that contain data. Forms allow you to view and maintain data. Forms can also be used to print data, but reports are more commonly used for that purpose. The simplest type of form in Access is one that includes all the fields in a table stacked one above the other. The following steps use the Form button to create a form. *Why? Using the Form button is the simplest way to create this type of form. The steps use the form to view records and then save the form.*

1

- Select the Account table in the Navigation Pane.

- If necessary, click Create on the ribbon to display the Create tab (Figure 1–63).

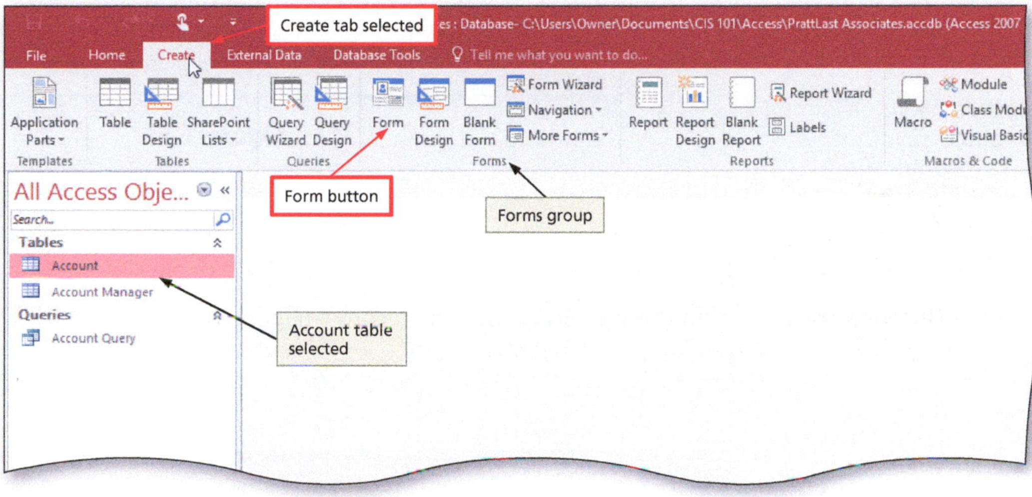

Figure 1–63

2

- Click the Form button (Create tab | Forms group) to create a simple form (Figure 1–64).

Q&A A Field list appeared on my screen. What should I do?
Click the 'Add Existing Fields' button (Form Layout Tools Design tab | Tools group) to remove the Field list from the screen.

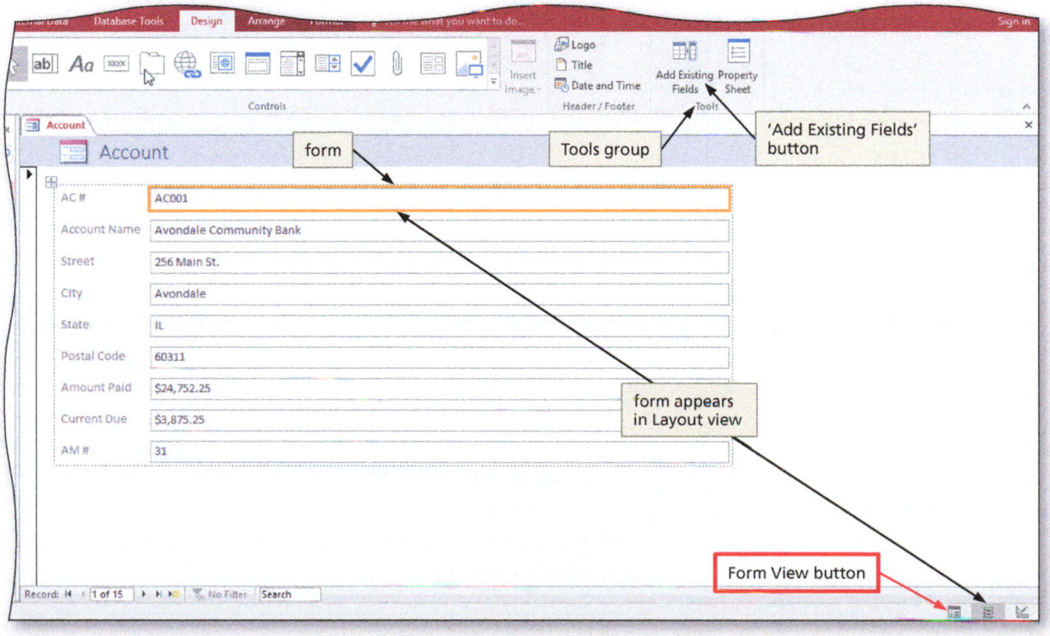

Figure 1–64

3

- Click the Form View button on the Access status bar to display the form in Form view rather than Layout view.

Q&A

What is the difference between Layout view and Form view?
Layout view allows you to make changes to the look of the form. Form view is the view you use to examine or make changes to the data.

How can I tell when I am in Layout view?
Access identifies Layout view in three ways. The left side of the status bar will contain the words, Layout View; shading will appear around the outside of the selected field in the form; and the Layout View button will be selected on the right side of the status bar.

- Click the Next record button three times to move to record 4 (Figure 1–65).

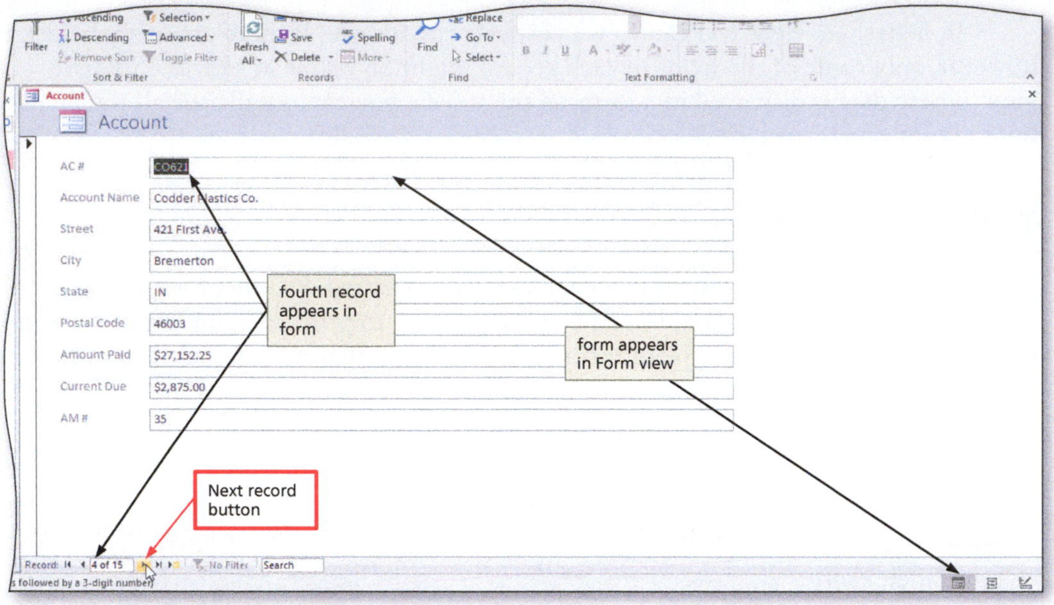

Figure 1–65

4

- Click the Save button on the Quick Access Toolbar to display the Save As dialog box (Figure 1–66).

Q&A

Do I have to click the Next record button before saving?
No. The only reason you were asked to click the button was so that you could experience navigation within the form.

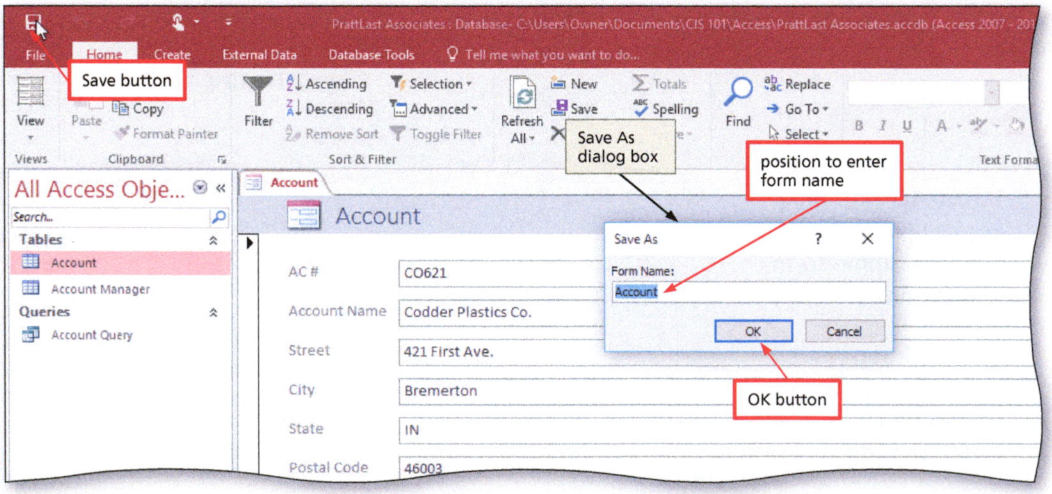

Figure 1–66

5

- Type **Account Form** as the form name, and then click the OK button to save the form.

- Click the Close button for the form to close the form.

Other Ways

1. Click View button (Form Layout Tools Design tab | Views group)

Using a Form

After you have saved a form, you can use it at any time by right-clicking the form in the Navigation Pane and then clicking Open on the shortcut menu. In addition to viewing data in the form, you can also use it to enter or update data, a process that is very similar to updating data using a datasheet. If you plan to use the form to enter or revise data, you must ensure you are viewing the form in Form view.

Break Point: If you wish to take a break, this is a good place to do so. You can exit Access now. To resume at a later time, run Access, open the database called PrattLast Associates, and continue following the steps from this location forward.

Creating and Printing Reports

PrattLast Associates wants to be able to present account financial data in a useful format. To do so, they will create the Account Financial Report shown in Figure 1–67. To create this report, you will first create a simple report containing all records. Then, you will modify the report to match the one shown in Figure 1–67.

Account Number	Account Name	Amount Paid	Current Due	Account Manager Number
AC001	Avondale Community Bank	$24,752.25	$3,875.25	31
BL235	Bland Corp.	$29,836.65	$2,765.30	35
CA043	Carlton Regional Clinic	$30,841.05	$3,074.30	58
CO621	Codder Plastics Co.	$27,152.25	$2,875.00	35
EC010	Eco Clothes Inc.	$19,620.00	$1,875.00	58
HL111	Halko Legal Associates	$25,702.20	$3,016.75	58
JM323	JSP Manufacturing Inc.	$19,739.70	$2,095.00	31
KV089	KAL Veterinary Services	$34,036.50	$580.00	35
KC156	Key Community College System	$10,952.25	$0.00	31
LC005	Lancaster County Hospital	$44,025.60	$3,590.80	58
LI268	Lars-Idsen Inc.	$0.00	$1,280.75	35
MI345	Midwest Library Consortium	$21,769.20	$2,890.60	31
ML008	Mums Landscaping Co.	$13,097.10	$2,450.00	35
TP098	TAL Packaging Systems	$22,696.95	$3,480.45	58
TW001	Tri-County Waste Disposal	$15,345.00	$2,875.50	31
		$339,566.70	$36,724.70	

Account Financial Report
Tuesday, September 12, 2017
7:54:24 PM

Figure 1–67

To Create a Report

1 CREATE FIRST TABLE | 2 ADD RECORDS | 3 PRINT CONTENTS | 4 IMPORT RECORDS
5 MODIFY SECOND TABLE | 6 CREATE QUERY | 7 CREATE FORM | **8 CREATE REPORT**

You will first create a report containing all fields. *Why? It is easiest to create a report with all the fields and then delete the fields you do not want.* The following steps create and save the initial report. They also modify the report title.

1

- Be sure the Account table is selected in the Navigation Pane.

- Click Create on the ribbon to display the Create tab (Figure 1–68).

Q&A Do I need to select the Account table prior to clicking Create on the ribbon?

You do not need to select the table at that point. You do need to select a table prior to clicking the Report button, because Access will include all the fields in whichever table or query is currently selected.

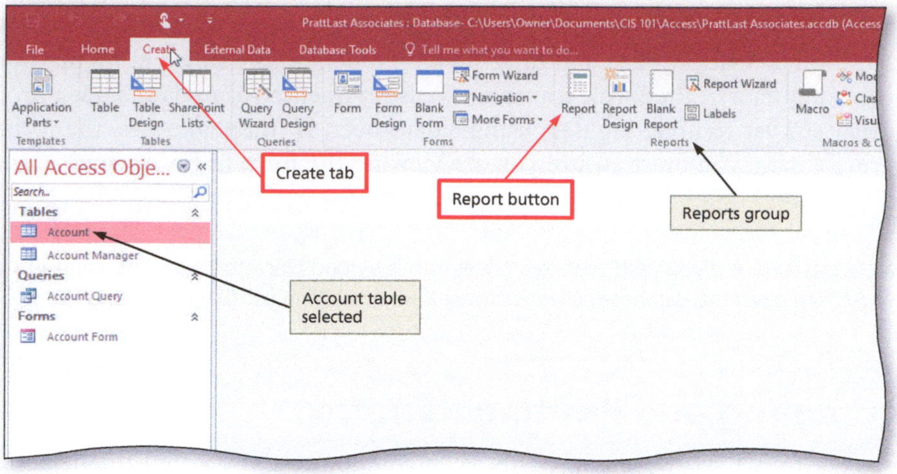

Figure 1–68

2

- Click the Report button (Create tab | Reports group) to create the report (Figure 1–69).

Q&A Why is the report title Account?

Access automatically assigns the name of the table or query as the title of the report. It also automatically includes the date and time. You can change either of these later.

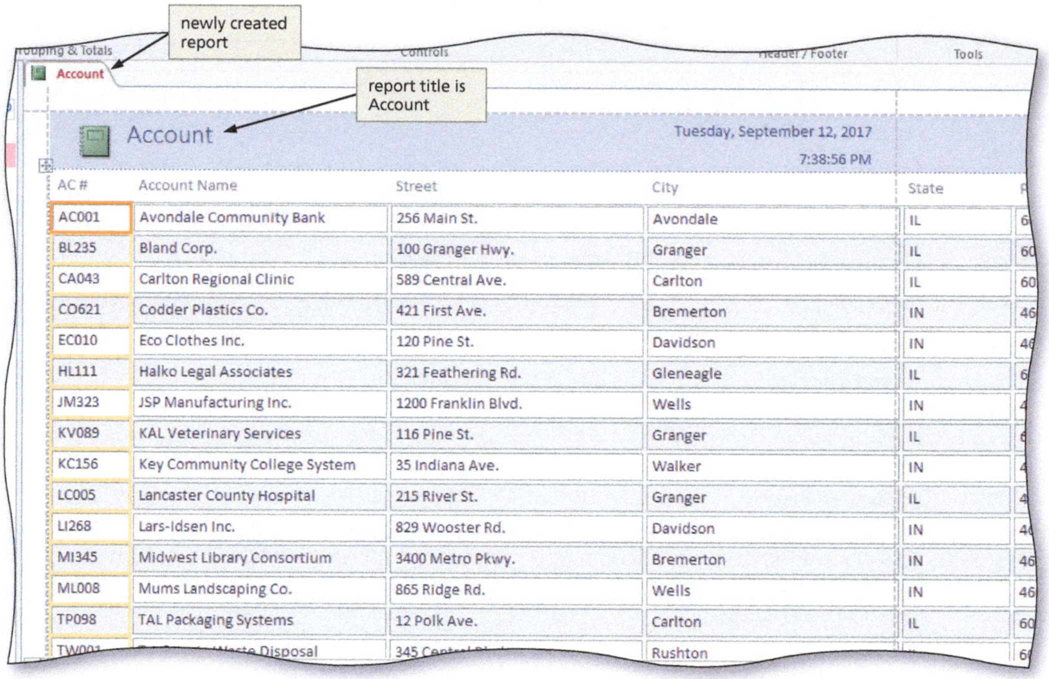

Figure 1–69

3

- Click the Save button on the Quick Access Toolbar to display the Save As dialog box, and then type Account Financial Report as the name of the report (Figure 1–70).

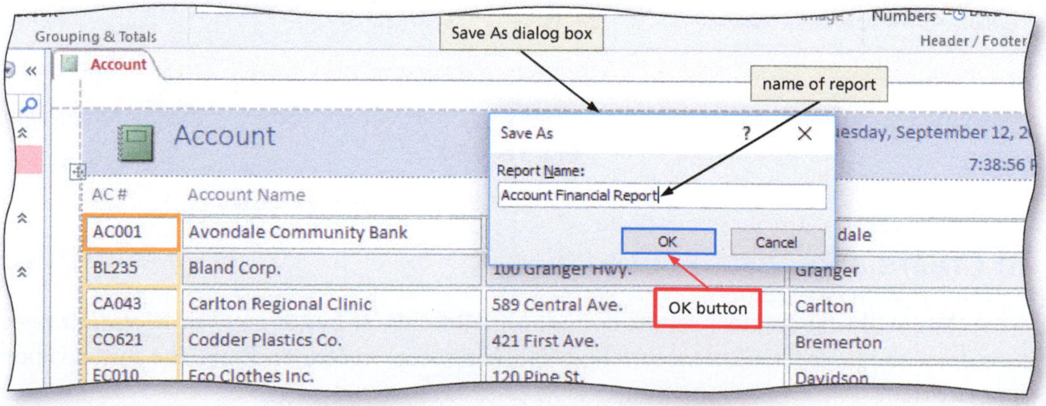

Figure 1–70

4
- Click the OK button (Save As dialog box) to save the report (Figure 1–71).

Q&A The name of the report changed. Why did the report title not change?
The report title is assigned the same name as the report by default. Changing the name of the report does not change the report title. You can change the title at any time to anything you like.

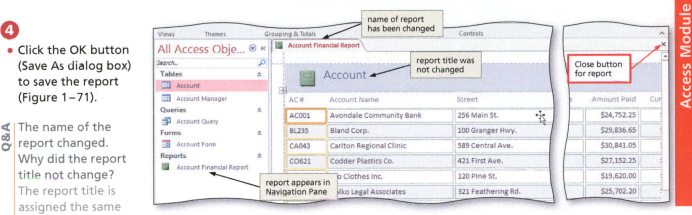

Figure 1–71

5
- Close the report by clicking its Close button.

Using Layout View in a Report

Access has four different ways to view reports: Report view, Print Preview, Layout view, and Design view. Report view shows the report on the screen. Print Preview shows the report as it will appear when printed. Layout view is similar to Report view in that it shows the report on the screen, but it also allows you to make changes to the report. Layout view is usually the easiest way to make such changes. Design view also allows you to make changes, but does not show you the actual report. Design view is most useful when the changes you need to make are especially complex. In this module, you will use Layout view to modify the report.

BTW
Report Navigation
When previewing a report, you can use the Navigation buttons on the status bar to move from one page to another.

To Modify Report Column Headings and Resize Columns

1 CREATE FIRST TABLE | 2 ADD RECORDS | 3 PRINT CONTENTS | 4 IMPORT RECORDS
5 MODIFY SECOND TABLE | 6 CREATE QUERY | 7 CREATE FORM | **8 CREATE REPORT**

To make the report match the one shown in Figure 1–67, you need to change the title, remove some columns, modify the column headings, and also resize the columns. The following steps use Layout view to make the necessary modifications to the report. *Why? Working in Layout view gives you all the tools you need to make the desired modifications. You can view the results of the modifications immediately.*

1
- Right-click Account Financial Report in the Navigation Pane, and then click Layout View on the shortcut menu to open the report in Layout view.

- If a Field list appears, click the 'Add Existing Fields' button (Report Layout Tools Design tab | Tools group) to remove the Field list from the screen.

- Close the Navigation Pane.

- Click the report title once to select it.

- Click the report title a second time to produce an insertion point (Figure 1–72).

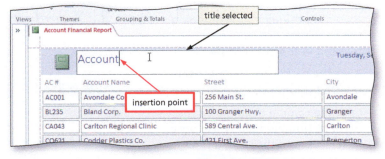

Figure 1–72

Q&A My insertion point is in the middle of Account. How do I produce an insertion point at the position shown in the figure?
You can use the RIGHT ARROW key to move the insertion point to the position in the figure, or you can click the desired position.

2

- Press the SPACEBAR to insert a space, and then type **Financial Report** to complete the title.
- Click the column heading for the Street field to select it.
- Press and hold the CTRL key and then click the column headings for the City, State, and Postal Code fields to select multiple column headings.

What happens if I do not hold down the CTRL key?

When you click another column heading, it will be the only one that is selected. To select multiple objects, you need to hold the CTRL key down for every object after the first selection.

I selected the wrong collection of objects. What should I do?

You can click somewhere else on the report so that the objects you want are not selected, and then begin the process again. Alternatively, you can repeatedly click the Undo button on the Quick Access Toolbar to undo your selections. Once you have done so, you can select the objects you want.

- Click Arrange on the ribbon to display the Report Layout Tools Arrange tab (Figure 1–73).

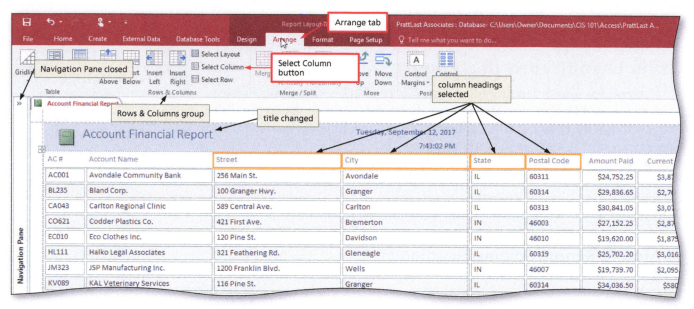

Figure 1–73

3

- Click the Select Column button (Report Layout Tools Arrange tab | Rows & Columns group) to select the entire columns corresponding to the column headings you selected in the previous step.

- Press the DELETE key to delete the selected columns.

- Click the column heading for the Account Number field twice, once to select it and the second time to produce an insertion point (Figure 1–74).

I selected the wrong field. What should I do?

Click somewhere outside the various fields to deselect the one you have selected. Then, click the Account Number field twice.

Figure 1–74

4

- Use the DELETE or BACKSPACE keys as necessary to erase the current entry, and then type **Account Number** as the new entry.

- Click the heading for the Account Manager Number field twice, erase the current entry, and then type **Account Manager Number** as the new entry.

- Click the Account Number field heading to select it, point to the lower boundary of the heading for the Account Number field so that the pointer changes to a two-headed arrow, and then drag the lower boundary to the approximate position shown in Figure 1–75 to expand the column headings.

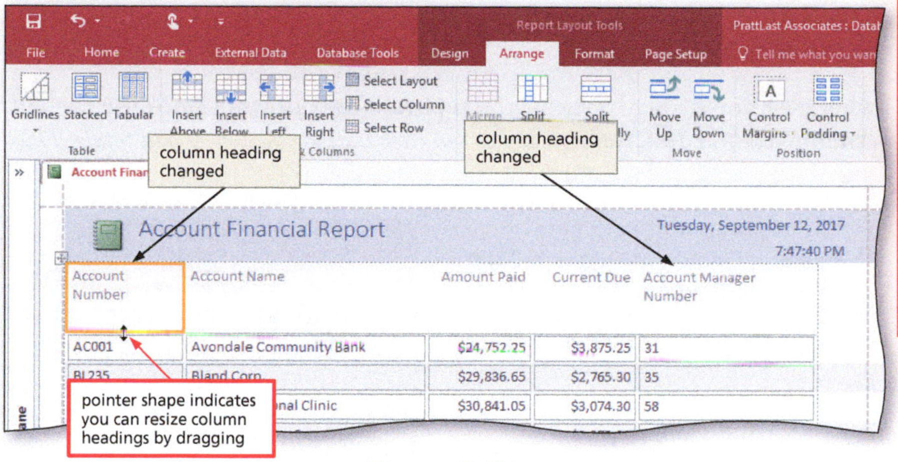

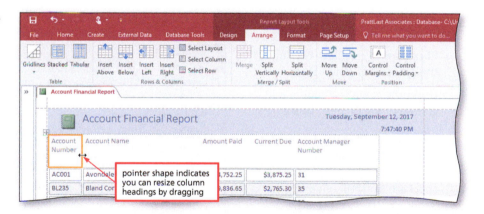

Figure 1–75

I did something wrong when I dragged and now my report looks strange. What should I do?
Click the Undo button on the Quick Access Toolbar to undo the change. Depending on the specific action you took, you might need to click it more than once.

My screen displays Account Manager Number on one line, not two. Is this a problem?
No. You will adjust the column heading in a later step.

5

- Point to the right boundary of the heading for the Account Number field so that the pointer changes to a two-headed arrow, and then drag the right boundary to the approximate position shown in Figure 1–76 to reduce the width of the column.

Figure 1–76

6

- Using the same technique, resize the other columns to the sizes shown in Figure 1–77.

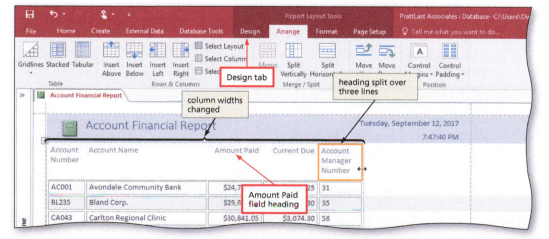

Figure 1–77

To Add Totals to a Report

The report in Figure 1–67 contains totals for the Amount Paid and Current Due columns. You can use Layout view to add these totals. Once you have added the totals, Access will calculate the appropriate values whenever you display or print the report. The following steps use Layout view to include totals for these three columns. *Why? In Layout view you can click a single button to add totals. This button sums all the values in the field.*

1

- Click the Amount Paid field heading (shown in Figure 1–77) to select the field.

Q&A
Do I have to click the heading? Could I click the field on one of the records?
You do not have to click the heading. You also could click the Amount Paid field on any record.

- Click Design on the ribbon to display the Design tab.

- Click the Totals button (Report Layout Tools Design tab | Grouping & Totals group) to display the Totals menu containing a list of available calculations (Figure 1–78).

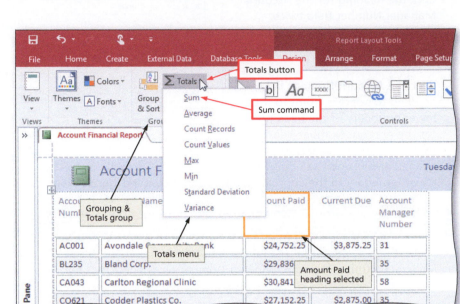

Figure 1–78

2

- Click Sum to calculate the sum of the amount of paid values.

- Using the same technique, add totals for the Current Due column.

Q&A
When I clicked the Totals button after selecting the Current Due field heading, Sum was already checked. Do I still need to click Sum?
No. In fact, if you do click it, you will remove the check mark, which will remove the total from the column.

- Scroll down to the bottom of the report to verify that the totals are included. If necessary, expand the size of the total controls so they appear completely by dragging the lower boundary of the controls to the approximate position shown in Figure 1–79.

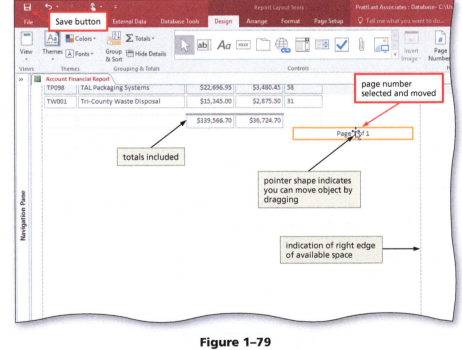

Figure 1–79

- Click the page number to select it, and then drag it to the approximate position shown in Figure 1–79.

Q&A
Why did I need to move the page number?
The dotted line near the right-hand edge of the screen indicates the right-hand border of the available space on the printed page, based on whatever margins and orientation are currently selected. A portion of the page number extends beyond this border. By moving the page number, it no longer extends beyond the border.

3
- Click the Save button on the Quick Access Toolbar to save your changes to the report layout.
- Close the report.

To Print a Report

The following steps print the report.

1 Open the Navigation Pane, if necessary, confirm that the Account Financial Report is selected, and then click File on the ribbon to open the Backstage view.

2 Click the Print tab in the Backstage view to display the Print gallery.

3 Click the Quick Print button to print the report.

Q&A | When I print the report, I have pound signs (####) rather than numbers where the totals should be for the Amount Paid and Current Due columns. The report looked fine on the screen. How can I correct it?
The columns are not wide enough to display the complete number. Open the report in Layout view and slightly increase the width of the Amount Paid and Current Due columns by dragging the right boundary of the column headings.

How can I print multiple copies of my report?
Click File on the ribbon to open the Backstage view. Click the Print tab, click Print in the Print gallery to display the Print dialog box, increase the number in the Number of Copies box, and then click the OK button .

How can I print a range of pages rather than printing the whole report?
Click File on the ribbon to open the Backstage view. Click the Print tab, click Print in the Print gallery to display the Print dialog box, click the Pages option button in the Print Range area, enter the desired page range, and then click the OK button (Print dialog box).

BTW
Distributing a Document
Instead of printing and distributing a hard copy of a document, you can distribute the document electronically. Options include sending the document via email; posting it on cloud storage (such as OneDrive) and sharing the file with others; posting it on social media, a blog, or other website; and sharing a link associated with an online location of the document. You also can create and share a PDF or XPS image of the document, so that users can view the file in Acrobat Reader or XPS Viewer instead of in Access.

Database Properties

Access helps you organize and identify your databases by using **database properties,** which are the details about a file. Database properties, also known as **metadata,** can include such information as the project author, title, or subject. **Keywords** are words or phrases that further describe the database. For example, a class name or database topic can describe the file's purpose or content.

Five different types of database properties exist, but the more common ones used in this book are standard and automatically updated properties. **Standard properties** are associated with all Microsoft Office documents and include author, title, and subject. **Automatically updated properties** include file system properties, such as the date you create or change a file, and statistics, such as the file size.

BTW
Exporting a Report as a PDF or XPS File
To export a report as a PDF or XPS file, display the External Data tab, and then click the PDF or XPS button (External Data tab | Export group). Enter the appropriate information in the Publish to PDF or XPS dialog box and click the Publish button.

Why would you want to assign database properties to a database?
Database properties are valuable for a variety of reasons:

- Users can save time locating a particular file because they can view a file's database properties without opening the database.
- By creating consistent properties for files having similar content, users can better organize their databases.
- Some organizations require Access users to add database properties so that other employees can view details about these files.

CONSIDER THIS

To Change Database Properties

To change database properties, you would follow these steps.

1 Click File on the ribbon to open the Backstage view and then, if necessary, click the Info tab in the Backstage view to display the Info gallery.

2 Click the 'View and edit database properties' link in the right pane of the Info gallery to display the PrattLast Associates Properties dialog box.

◄ | Why are some of the database properties already filled in?
Q&A | The person who installed Office 2016 on your computer or network might have set or customized the properties.

3 If the property you want to change is displayed in the Properties dialog box, click the text box for the property and make the desired change. Skip the remaining steps.

4 If the property you want to change is not displayed in the Properties dialog box, click the appropriate tab so the property is displayed and then make the desired change.

5 Click the OK button in the Properties dialog box to save your changes and remove the dialog box from the screen.

Special Database Operations

Additional operations involved in maintaining a database are backup, recovery, compacting, and repairing.

Backup and Recovery

It is possible to damage or destroy a database. Users can enter data that is incorrect; programs that are updating the database can end abnormally during an update; a hardware problem can occur; and so on. After any such event has occurred, the database may contain invalid data or it might be totally destroyed.

Obviously, you cannot allow a situation in which data has been damaged or destroyed to go uncorrected. You must somehow return the database to a correct state. This process is called recovery; that is, you **recover** the database.

The simplest approach to recovery involves periodically making a copy of the database (called a **backup copy** or a **save copy**). This is referred to as **backing up** the database. If a problem occurs, you correct the problem by overwriting the actual database — often referred to as the **live database** — with the backup copy.

To back up the database that is currently open, you use the Back Up Database command on the Save As tab in the Backstage view. In the process, Access suggests a name that is a combination of the database name and the current date. For example, if you back up the PrattLast Associates database on October 20, 2017, Access will suggest the name, PrattLast Associates_2017-10-20. You can change this name if you desire, although it is a good idea to use this name. By doing so, it will be easy to distinguish between all the backup copies you have made to determine which is the most recent. In addition, if you discover that a critical problem occurred on October 18, 2017, you may want to go back to the most recent backup before October 18. If, for example, the database was not backed up on October 17 but was backed up on October 16, you would use PrattLast Associates_2017-10-16.

TO BACK UP A DATABASE

You would use the following steps to back up a database to a file on a hard disk, high-capacity removable disk, or other storage location.

1. Open the database to bc backed up.
2. Click File on the ribbon to open the Backstage view, and then click the Save As tab.
3. With Save Database As selected in the File Types area, click 'Back Up Database' in the Save Database As area, and then click the Save As button.
4. Navigate to the desired location in the Save As box. If you do not want the name Access has suggested, enter the desired name in the File name text box.
5. Click the Save button to back up the database.

Access creates a backup copy with the desired name in the desired location. Should you ever need to recover the database using this backup copy, you can simply copy it over the live version.

Compacting and Repairing a Database

As you add more data to a database, it naturally grows larger. When you delete an object (records, tables, forms, or queries), the space previously occupied by the object does not become available for additional objects. Instead, the additional objects are given new space; that is, space that was not already allocated. To remove this empty space from the database, you must **compact** the database. The same option that compacts the database also repairs problems that might have occurred in the database.

TO COMPACT AND REPAIR A DATABASE

You would use the following steps to compact and repair a database.

1. Open the database to be compacted.
2. Click File on the ribbon to open the Backstage view, and then, if necessary, select the Info tab.
3. Click the 'Compact & Repair Database' button in the Info gallery to compact and repair the database.

The database now is the compacted form of the original.

Additional Operations

Additional special operations include opening another database, closing a database without exiting Access, and saving a database with another name. They also include deleting a table (or other object) as well as renaming an object.

When you are working in a database and you open another database, Access will automatically close the database that was previously open. Before deleting or renaming an object, you should ensure that the object has no dependent objects; that is, other objects that depend on the object you want to delete.

TO CLOSE A DATABASE WITHOUT EXITING ACCESS

You would use the following steps to close a database without exiting Access.

1. Click File on the ribbon to open the Backstage view.
2. Click Close.

TO SAVE A DATABASE WITH ANOTHER NAME

To save a database with another name, you would use the following steps.

1. Click File on the ribbon to open the Backstage view, and then select the Save As tab.
2. With Save Database As selected in the File Types area and Access Database selected in the Save Database As area, click the Save As button.
3. Enter a name and select a location for the new version.
4. Click the Save button.

If you want to make a backup, could you just save the database with another name?
You could certainly do that. Using the backup procedure discussed earlier is useful because doing so automatically includes the current database name and the date in the name of the file it creates.

TO DELETE A TABLE OR OTHER OBJECT IN THE DATABASE

You would use the following steps to delete a database object.

1. Right-click the object in the Navigation Pane.
2. Click Delete on the shortcut menu.
3. Click the Yes button in the Microsoft Access dialog box.

TO RENAME AN OBJECT IN THE DATABASE

You would use the following steps to rename a database object.

1. Right-click the object in the Navigation Pane.
2. Click Rename on the shortcut menu.
3. Type the new name and press the ENTER key.

BTW

Access Help

At any time while using Access, you can find answers to questions and display information about various topics through Access Help. Used properly, this form of assistance can increase your productivity and reduce your frustrations by minimizing the time you spend learning how to use Access. For instructions about Access Help and exercises that will help you gain confidence in using it, read the Office and Windows module at the beginning of this book.

To Exit Access

All the steps in this module are now complete.

1 If desired, sign out of your Microsoft account.

2 Exit Access.

Database Design

BTW

Determining Database Requirements

The determination of database requirements is part of a process known as systems analysis. A systems analyst examines existing and proposed documents, and examines organizational policies to determine exactly the type of data needs the database must support.

This section illustrates the **database design** process, that is, the process of determining the tables and fields that make up the database. It does so by showing how you would design the database for PrattLast Associates from a set of requirements. In this section, you will use commonly accepted shorthand to represent the tables and fields that make up the database as well as the primary keys for the tables. For each table, you give the name of the table followed by a set of parentheses. Within the parentheses is a list of the fields in the table separated by commas. You underline the primary key. For example,

Product (Product Code, Description, On Hand, Price)

represents a table called Product. The Product table contains four fields: Product Code, Description, On Hand, and Price. The Product Code field is the primary key.

Database Requirements

The PrattLast Associates database must maintain information on both accounts and account managers. The business currently keeps this data in two Word tables and two Excel workbooks, as shown in Figure 1–80. They use Word tables for address information and Excel workbooks for financial information.

- For accounts, PrattLast needs to maintain address data. It currently keeps this data in a Word table (Figure 1–80a).

- PrattLast also maintains financial data for each account. This includes the amount paid and current amount due for the account. It keeps these amounts, along with the account name and number, in the Excel worksheet shown in Figure 1–80b.

- PrattLast keeps account manager address data in a Word table, as shown in Figure 1–80c.

- Just as with accounts, it keeps financial data for account managers, including their start date, salary, and bonus rate, in a separate Excel worksheet, as shown in Figure 1–80d.

Finally, PrattLast keeps track of which accounts are assigned to which account managers. Each account is assigned to a single account manager, but each account manager might be assigned many accounts. Currently, for example, accounts AC001 (Avondale Community Bank), JM323 (JSP Manufacturing Inc.), KC156 (Key Community College System), MI345 (Midwest Library Consortium), and TW001 (Tri-County Waste Disposal) are assigned to account manager 31 (Haydee Rivera). Accounts BL235 (Bland Corp.), CO621 (Codder Plastics Co.), KV089 (KAL Veterinary Services), LI268 (Lars-Idsen Inc.), and ML008 (Mums Landscaping Co.) are assigned to account manager 35 (Mark Simson). Accounts CA043 (Carlton Regional Clinic), EC010 (Eco Clothes Inc.), HL111 (Halko Legal Associates), LC005 (Lancaster County Hospital), and TP098 (TAL Packaging Systems) are assigned to account manager 58 (Karen Murowski). PrattLast has an additional account manager, Peter Lu, whose number has been assigned as 42, but who has not yet been assigned any accounts.

BTW

Additional Data for PrattLast Associates
PrattLast could include other types of data in the database. The Account table could include data on a contact person at each organization, such as name, telephone number, and email address. The Account Manager table could include the mobile telephone number, email address, and emergency contact information for the account manager.

Account Number	Account Name	Street	City	State	Postal Code
AC001	Avondale Community Bank	256 Main St.	Avondale	IL	60311
BL235	Bland Corp.	100 Granger Hwy.	Granger	IL	60314
CA043	Carlton Regional Clinic	589 Central Ave.	Carlton	IL	60313
CO621	Codder Plastics Co.	421 First Ave.	Bremerton	IN	46003
EC010	Eco Clothes Inc.	120 Pine St.	Davidson	IN	46010
HL111	Halko Legal Associates	321 Feathering Rd.	Gleneagle	IL	60319
JM323	JSP Manufacturing Inc.	1200 Franklin Blvd.	Wells	IN	46007
KC156	Key Community College System	35 Indiana Ave.	Walker	IN	46004
KV089	KAL Veterinary Services	116 Pine St.	Granger	IL	60314
LC005	Lancaster County Hospital	215 River St.	Granger	IL	46004
LI268	Lars-Idsen Inc.	829 Wooster Rd.	Davidson	IN	46010
MI345	Midwest Library Consortium	3400 Metro Pkwy.	Bremerton	IN	46003
ML008	Mums Landscaping Co.	865 Ridge Rd.	Wells	IN	46007
TP098	TAL Packaging Systems	12 Polk Ave.	Carlton	IL	60313
TW001	Tri-County Waste Disposal	345 Central Blvd.	Rushton	IL	60321

Figure 1–80a Account Addresses

A1	▼	:	✕	✓	fx	Account Number					

	A	B	C	D	E	F	G	H	I	J
1	Account Number	Account Name	Amount Paid	Current Due						
2	AC001	Avondale Community Bank	24,752.25	3,875.25						
3	BL235	Bland Corp.	29,836.65	2,765.30						
4	CA043	Carlton Regional Clinic	30,841.05	3,074.30						
5	CO621	Codder Plastics Co.	27,152.25	2,875.00						
6	EC010	Eco Clothes Inc.	19,620.00	1,875.00						
7	HL111	Halko Legal Associates	25,702.20	3,016.75						
8	JM323	JSP Manufacturing Inc.	19,739.70	2,095.00						
9	KV089	KAL Veterinary Services	34,036.50	580.00						
10	KC156	Key Community College System	10,952.25	0.00						
11	LC005	Lancaster County Hospital	44,025.60	3,590.80						
12	LI268	Lars-Idsen Inc.	0.00	1,280.75						
13	MI345	Midwest Library Consortium	21,769.20	2,890.60						
14	ML008	Mums Landscaping Co.	13,097.10	2,450.00						
15	TP098	TAL Packaging Systems	22,696.95	3,480.45						
16	TW001	Tri-County Waste Disposal	15,345.00	2,875.50						

Figure 1–80b Account Financial Data

Account Manager Number	Last Name	First Name	Street	City	State	Postal Code
31	Rivera	Haydee	325 Twiddy St.	Avondale	IL	60311
35	Simson	Mark	1467 Hartwell St.	Walker	IN	46004
42	Lu	Peter	5624 Murray Ave.	Davidson	IN	46007
58	Murowski	Karen	168 Truesdale Dr.	Carlton	IL	60313

Figure 1–80c Account Manager Addresses

	A	B	C	D	E	F	G	H	I
1	Account Manager Number	Last Name	First Name	Start Date	Salary	Bonus Rate			
2	31	Rivera	Haydee	6/3/2013	48,750.00	0.15			
3	35	Simson	Mark	5/19/2014	40,500.00	0.12			
4	42	Lu	Peter	8/3/2015	36,750.00	0.09			
5	58	Murowski	Karen	11/9/2016	24,000.00	0.08			
6									

Figure 1–80d Account Manager Financial Data

Database Design Process

The database design process involves several steps.

CONSIDER THIS

What is the first step in the process?
Identify the tables. Examine the requirements for the database to identify the main objects that are involved. There will be a table for each object you identify.

In a database for one organization, for example, the main objects might be departments and employees. This would require two tables: one for departments and the other for employees. In the database for another organization, the main objects might be accounts and account managers. In this case, there also would be two tables: one for accounts and the other for account managers. In still another organization's database, the main objects might be books, publishers, and authors. This database would require three tables: one for books, a second for publishers, and a third for authors.

Identifying the Tables

For the PrattLast Associates database, the main objects are accounts and account managers. This leads to two tables, which you must name. Reasonable names for these two tables are:

Account

Account Manager

After identifying the tables, what is the second step in the database design process?
Determine the primary keys. Recall that the primary key is the unique identifier for records in the table. For each table, determine the unique identifier. In a Department table, for example, the unique identifier might be the Department Code. For a Book table, the unique identifier might be the ISBN (International Standard Book Number).

Determining the Primary Keys

The next step is to identify the fields that will be the unique identifiers, or primary keys. Account numbers uniquely identify accounts, and account manager numbers uniquely identify account managers. Thus, the primary key for the Account table is the account number, and the primary key for the Account Manager table is the account manager number. Reasonable names for these fields would be Account Number and Account Manager Number, respectively. Adding these primary keys to the tables gives:

Account (<u>Account Number</u>)

Account Manager (<u>Account Manager Number</u>)

What is the third step in the database design process after determining the primary keys?
Determine the additional fields. The primary key will be a field or combination of fields in a table. A table will typically contain many additional fields, each of which contains a type of data. Examine the project requirements to determine these additional fields. For example, in an Employee table, additional fields might include Employee Name, Street Address, City, State, Postal Code, Date Hired, and Salary.

Determining Additional Fields

After identifying the primary keys, you need to determine and name the additional fields. In addition to the account number, the Account Address Information shown in Figure 1–80a contains the account name, street, city, state, and postal code. These would be fields in the Account table. The Account Financial Information shown in Figure 1–80b also contains the account number and account name, which are already included in the Account table. The financial information also contains the amount paid and current due. Adding the amount paid and current due fields to those already identified in the Account table and assigning reasonable names gives:

Account (<u>Account Number</u>, Account Name, Street, City, State, Postal Code, Amount Paid, Current Due)

Similarly, examining the Account Manager Address Information in Figure 1–80c adds the last name, first name, street, city, state, and postal code fields to the Account Manager table. In addition to the account manager number, last name, and first name, the Account Manager Financial Information in Figure 1–80d would add the start date, salary, and bonus rate. Adding these fields to the Account Manager table and assigning reasonable names gives:

Account Manager (<u>Account Manager Number</u>, Last Name, First Name, Street, City, State, Postal Code, Start Date, Salary, Bonus Rate)

BTW

Database Design Language (DBDL)
Database Design Language (DBDL) is a commonly accepted shorthand representation for showing the structure of a relational database. You write the name of the table and then within parentheses you list all the columns in the table. If the columns continue beyond one line, indent the subsequent lines.

What happens as the fourth step, after determining additional fields?
Determine relationships between the tables. A relationship is an association between objects. In a database containing information about departments and employees, there is an association between the departments and the employees. A department is associated with all the employees in the department, and an employee is associated with the department to which he or she is assigned. Technically, you say that a department is related to all the employees in the department, and an employee is related to his or her department.

The relationship between department and employees is an example of a **one-to-many relationship** because one employee is associated with one department, but each department can be associated with many employees. The Department table would be the "one" table in the relationship. The Employee table would be the "many" table in the relationship.

When you have determined that two tables are related, follow these general guidelines:

- Identify the "one" table.
- Identify the "many" table.
- Include the primary key from the "one" table as a field in the "many" table.

Determining and Implementing Relationships between the Tables

According to the requirements, each account has one account manager, but each account manager can have many accounts. Thus, the Account Manager table is the "one" table, and the Account table is the "many" table. To implement this one-to-many relationship between account managers and accounts, add the Account Manager Number field (the primary key of the Account Manager table) to the Account table. This produces:

Account (<u>Account Number</u>, Account Name, Street, City, State, Postal Code, Amount Paid, Current Due, Account Manager Number)

Account Manager (<u>Account Manager Number</u>, Last Name, First Name, Street, City, State, Postal Code, Start Date, Salary, Bonus Rate)

After creating relationships between tables, what is the fifth step in the database design process?
Determine data types for the fields, that is, the type of data that can be stored in the field.

Assigning Data Types to the Fields

See the earlier section Determing Data Types for the Fields for a discussion of the available data types and their use in the PrattLast Associates database. That section also discusses other properties that can be assigned, such as captions, field size, and the number of decimal places.

BTW
Postal Codes
Some organizations with accounts throughout the country have a separate table of postal codes, cities, and states. When placing an order, you typically are asked for your postal code (or ZIP code), rather than city, state, and postal code. You then are asked to confirm that the city and state correspond to that postal code.

Identifying and Removing Redundancy

Redundancy means storing the same fact in more than one place. It usually results from placing too many fields in a table — fields that really belong in separate tables — and often causes serious problems. If you had not realized there were two objects, such as accounts and account managers, you might have placed all the data in a single Account table. Figure 1–81 shows an example of a table that includes both account and account manager information. Notice that the data for a given account manager (number, name, address, and so on) occurs on more than one record. The data for rep 35, Mark Simson, is repeated in the figure. Storing this data on multiple records is an example of redundancy.

Account table

Account Number	Account Name	Street	...	Account Manager Number	Last Name	First Name
AC001	Avondale Community Bank	256 Main St.	...	31	Rivera	Haydee
BL235	Bland Corp.	100 Granger Hwy.	...	35	Simson	Mark
CA043	Carlton Regional Clinic	589 Central Ave.	...	58	Murowski	Karen
CO621	Codder Plastics Co.	421 First Ave.	...	35	Simson	Mark
EC010	Eco Clothes Inc.	120 Pine St.	...	58	Murowski	Karen
...	...	...	...	...	...	...
...	...	...	...	...	...	...

Account Manager numbers are 35

name of Account Manager 35 appears more than once

Figure 1–81

What problems does this redundancy cause?

Redundancy results in several problems, including:

1. Wasted storage space. The name of account manager 35, Mark Simson, for example, should be stored only once. Storing this information several times is wasteful.

2. More complex database updates. If, for example, Mark Simson's name is spelled incorrectly and needs to be changed in the database, his name would need to be changed in several different places.

3. Possible inconsistent data. Nothing prohibits the account manager's last name from being Simson on account BL235's record and Stimson on account CO621's record. The data would be inconsistent. In both cases, the account manager number is 35, but the last names are different.

How do you eliminate redundancy?

The solution to the problem is to place the redundant data in a separate table, one in which the data will no longer be redundant. If, for example, you place the data for account managers in a separate table (Figure 1–82), the data for each account manager will appear only once.

Account table

Account Number	Account Name	Street	...	Account Manager Number
AC001	Avondale Community Bank	256 Main St.	...	31
BL235	Bland Corp.	100 Granger Hwy.	...	35
CA043	Carlton Regional Clinic	589 Central Ave.	...	58
CO621	Codder Plastics Co.	421 First Ave.	...	35
EC010	Eco Clothes Inc.	120 Pine St.	...	58
...	...	...	...	...
...	...	...	...	...

Account Manager numbers are 35

Account Manager Table

Account Manager Number	Last Name	First Name	...
31	Rivera	Haydee	...
35	Simson	Mark	...
42	Lu	Peter	...
58	Murowski	Karen	...

name of Account Manager 35 appears only once

Figure 1–82

Notice that you need to have the account manager number in both tables. Without it, there would be no way to tell which account manager is associated with which account. The remaining account manager data, however, was removed from the Account table and placed in the Account Manager table. This new arrangement corrects the problems of redundancy in the following ways:

- Because the data for each account manager is stored only once, space is not wasted.

- Changing the name of an account manager is easy. You need to change only one row in the Account Manager table.

- Because the data for an account manager is stored only once, inconsistent data cannot occur.

Designing to omit redundancy will help you to produce good and valid database designs. You should always examine your design to see if it contains redundancy. If it does, you should decide whether you need to remove the redundancy by creating a separate table.

If you examine your design, you will see that there is one area of redundancy (see the data in Figure 1–1). Cities and states are both repeated. Every account whose postal code is 60314, for example, has Granger as the city and IL as the state. To remove this redundancy, you would create a table with the primary key Postal Code and City and State as additional fields. City and State would be removed from the Account table. Having City, State, and Postal Code in a table is very common, however, and usually you would not take such action. No other redundancy exists in your tables.

Summary

In this module you have learned to create an Access database, create tables and add records to a database, print the contents of tables, import data, create queries, create forms, create reports, and change database properties. You have also learned how to design a database.

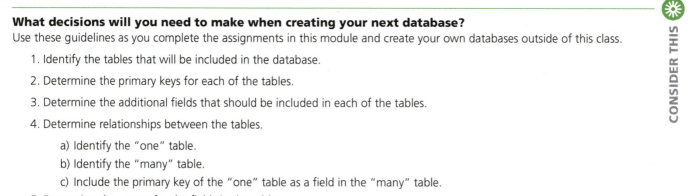

What decisions will you need to make when creating your next database?

Use these guidelines as you complete the assignments in this module and create your own databases outside of this class.

1. Identify the tables that will be included in the database.

2. Determine the primary keys for each of the tables.

3. Determine the additional fields that should be included in each of the tables.

4. Determine relationships between the tables.

    a) Identify the "one" table.

    b) Identify the "many" table.

    c) Include the primary key of the "one" table as a field in the "many" table.

5. Determine data types for the fields in the tables.

6. Determine additional properties for fields.

    a) Determine if a caption is warranted.

    b) Determine if a description of the field is warranted.

    c) Determine field sizes.

    d) Determine formats.

7. Identify and remove any unwanted redundancy.

8. Determine a storage location for the database.

9. Determine the best method for distributing the database objects.

CONSIDER THIS

How should you submit solutions to questions in the assignments identified with a symbol?
Every assignment in this book contains one or more questions identified with a symbol. These questions require you to think beyond the assigned database. Present your solutions to the questions in the format required by your instructor. Possible formats may include one or more of these options: write the answer; create a document that contains the answer; present your answer to the class; discuss your answer in a group; record the answer as audio or video using a webcam, smartphone, or portable media player; or post answers on a blog, wiki, or website.

Apply Your Knowledge

Reinforce the skills and apply the concepts you learned in this module.

Adding a Caption, Changing a Data Type, and Creating a Query, Form, and Report

Note: To complete this assignment, you will be required to use the Data Files. Please contact your instructor for information about accessing the Data Files.

Instructions: Friendly Janitorial Services provides janitorial services to local businesses. The company uses a team-based approach and each team has a team leader or supervisor. Friendly Janitorial Services has a database that keeps track of its supervisors and its clients. Each client is assigned to a single supervisor; each supervisor may be assigned many clients. The database has two tables. The Client table contains data on the clients who use Friendly Janitorial Services. The Supervisor table contains data on the supervisors. You will add a caption, change a data type, and create a query, a form, and a report, as shown in Figure 1–83.

Perform the following tasks:

1. Run Access, open the Apply Friendly Janitorial Services database from the Data Files, and enable the content.

2. Open the Supervisor table in Datasheet view, add SU # as the caption for the Supervisor Number field, and resize all columns to best fit the data. Save the changes to the layout of the table and close the table.

3. Open the Client table in Design view and change the data type for the Supervisor Number field to Short Text. Change the field size for the field to 3 and add SU # as the caption for the Supervisor Number field. Save the changes to the table and close the table. Then, open the Client table in Datasheet view and resize all columns to best fit the data. Save the changes to the layout of the table and close the table.

4. Use the Simple Query Wizard to create a query for the Client table that contains the Client Number, Client Name, Amount Paid, Current Due, and Supervisor Number. The query is a detail query. Use the name Client Query for the query and close the query.

5. Create a simple form for the Supervisor table. Save the form and use the name Supervisor for the form. Close the form.

6. Create the report shown in Figure 1–83 for the Client table. The report includes totals for both the Amount Paid and Current Due fields. Be sure the totals appear completely. You might need to expand the size of the total controls. Move the page number so that it is within the margins. Save the report as Client Financial Report.

7. If requested by your instructor, add your last name to the title of the report, that is, change the title to Client Financial Report LastName where LastName is your actual last name.

8. Compact and repair the database.

9. Submit the revised database in the format specified by your instructor.

10. ✳ How would you change the field name of the Street field in the Client table to Address?

Continued >

Apply Your Knowledge *continued*

Client Financial Report			Tuesday, September 12, 2017	
			6:19:45 PM	
Client Number	Client Name	Amount Paid	Current Due	Supervisor Number
AT13	Atlas Repair	$5,400.00	$600.00	103
AZ01	AZ Auto	$9,250.00	$975.00	110
BB35	Babbage Bookkeeping	$8,820.00	$980.00	110
BL24	Blanton Shoes	$1,850.75	$210.25	120
MM01	Moss Manufacturing	$10,456.25	$1,125.00	114
PL03	Prime Legal Associates	$19,905.00	$2,245.00	110
PS67	PRIM Staffing	$4,500.00	$500.00	114
TE15	Telton-Edwards	$0.00	$700.00	120
		$129,979.20	$14,542.55	

Figure 1–83

Extend Your Knowledge

Extend the skills you learned in this module and experiment with new skills. You may need to use Help to complete the assignment.

Using a Database Template to Create an Events Database

Instructions: Access includes both desktop database templates and web-based templates. You can use a template to create a beginning database that can be modified to meet your specific needs. You will use a template to create an Events database. The database template includes sample tables, queries, forms, and reports. You will modify the database and create the Events Query shown in Figure 1–84.

Perform the following tasks:
1. Run Access.
2. Select the Desktop event management template in the template gallery and create a new database with the file name Extend Events.
3. Enable the content and close the Event List form.
4. Open the Navigation Pane and change the organization to Object Type.
5. Open the Events table in Datasheet view and delete the Attachments field in the table. The Attachments field has a paperclip as the column heading.
6. Add the Event Type field to the end of the table. Assign the Short Text data type with a field size of 15.
7. Save the changes to the Events table and close the table.
8. Use the Simple Query Wizard to create the Events Query shown in Figure 1–84. Close the query.

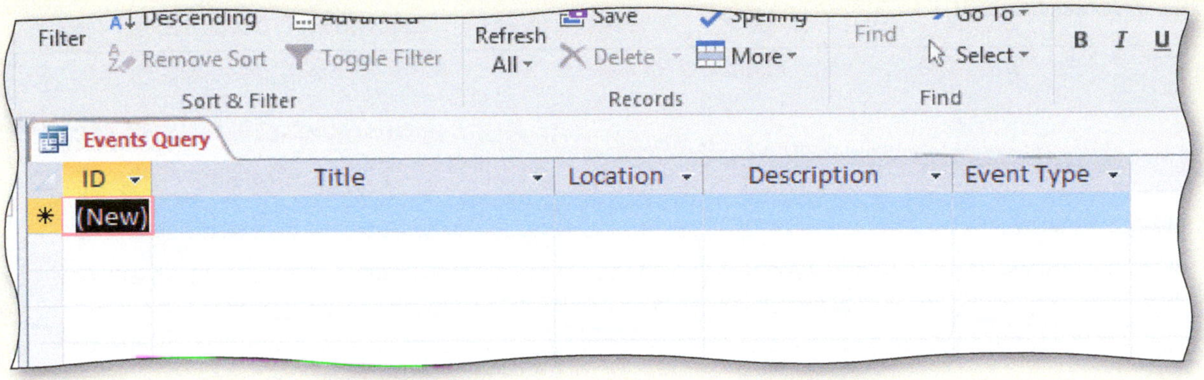

Figure 1–84

9. Open the Current Events report in Layout view. Delete the controls containing the current date and current time in the upper-right corner of the report. Change the title of the report to Current Events List.

10. Save the changes to the report.

11. If requested to do so by your instructor, add your first and last names to the end of the title and save the changes to the report.

12. Submit the revised database in the format specified by your instructor.

13. a. Why would you use a template instead of creating a database from scratch with just the fields you need?

   b. The Attachment data type allows you to attach files to a database record. If you were using this database to keep track of events for a 4th of July celebration in a small town, what specific documents might you attach to an Events record?

Expand Your World

Create a solution, which uses cloud and web technologies, by learning and investigating on your own from general guidance.

Problem: You and two friends recently started a business that provides temporary non-medical help to individuals and families in need of assistance. You want to be able to share query results and reports, so you have decided to store the items in the cloud. You are still learning Access, so you are going to create a sample query and the report shown in Figure 1–85, export the results, and save to a cloud storage location, such as Microsoft OneDrive, Dropbox, or Google Drive.

Note: To complete this assignment, you will be required to use the Data Files. Please contact your instructor for information about accessing the Data Files.

Instructions:

1. Open the Expand Temporary Help database from the Data Files and enable the content.

2. Use the Simple Query Wizard to create a query that includes the Client Number, First Name, Last Name, Balance, and Helper Number. Save the query as Client Query.

3. Export the Client Query as an XPS document to a cloud-based storage location of your choice.

4. Create the report shown in Figure 1–85. Save the report as Client Status Report.

Continued >

Expand Your World *continued*

Client Status Report			Tuesday, September 12, 2017	
			6:22:36 PM	

Client Number	Last Name	First Name	Balance	Helper Number
AB10	Autley	Francis	$55.00	203
BR16	Behrens	Alexa	$90.00	205
FF45	Ferdon		$0.00	207
		Libby	$0.00	207
PR80	Priestly	Martin	$85.00	205
SA23	Sanders	Marya	$0.00	207
TR35	Teeter	Rich	$50.00	205
			$469.00	

Figure 1–85

5. Export the Client Status Report as a PDF document to a cloud-based storage location of your choice. You do not need to change any optimization or export settings. Do not save the export steps.

6. If requested to do so by your instructor, open the Helper table and change the last name and first name for helper 203 to your last name and your first name.

7. Submit the assignment in the format specified by your instructor.

8. Which cloud-based storage location did you use for this assignment? Why?

In the Labs

Design, create, modify, and/or use a database following the guidelines, concepts, and skills presented in this module. Labs are listed in order of increasing difficulty. Labs 1 and 2, which increase in difficulty, require you to create solutions based on what you learned in the module; Lab 3 requires you to apply your creative thinking and problem-solving skills to design and implement a solution.

Lab 1: Creating Objects for the Garden Naturally Database

Problem: Garden Naturally is a company that provides products for the organic gardening community. Sales representatives are responsible for selling to distributors, nurseries, and retail stores. The company recently decided to store its customer and sales rep data in a database. Each customer is assigned to a single sales rep, but each sales rep may be assigned many customers. The database and the Sales Rep table have been created, but the Salary YTD field needs to be added to the table. The records shown in Table 1–6 must be added to the Sales Rep table. The company plans to import the Customer table from the Excel worksheet shown in Figure 1–86. Garden Naturally would like to finish storing this data in a database and has asked you to help.

Note: To complete this assignment, you will be required to use the Data Files. Please contact your instructor for information about accessing the Data Files.

Instructions: Perform the following tasks:

1. Run Access, open the Lab 1 Garden Naturally database from the Data Files, and enable the content.

2. Open the Sales Rep table in Datasheet view and add the Salary YTD field to the end of the table. The field has the Currency data type. Assign the caption SR # to the Sales Rep Number field.

3. Add the records shown in Table 1–6.

Table 1–6 Data for Sales Rep Table									
Sales Rep Number	Last Name	First Name	Street	City	State	Postal Code	Start Date	Commission Rate	Salary YTD
32	Ortiz	Gloria	982 Victoria Ln.	Chesnee	NJ	07053	9/12/2015	.05	$32,555.65
35	Sinson	Mike	45 Elm St.	Quaker	DE	19719	8/28/2017	.04	$1,500.00
29	Gupta	Rufus	678 Hillcrest Rd.	Gossett	PA	19157	6/1/2015	.06	$35,075.30
26	Jones	Pat	43 Third St.	Greer	PA	19158	5/16/2016	.05	$33,100.50

4. Resize the columns to best fit the data. Save the changes to the layout of the table.

5. Import the Lab 1–1 Customer workbook shown in Figure 1–86 into the database. The first row of the workbook contains the column headings. Customer Number is the primary key for the new table. Assign the name Customer to the table. Save the Import steps, and assign the name Import-Customer Workbook to the steps. Assign Import Customer Workbook as the description.

	A	B	C	D	E	F	G	H	I
1	Customer Number	Customer Name	Address	City	State	Postal Code	Amount Paid	Balance Due	Sales Rep Number
2	AA30	All About Gardens	47 Berton St.	Greer	PA	19158	$1,190.00	$365.00	26
3	CT02	Christmas Tree Farm	483 Cantor Rd.	Pleasantburg	NJ	07025	$2,285.50	$825.35	29
4	GG01	Garden Gnome	10 Main St.	Gossett	PA	19157	$1,300.00	$297.50	29
5	GT34	Green Thumb Growers	26 Jefferson Hwy.	Pleasantburg	NJ	07025	$3,325.45	$865.50	32
6	LH15	Lawn & Home Store	33 Maple St.	Chambers	NJ	07037	$895.00	$515.00	26
7	ML25	Mum's Landscaping	196 Lincoln Ave.	Quaker	DE	19719	$0.00	$1,805.00	29
8	OA45	Outside Architects	234 Magnolia Rd.	Gaston	DE	19723	$4,205.50	$945.00	32
9	PL10	Pat's Landscaping	22 Main St.	Chesnee	NJ	07053	$1,165.00	$180.00	26
10	PN18	Pyke Nurseries	10 Grant Blvd.	Adelphia	PA	19159	$2,465.00	$530.00	32
11	SL25	Summit Lawn Service	345 Oaktree Rd.	Chesnee	NJ	07053	$3,225.45	$675.50	26
12	TG38	TriState Growers	24 Main St.	Gaston	DE	19723	$1,075.00	$0.00	29
13	TW34	TAL Wholesalers	234 Cantor Rd.	Pleasantburg	NJ	07025	$4,125.00	$350.00	26
14	TY03	TLC Yard Care	24 Berton St.	Greer	PA	19158	$1,845.00	$689.45	29
15	YS04	Yard Shoppe	124 Elm St.	Quaker	DE	19719	$445.00	$575.00	32
16	YW01	Young's Wholesalers	5239 Lancaster Hwy.	Adelphia	PA	19156	$1,785.50	$345.60	32
17									
18									
19									
20									
21									

Figure 1–86

Continued >

In the Labs continued

6. Open the Customer table in Design view and make the following changes:

   a. Change the field size for the Customer Number field to 4. Change the field size for the Customer Name field to 30. Change the field size for the Address field to 25 and the field size for the City field to 20. Change the field size for the State field to 2 and the field size for the Postal Code field to 5. Change the field size for the Sales Rep Number field to 2.

   b. Add the caption CU # to the Customer Number field.

   c. Add the caption SR # to the Sales Rep Number field.

7. Save the changes to the Customer table. If a Microsoft Access dialog box appears with the 'Some data may be lost' message, click the Yes button.

8. Open the Customer table in Datasheet view and resize all columns to best fit the data. Save the changes to the layout of the table.

9. Create a query using the Simple Query Wizard for the Customer table that displays the Customer Number, Customer Name, Amount Paid, Balance Due, and Sales Rep Number. Save the query as Customer Query.

Customer Financial Report				Tuesday, September 12, 2017 6:25:09 PM
Customer Number	Customer Name	Amount Paid	Balance Due	Sales Rep Number
AA30	All About Gardens	$1,190.00	$365.00	26
CT02	Christmas Tree Farm	$2,285.50	$825.35	29
TG38	TriState Growers	$1,075.00	$0.00	29
TW34	TAL Wholesalers	$4,125.00	$350.00	26
TY03	TLC Yard Care	$1,845.00	$689.45	29
YS04	Yard Shoppe	$445.00	$575.00	32
YW01	Young's Wholesalers	$1,785.50	$345.60	32
		$29,332.40	$8,963.90	

Figure 1–87

10. Create the report shown in Figure 1–87 for the Customer table. The report should include the Customer Number, Customer Name, Amount Paid, Balance Due, and Sales Rep Number fields. Include totals for the Amount Paid and Balance Due fields. Be sure to change the column headings to those shown in Figure 1–87. Save the report as Customer Financial Report.

11. If requested to do so by your instructor, change the address for Pat Jones in the Sales Rep table to your address. If your address is longer than 20 characters, simply enter as much as you can.

12. Submit the revised database in the format specified by your instructor.

13. The Commission Rate field has a field size of Single. If you changed the field size to Integer, what values would appear in the Commission Rate column? Why?

Lab 2: **Creating the Museum Gift Shop Database**

Problem: The local science museum operates a gift shop that sells science-related items. The gift shop purchases the items from vendors that deal in science-related games, toys, and other merchandise. Currently, the information about the items and the vendors is stored in two Excel workbooks. Each item is assigned to a single vendor, but each vendor may be assigned many items. You are to create a database that will store the item and vendor information. You have already determined that you need two tables, a Vendor table and an Item table, in which to store the information.

Note: To complete this assignment, you will be required to use the Data Files. Please contact your instructor for information about accessing the Data Files.

Instructions: Perform the following tasks:

1. Use the Blank desktop database option to create a new database in which to store all objects related to the items for sale. Call the database Lab 2 Museum Gift Shop.

2. Import the Lab 1–2 Vendor Data Excel workbook into the database. The first row of the workbook contains the column headings. Vendor Code is the primary key for the new table. Assign the name Vendor to the table. Do not save the Import steps.

3. Open the Vendor table in Datasheet view. Change the field size for the Vendor Code field to 2; the field size for the Vendor Name field to 25; and the field size for the Telephone Number field to 12. Assign the caption VC to the Vendor Code field.

4. Import the Lab 1–2 Item Data Excel workbook into the database. The first row of the workbook contains the column headings. Item Number is the primary key for this table. Assign the name Item to the table. Do not save the Import steps.

5. Open the Item table in Design view. Change the field size for the Item Number field to 4. Change the field size for the Description field to 28. Add the caption Wholesale for the Wholesale Cost field, the caption Retail for the Retail Price field, and the caption VC for the vendor code. The On Hand field should be an Integer field. Be sure that the field size for the Vendor Code in the Item table is identical to the field size for the Vendor Code in the Vendor table. Save the changes to the table and close the table.

6. Open the Item table in Datasheet view and resize the columns to best fit the data. Save the changes to the layout of the table and close the table.

7. Create a query for the Item table. Include the Item Number, Description, Wholesale Cost, Retail Price, and Vendor Code. Save the query as Item Query.

8. Create a simple form for the Item table. Use the name Item for the form.

9. Create the report shown in Figure 1–88 for the Item table. Do not add any totals. Save the report as Item Status Report.

Item Status Report

Tuesday, September 12, 2017
6:26:31 PM

Item Number	Description	On Hand	Wholesale Price
3663	Agate Bookends	4	$16.25
3673	Amazing Science Fun	8	$13.50
4553	Cosmos Uncovered	9	$8.95
4573	Crystal Growing Kit	7	$6.75
4583	Dinosaur Egg Ornament	12	$7.50

Figure 1–88

Continued >

In the Labs *continued*

10. If requested to do so by your instructor, change the telephone number for Atherton Wholesalers to your telephone number.

11. Submit the database in the format specified by your instructor.

12. ✳ If you had designed this database, could you have used the field name, Name, for the Vendor Name field name? If not, why not?

Lab 3: **Consider This: Your Turn**

Apply your creative thinking and problem solving skills to design and implement a solution.

Creating the Camshay Marketing Database

Note: To complete this assignment, you will be required to use the Data Files. Please contact your instructor for information about accessing the Data Files.

Part 1: Camshay Marketing Associates is a small company that specializes in data mining for marketing research and analysis. The company focuses on the service, nonprofit, and retail sectors. Camshay uses marketing analysts to work collaboratively with clients. Marketing analysts are paid a base salary and can earn incentive pay for maintaining and expanding client relationships. Based on the information in the Lab 1–3 Camshay Marketing workbook, use the concepts and techniques presented in this module to design and create a database to store the Camshay Marketing data. Change data types and field sizes as necessary. Add captions where appropriate. Create a form for the Client table and a report for the Client table similar to the Account Financial Report shown in Figure 1-67. Use the simple query wizard to create a query for the Client table that includes the Client Number, Client Name, Current Due and Marketing Analyst Number. Open the query and add a criterion to the query results to find only those clients whose amount due is $0.00 and save this modified query with a different name. Submit your assignment in the format specified by your instructor.

Part 2: You made several decisions while determining the table structures and adding data to the tables in this assignment. What method did you use to add the data to each table? Are there any other methods that would also have worked?

PrattLast Associates : Database- C:\Users\Owner\Documents\CI

File   Home   Create   External Data   Database Tools   ♀ Tell me what you want to do...

Microsoft Access 2016

2 Querying a Database

Objectives

You will have mastered the material in this module when you can:

- Create queries using Design view
- Include fields in the design grid
- Use text and numeric data in criteria
- Save a query and use the saved query
- Create and use parameter queries
- Use compound criteria in queries
- Sort data in queries

- Join tables in queries
- Create a report and a form from a query
- Export data from a query to another application
- Perform calculations and calculate statistics in queries
- Create crosstab queries
- Customize the Navigation Pane

Introduction

One of the primary benefits of using a database management system such as Access is having the ability to find answers to questions related to data stored in the database. When you pose a question to Access, or any other database management system, the question is called a query. A **query** is simply a question presented in a way that Access can process.

To find the answer to a question, you first create a corresponding query using the techniques illustrated in this module. After you have created the query, you instruct Access to run the query, that is, to perform the steps necessary to obtain the answer. Access then displays the answer in Datasheet view.

For an introduction to Windows and instructions about how to perform basic Windows tasks, read the Office and Windows module at the beginning of this book, where you can learn how to resize windows, change screen resolution, create folders, move and rename files, use Windows Help, and much more

Project — Querying a Database

Examples of questions related to the data in the PrattLast Associates database are shown in Figure 2–1.

In addition to these questions, PrattLast managers need to find information about accounts located in a specific city, but they want to enter a different city each time they ask the question. The company can use a parameter query to accomplish this task. PrattLast managers also want to summarize data in a specific way, which might involve performing calculations, and they can use a crosstab query to present the data in the desired form.

Microsoft Access 2016

File   Home   Create   External Data   Database Tools   Tell me what you want to do...

PrattLast Associates : Database- C:\Users\Owner\Documents\CIS

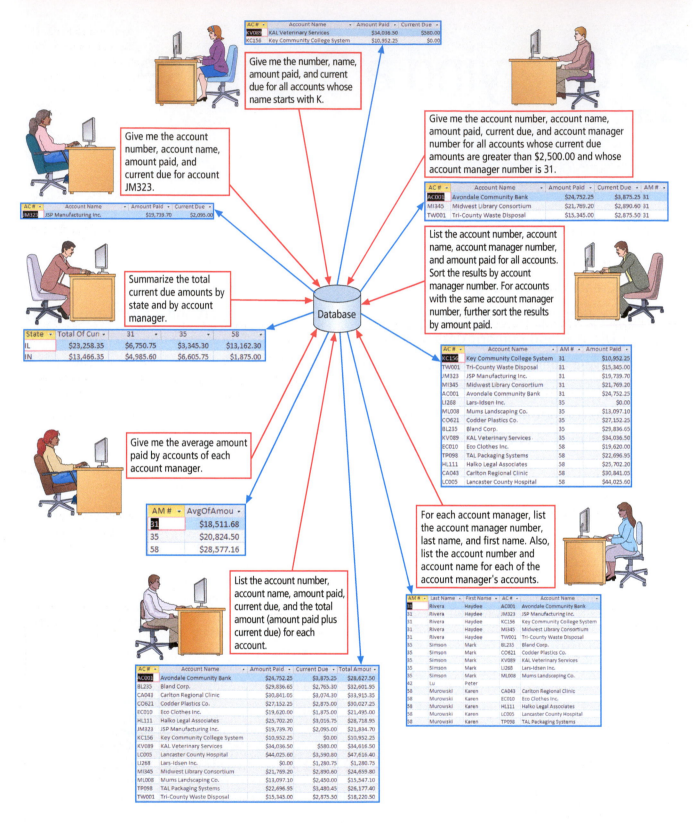

Figure 2–1

In this module, you will learn how to create and use the queries shown in Figure 2–1. The following roadmap identifies general activities you will perform as you progress through this module:

1. **CREATE QUERIES** in Design view.

2. **USE CRITERIA** in queries.

3. **SORT DATA** in queries.

4. **JOIN TABLES** in queries.

5. **EXPORT** query **RESULTS.**

6. **PERFORM CALCULATIONS** in queries.

7. **CREATE** a **CROSSTAB** query.

8. **CUSTOMIZE** the **NAVIGATION PANE**.

Creating Queries

As you learned in Module 1, you can use queries in Access to find answers to questions about the data contained in the database. *Note:* In this module, you will save each query example. When you use a query for another task, such as to create a form or report, you will assign a specific name to a query, for example, Manager-Account Query. In situations in which you will not use the query again, you will assign a name using a convention that includes the module number and a query number, for example, m02q01. Queries are numbered consecutively.

BTW

Select Queries
The queries you create in this module are select queries. In a select query, you retrieve data from one or more tables using criteria that you specify and display the data in a datasheet.

To Create a Query in Design View

1 CREATE QUERIES | 2 USE CRITERIA | 3 SORT DATA | 4 JOIN TABLES | 5 EXPORT RESULTS
6 PERFORM CALCULATIONS | 7 CREATE CROSSTAB | 8 CUSTOMIZE NAVIGATION PANE

In Module 1, you used the Simple Query Wizard to create a query. Most of the time, however, you will use Design view, which is the primary option for creating queries. *Why? Once you have created a new query in Design view, you have more options than with the wizard and can specify fields, criteria, sorting, calculations, and so on.* The following steps create a new query in Design view.

1
- Run Access and open the database named PrattLast Associates from your hard disk, OneDrive, or other storage location.

- Click the 'Shutter Bar Open/Close Button' to close the Navigation Pane.

- Click Create on the ribbon to display the Create tab (Figure 2–2).

Figure 2–2

2

- Click the Query Design button (Create tab | Queries group) to create a new query (Figure 2–3).

Q&A
Is it necessary to close the Navigation Pane?
No. Closing the pane gives you more room for the query, however, so it is usually a good practice.

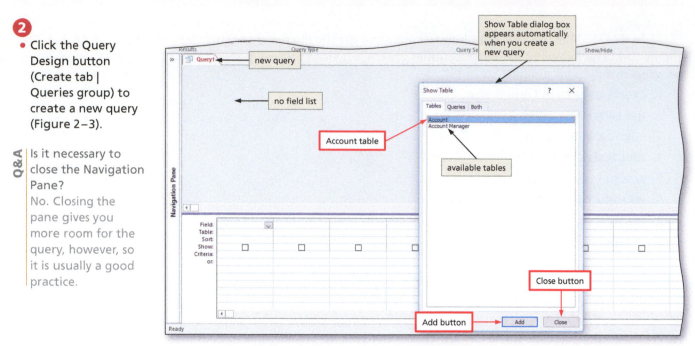

Figure 2–3

3

- Ensure the Account table (Show Table dialog box) is selected. If it is not, click the Account table to select it.
- Click the Add button to add the selected table to the query.
- Click the Close button to remove the dialog box from the screen.

Q&A
What if I inadvertently add the wrong table?
Right-click the table that you added in error and click Remove Table on the shortcut menu. You also can just close the query, indicate that you do not want to save it, and then start over.

- Drag the lower edge of the field list down far enough so all fields in the table appear (Figure 2–4).

Q&A
Is it essential that I resize the field list?
No. You can always scroll through the list of fields using the scroll bar. Resizing the field list so that all fields appear is usually more convenient.

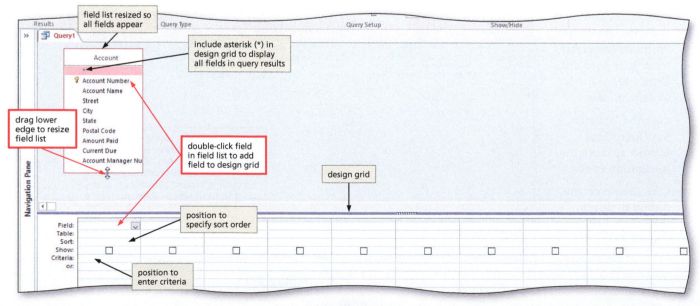

Figure 2–4

1 CREATE QUERIES | 2 USE CRITERIA | 3 SORT DATA | 4 JOIN TABLES | 5 EXPORT RESULTS
6 PERFORM CALCULATIONS | 7 CREATE CROSSTAB | 8 CUSTOMIZE NAVIGATION PANE

To Add Fields to the Design Grid

Once you have a new query displayed in Design view, you are ready to make entries in the **design grid**, the portion of the window where you specify fields and criteria for the query. The design grid is located in the lower pane of the window. You add the fields you want included in the query to the Field row in the grid. **Why add fields to the grid?** *Only the fields that appear in the design grid are included in the query results.* The following step begins creating a query that PrattLast Associates might use to obtain the account number, account name, amount paid, and current due for a particular account.

1

- Double-click the Account Number field in the field list to add the field to the query.

Q&A What if I add the wrong field?
Click just above the field name in the design grid to select the column and then press the DELETE key to remove the field.

- Double-click the Account Name field in the field list to add the field to the query.

- Add the Amount Paid field to the query.

- Add the Current Due field to the query (Figure 2–5).

Q&A What if I want to include all fields? Do I have to add each field individually?
No. Instead of adding individual fields, you can double-click the asterisk (*) to add the asterisk to the design grid. The asterisk is a shortcut indicating all fields are to be included.

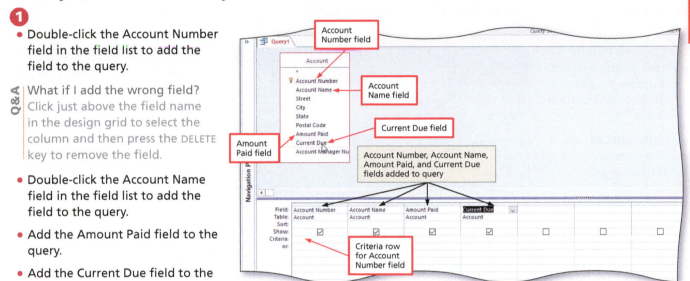

Figure 2–5

Determining Criteria

When you use queries, usually you are looking for those records that satisfy some criterion. In the simple query you created in the previous module, for example, you entered a criterion to restrict the records to those with the account manager number 35. In another query, you might want the name, amount paid, and current due amounts for the account whose number is JM323, for example, or for those accounts whose names start with the letters, La. You enter criteria in the Criteria row in the design grid below the field name to which the criterion applies. For example, to indicate that the account number must be JM323, you first must add the Account Number field to the design grid. You then would type JM323 in the Criteria row below the Account Number field.

Running the Query

After adding the appropriate fields and defining the query's criteria, you must run the query to get the results. To view the results of the query from Design view, click the Run button to instruct Access to run the query, that is, to perform the necessary actions to produce and display the results in Datasheet view.

To Use Text Data in a Criterion

To use **text data** (data in a field whose data type is Short Text) in criteria, simply type the text in the Criteria row below the corresponding field name, just as you did in Module 1. In Access, you do not need to enclose text data in quotation marks as you do in many other database management systems. *Why? Access will enter the quotation marks automatically, so you can simply type the desired text.* The following steps finish creating a query that PrattLast Associates might use to obtain the account number, account name, amount paid, and current due amount of account JM323. These steps add the appropriate criterion so that only the desired account will appear in the results. The steps also save the query.

1

- Click the Criteria row for the Account Number field to produce an insertion point.

- Type **JM323** as the criterion (Figure 2–6).

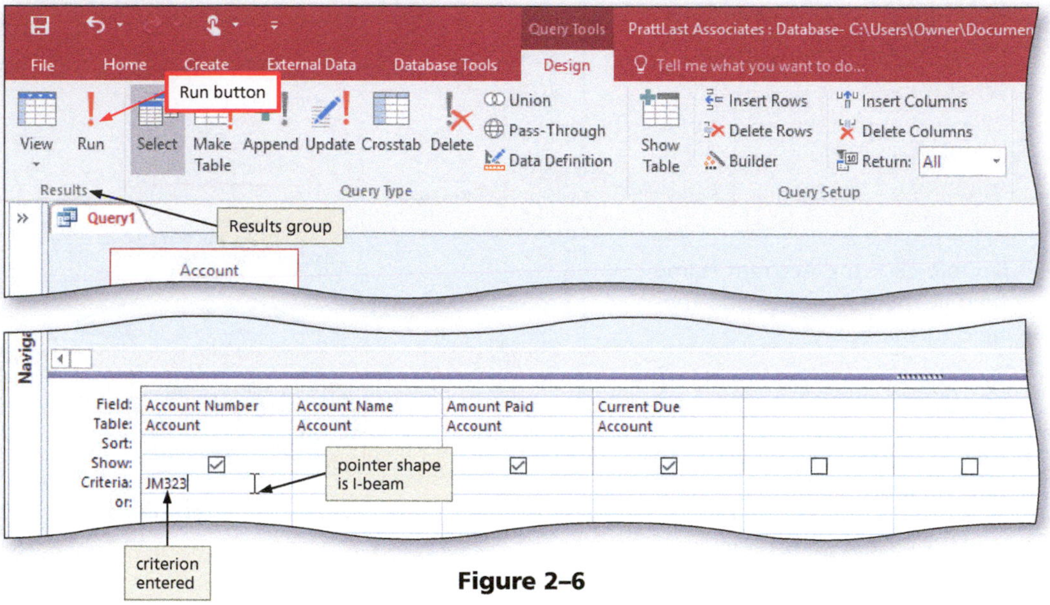

Figure 2–6

2

- Click the Run button (Query Tools Design tab | Results group) to run the query (Figure 2–7).

Q&A Can I also use the View button in the Results group to run the query?
Yes. You can click the View button to view the query results in Datasheet view.

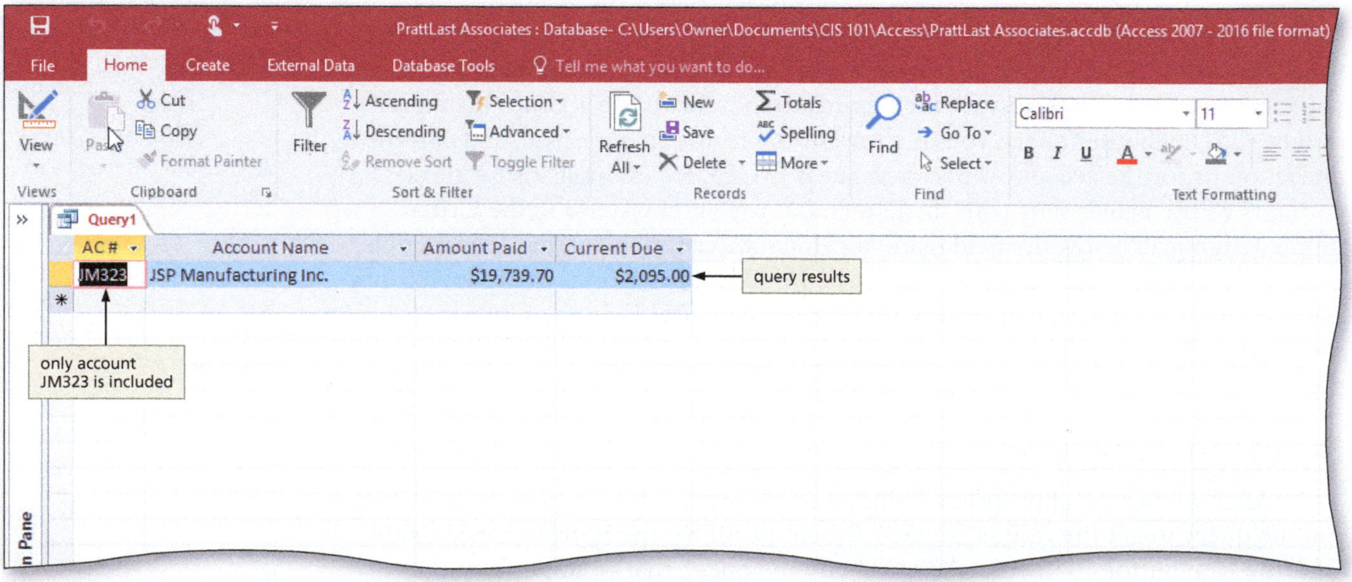

Figure 2–7

3

- Click the Save button on the Quick Access Toolbar to display the Save As dialog box.

- Type **m02q01** as the name of the query (Figure 2–8).

 Can I also save from Design view?
Yes. You can save the query when you view it in Design view just as you can save it when you view query results in Datasheet view.

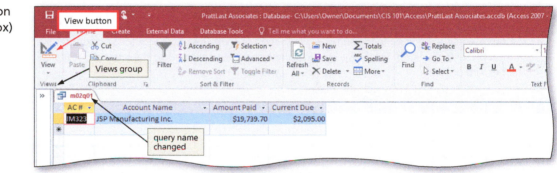

Figure 2–8

4

- Click the OK button (Save As dialog box) to save the query (Figure 2–9).

Figure 2–9

Other Ways

1. Right-click query tab, click Save on shortcut menu   2. Press CTRL+S

Using Saved Queries

After you have created and saved a query, you can use it in a variety of ways:

- To view the results of a query that is not currently open, open it by right-clicking the query in the Navigation Pane and clicking Open on the shortcut menu.

- If you want to change the design of a query that is already open, return to Design view and make the changes.

- If you want to change the design of a query that is not currently open, right-click the query in the Navigation Pane and then click Design View on the shortcut menu to open the query in Design view.

- To print the results with a query open, click File on the ribbon, click the Print tab in the Backstage view, and then click Quick Print.

BTW

The Ribbon and Screen Resolution
Access may change how the groups and buttons within the groups appear on the ribbon, depending on the computer or mobile device's screen resolution. Thus, your ribbon may look different from the ones in this book if you are using a screen resolution other than 1366 x 768.

- To print a query without first opening it, be sure the query is selected in the Navigation Pane and click File on the ribbon, click the Print tab in the Backstage view, and then click Quick Print.

- You can switch between views of a query using the View button (Home tab | Views group). Clicking the arrow at the bottom of the button produces the View button menu. You then click the desired view in the menu. The two query views you use in this module are Datasheet view (to see the results) and Design view (to change the design). You can also click the top part of the View button, in which case you will switch to the view identified by the icon on the button. In Figure 2–9, the View button displays the icon for Design view, so clicking the button would change to Design view. For the most part, the icon on the button represents the view you want, so you can usually simply click the button.

Wildcards

Microsoft Access supports wildcards. **Wildcards** are symbols that represent any character or combination of characters. One common wildcard, the **asterisk (*)**, represents any collection of characters. Another wildcard symbol is the **question mark (?)**, which represents any individual character.

What does S* represent? What does T?m represent?

S* represents the letter, S, followed by any collection of characters. A search for S* might return System, So, or Superlative. T?m represents the letter, T, followed by any single character, followed by the letter, m. A search for T?m might return the names Tim or Tom.

To Use a Wildcard

1 CREATE QUERIES | **2 USE CRITERIA** | 3 SORT DATA | 4 JOIN TABLES | 5 EXPORT RESULTS
6 PERFORM CALCULATIONS | 7 CREATE CROSSTAB | 8 CUSTOMIZE NAVIGATION PANE

The following steps modify the previous query to use the asterisk wildcard so that PrattLast Associates can select only those accounts whose names begin with K. *Why? Because you do not know how many characters will follow the K, the asterisk wildcard symbol is appropriate.* The steps also save the query with a new name using the Save As command.

1

- Click the View button (Home tab | Views group), shown in Figure 2–9, to return to Design view.

- If necessary, click the Criteria row below the Account Number field to produce an insertion point.

Q&A The text I entered now has quotation marks surrounding it. What happened?
Criteria for text data needs to be enclosed in quotation marks. You do not have to type the quotation marks; Access adds them automatically.

- Use the DELETE or BACKSPACE key as necessary to delete the current entry.

- Click the Criteria row below the Account Name field to produce an insertion point.

- Type **K*** as the criterion (Figure 2–10).

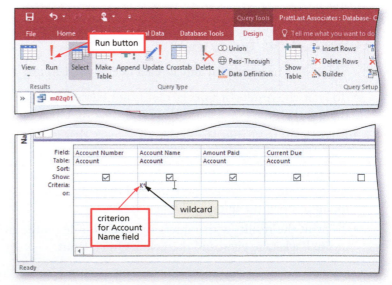

Figure 2–10

2
- Run the query by clicking the Run button (Query Tools Design tab | Results group) (Figure 2–11).

🔎 **Experiment**
- Change the letter K to lowercase in the criterion and run the query to determine whether case makes a difference when entering a wildcard.

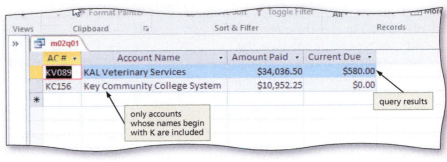

Figure 2–11

3
- Click File on the ribbon to open the Backstage view.
- Click the Save As tab in the Backstage view to display the Save As gallery.
- Click 'Save Object As' in the File Types area (Figure 2–12).

Q&A Can I just click the Save button on the Quick Access Toolbar as I did when saving the previous query?
If you clicked the Save button, you

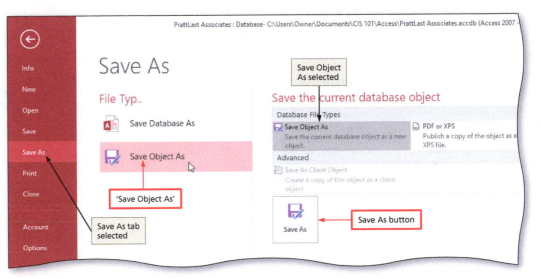

Figure 2–12

would replace the previous query with the version you just created. Because you want to save both the previous query and the new one, you need to save the new version with a different name. To do so, you must use Save Object As, which is available through the Backstage view.

4
- With Save Object As selected in the File Types gallery, click the Save As button to display the Save As dialog box.
- Erase the name of the current query and type **m02q02** as the name for the saved query (Figure 2–13).

Q&A The current entry in the As text box is Query. Could I save the query as some other type of object?

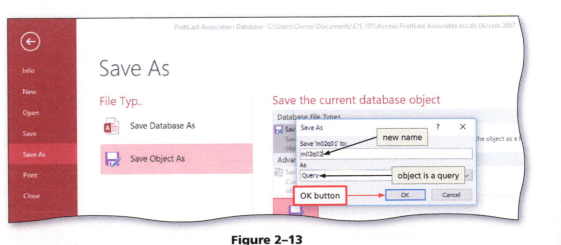

Figure 2–13

Although you usually would want to save the query as another query, you can also save it as a form or report by changing the entry in the As text box. If you do, Access would create either a simple form or a simple report for the query.

5

- Click the OK button (Save As dialog box) to save the query with the new name and close the Backstage view (Figure 2–14).

How can I tell that the query was saved with the new name?
The new name will appear on the tab.

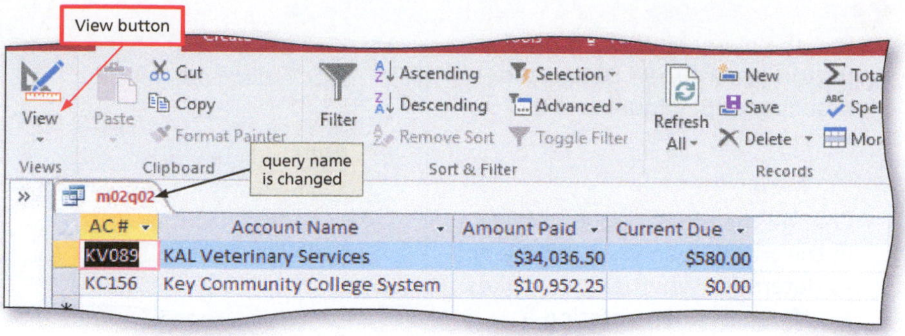

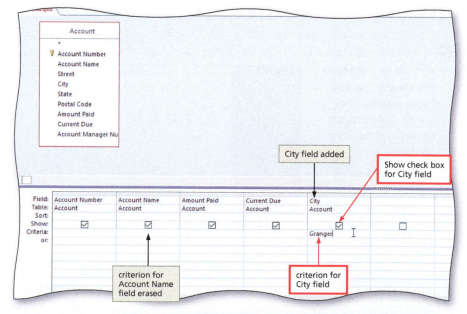

Figure 2–14

Other Ways

1. Click Design View button on status bar

To Use Criteria for a Field Not Included in the Results

1 CREATE QUERIES | **2 USE CRITERIA** | 3 SORT DATA | 4 JOIN TABLES | 5 EXPORT RESULTS
6 PERFORM CALCULATIONS | 7 CREATE CROSSTAB | 8 CUSTOMIZE NAVIGATION PANE

In some cases, you might require criteria for a particular field that should not appear in the results of the query. For example, you may want to see the account number, account name, amount paid, and current due for all accounts located in Granger. The criteria involve the City field, but you do not want to include the City field in the results.

To enter a criterion for the City field, it must be included in the design grid. Normally, it would then appear in the results. To prevent this from happening, remove the check mark from its check box in the Show row of the grid. **Why?** *A check mark in the Show check box instructs Access to show the field in the result. If you remove the check mark, you can use the field in the query without displaying it in the query results.*

The following steps modify the previous query so that PrattLast Associates can select only those accounts located in Granger. PrattLast does not want the city to appear in the results, however. The steps also save the query with a new name.

1

- Click the View button (Home tab | Views group), shown in Figure 2–14, to return to Design view.

The text I entered is now preceded by the word, Like. What happened?
Criteria that include wildcards need to be preceded by the word, Like. However, you do not have to type it; Access adds the word automatically to any criterion involving a wildcard.

- Erase the criterion in the Criteria row of the Account Name field.

- Add the City field to the query.

- Type **Granger** as the criterion for the City field (Figure 2–15).

Figure 2–15

2
- Click the Show check box for the City field to remove the check mark (Figure 2–16).

Q&A Could I have removed the check mark before entering the criterion?
Yes. The order in which you perform the two operations does not matter.

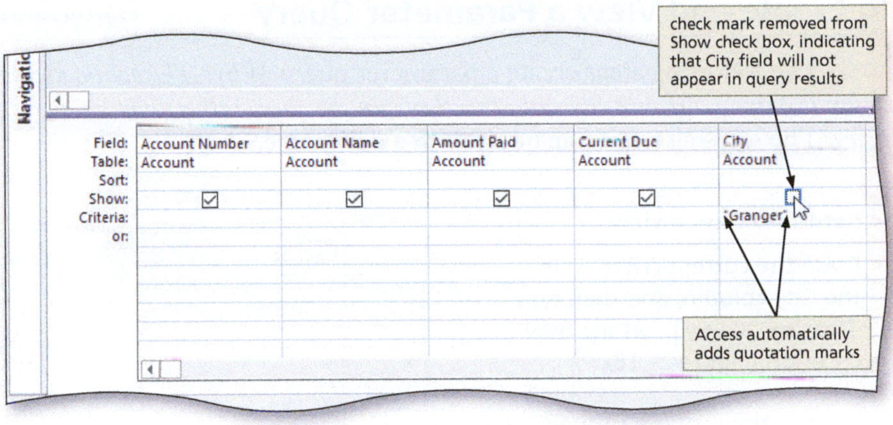

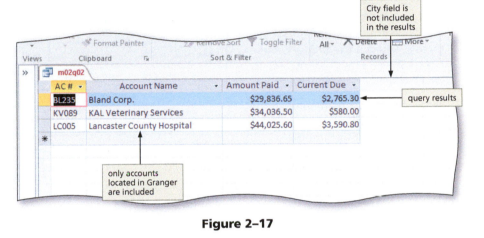

check mark removed from Show check box, indicating that City field will not appear in query results

Access automatically adds quotation marks

Figure 2–16

3
- Run the query (Figure 2–17).

Experiment
- Click the View button to return to Design view, enter a different city name as the criterion, and run the query. Repeat this process with additional city names, including at least one city name that is not in the database. When finished, change the criterion back to Granger.

City field is not included in the results

query results

only accounts located in Granger are included

Figure 2–17

Creating a Parameter Query

If you wanted to find accounts located in Wells instead of Granger, you would either have to create a new query or modify the existing query by replacing Granger with Wells as the criterion. Rather than giving a specific criterion when you first create the query, occasionally you may want to be able to enter part of the criterion when you run the query and then have the appropriate results appear. For example, you might want a query to return the account number, account name, amount paid, and current due for all accounts in a specific city, specifying a different city each time you run the query. A user could run the query, enter Wells as the city, and then see all the accounts in Wells. Later, the user could use the same query but enter Granger as the city, and then see all the accounts in Granger.

To enable this flexibility, you create a **parameter query**, which is a query that prompts for input whenever it is used. You enter a parameter (the prompt for the user) rather than a specific value as the criterion. You create the parameter by enclosing the criterion value in square brackets. It is important that the value in the brackets does not match the name of any field. If you enter a field name in square brackets, Access assumes you want that particular field and does not prompt the user for input. To prompt the user to enter the city name as the input, you could place [Enter City] as the criterion in the City field.

BTW

Designing Queries
Before creating queries, examine the contents of the tables involved. You need to know the data type for each field and how the data for the field is stored. If a query includes a state, for example, you need to know whether state is stored as the two-character abbreviation or as the full state name.

To Create and View a Parameter Query

The following steps create a parameter query. *Why? The parameter query will give users at PrattLast the ability to enter a different city each time they run the query rather than having a specific city as part of the criterion in the query.* The steps also save the query with a new name.

1

- Return to Design view.

- Erase the current criterion in the City column, and then type **[Enter City]** as the new criterion (Figure 2–18).

Q&A

What is the purpose of the square brackets?

The square brackets indicate that the text entered is not text that the value in the column must match. Without the brackets, Access would search for records in which the city is Enter City.

What if I typed a field name in the square brackets?

Access would simply use the value in that field. To create a parameter query, you must not use a field name in the square brackets.

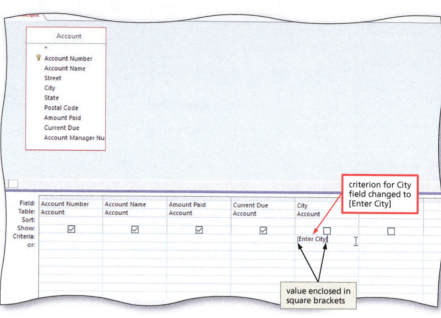

Figure 2–18

2

- Click the Run button (Query Tools Design tab | Results group) to display the Enter Parameter Value dialog box (Figure 2–19).

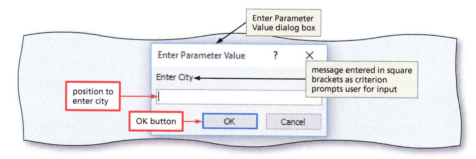

Figure 2–19

3

- Type **Wells** as the parameter value in the Enter City text box, and then click the OK button (Enter Parameter Value dialog box) to close the dialog box and view the query (Figure 2–20).

Experiment

- Try using other characters between the square brackets. In each case, run the query. When finished, change the characters between the square brackets back to Enter City.

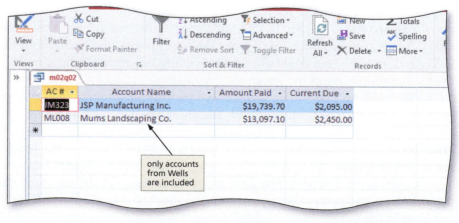

Figure 2–20

4

- Click File on the ribbon to open the Backstage view.

- Click the Save As tab in the Backstage view to display the Save As gallery.

- Click 'Save Object As' in the File Types area.

- With Save Object As selected in the File Types area, click the Save As button to display the Save As dialog box.

- Type `Account-City Query` as the name for the saved query.

- Click the OK button (Save As dialog box) to save the query with the new name and close the Backstage view (Figure 2–21).

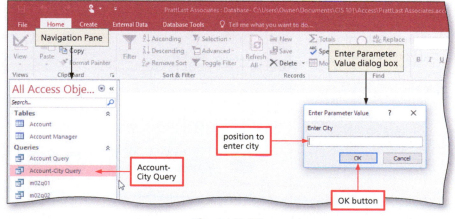

Figure 2–21

5

- Click the Close button for the Account-City Query to close the query.

To Use a Parameter Query

1 CREATE QUERIES | **2 USE CRITERIA** | 3 SORT DATA | 4 JOIN TABLES | 5 EXPORT RESULTS
6 PERFORM CALCULATIONS | 7 CREATE CROSSTAB | 8 CUSTOMIZE NAVIGATION PANE

You use a parameter query like any other saved query. You can open it or you can print the query results. In either case, Access prompts you to supply a value for the parameter each time you use the query. If changes have been made to the data since the last time you ran the query, the results of the query may be different, even if you enter the same value for the parameter. *Why? In addition to the ability to enter different field values each time the parameter query is run, the query always uses the data that is currently in the table.* The following steps use the parameter query named Account-City Query.

1

- Open the Navigation Pane.

- Right-click the Account-City Query to produce a shortcut menu.

- Click Open on the shortcut menu to open the query and display the Enter Parameter Value dialog box (Figure 2–22).

Q&A

The title bar for my Navigation Pane contains Tables and Related Views rather than All Access Objects as it did in Module 1. What should I do?
Click the Navigation Pane arrow and then click 'All Access Objects'.

Figure 2–22

I do not have the Search bar at the top of the Navigation Pane that I had in Module 1. What should I do?
Right-click the Navigation Pane title bar arrow to display a shortcut menu, and then click Search Bar.

2

- Type **Wells** in the Enter City text box, and then click the OK button (Enter Parameter Value dialog box) to display the results using Wells as the city, as shown in Figure 2–21.

- Close the query.

---

1 CREATE QUERIES | 2 USE CRITERIA | 3 SORT DATA | 4 JOIN TABLES | 5 EXPORT RESULTS
6 PERFORM CALCULATIONS | 7 CREATE CROSSTAB | 8 CUSTOMIZE NAVIGATION PANE

To Use a Number in a Criterion

To enter a number in a criterion, type the number without any dollar signs or commas. *Why? If you enter a dollar sign, Access assumes you are entering text. If you enter a comma, Access considers the criterion invalid.* The following steps create a query that PrattLast Associates might use to display all accounts whose current due amount is $0. The steps also save the query with a new name.

1

- Close the Navigation Pane.

- Click Create on the ribbon to display the Create tab.

- Click the Query Design button (Create tab | Queries group) to create a new query.

- If necessary, click the Account table (Show Table dialog box) to select the table.

- Click the Add button to add the selected table to the query.

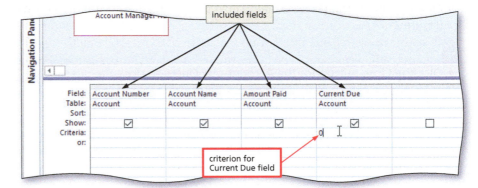

Figure 2–23

- Click the Close button to remove the dialog box from the screen.

- Drag the lower edge of the field list down far enough so all fields in the list are displayed.

- Include the Account Number, Account Name, Amount Paid, and Current Due fields in the query.

- Type **0** as the criterion for the Current Due field (Figure 2–23).

Q&A Do I need to enter a dollar sign and decimal point?

No. Access will interpret 0 as $0 because the data type for the Current Due field is currency.

2

- Run the query (Figure 2–24).

Q&A Why did Access display the results as $0.00 when I only entered 0?

Access uses the format for the field to determine how to display the result. In this case, the format indicated that Access should include the dollar sign, decimal point, and two decimal places.

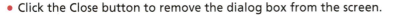

Figure 2–24

3

- Save the query as m02q03.

◁ How do I know when to use the Save button to save a query or use the Backstage view to perform a Save As?

If you are saving a new query, the simplest way is to use the Save button on the Quick Access Toolbar. If you are saving changes to a previously saved query but do not want to change the name, use the Save button. If you want to save a previously saved query with a new name, you must use the Backstage view and perform a Save Object As.

- Close the query.

Comparison Operators

Unless you specify otherwise, Access assumes that the criteria you enter involve equality (exact matches). In the last query, for example, you were requesting those accounts whose current due amount is equal to 0 (zero). In other situations, you might want to find a range of results; for example, you could request accounts whose current due is greater than $1,000.00. If you want a query to return something other than an exact match, you must enter the appropriate **comparison operator**. The comparison operators are > (greater than), < (less than), >= (greater than or equal to), <= (less than or equal to), and NOT (not equal to).

To Use a Comparison Operator in a Criterion

1 CREATE QUERIES | **2 USE CRITERIA** | 3 SORT DATA | 4 JOIN TABLES | 5 EXPORT RESULTS
6 PERFORM CALCULATIONS | 7 CREATE CROSSTAB | 8 CUSTOMIZE NAVIGATION PANE

The following steps use the > operator to create a query that PrattLast Associates might use to find all account managers whose start date is after 1/1/2015. *Why? A date greater than 1/1/2015 means the date comes after 1/1/2015.* The steps also save the query with a new name.

1

- Start a new query using the Account Manager table.

- Include the Account Manager Number, Last Name, First Name, and Start Date fields.

- Type **>1/01/2015** as the criterion for the Start Date field (Figure 2–25).

◁ Why did I not have to type the leading zero in the Month portion of the date?

It is fine as you typed it. You also could have typed 01/1/2015. Some people often type the day using two digits, such as 1/01/2015. You also could have typed a leading zero for both the month and the day: 01/01/2015.

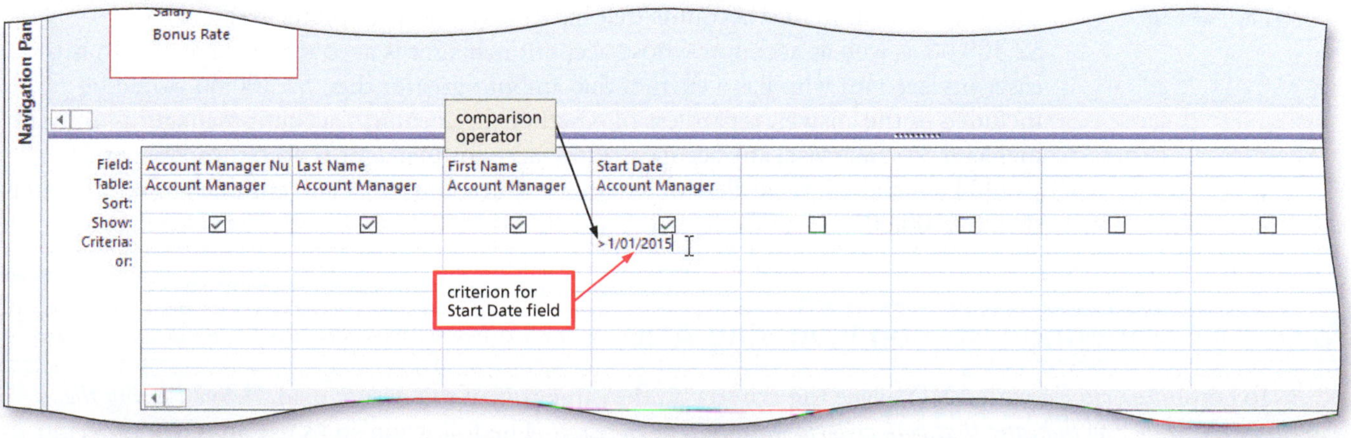

Figure 2–25

2

- Run the query (Figure 2–26).

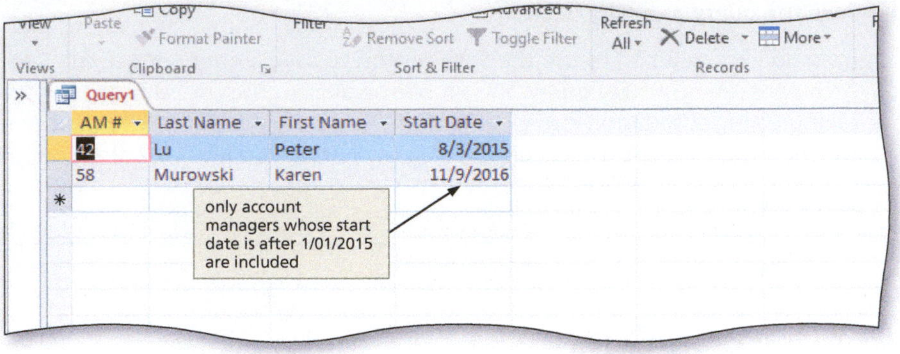

Experiment

- Return to Design view. Try a different criterion involving a comparison operator in the Start Date field and run the query. When finished, return to Design view, enter the original criterion (>1/01/2015) in the Start Date field, and run the query.

Figure 2–26

Q&A

I returned to Design view and noticed that Access changed 1/01/2015 to #1/01/2015#. Why does the date now have number signs around it?
This is the date format in Access. You usually do not have to enter the number signs because in most cases Access will insert them automatically.

My records are in a different order. Is this a problem?
No. The important thing is which records are included in the results. You will see later in this module how you can specify the specific order you want for cases when the order is important.

Can I use the same comparison operators with text data?
Yes. Comparison operators function the same whether you use them with number fields, currency fields, date fields, or text fields. With a text field, comparison operators use alphabetical order in making the determination.

3

- Save the query as m02q04.

- Close the query.

BTW

Queries: Query-by-Example
Query-By-Example, often referred to as QBE, was a query language first proposed in the mid-1970s. In this approach, users asked questions by filling in a table on the screen. The Access approach to queries is based on Query-By-Example.

Using Compound Criteria

Often your search data must satisfy more than one criterion. This type of criterion is called a **compound criterion** and is created using the words AND or OR.

In an **AND criterion**, each individual criterion must be true in order for the compound criterion to be true. For example, an AND criterion would allow you to find accounts that have current due amounts greater than $2,500.00 and whose account manager is manager 31.

An **OR criterion** is true if either individual criterion is true. An OR criterion would allow you to find accounts that have current due amounts greater than $2,500.00 as well as accounts whose account manager is account manager 31. In this case, any account who has a current due amount greater than $2,500.00 would be included in the answer, regardless of whether the account's account manager is account manager 31. Likewise, any account whose account manager is account manager 31 would be included, regardless of whether the account has a current due amount greater than $2,500.00.

1 CREATE QUERIES | **2 USE CRITERIA** | 3 SORT DATA | 4 JOIN TABLES | 5 EXPORT RESULTS
6 PERFORM CALCULATIONS | 7 CREATE CROSSTAB | 8 CUSTOMIZE NAVIGATION PANE

To Use a Compound Criterion Involving AND

To combine criteria with AND, place the criteria on the same row of the design grid. **Why?** *Placing the criteria in the same row indicates that both criteria must be true in Access.* The following steps use an AND criterion to enable PrattLast to find those accounts who have a current due amount greater than $2,500.00 and whose account manager is manager 31. The steps also save the query.

1
- Start a new query using the Account table.

- Include the Account Number, Account Name, Amount Paid, Current Due, and Account Manager Number fields.

- Type **>2500** as the criterion for the Current Due field.

- Type **31** as the criterion for the Account Manager Number field (Figure 2–27).

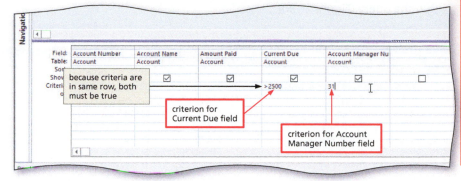

Figure 2–27

2
- Run the query (Figure 2–28).

3
- Save the query as m02q05.

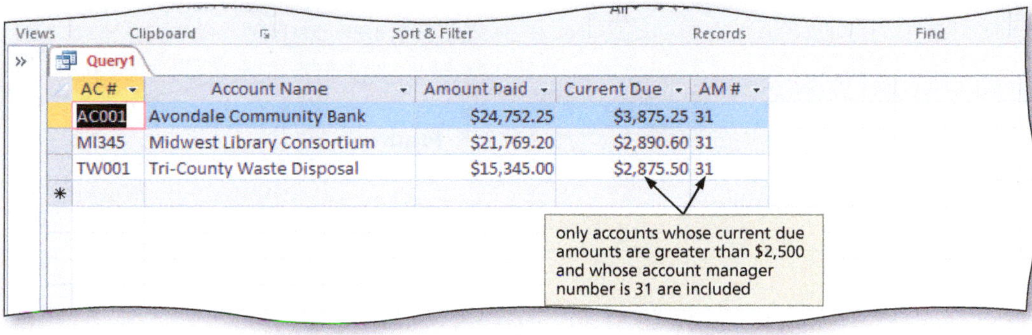

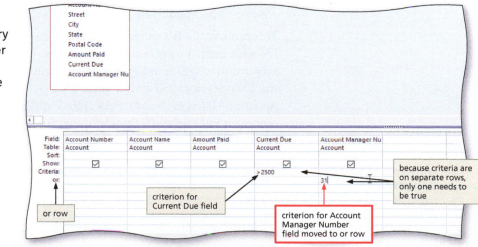

Figure 2–28

1 CREATE QUERIES | **2 USE CRITERIA** | 3 SORT DATA | 4 JOIN TABLES | 5 EXPORT RESULTS

6 PERFORM CALCULATIONS | 7 CREATE CROSSTAB | 8 CUSTOMIZE NAVIGATION PANE

To Use a Compound Criterion Involving OR

To combine criteria with OR, each criterion must go on separate rows in the Criteria area of the grid. *Why? Placing criteria on separate rows indicates at least one criterion must be true in Access.* The following steps use an OR criterion to enable PrattLast to find those accounts who have a current due amount greater than $2,500.00 or whose account manager is manager 31 (or both). The steps also save the query with a new name.

1
- Return to Design view.

- If necessary, click the Criteria entry for the Account Manager Number field and then use the BACKSPACE key or the DELETE key to erase the entry ("31").

- Click the or row (the row below the Criteria row) for the Account Manager Number field, and then type **31** as the entry (Figure 2–29).

Figure 2–29

2

- Run the query (Figure 2–30).

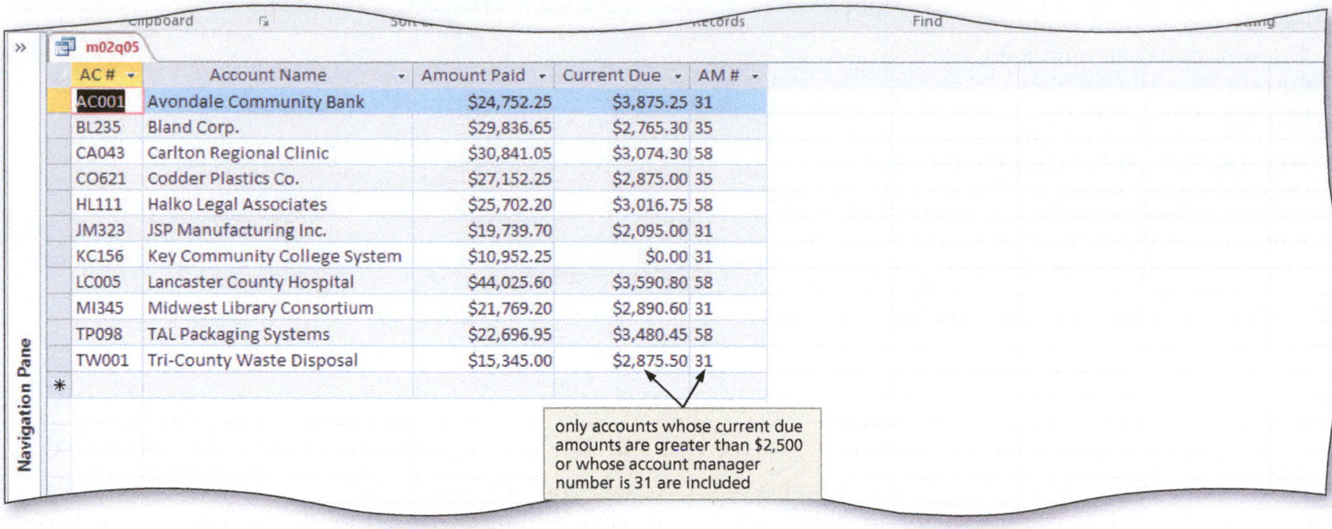

Clipboard
Records
Find
m02q05
AC # | Account Name | Amount Paid | Current Due | AM #
AC001 Avondale Community Bank $24,752.25 $3,875.25 31
BL235 Bland Corp. $29,836.65 $2,765.30 35
CA043 Carlton Regional Clinic $30,841.05 $3,074.30 58
CO621 Codder Plastics Co. $27,152.25 $2,875.00 35
HL111 Halko Legal Associates $25,702.20 $3,016.75 58
JM323 JSP Manufacturing Inc. $19,739.70 $2,095.00 31
KC156 Key Community College System $10,952.25 $0.00 31
LC005 Lancaster County Hospital $44,025.60 $3,590.80 58
MI345 Midwest Library Consortium $21,769.20 $2,890.60 31
TP098 TAL Packaging Systems $22,696.95 $3,480.45 58
TW001 Tri-County Waste Disposal $15,345.00 $2,875.50 31
Navigation Pane
only accounts whose current due amounts are greater than $2,500 or whose account manager number is 31 are included

Figure 2–30

3

- Save the query as m02q06.

Special Criteria

You can use three special criteria in queries:

1. If you want to create a criterion involving a range of values in a single field, you can use the **AND operator**. You place the word AND between the individual conditions. For example, if you wanted to find all accounts whose amount paid is greater than or equal to $20,000.00 and less than or equal to $40,000.00, you would enter >= 20000 AND <= 40000 as the criterion in the Amount Paid column.
2. You can select values in a given range by using the **BETWEEN operator**. This is often an alternative to the AND operator. For example, to find all accounts whose amount paid is between $20,000.00 and $40,000.00, inclusive, you would enter BETWEEN 20000 AND 40000 as the criterion in the Amount Paid column. This is equivalent to entering >=20000 and <=40000.
3. You can select a list of values by using the **IN operator**. You follow the word IN with the list of values in parentheses. For example, to find accounts whose account manager number is 31 and accounts whose account manager is 35 using the IN operator, you would enter IN ("31","35") on the Criteria row in the Account Manager Number column. Unlike when you enter a simple criterion, you must enclose text values in quotation marks.

BTW

Rearranging Fields in a Query

To move a field in the design grid, click the column selector for the field to select the field and drag it to the appropriate location.

CONSIDER THIS

How would you find accounts whose account manager number is 31 or 35 without using the IN operator?

Place the number 31 in the Criteria row of the Account Manager Number column. Place the number 35 in the or row of the Account Manager Number column.

Sorting

In some queries, the order in which the records appear is irrelevant. All you need to be concerned about are the records that appear in the results. It does not matter which one is first or which one is last.

In other queries, however, the order can be very important. You may want to see the cities in which accounts are located and would like them arranged alphabetically. Perhaps you want to see the accounts listed by account manager number. Further, within all the accounts of any given account manager, you might want them to be listed by amount paid from largest amount to smallest.

To order the records in a query result in a particular way, you **sort** the records. The field or fields on which the records are sorted is called the **sort key**. If you are sorting on more than one field (such as sorting by amount paid within account manager number), the more important field (Account Manager Number) is called the **major key** (also called the **primary sort key**) and the less important field (Amount Paid) is called the **minor key** (also called the **secondary sort key**).

To sort in Microsoft Access, specify the sort order in the Sort row of the design grid below the field that is the sort key. If you specify more than one sort key, the sort key on the left will be the major sort key, and the one on the right will be the minor key.

BTW

Sorting Data in a Query
When sorting data in a query, the records in the underlying tables (the tables on which the query is based) are not actually rearranged. Instead, the DBMS determines the most efficient method of simply displaying the records in the requested order. The records in the underlying tables remain in their original order.

BTW

Clearing the Design Grid
You can also clear the design grid using the ribbon. To do so, click the Home tab, click the Advanced button to display the Advanced menu, and then click Clear Grid on the Advanced menu.

To Clear the Design Grid

1 CREATE QUERIES | 2 USE CRITERIA | 3 SORT DATA | 4 JOIN TABLES | 5 EXPORT RESULTS
6 PERFORM CALCULATIONS | 7 CREATE CROSSTAB | 8 CUSTOMIZE NAVIGATION PANE

Why? *If the fields you want to include in the next query are different from those in the previous query, it is usually simpler to start with a clear grid, that is, one with no fields already in the design grid.* You always can clear the entries in the design grid by closing the query and then starting over. A simpler approach to clearing the entries is to select all the entries and then press the DELETE key. The following steps return to Design view and clear the design grid.

1

- Return to Design view.

- Click just above the Account Number column heading in the grid to select the column.

Q&A I clicked above the column heading, but the column is not selected. What should I do?
You did not point to the correct location. Be sure the pointer changes into a down-pointing arrow and then click again.

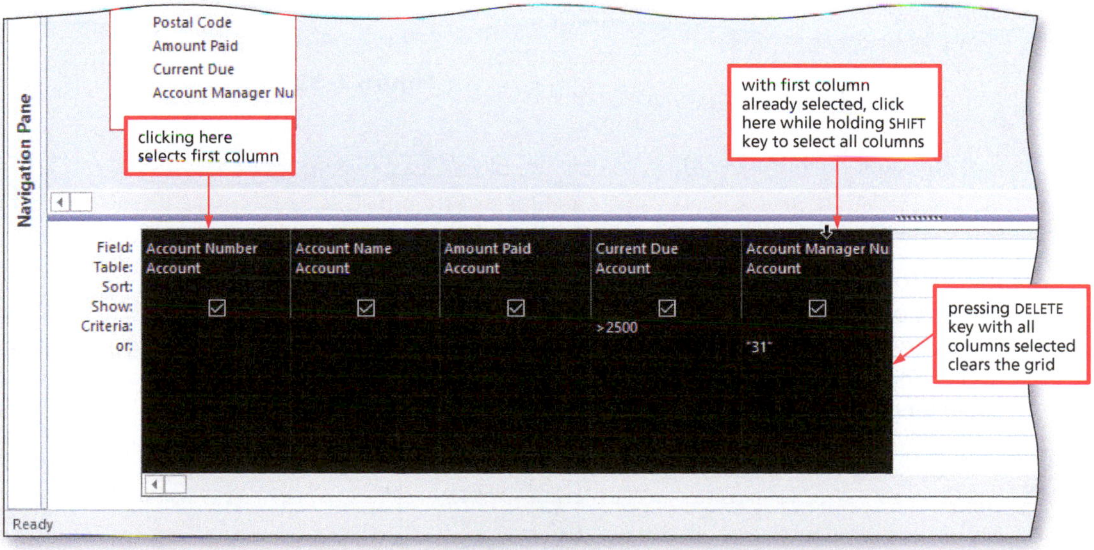

Figure 2–31

- Hold the SHIFT key down and click just above the Account Manager Number column heading to select all the columns (Figure 2–31).

2

- Press the DELETE key to clear the design grid.

To Sort Data in a Query

If you determine that the query results should be sorted, you will need to specify the sort key. The following steps sort the cities in the Account table by indicating that the City field is to be sorted. The steps specify Ascending sort order. **Why?** *When sorting text data, Ascending sort order arranges the results in alphabetical order.*

1

- Include the City field in the design grid.
- Click the Sort row in the City field column, and then click the Sort arrow to display a menu of possible sort orders (Figure 2–32).

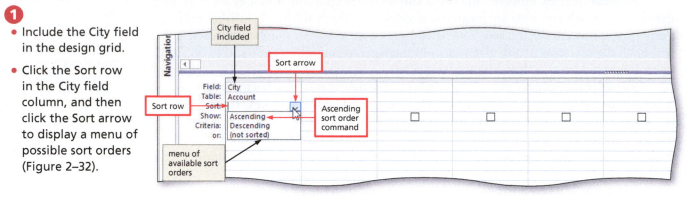

Figure 2–32

2

- Click Ascending to select the sort order (Figure 2–33).

Figure 2–33

3

- Run the query (Figure 2–34).

Experiment

- Return to Design view and change the sort order to Descending. Run the query. Return to Design view and change the sort order back to Ascending. Run the query.

Q&A
Why do some cities appear more than once?
More than one account is located in those cities.

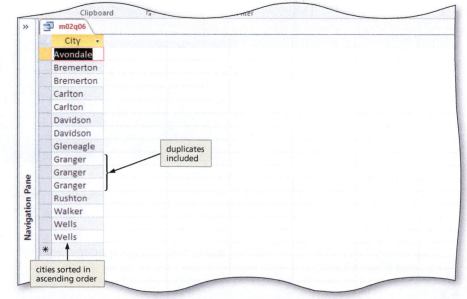

Figure 2–34

To Omit Duplicates

When you sort data, duplicates normally are included. In the query shown in Figure 2–34, for example, Bremerton appears twice. Several other cities appear multiple times as well. You eliminate duplicates using the query's property sheet. A **property sheet** is a window containing the various properties of the object. To omit duplicates, you will use the property sheet to change the Unique Values property from No to Yes.

The following steps create a query that PrattLast Associates might use to obtain a sorted list of the cities in the Account table in which each city is listed only once. *Why? Unless you wanted to know how many accounts were located in each city, the duplicates typically do not add any value.* The steps also save the query with a new name.

1
- Return to Design view.
- Click the second field (the empty field to the right of City) in the design grid to produce an insertion point.
- If necessary, click Design on the ribbon to display the Design tab.
- Click the Property Sheet button (Query Tools Design tab | Show/Hide group) to display the property sheet (Figure 2–35).

Q&A
My property sheet looks different. What should I do?
If your sheet looks different, close the property sheet and repeat this step.

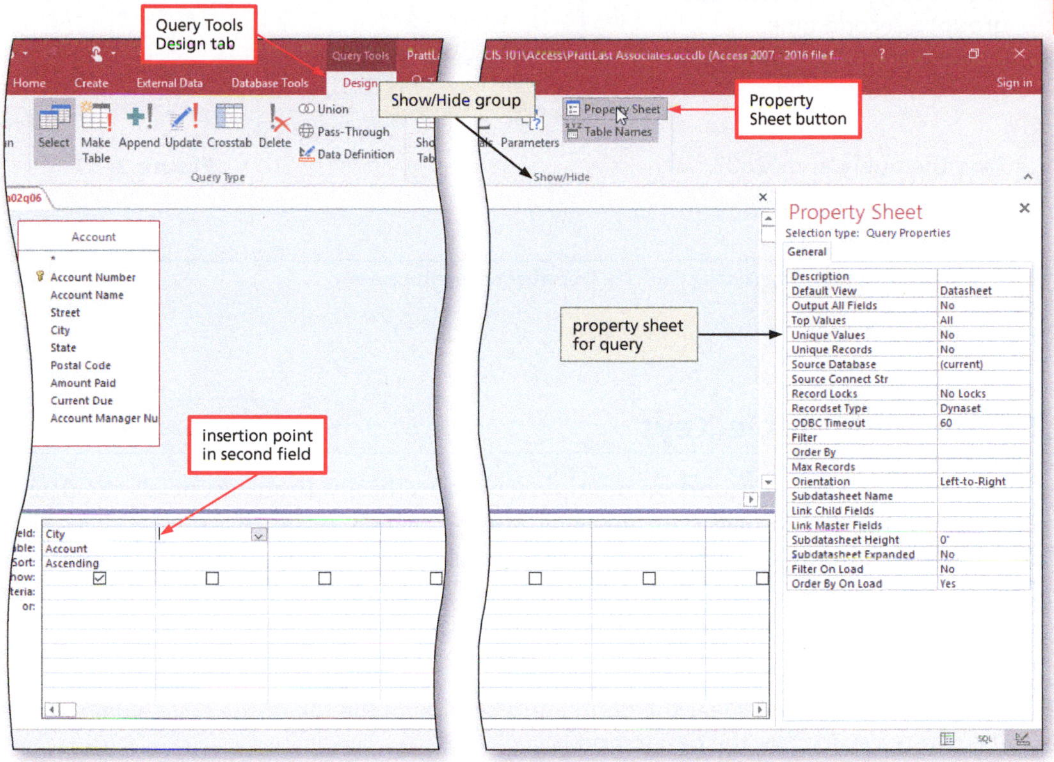

Figure 2–35

2
- Click the Unique Values property box, and then click the arrow that appears to display a list of available choices (Figure 2–36).

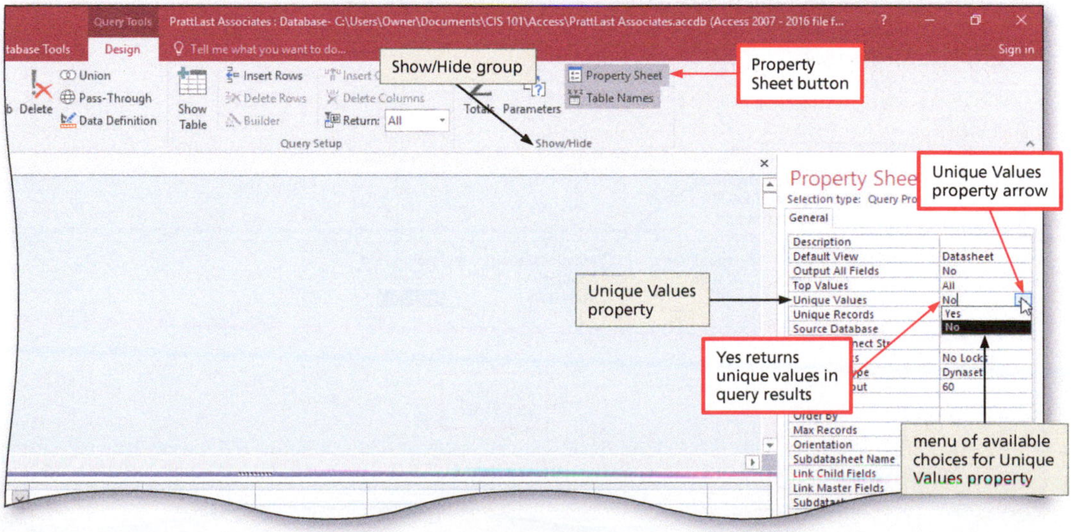

Figure 2–36

3

- Click Yes to indicate that the query will return unique values, which means that each value will appear only once in the query results.

- Close the Query Properties property sheet by clicking the Property Sheet button (Query Tools Design tab | Show/Hide group) a second time.

- Run the query (Figure 2–37).

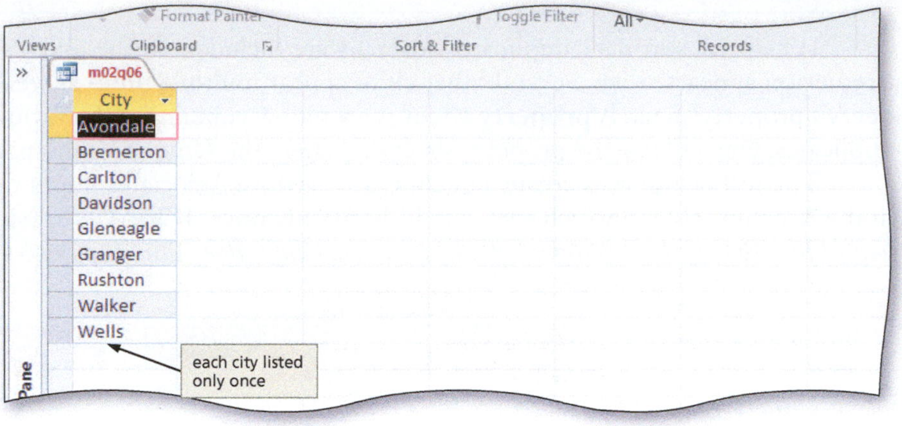

4

- Save the query as m02q07.

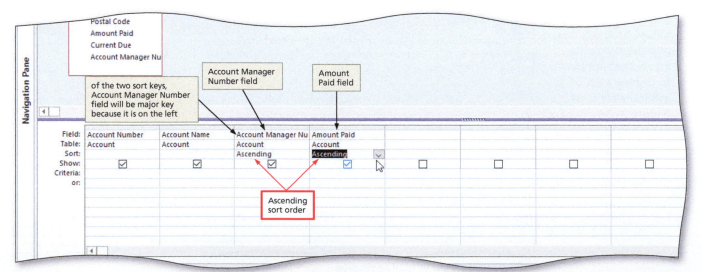

each city listed only once

Figure 2–37

Other Ways

1. Right-click second field in design grid, click Properties on shortcut menu

---

1 CREATE QUERIES | 2 USE CRITERIA | 3 SORT DATA | 4 JOIN TABLES | 5 EXPORT RESULTS
6 PERFORM CALCULATIONS | 7 CREATE CROSSTAB | 8 CUSTOMIZE NAVIGATION PANE

To Sort on Multiple Keys

The following steps sort on multiple keys. Specifically, PrattLast needs the data to be sorted by amount paid (low to high) within account manager number, which means that the Account Manager Number field is the major key and the Amount Paid field is the minor key. The steps place the Account Manager Number field to the left of the Amount Paid field. *Why? In Access, the major key must appear to the left of the minor key.* The steps also save the query with a new name.

1

- Return to Design view. Clear the design grid by clicking the top of the first column in the grid, and then pressing the DELETE key to clear the design grid.

- In the following order, include the Account Number, Account Name, Account Manager Number, and Amount Paid fields in the query.

- Select Ascending as the sort order for both the Account Manager Number field and the Amount Paid field (Figure 2–38).

Figure 2–38

2

- Run the query (Figure 2–39).

🔍 **Experiment**

- Return to Design view and try other sort combinations for the Account Manager Number and Amount Paid fields, such as Ascending for Account Manager Number and Descending for Amount Paid. In each case, run the query to see the effect of the changes. When finished, select Ascending as the sort order for both fields.

Q&A

What if the Amount Paid field is to the left of the Account Manager Number field?

It is important to remember that the major sort key must appear to the left of the minor sort key in the design grid. If you attempted to sort by amount paid within account manager number, but placed the Amount Paid field to the left of the Account Manager Number field, your results would not accurately represent the intended sort.

AC #	Account Name	AM #	Amount Paid
KC156	Key Community College System	31	$10,952.25
TW001	Tri-County Waste Disposal	31	$15,345.00
JM323	JSP Manufacturing Inc.	31	$19,739.70
MI345	Midwest Library Consortium	31	$21,769.20
AC001	Avondale Community Bank	31	$24,752.25
LI268	Lars-Idsen Inc.	35	$0.00
ML008	Mums Landscaping Co.	35	$13,097.10
CO621	Codder Plastics Co.	35	$27,152.25
BL235	Bland Corp.	35	$29,836.65
KV089	KAL Veterinary Services	35	$34,036.50
EC010	Eco Clothes Inc.	58	$19,620.00
TP098	TAL Packaging Systems	58	$22,696.95
HL111	Halko Legal Associates	58	$25,702.20
CA043	Carlton Regional Clinic	58	$30,841.05
LC005	Lancaster County Hospital	58	$44,025.60

within group of accounts with the same account manager number, rows are sorted by amount paid in ascending order

overall order is by account manager number in ascending order

Figure 2–39

3

- Save the query as m02q08.

Is there any way to sort the records in this same order, but have the Amount Paid field appear to the left of the Account Manager Number field in the query results?

Yes. Remove the check mark from the Account Manager Number field, and then add an additional Account Manager Number field at the end of the query. The first Account Manager Number field will be used for sorting but will not appear in the results. The second will appear in the results, but will not be involved in the sorting process.

CONSIDER THIS

How do you approach the creation of a query that might involve sorting?

Examine the query or request to see if it contains words such as *order* or *sort*. Such words imply that the order of the query results is important. If so, you need to sort the query.

- If sorting is required, identify the field or fields on which the results are to be sorted. In the request, look for language such as *ordered by* or *sort the results by*, both of which would indicate that the specified field is a sort key.

- If using multiple sort keys, determine the major and minor keys. If you are using two sort keys, determine which one is the more important, or the major key. Look for language such as *sort by amount paid within account manager number*, which implies that the overall order is by account manager number. In this case, the Account Manager Number field would be the major sort key and the Amount Paid field would be the minor sort key.

- Determine sort order. Words such as *increasing*, *ascending*, or *low-to-high* imply Ascending order. Words such as *decreasing*, *descending*, or *high-to-low* imply Descending order. Sorting in *alphabetical order* implies Ascending order. If there were no words to imply a particular order, you would typically use Ascending.

- Examine the query or request to see if there are any special restrictions. One common restriction is to exclude duplicates. Another common restriction is to list only a certain number of records, such as the first five records.

CONSIDER THIS

To Create a Top-Values Query

Rather than show all the results of a query, you may want to show only a specified number of records or a percentage of records. **Why?** *You might not need to see all the records, just enough to get a general idea of the results.* Creating a **top-values query** allows you to restrict the number of records that appear. When you sort records, you can limit results to those records having the highest (descending sort) or lowest (ascending sort) values. To do so, first create a query that sorts the data in the desired order. Next, use the Return box on the Design tab to change the number of records to be included from All to the desired number or percentage.

The following steps create a query for PrattLast Associates that shows only the first five records that were included in the results of the previous query. The steps also save the resulting query with a new name.

1

• Return to Design view.

• If necessary, click Design on the ribbon to display the Design tab.

• Click the Return arrow (Query Tools Design tab | Query Setup group) to display the Return menu (Figure 2–40).

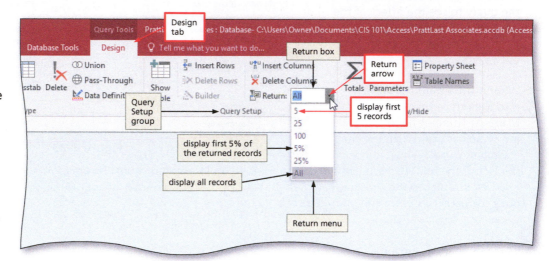

Figure 2–40

2

• Click 5 in the Return menu to specify that the query results should contain the first five rows.

Q&A Could I have typed the 5? What about other numbers that do not appear in the list?
Yes, you could have typed the 5. For numbers not appearing in the list, you must type the number.

• Run the query (Figure 2–41).

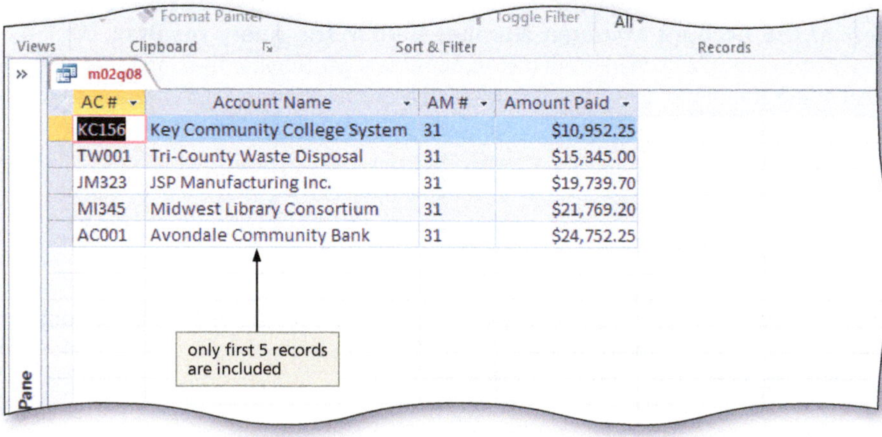

3

• Save the query as m02q09.

• Close the query.

Figure 2–41

Q&A Do I need to close the query before creating my next query?
Not necessarily. When you use a top-values query, however, it is important to change the value in the Return box back to All. If you do not change the Return value back to All, the previous value will remain in effect. Consequently, you might not get all the records you should in the next query. A good practice whenever you use a top-values query is to close the query as soon as you are done. That way, you will begin your next query from scratch, which ensures that the value is reset to All.

Joining Tables

In designing a query, you need to determine whether more than one table is required. For example, if the question being asked involves data from both the Account and Account Manager tables, then both tables are required for the query. For example, you might want a query that gives the number and name of each account (from the Account table) along with the number and name of the account's account manager (from the Account Manager table). Both the Account and Account Manager tables are required for this query. You need to **join** the tables to find records in the two tables that have identical values in matching fields (Figure 2–42). In this example, you need to find records in the Account table and the Account Manager table that have the same value in the Account Manager Number fields.

BTW

Ad Hoc Relationships
When you join tables in a query, you are creating an ad hoc relationship, that is, a relationship between tables created for a specific purpose. In Module 3, you will create general-purpose relationships using the Relationships window.

Account Table

AC #	Account Name	...	AM #
AC001	Avondale Community Bank	...	31
BL235	Bland Corp.	...	35
CA043	Carlton Regional Clinic	...	58
CO621	Codder Plastics Co.	...	35
EC010	Eco Clothes Inc.	...	58
HL111	Halko Legal Associates	...	58
JM323	JSP Manufacturing Inc.	...	31
KC156	Key Community College System	...	31
KV089	KAL Veterinary Services	...	35
LC005	Lancaster County Hospital	...	58
LI268	Lars-Idsen Inc.	...	35
MI345	Midwest Library Consortium	...	31
ML008	Mums Landscaping Co.	...	35
TP098	TAL Packaging Systems	...	58
TW001	Tri-County Waste Disposal	...	31

Give me the number and name of each account along with the number and name of the account manager.

Account Manager Table

AM #	Last Name	First Name	...
31	Rivera	Haydee	...
35	Simson	Mark	...
42	Lu	Peter	...
58	Murowski	Karen	...

BTW

Join Line
If you do not get a join line automatically, there may be a problem with one of your table designs. Open each table in Design view and make sure that the data types are the same for the matching field in both tables and that one of the matching fields is the primary key in a table. Correct these errors and create the query again.

Account Table

AC #	Account Name	...	AM #	Last Name	First Name	...
AC001	Avondale Community Bank	...	31	Rivera	Haydee	...
BL235	Bland Corp.	...	35	Simson	Mark	...
CA043	Carlton Regional Clinic	...	58	Murowski	Karen	...
CO621	Codder Plastics Co.	...	35	Simson	Mark	...
EC010	Eco Clothes Inc.	...	58	Murowski	Karen	...
HL111	Halko Legal Associates	...	58	Murowski	Karen	...
JM323	JSP Manufacturing Inc.	...	31	Rivera	Haydee	...
KV089	KAL Veterinary Services	...	35	Simson	Mark	...
KC156	Key Community College System	...	31	Rivera	Haydee	...
LC005	Lancaster County Hospital	...	58	Murowski	Karen	...
LI268	Lars-Idsen Inc.	...	35	Simson	Mark	...
MI345	Midwest Library Consortium	...	31	Rivera	Haydee	...
ML008	Mums Landscaping Co.	...	35	Simson	Mark	...
TP098	TAL Packaging Systems	...	58	Murowski	Karen	...
TW001	Tri-County Waste Disposal	...	31	Rivera	Haydee	...

BTW

Join Types
The type of join that finds records from both tables that have identical values in matching fields is called an inner join. An inner join is the default join in Access. Outer joins are used to show all the records in one table as well as the common records; that is, the records that share the same value in the join field. In a left outer join, all rows from the table on the left are included. In a right outer join, all rows from the table on the right are included.

Figure 2–42

1 CREATE QUERIES | 2 USE CRITERIA | 3 SORT DATA | **4 JOIN TABLES** | 5 EXPORT RESULTS
6 PERFORM CALCULATIONS | 7 CREATE CROSSTAB | 8 CUSTOMIZE NAVIGATION PANE

To Join Tables

If you have determined that you need to join tables, you first will bring field lists for both tables to the upper pane of the Query window while working in Design view. Access will draw a line, called a **join line**, between matching fields in the two tables, indicating that the tables are related. You then can select fields from either table. Access joins the tables automatically.

The first step is to create a new query and add the Account Manager table to the query. Then, add the Account table to the query. A join line should appear, connecting the Account Manager Number fields in the two field lists. ***Why might the join line not appear?*** *If the names of the matching fields differ from one table to the other, Access will not insert the line. You can insert it manually, however, by clicking one of the two matching fields and dragging the pointer to the other matching field.*

The following steps create a query to display information from both the Account table and the Account Manager table.

1
- Click Create on the ribbon to display the Create tab.
- Click the Query Design button (Create tab | Queries group) to create a new query.
- If necessary, click the Account Manager table (Show Table dialog box) to select the table.
- Click the Add button (Show Table dialog box) to add a field list for the Account Manager Table to the query (Figure 2–43).

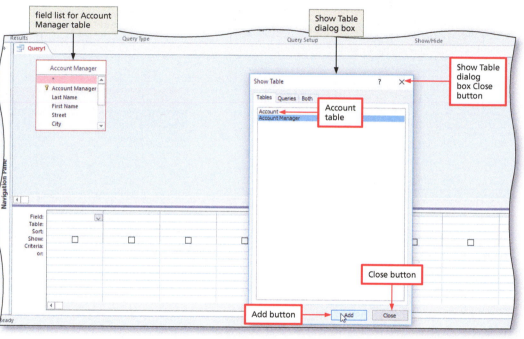

Figure 2–43

2
- Click the Account table (Show Table dialog box).
- Click the Add button (Show Table dialog box) to add a field list for the Account table.
- Close the Show Table dialog box by clicking the Close button.
- Expand the size of the two field lists so all the fields in the Account Manager and Account tables appear (Figure 2–44).

I did not get a join line. What should I do?
Ensure that the names of the matching fields are the same, the data types are the same, and the matching field is the primary key in one of the two tables. If all of these factors are true and you still do not have a join line, you can produce one by pointing to a matching field and dragging to the other matching field.

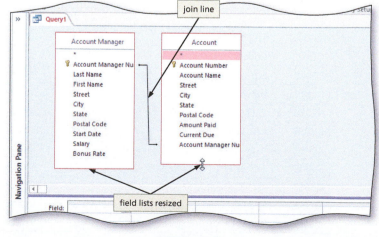

Figure 2–44

3

- In the design grid, include the Account Manager Number, Last Name, and First Name fields from the Account Manager Table as well as the Account Number and Account Name fields from the Account table.

- Select Ascending as the sort order for both the Account Manager Number field and the Account Number field (Figure 2–45).

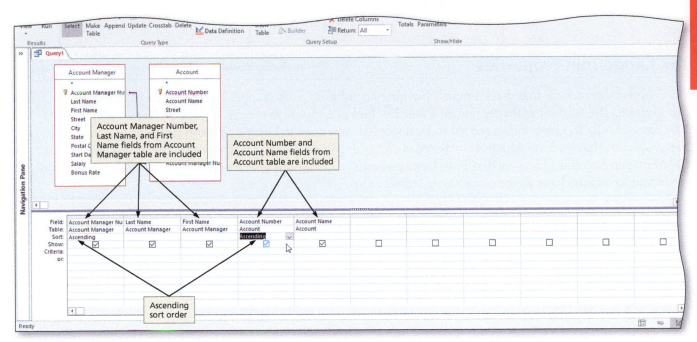

Figure 2–45

4

- Run the query (Figure 2–46).

Figure 2–46

5

- Click the Save button on the Quick Access Toolbar to display the Save As dialog box.

- Type **Manager-Account Query** as the query name.

- Click the OK button (Save As dialog box) to save the query.

To Change Join Properties

1 CREATE QUERIES | 2 USE CRITERIA | 3 SORT DATA | **4 JOIN TABLES** | 5 EXPORT RESULTS
6 PERFORM CALCULATIONS | 7 CREATE CROSSTAB | 8 CUSTOMIZE NAVIGATION PANE

Normally, records that do not match the query conditions do not appear in the results of a join query. For example, the account manager named Peter Lu does not appear in the results. ***Why?*** *He currently does not have any accounts.* To cause such a record to be displayed, you need to change the **join properties**, which are the properties that indicate which records appear in a join. The following steps change the join properties of the Manager-Account Query so that PrattLast can include all account managers in the results, rather than only those managers who have already been assigned accounts.

1

- Return to Design view.

- Right-click the join line to produce a shortcut menu (Figure 2–47).

Q&A | I do not see Join Properties on my shortcut menu. What should I do?
If Join Properties does not appear on your shortcut menu, you did not point to the appropriate portion of the join line. You will need to point to the correct (middle) portion and right-click again.

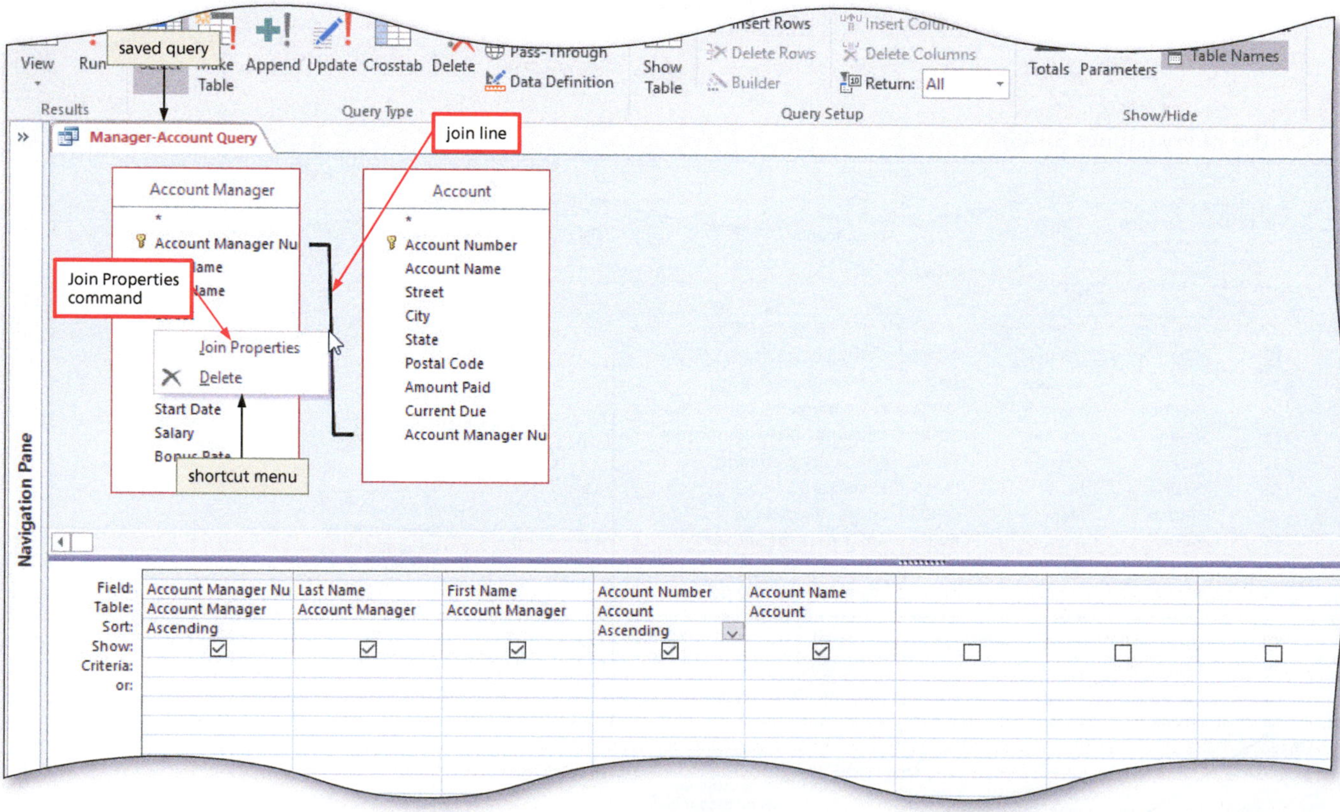

Figure 2–47

2

- Click Join Properties on the shortcut menu to display the Join Properties dialog box (Figure 2–48).

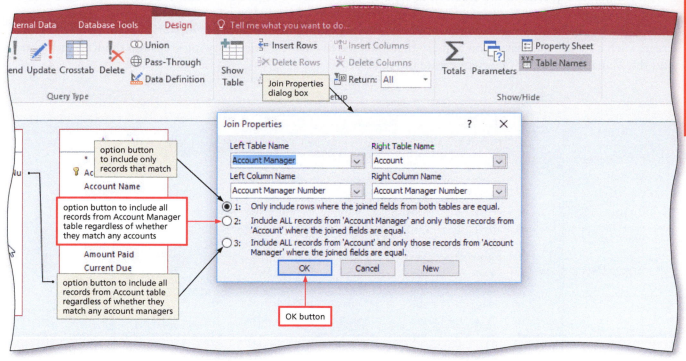

Figure 2–48

3

- Click option button 2 (Join Properties dialog box) to include all records from the Account Manager Table regardless of whether they match any accounts.

- Click the OK button (Join Properties dialog box) to modify the join properties.

- Run the query (Figure 2–49).

🔍 **Experiment**

- Return to Design view, change the Join properties, and select option button 3. Run the query to see the effect of this option. When done, return to Design view, change the join properties, and once again select option button 2.

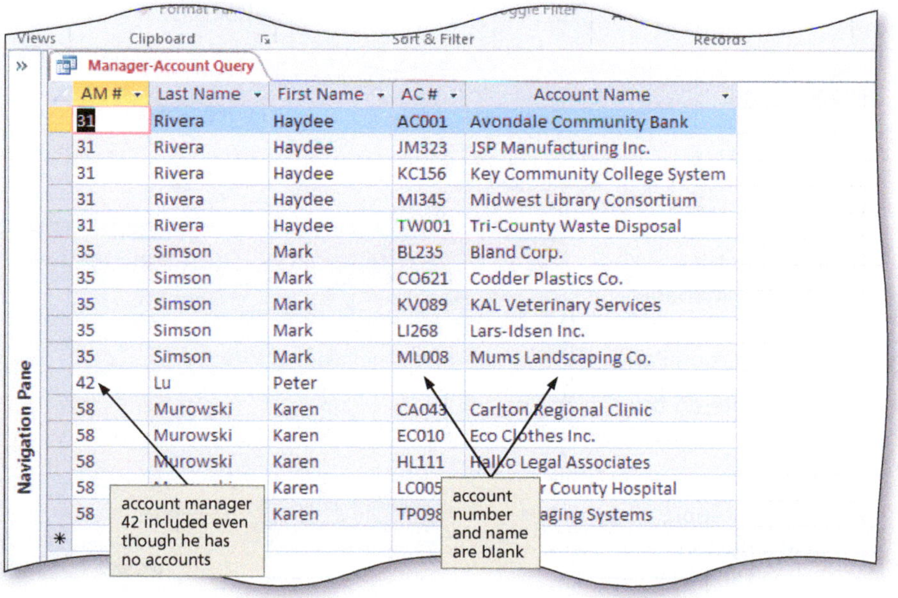

Figure 2–49

4

- Click the Save button on the Quick Access Toolbar to save the changes to the query.

- Close the Manager-Account Query.

Q&A I see a dialog box that asks if I want to save the query. What should I do?
Click the OK button to save the query.

To Create a Report from a Query

You can use queries in the creation of reports. The report in Figure 2–50 involves data from more than one table. *Why? The Last Name and First Name fields are in the Account Manager table. The Account Number and Account Name fields are in the Account table. The Account Manager Number field is in both tables.* The easiest way to create such a report is to base it on a query that joins the two tables. The following steps use the Report Wizard and the Manager-Account Query to create the report.

Manager-Account Report

AM #	Last Name	First Name	AC #	Account Name
31	Rivera	Haydee	AC001	Avondale Community Bank
31	Rivera	Haydee	JM323	JSP Manufacturing Inc.
31	Rivera	Haydee	KC156	Key Community College System
31	Rivera	Haydee	MI345	Midwest Library Consortium
31	Rivera	Haydee	TW001	Tri-County Waste Disposal
35	Simson	Mark	BL235	Bland Corp.
35	Simson	Mark	CO621	Codder Plastics Co.
35	Simson	Mark	KV089	KAL Veterinary Services
35	Simson	Mark	LI268	Lars-Idsen Inc.
35	Simson	Mark	ML008	Mums Landscaping Co.
42	Lu	Peter		
58	Murowski	Karen	CA043	Carlton Regional Clinic
58	Murowski	Karen	EC010	Eco Clothes Inc.
58	Murowski	Karen	HL111	Halko Legal Associates
58	Murowski	Karen	LC005	Lancaster County Hospital
58	Murowski	Karen	TP098	TAL Packaging Systems

Figure 2–50

1

- Open the Navigation Pane, and then select the Manager-Account Query in the Navigation Pane.

- Click Create on the ribbon to display the Create tab.

- Click the Report Wizard button (Create tab | Reports group) to display the Report Wizard dialog box (Figure 2–51).

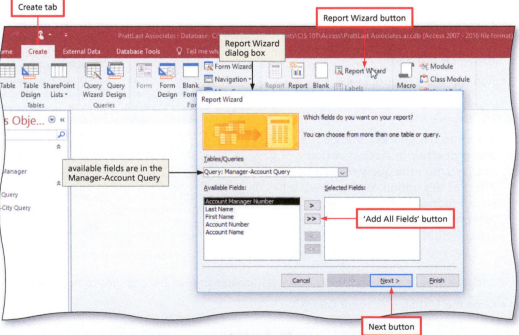

Figure 2–51

2

- Click the 'Add All Fields' button (Report Wizard dialog box) to add all the fields in the Manager-Account Query.

- Click the Next button to display the next Report Wizard screen (Figure 2–52).

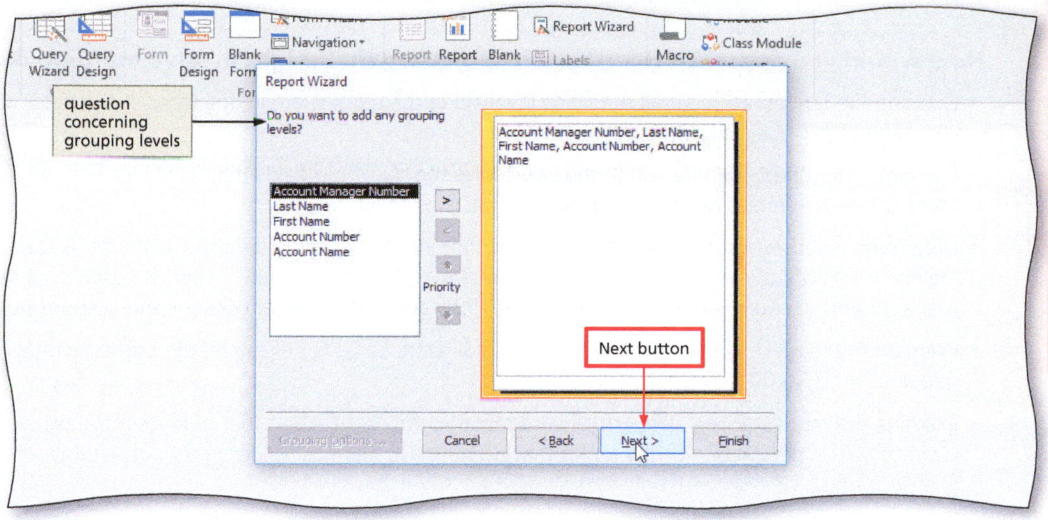

Figure 2–52

3

- Because you will not specify any grouping, click the Next button in the Report Wizard dialog box to display the next Report Wizard screen.

- Because you already specified the sort order in the query, click the Next button again to display the next Report Wizard screen.

- Make sure that Tabular is selected as the Layout and Portrait is selected as the Orientation.

- Click the Next button to display the next Report Wizard screen.

- Erase the current title, and then type **Manager-Account Report** as the new title.

- Click the Finish button to produce the report (Figure 2–53).

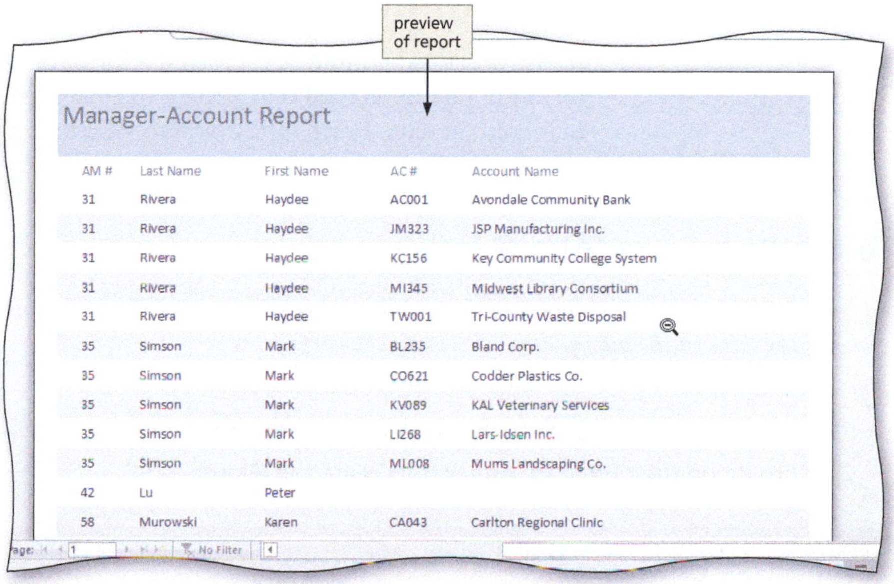

Figure 2–53

Q&A   My report is very small and does not look like the one in the figure. What should I do?
Click the pointer, which should look like a magnifying glass, anywhere in the report to magnify the report.

- Close the Manager-Account Report.

To Print a Report

The following steps print a hard copy of the report.

1   With the Manager-Account Report selected in the Navigation Pane, click File on the ribbon to open the Backstage view.

2   Click the Print tab in the Backstage view to display the Print gallery.

3   Click the Quick Print button to print the report.

How would you approach the creation of a query that might involve multiple tables?

• Examine the request to see if all the fields involved in the request are in one table. If the fields are in two (or more) tables, you need to join the tables.

• If joining is required, identify within the two tables the matching fields that have identical values. Look for the same column name in the two tables or for column names that are similar.

• Determine whether sorting is required. Queries that join tables often are used as the basis for a report. If this is the case, it may be necessary to sort the results. For example, the Manager-Account Report is based on a query that joins the Account Manager and Account tables. The query is sorted by account manager number and account number.

• Examine the request to see if there are any special restrictions. For example, the user may only want accounts whose current due amount is $0.00.

• Examine the request to see if you only want records from both tables that have identical values in matching fields. If you want to see records in one of the tables that do not have identical values in the other table, then you need to change the join properties.

Creating a Form for a Query

In the previous module, you created a form for the Account table. You can also create a form for a query. Recall that a **form** in a database is a formatted document with fields that contain data. Forms allow you to view and maintain data.

To Create a Form for a Query

1 CREATE QUERIES | 2 USE CRITERIA | 3 SORT DATA | 4 JOIN TABLES | 5 EXPORT RESULTS
6 PERFORM CALCULATIONS | 7 CREATE CROSSTAB | 8 CUSTOMIZE NAVIGATION PANE

The following steps create a form, then save the form. *Why? The form will be available for future use in viewing the data in the query.*

1
• If necessary, select the Manager-Account Query in the Navigation Pane.

• Click Create on the ribbon to display the Create tab (Figure 2–54).

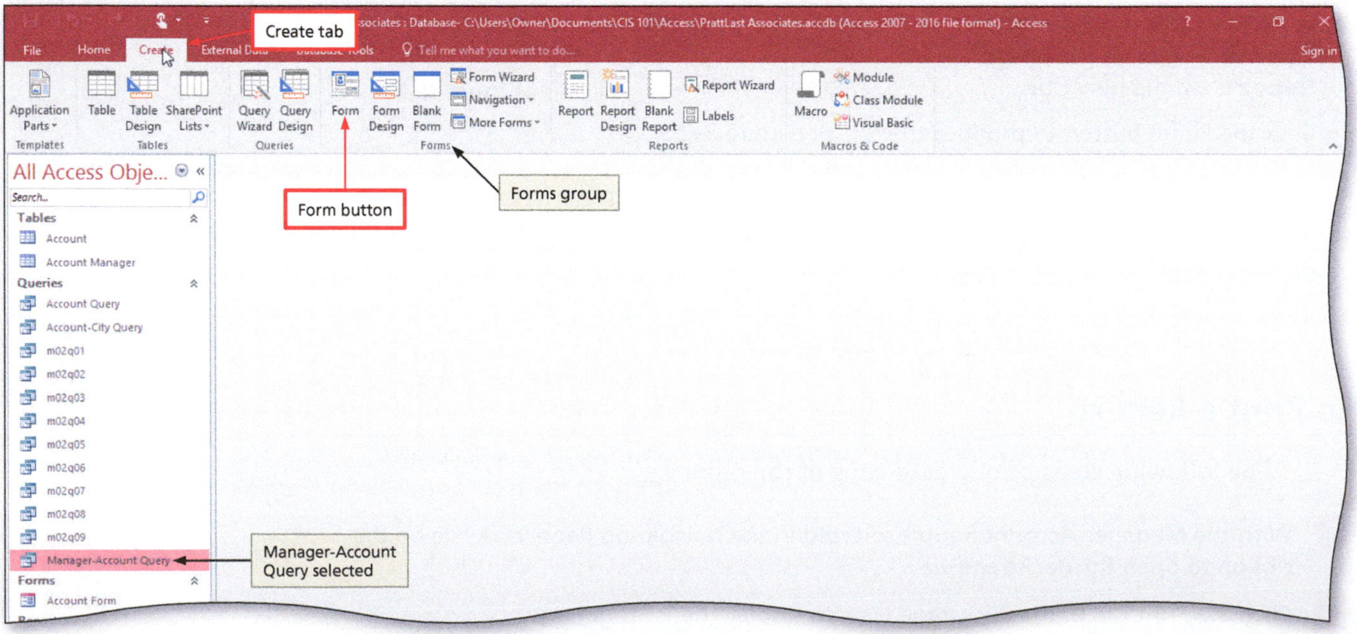

Figure 2–54

2

- Click the Form button (Create tab | Forms group) to create a simple form (Figure 2–55).

Q&A I see a field list also. What should I do?
Click the Close button for the Field List.

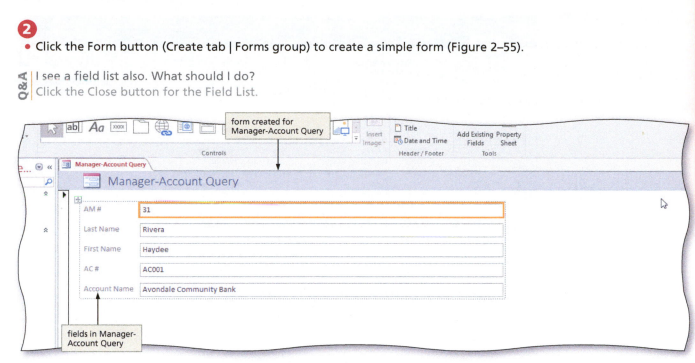

Figure 2–55

3

- Click the Save button on the Quick Access Toolbar to display the Save As dialog box.
- Type **Manager-Account Form** as the form name.
- Click the OK button to save the form.
- Click the Close button for the form to close the form.

Using a Form

After you have saved a form, you can use it at any time by right-clicking the form in the Navigation Pane and then clicking Open on the shortcut menu. If you plan to use the form to enter data, you must ensure you are viewing the form in Form view.

Break Point: If you wish to take a break, this is a good place to do so. You can exit Access now. To resume later, run Access, open the database called PrattLast Associates, and continue following the steps from this location forward.

Exporting Data From Access to Other Applications

You can **export**, or copy, tables or queries from an Access database so that another application (for example, Excel or Word) can use the data. The application that will receive the data determines the export process to be used. You can export to text files in a variety of formats. For applications to which you cannot directly export data, you often can export an appropriately formatted text file that the other application can import. Figure 2–56 shows the workbook produced by exporting the Manager-Account Query to Excel. The columns in the workbook have been resized to best fit the data.

BTW

Exporting Data
You frequently need to export data so that it can be used in other applications and by other users in an organization. For example, the Accounting department might require financial data in an Excel format to perform certain financial functions. Marketing might require a list of account names and addresses in Word or RTF format for marketing campaigns.

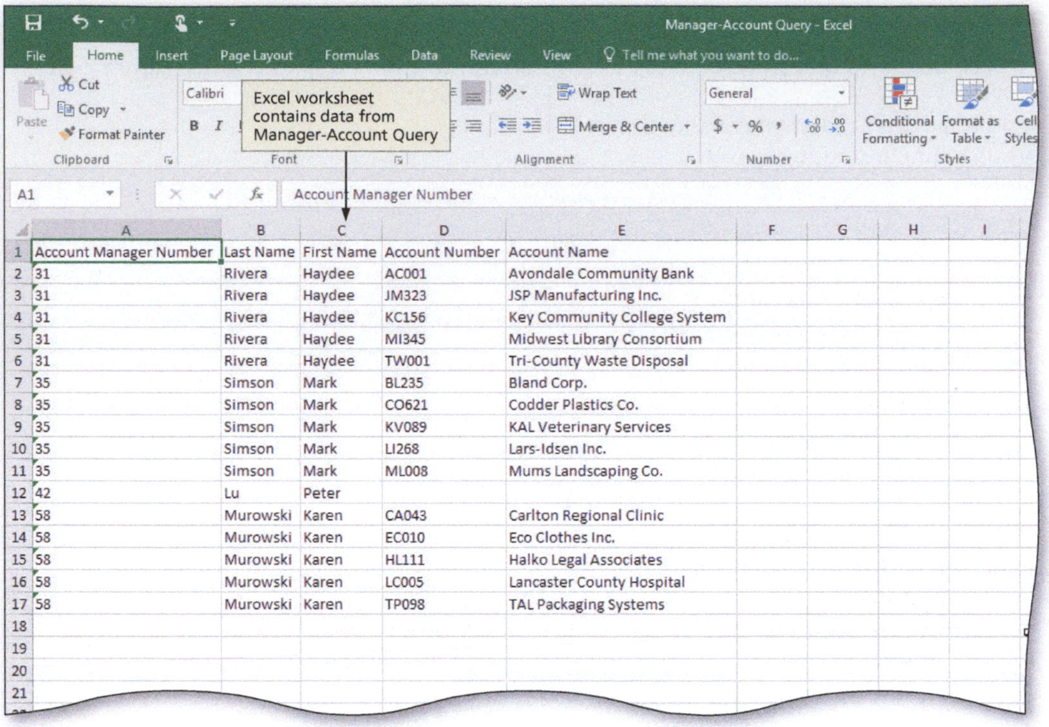

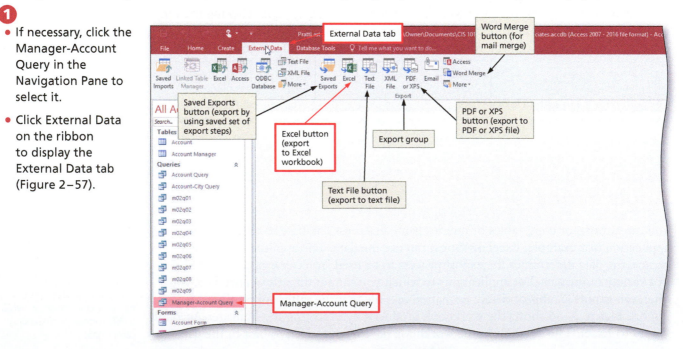

Figure 2–56

To Export Data to Excel

1 CREATE QUERIES | 2 USE CRITERIA | 3 SORT DATA | 4 JOIN TABLES | **5 EXPORT RESULTS**
6 PERFORM CALCULATIONS | 7 CREATE CROSSTAB | 8 CUSTOMIZE NAVIGATION PANE

For PrattLast Associates to make the Manager-Account Query available to Excel users, it needs to export the data. To export data to Excel, select the table or query to be exported and then click the Excel button in the Export group on the External Data tab. The following steps export the Manager-Account Query to Excel and save the export steps. *Why save the export steps? By saving the export steps, you could easily repeat the export process whenever you like without going through all the steps.* You would use the saved steps to export data in the future by clicking the Saved Exports button (External Data tab | Export group) and then selecting the steps you saved.

❶

- If necessary, click the Manager-Account Query in the Navigation Pane to select it.

- Click External Data on the ribbon to display the External Data tab (Figure 2–57).

Figure 2–57

2

- Click the Excel button (External Data tab | Export group) to display the Export-Excel Spreadsheet dialog box.

- Click the Browse button (Export-Excel Spreadsheet dialog box), and then navigate to the location where you want to export the query (your hard disk, OneDrive, or other storage location).

- Confirm that the file format is Excel Workbook (*.xlsx), and the file name is Manager-Account Query, and then click the Save button (File Save dialog box) to select the file name and location (Figure 2–58).

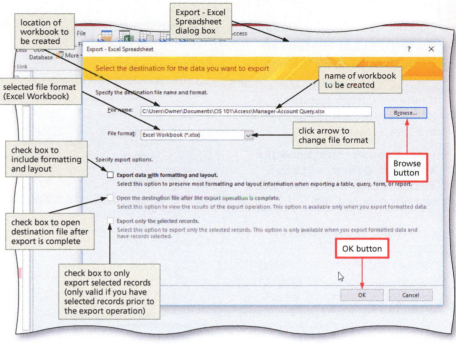

Figure 2–58

Q&A Did I need to browse?
No. You could type the appropriate file location.

Could I change the name of the file?
You could change it. Simply replace the current file name with the one you want.

What if the file I want to export already exists?
Access will indicate that the file already exists and ask if you want to replace it. If you click the Yes button, the file you export will replace the old file. If you click the No button, you must either change the name of the export file or cancel the process.

- Click the OK button (Export-Excel Spreadsheet dialog box) to export the data (Figure 2–59).

Figure 2–59

3

- Click the 'Save export steps' check box (Export-Excel Spreadsheet dialog box) to display the Save Export Steps options.

- If necessary, type **Export-Manager-Account Query** in the Save as text box.

- Type **Export the Manager-Account Query without formatting** in the Description text box (Figure 2–60).

Q&A How could I re-use the export steps?

You can use these steps to export data in the future by clicking the Saved Exports button (External Data tab | Export group) and then selecting the steps you saved.

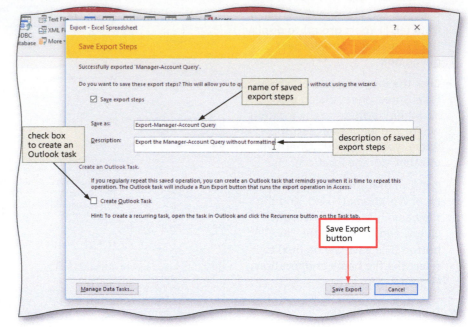

Figure 2–60

4

- Click the Save Export button (Export-Excel Spreadsheet dialog box) to save the export steps.

Other Ways

1. Right-click database object in Navigation Pane, click Export.

BTW

Saving Export Steps
Because query results are based on the data in the underlying tables, a change to an underlying table would result in a new query answer. For example, if the last name for account manager 35 changed from Simson to Smith, the change would be made in the Account Manager table. If you run the Manager-Account Query again and export the query using the saved export steps, the Excel workbook would show the changed name.

TO EXPORT DATA TO WORD

It is not possible to export data from Access to the standard Word format. It is possible, however, to export the data as a rich text format (RTF) file, which Word can use. To export data from a query or table to an RTF file, you would use the following steps.

1. With the query or table to be exported selected in the Navigation Pane, click the More button (External Data tab | Export group) and then click Word on the More menu to display the Export-RTF File dialog box.

2. Navigate to the location in which to save the file and assign a file name.

3. Click the Save button, and then click the OK button to export the data.

4. Save the export steps if you want, or simply click the Close button in the Export-RTF File dialog box to close the dialog box without saving the export steps.

Text Files

You can also export Access data to text files, which can be used for a variety of purposes. Text files contain unformatted characters, including alphanumeric characters, and some special characters, such as tabs, carriage returns, and line feeds.

In **delimited files**, each record is on a separate line and the fields are separated by a special character, called the **delimiter**. Common delimiters are tabs, semicolons, commas, and spaces. You can also choose any other value that does not appear within the field contents as the delimiter. The comma-separated values (CSV) file often used in Excel is an example of a delimited file.

In **fixed-width files**, the width of any field is the same on every record. For example, if the width of the first field on the first record is 12 characters, the width of the first field on every other record must also be 12 characters.

TO EXPORT DATA TO A TEXT FILE

When exporting data to a text file, you can choose to export the data with formatting and layout. This option preserves much of the formatting and layout in tables, queries, forms, and reports. For forms and reports, this is the only option for exporting to a text file.

If you do not need to preserve the formatting, you can choose either delimited or fixed-width as the format for the exported file. The most common option, especially if formatting is not an issue, is delimited. You can choose the delimiter. You can also choose whether to include field names on the first row. In many cases, delimiting with a comma and including the field names is a good choice.

To export data from a table or query to a comma-delimited file in which the first row contains the column headings, you would use the following steps.

1. With the query or table to be exported selected in the Navigation Pane, click the Text File button (External Data tab | Export group) to display the Export-Text File dialog box.

2. Select the name and location for the file to be created.

3. If you need to preserve formatting and layout, be sure the 'Export data with formatting and layout' check box is checked. If you do not need to preserve formatting and layout, make sure the check box is not checked. Once you have made your selection, click the OK button in the Export-Text File dialog box.

4. To create a delimited file, be sure the Delimited option button is selected in the Export Text Wizard dialog box. To create a fixed-width file, be sure the Fixed Width option button is selected. Once you have made your selection, click the Next button.

5. a. If you are exporting to a delimited file, choose the delimiter that you want to separate your fields, such as a comma. Decide whether to include field names on the first row and, if so, click the 'Include Field Names on First Row' check box. If you want to select a text qualifier, select it in the Text Qualifier list. When you have made your selections, click the Next button.

   b. If you are exporting to a fixed-width file, review the position of the vertical lines that separate your fields. If any lines are not positioned correctly, follow the directions on the screen to reposition them. When you have finished, click the Next button.

6. Click the Finish button to export the data.

7. Save the export steps if you want, or simply click the Close button in the Export-Text File dialog box to close the dialog box without saving the export steps.

Adding Criteria to a Join Query

Sometimes you will want to join tables, but you will not want to include all possible records. For example, you would like to create a report showing only those accounts whose amount paid is greater than $20,000.00. In this case, you would relate the tables and include fields just as you did before. You will also include criteria. To include only those accounts whose amount paid is more than $20,000.00, you will include >20000 as a criterion for the Amount Paid field.

BTW

Distributing a Document
Instead of printing and distributing a hard copy of a document, you can distribute the document electronically. Options include sending the document via email; posting it on cloud storage (such as OneDrive) and sharing the file with others; posting it on social media, a blog, or other website; and sharing a link associated with an online location of the document. You also can create and share a PDF or XPS image of the document, so that users can view the file in Acrobat Reader or XPS Viewer instead of in Access.

To Restrict the Records in a Join

The following steps modify the Manager-Account Query so that the results for PrattLast Associates include a criterion. ***Why?*** *PrattLast wants to include only those accounts whose amount paid is more than $20,000.00.*

1

- Open the Navigation Pane, if necessary, and then right-click the Manager-Account Query to produce a shortcut menu.
- Click Design View on the shortcut menu to open the Manager-Account Query in Design view.

Figure 2–61

- Close the Navigation Pane.
- Add the Amount Paid field to the query.
- Type **>20000** as the criterion for the Amount Paid field (Figure 2–61).

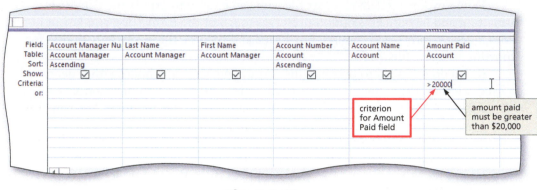

2

- Run the query (Figure 2–62).

3

- Close the query.
- When asked if you want to save your changes, click the No button.

Q&A What would happen if I saved the changes?

The next time you used this query, you would only see accounts whose amount paid is more than $20,000.00.

AM #	Last Name	First Name	AC #	Account Name	Amount Paid
31	Rivera	Haydee	AC001	Avondale Community Bank	$24,752.25
31	Rivera	Haydee	MI345	Midwest Library Consortium	$21,769.20
35	Simson	Mark	BL235	Bland Corp.	$29,836.65
35	Simson	Mark	CO621	Codder Plastics Co.	$27,152.25
35	Simson	Mark	KV089	KAL Veterinary Services	$34,036.50
58	Murowski	Karen	CA043	Carlton Regional Clinic	$30,841.05
58	Murowski	Karen	HL111	Halko Legal Associates	$25,702.20
58	Murowski	Karen	LC005	Lancaster County Hospital	$44,025.60
58	Murowski	Karen	TP098	TAL Packaging Systems	$22,696.95

Figure 2–62

BTW

Expression Builder

Access includes a tool to help you create complex expressions. If you click Build on the shortcut menu (see Figure 2–63), Access displays the Expression Builder dialog box, which includes an expression box, operator buttons, and expression elements. You can type parts of the expression directly and paste operator buttons and expression elements into the box. You also can use functions in expressions.

Calculations

If a special calculation is required for a query, you need to determine whether the calculation is an **individual record calculation** (for example, adding the values in two fields for one record) or a **group calculation** (for example, finding the total of the values in a particular field on all the records).

PrattLast Associates might want to know the total amount (amount paid and current due) for each account. This would seem to pose a problem because the Account table does not include a field for total amount. You can calculate it, however, because the total amount is equal to the amount paid plus the current due. A field that can be computed from other fields is called a **calculated field** or a **computed field** and is not usually included in the table. Including it introduces the possibility for errors in the table. If the value in the field does not happen to match the results

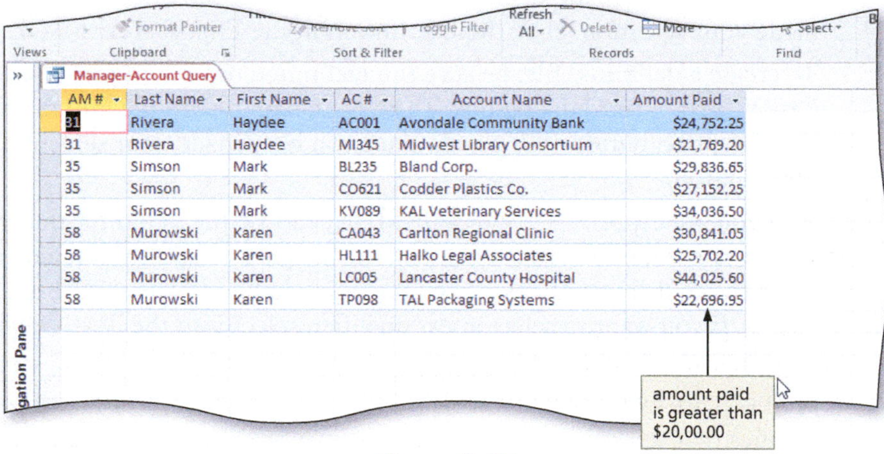

of the calculation, the data is inconsistent. A calculated field is an individual record calculation because each calculation only involves fields in a single record.

PrattLast might also want to calculate the average amount paid for the accounts of each account manager. That is, they may want the average for accounts of account manager 31, the average for accounts of account manager 35, and so on. This type of calculation is called a **group calculation** because each calculation involves groups of records. In this example, the accounts of account manager 31 would form one group, the accounts of account manager 35 would be a second group, and the accounts of account manager 58 would form a third group.

To Use a Calculated Field in a Query

1 CREATE QUERIES | 2 USE CRITERIA | 3 SORT DATA | 4 JOIN TABLES | 5 EXPORT RESULTS
6 PERFORM CALCULATIONS | 7 CREATE CROSSTAB | 8 CUSTOMIZE NAVIGATION PANE

If you need a calculated field in a query, you enter a name, or alias, for the calculated field, a colon, and then the calculation in one of the columns in the Field row of the design grid for the query. Any fields included in the expression must be enclosed in square brackets ([ ]). For example, for the total amount, you will type Total Amount:[Amount Paid]+[Current Due] as the expression.

You can type the expression directly into the Field row in Design view. The preferred method, however, is to select the column in the Field row and then use the Zoom command on its shortcut menu. When Access displays the Zoom dialog box, you can enter the expression. *Why use the Zoom command? You will not be able to see the entire entry in the Field row, because the space available is not large enough.*

You can use addition (+), subtraction (-), multiplication (*), or division (/) in calculations. If you have multiple calculations in an expression, you can include parentheses to indicate which calculations should be done first.

The following steps create a query that PrattLast Associates might use to obtain financial information on its accounts, including the total amount (amount paid + current due), which is a calculated field.

1
- Create a query with a field list for the Account table.
- Add the Account Number, Account Name, Amount Paid, and Current Due fields to the query.
- Right-click the Field row in the first open column in the design grid to display a shortcut menu (Figure 2–63).

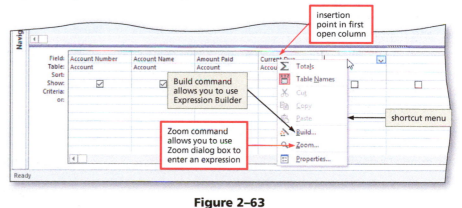

Figure 2–63

2
- Click Zoom on the shortcut menu to display the Zoom dialog box.
- Type `Total Amount:[Amount Paid]+[Current Due]` in the Zoom dialog box (Figure 2–64).

Q&A
Do I always need to put square brackets around field names?
If the field name does not contain spaces, square brackets are technically not required. It is a good practice, however, to get in the habit of using the brackets in field calculations.

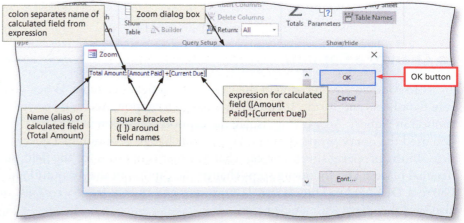

Figure 2–64

3
- Click the OK button (Zoom dialog box) to enter the expression (Figure 2–65).

Current Due
Account Manager Nu

only part of
expression
is visible

Field:	Account Number	Account Name	Amount Paid	Current Due	Total Amount: [Am			
Table:	Account	Account	Account	Account				
Sort:								
Show:	☑	☑	☑	☑	☑	☐	☐	☐
Criteria:								
or:								

Figure 2–65

4
- Run the query (Figure 2–66).

Experiment

- Return to Design view and try other expressions. In at least one case, omit the Total Amount and the colon. In at least one case, intentionally misspell a field name. In each case, run the query to see the effect of your changes. When finished, reenter the original expression.

AC #	Account Name	Amount Paid	Current Due	Total Amour
AC001	Avondale Community Bank	$24,752.25	$3,875.25	$28,627.50
BL235	Bland Corp.	$29,836.65	$2,765.30	$32,601.95
CA043	Carlton Regional Clinic	$30,841.05	$3,074.30	$33,915.35
CO621	Codder Plastics Co.	$27,152.25	$2,875.00	$30,027.25
EC010	Eco Clothes Inc.	$19,620.00	$1,875.00	$21,495.00
HL111	Halko Legal Associates	$25,702.20	$3,016.75	$28,718.95
JM323	JSP Manufacturing Inc.	$19,739.70	$2,095.00	$21,834.70
KC156	Key Community College System	$10,952.25	$0.00	$10,952.25
KV089	KAL Veterinary Services	$34,036.50	$580.00	$34,616.50
LC005	Lancaster County Hospital	$44,025.60	$3,590.80	$47,616.40
LI268	Lars-Idsen Inc.	$0.00	$1,280.75	$1,280.75
MI345	Midwest Library Consortium	$21,769.20	$2,890.60	$24,659.80
ML008	Mums Landscaping Co.	$13,097.10	$2,450.00	$15,547.10
TP098	TAL Packaging Systems	$22,696.95	$3,480.45	$26,177.40
TW001	Tri-County Waste Disposal	$15,345.00	$2,875.50	$18,220.50

results are calculated by adding amount paid and current due

Total Amount field

Figure 2–66

Other Ways

1. Press SHIFT+F2

1 CREATE QUERIES | 2 USE CRITERIA | 3 SORT DATA | 4 JOIN TABLES | 5 EXPORT RESULTS
6 PERFORM CALCULATIONS | 7 CREATE CROSSTAB | 8 CUSTOMIZE NAVIGATION PANE

To Change a Caption

In Module 1, you changed the caption for a field in a table. When you assigned a caption, Access displayed it in datasheets and forms. If you did not assign a caption, Access displayed the field name. You can also change a caption in a query. Access will display the caption you assign in the query results. When you omitted duplicates, you used the query property sheet. When you change a caption in a query, you use the property sheet for the field. In the property sheet, you can change other properties for the field, such as the format and number of decimal places. The following steps change the caption of the Amount Paid field to Paid and the caption of the Current Due field to Due. *Why? These changes give shorter, yet very readable, column headings for the fields.* The steps also save the query with a new name.

1

- Return to Design view.

- If necessary, click Design on the ribbon to display the Query Tools Design tab.

- Click the Amount Paid field in the design grid, and then click the Property Sheet button (Query Tools Design tab | Show/Hide group) to display the properties for the Amount Paid field.

- Click the Caption box, and then type **Paid** as the caption (Figure 2–67).

Q&A | My property sheet looks different. What should I do?
Close the property sheet and repeat this step.

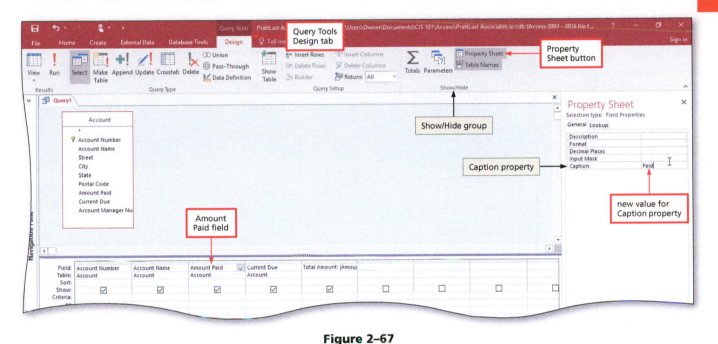

Figure 2–67

2

- Click the Current Due field in the design grid to view its properties in the Property Sheet.

- Click the Caption box, and then type **Due** as the caption.

- Close the Property Sheet by clicking the Property Sheet button a second time.

- Run the query (Figure 2–68).

3

- Save the query as m02q10.

- Close the query.

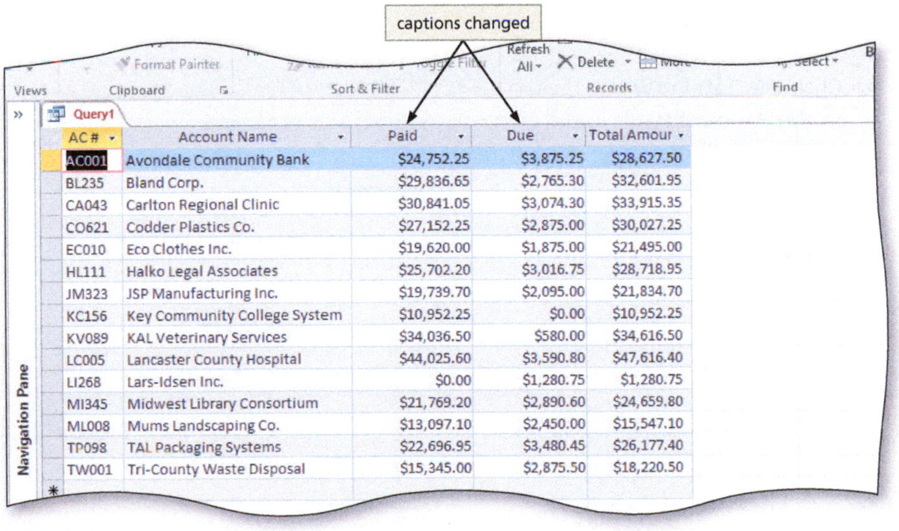

Figure 2–68

Other Ways

1. Right-click field in design grid, click Properties on shortcut menu

To Calculate Statistics

For group calculations, Microsoft Access supports several built-in statistics: COUNT (count of the number of records), SUM (total), AVG (average), MAX (largest value), MIN (smallest value), STDEV (standard deviation), VAR (variance), FIRST (first value), and LAST (last value). These statistics are called aggregate functions. An **aggregate function** is a function that performs some mathematical function against a group of records. To use an aggregate function in a query, you include it in the Total row in the design grid. In order to do so, you must first include the Total row by clicking the Totals button on the Design tab. *Why? The Total row usually does not appear in the grid.*

The following steps create a new query for the Account table. The steps include the Total row in the design grid, and then calculate the average amount paid for all accounts.

1
- Create a new query with a field list for the Account table.

- Click the Totals button (Query Tools Design tab | Show/Hide group) to include the Total row in the design grid.

- Add the Amount Paid field to the query (Figure 2–69).

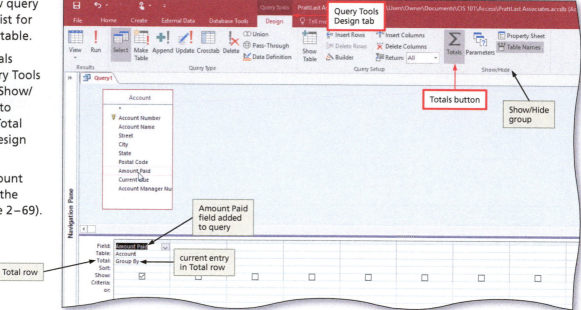

Figure 2–69

2
- Click the Total row in the Amount Paid column to display the Total arrow.

- Click the Total arrow to display the Total list (Figure 2–70).

Figure 2–70

3
- Click Avg to select the calculation that Access is to perform (Figure 2–71).

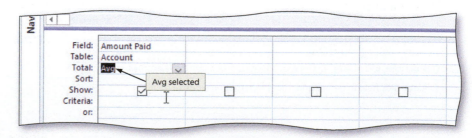

Figure 2–71

4
- Run the query (Figure 2–72).

Experiment
- Return to Design view and try other aggregate functions. In each case, run the query to see the effect of your selection. When finished, select Avg once again.

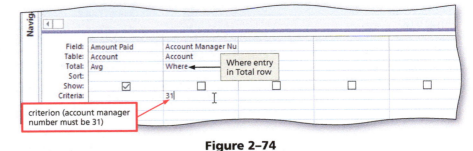

Figure 2–72

To Use Criteria in Calculating Statistics

1 CREATE QUERIES | 2 USE CRITERIA | 3 SORT DATA | 4 JOIN TABLES | 5 EXPORT RESULTS
6 PERFORM CALCULATIONS | 7 CREATE CROSSTAB | 8 CUSTOMIZE NAVIGATION PANE

Why? Sometimes calculating statistics for all the records in the table is appropriate. In other cases, however, you will need to calculate the statistics for only those records that satisfy certain criteria. To enter a criterion in a field, first you select Where as the entry in the Total row for the field, and then enter the criterion in the Criteria row. Access uses the word, Where, to indicate that you will enter a criterion. The following steps use this technique to calculate the average amount paid for accounts of account manager 31. The steps also save the query with a new name.

1
- Return to Design view.
- Include the Account Manager Number field in the design grid.
- Click the Total row in the Account Manager Number column.
- Click the Total arrow in the Account Manager Number column to produce a Total list (Figure 2–73).

Figure 2–73

2
- Click Where to be able to enter a criterion.
- Type **31** as the criterion for the Account Manager Number field (Figure 2–74).

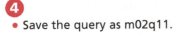

Figure 2–74

3
- Run the query (Figure 2–75).

4
- Save the query as m02q11.

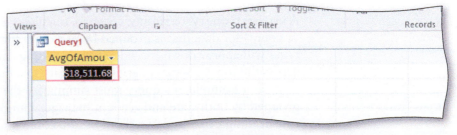

Figure 2–75

To Use Grouping

Why? *Statistics are often used in combination with grouping; that is, statistics are calculated for groups of records. For example, PrattLast could calculate the average amount paid for the accounts of each account manager, which would require the average for the accounts of account manager 31, account manager 35, and so on.* **Grouping** means creating groups of records that share some common characteristic. In grouping by Account Manager Number, for example, the accounts of account manager 31 would form one group, the accounts of account manager 35 would form a second, and the accounts of account manager 58 would form a third group. The calculations are then made for each group. To indicate grouping in Access, select Group By as the entry in the Total row for the field to be used for grouping.

The following steps create a query that calculates the average amount paid for the accounts of each account manager at PrattLast Associates. The steps also save the query with a new name.

1
- Return to Design view and clear the design grid.
- Include the Account Manager Number field in the query.
- Include the Amount Paid field in the query.
- Select Avg as the calculation in the Total row for the Amount Paid field (Figure 2–76).

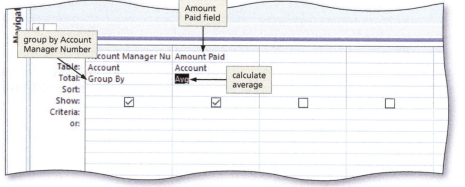

Figure 2–76

Why was it not necessary to change the entry in the Total row for the Account Manager Number field?
Group By, which is the initial entry in the Total row when you add a field, is correct. Thus, you did not need to change the entry.

2
- Run the query (Figure 2–77).

3
- Save the query as m02q12.
- Close the query.

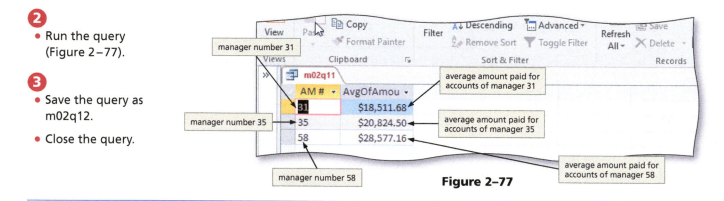

Figure 2–77

Crosstab Queries

A **crosstab query**, or simply, crosstab, calculates a statistic (for example, sum, average, or count) for data that is grouped by two different types of information. One of the types will appear down the side of the resulting datasheet, and the other will appear across the top. Crosstab queries are useful for summarizing data by category or group.

For example, if a query must summarize the sum of the current due amounts grouped by both state and account manager number, you could have states as the row headings, that is, down the side. You could have account manager numbers as the column headings, that is, across the top. The entries within the datasheet represent the total of the current due amounts. Figure 2–78 shows a crosstab in which the total of current due amounts is grouped by both state and account manager number, with states down the left side and account manager numbers across the top. For example, the entry in the row labeled IL and in the column labeled 31 represents the total of the current due amounts by all accounts of account manager 31 who are located in Illinois.

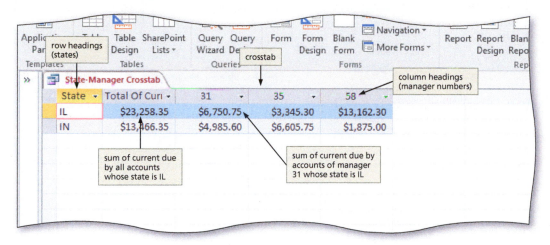

Figure 2–78

How do you know when to use a crosstab query?

If data is to be grouped by two different types of information, you can use a crosstab query. You will need to identify the two types of information. One of the types will form the row headings and the other will form the column headings in the query results.

To Create a Crosstab Query

1 CREATE QUERIES | 2 USE CRITERIA | 3 SORT DATA | 4 JOIN TABLES | 5 EXPORT RESULTS
6 PERFORM CALCULATIONS | 7 CREATE CROSSTAB | 8 CUSTOMIZE NAVIGATION PANE

The following steps use the Crosstab Query Wizard to create a crosstab query. *Why? PrattLast Associates wants to group data on current due amounts by two types of information: state and account manager.*

1
- Click Create on the ribbon to display the Create tab.
- Click the Query Wizard button (Create tab | Queries group) to display the New Query dialog box (Figure 2–79).

Figure 2–79

2

- Click Crosstab Query Wizard (New Query dialog box).

- Click the OK button to display the Crosstab Query Wizard dialog box (Figure 2–80).

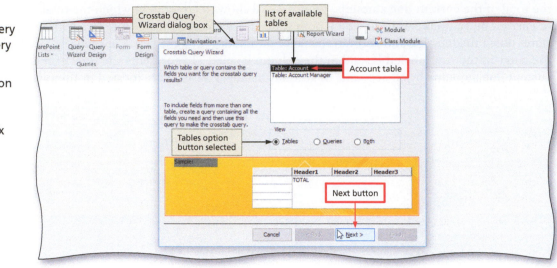

Figure 2–80

3

- With the Tables option button selected, click Table: Account to select the Account table, and then click the Next button to display the next Crosstab Query Wizard screen.

- Click the State field, and then click the Add Field button to select the State field for row headings (Figure 2–81).

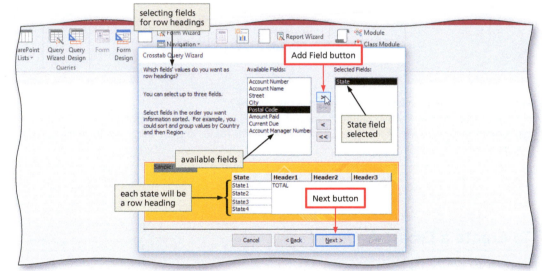

Figure 2–81

4

- Click the Next button to display the next Crosstab Query Wizard screen.

- Click the Account Manager Number field to select the field for column headings (Figure 2–82).

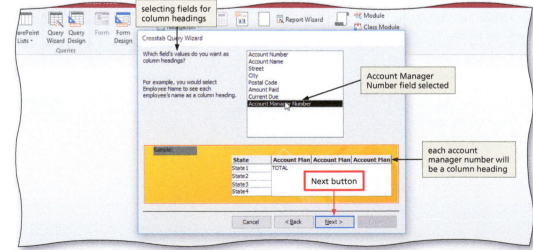

Figure 2–82

5

- Click the Next button to display the next Crosstab Query Wizard screen.

- Click the Current Due field to select the field for calculations.

🔍 **Experiment**

- Click other fields. For each field, examine the list of calculations that are available. When finished, click the Current Due field again.

- Click Sum to select the calculation to be performed (Figure 2–83).

Q&A My list of functions is different. What did I do wrong?
Either you clicked the wrong field, or the Current Due field has the wrong data type. For example, if you mistakenly assigned it the Short Text data type, you would not see Sum in the list of available calculations.

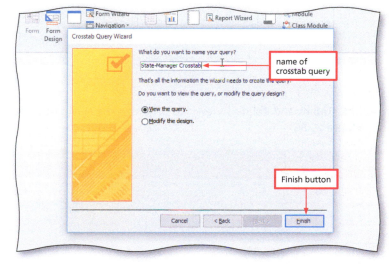

Figure 2–83

6

- Click the Next button to display the next Crosstab Query Wizard screen.

- Erase the text in the name text box and type **State-Manager Crosstab** as the name of the query (Figure 2–84).

7

- If requested to do so by your instructor, name the crosstab query as FirstName LastName Crosstab where FirstName and LastName are your first and last names.

- Click the Finish button to produce the crosstab shown in Figure 2–78.

- Close the query.

Figure 2–84

Customizing the Navigation Pane

Currently, the entries in the Navigation Pane are organized by object type. That is, all the tables are together, all the queries are together, and so on. You might want to change the way the information is organized. For example, you might want to have the Navigation Pane organized by table, with all the queries, forms, and reports associated with a particular table appearing after the name of the table. You can also use the Search bar to restrict the objects that appear to only those that have a certain collection of characters in their name. For example, if you entered the letters, Ma, only those objects containing Ma somewhere within the name will be included.

BTW

Access Help
At any time while using Access, you can find answers to questions and display information about various topics through Access Help. Used properly, this form of assistance can increase your productivity and reduce your frustrations by minimizing the time you spend learning how to use Access. For instructions about Access Help and exercises that will help you gain confidence in using it, read the Office and Windows module at the beginning of this book.

To Customize the Navigation Pane

The following steps change the organization of the Navigation Pane. They also use the Search bar to restrict the objects that appear. *Why? Using the Search bar, you can reduce the number of objects that appear in the Navigation Pane and just show the ones in which you are interested.*

1

- If necessary, click the 'Shutter Bar Open/ Close Button' to open the Navigation Pane.

- Click the Navigation Pane arrow to produce the Navigation Pane menu (Figure 2–85).

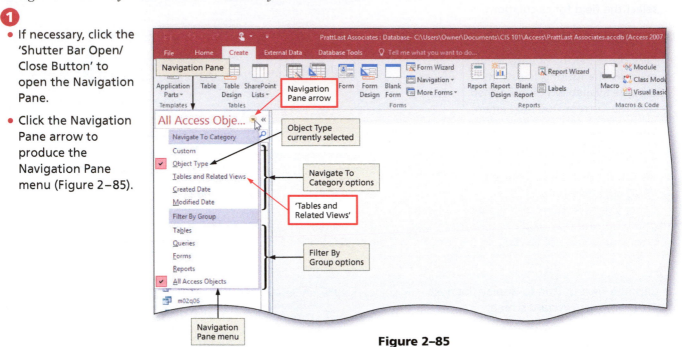

Figure 2–85

2

- Click 'Tables and Related Views' to organize the Navigation Pane by table rather than by the type of object (Figure 2–86).

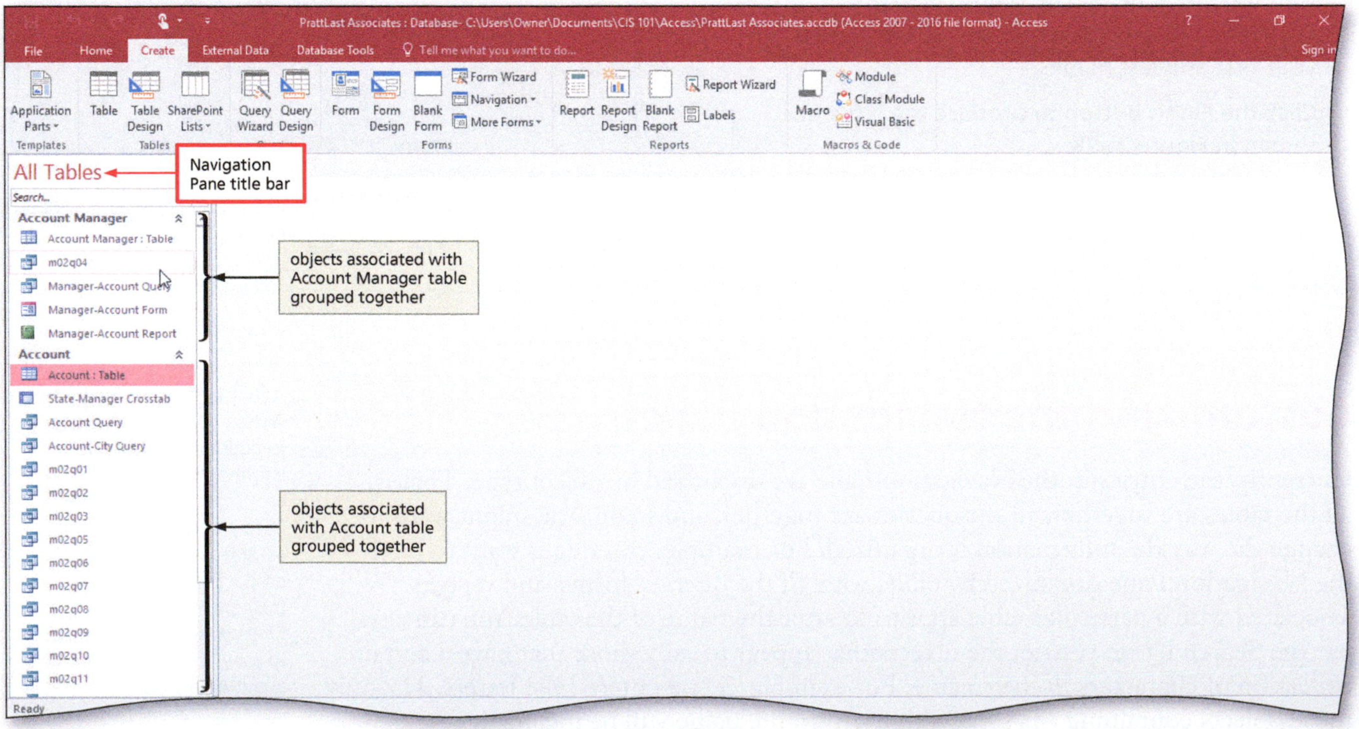

Figure 2–86

3

- Click the Navigation Pane arrow to produce the Navigation Pane menu.

- Click Object Type to once again organize the Navigation Pane by object type.

🔎 **Experiment**

- Select different Navigate To Category options to see the effect of the option. With each option you select, select different Filter By Group options to see the effect of the filtering. When you have finished experimenting, select the 'Object Type Navigate To Category' option and the 'All Access Objects Filter By Group' option.

- If the Search bar does not appear, right-click the Navigation Pane and click Search Bar on the shortcut menu.

- Click in the Search box to produce an insertion point.

- Type **Ma** as the search string to restrict the objects displayed to only those containing the desired string (Figure 2–87).

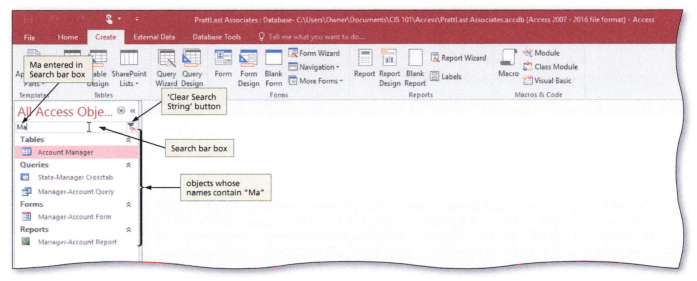

Figure 2–87

4

- Click the 'Clear Search String' button to remove the search string and redisplay all objects.

Q&A Did I have to click the button to redisplay all objects? Could I simply have erased the current string to achieve the same result?

You did not have to click the button. You could have used the DELETE or BACKSPACE keys to erase the current search string.

- If desired, sign out of your Microsoft account.

- Exit Access.

Summary

In this module you have learned to create queries, enter fields, enter criteria, use text and numeric data in queries, use wildcards, use compound criteria, create parameter queries, sort data in queries, join tables in queries, perform calculations in queries, and create crosstab queries. You also learned to create a report and a form that used a query, to export a query, and to customize the Navigation Pane.

What decisions will you need to make when creating queries?

Use these guidelines as you complete the assignments in this module and create your own queries outside of this class.

1. Identify the fields by examining the question or request to determine which fields from the tables in the database are involved.

2. Identify restrictions or the conditions that records must satisfy to be included in the results.

3. Determine whether special order is required.

   a) Determine the sort key(s).

   b) If using two sort keys, determine the major and minor key.

   c) Determine sort order. If there are no words to imply a particular order, you would typically use Ascending.

   d) Determine restrictions, such as excluding duplicates.

4. Determine whether more than one table is required.

   a) Determine which tables to include.

   b) Determine the matching fields.

   c) Determine whether sorting is required.

   d) Determine restrictions.

   e) Determine join properties.

5. Determine whether calculations are required.

   a) For individual record calculations, determine the calculation and a name for the calculated field.

   b) For group calculations, determine the calculation as well as the field to be used for grouping.

6. If data is to be summarized and the data is to be grouped by two different types of information, create a crosstab query.

How should you submit solutions to questions in the assignments identified with a symbol?

Every assignment in this book contains one or more questions identified with a symbol. These questions require you to think beyond the assigned database. Present your solutions to the questions in the format required by your instructor. Possible formats may include one or more of these options: write the answer; create a document that contains the answer; present your answer to the class; discuss your answer in a group; record the answer as audio or video using a webcam, smartphone, or portable media player; or post answers on a blog, wiki, or website.

Apply Your Knowledge

Reinforce the skills and apply the concepts you learned in this module.

Using Wildcards in a Query, Creating a Parameter Query, Joining Tables, and Creating a Report

Instructions: Run Access. Open the Apply Friendly Janitorial Services database that you modified in Apply Your Knowledge in Module 1. (If you did not complete the exercise, see your instructor for a copy of the modified database.)

Perform the following tasks:

1. Create a query for the Client table and add the Client Number, Client Name, Amount Paid, and Current Due fields to the design grid. Add a criterion to find all clients whose names start with the letter B. Run the query and then save it as Apply 2 Step 1 Query.

2. Create a query for the Client table and add the Client Number, Client Name, Amount Paid, and Supervisor Number fields to the design grid. Sort the records in descending order by Amount Paid. Add a criterion for the Supervisor Number field that allows the user to enter a different supervisor each time the query is run. Run the query and enter 114 as the supervisor number to test the query. Save the query as Apply 2 Step 2 Query.

3. Create a query for the Client table and add the Client Number, Client Name, and Current Due fields to the design grid. Add a criterion to find all clients whose current due amount is less than $500.00. Run the query and then save it as Apply 2 Step 3 Query.

4. Create a query that joins the Supervisor and Client tables. Add the Supervisor Number, Last Name, and First Name fields from the Supervisor table and the Client Number and Client Name fields from the Client table to the design grid. Sort the records in ascending order by Client Number within Supervisor Number. Run the query and save it as Supervisor-Client Query.

5. Create the report shown in Figure 2–88. The report uses the Supervisor-Client Query.

Supervisor-Client Report

SU #	Last Name	First Name	CL #	Client Name
103	Estevez	Enrique	AT13	Atlas Repair
103	Estevez	Enrique	CP03	Calder Plastics
103	Estevez	Enrique	HC17	Hill Crafts
103	Estevez	Enrique	KD15	Klean n Dri
110	Hillsdale	Rachel	AZ01	AZ Auto
110	Hillsdale	Rachel	BB35	Babbage Bookkeeping
110	Hillsdale	Rachel	CJ45	C Joe Diner
110	Hillsdale	Rachel	HN23	Hurley National Bank
110	Hillsdale	Rachel	PL03	Prime Legal Associates
114	Liu	Chou	CC25	Cramden Co.
114	Liu	Chou	MM01	Moss Manufacturing
114	Liu	Chou	PS67	PRIM Staffing
120	Short	Chris	BL24	Blanton Shoes
120	Short	Chris	KC12	Kady Regional Clinic
120	Short	Chris	TE15	Telton-Edwards

Figure 2–88

6. If requested to do so by your instructor, rename the Supervisor-Client Report in the Navigation Pane as LastName-Client Report where LastName is your last name.

7. Submit the revised database in the format specified by your instructor.

8. ✹ What criteria would you enter in the Street field if you wanted to find all clients whose businesses were on Beard?

Extend Your Knowledge

Extend the skills you learned in this module and experiment with new skills. You may need to use Help to complete the assignment.

Creating Crosstab Queries Using Criteria and Exporting a Query

Note: To complete this assignment, you will be required to use the Data Files. Please contact your instructor for information about accessing the Data Files.

Continued >

STUDENT ASSIGNMENTS

Extend Your Knowledge *continued*

Instructions: Run Access. Open the Extend TAL Maintenance database, which is located in the Data Files. TAL Maintenance is a small business that provides various outdoor maintenance services, such as painting, lawn maintenance, and parking lot re-paving, to commercial customers. The owner has created an Access database in which to store information about the customers the company serves and team leaders working for the company. You will create the crosstab query shown in Figure 2–89. You will also query the database using specified criteria and export a query.

Perform the following tasks:

1. Create the crosstab query shown in Figure 2–89. The crosstab groups the total of customers' balance by city and team leader number.

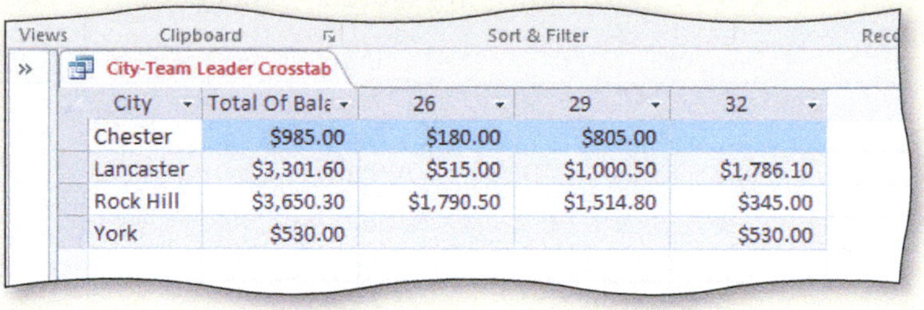

2. Create a query to find all customers who are not located in Rock Hill. Include the Customer Number, Customer Name, and Balance fields in the query results. Save the query as Extend 2 Step 2 Query.

Figure 2–89

3. Create a query to find all team leaders whose first name is either Alex or Alix. Include the Team Leader Number, First Name, and Last Name in the query results. Save the query as Extend 2 Step 3 Query.

4. Create a query to find all customers where the team leader number is either 29 or 32 and the balance is greater than $550.00. Include the Customer Number, Customer Name, Balance, and Team Leader Number fields in the design grid in that order. Use the IN operator in your query design. Sort the results by customer number within team leader number. Save the query as Extend 2 Step 4 Query.

5. Export the City-Team Leader Crosstab as a Word file with the name City-Team Leader Crosstab.rtf and save the export steps.

6. Open the Customer table and change the balance for account C04 to $1,000.50.

7. If requested to do so by your instructor, change the customer name of customer K10 from Kathy's Books to Last Name Books where Last Name is your last name.

8. Use the saved export steps to export the City-Team Leader Crosstab again. When asked if you want to replace the existing file, click Yes.

9. Submit the revised database and the exported RTF file in the format specified by your instructor.

10. ✹ How would you create the query in Step 4 without using the IN operator?

Expand Your World

Create a solution, which uses cloud and web technologies, by learning and investigating on your own from general guidance.

Problem: You are taking a general science course and the instructor would like you to gather some weather statistics and query the statistics as part of the unit on climate change.

Instructions:

1. Examine a website that contains historical weather data, such as accuweather.com or weatherunderground.com. Select weather data for the city in which you were born for the month of January, 2014. If you cannot find your city, then select a large city near your current location.

2. Create a database that contains one table and has the following fields: Day of the month (1 through 31), Day of the week, high temperature for the day, and low temperature for the day. (*Hint:* Use the autonumber data type to record the day of the month.)

3. Create queries that do the following:

   a. Display the five days with the highest high temperature.

   b. Display the five days with lowest low temperature.

   c. Display the average high and low temperature for the entire month.

   d. Calculate the difference between the high and low temperatures for each day.

   e. Display the high and low temperatures for each day in both Fahrenheit and Celsius. (*Hint:* Use the Internet to find the conversion formula.)

4. Submit the revised database in the format specified by your instructor.

5. Use an Internet search engine to find the historical average high and low temperatures in January for your city.

6. ✳ Which websites did you use to gather data and search for the historical averages? How does the query result in Step 3c differ from the historical average?

In the Labs

Design, create, modify, and/or use a database following the guidelines, concepts, and skills presented in this module. Labs are listed in order of increasing difficulty. Labs 1 and 2, which increase in difficulty, require you to create solutions based on what you learned in the module; Lab 3 requires you to apply your creative thinking and problem solving skills to design and implement a solution.

Lab 1: Querying the Garden Naturally Database

Problem: The management of Garden Naturally has determined a number of questions it wants the database management system to answer. You must obtain the answers to these questions.

Note: Use the database modified in Lab 1 of Module 1 for this assignment, or see your instructor for information on accessing the required files.

Instructions: Perform the following tasks:

1. Run Access. Open the Lab 1 Garden Naturally database you modified in Module 1 and create a new query for the Customer table. Add the Customer Number, Customer Name, Amount Paid, Balance Due, and Sales Rep Number fields to the design grid, and restrict the query results to only those customers where the sales rep number is 29. Save the query as Lab 2-1 Step 1 Query.

2. Create a query for the Customer table that includes the Customer Number, Customer Name, and Balance Due fields for all customers located in Delaware (DE) with a balance due greater than $1,000.00. Save the query as Lab 2-1 Step 2 Query.

3. Create a query for the Customer table that includes the Customer Number, Customer Name, Address, City, and State fields for all customers located in cities that begin with Ch. Save the query as Lab 2-1 Step 3 Query.

Continued >

In the Labs continued

4. Create a query for the Customer table that lists all states in ascending order. Each state should appear only once. Save the query as Lab 2-1 Step 4 Query.

5. Create a query for the Customer table that allows the user to type the name of the desired city when the query is run. The query results should display the Customer Number, Customer Name, Balance Due, and Amount Paid fields in that order. Test the query by searching for those records where the customer is located in Quaker. Save the query as Lab 2-1 Step 5 Query.

6. Create a query for the Sales Rep table that includes the First Name, Last Name, and Start Date for all sales reps who started after June 1, 2015. Save the query as Lab 2-1 Step 6 Query.

7. Create a query that joins the Sales Rep and Customer tables. Include the Sales Rep Number, Last Name, and First Name from the Sales Rep table. Include the Customer Number, Customer Name, and Amount Paid from the Customer table. Sort the records in ascending order by sales rep's last name and then by customer name. All sales reps should appear in the result even if they currently have no customers. Save the query as Lab 2-1 Step 7 Query.

8. Open the Lab 2-1 Step 7 Query in Design view and remove the Sales Rep table from the query. Add the Balance Due field to the design grid. Calculate the total of the balance and amount paid amounts. Assign the alias Total Amount to the calculated field. Change the caption for the Amount Paid field to Paid and the caption for the Balance Due field to Owed. Save the query as Lab 2-1 Step 8 Query.

9. Create a query for the Customer table to display the total amount paid for sales rep 26. Save the query as Lab 2-1 Step 9 Query.

10. Create a query for the Customer table to display the average balance due for each sales rep. Save the query as Lab 2-1 Step 10 Query.

11. Create the crosstab query shown in Figure 2–90. The crosstab groups the average of customers' amount paid by state and sales rep number. Save the crosstab as State-Sales Rep Crosstab.

State	Total Of Am	26	29	32
DE	$1,431.38		$537.50	$2,325.25
NJ	$2,503.57	$2,352.61	$2,285.50	$3,325.45
PA	$1,717.10	$1,190.00	$1,572.50	$2,125.25

Figure 2–90

12. If requested to do so by your instructor, open the Lab 2-1 Step 1 query and change the caption for the Sales Rep Number field to your last name.

13. Submit the revised database in the format specified by your instructor.

14. ✹ How would you modify the query in Step 7 to include only sales reps that currently have customers?

Lab 2: **Querying the Museum Gift Shop Database**

Problem: The manager of the Museum gift shop has determined a number of questions she wants the database management system to answer. You must obtain answers to these questions.

Note: Use the database created in Lab 2 of Module 1 for this assignment or see your instructor for information on accessing the required files.

Instructions: Perform the following tasks:

1. Run Access. Open the Lab 2 Museum Gift Shop database and create a query for the Item table that includes all fields and all records in the Item table. Name the query Lab 2-2 Step 1 Query.

2. Create a query for the Item table that includes the Item Number, Description, Wholesale Cost, and Vendor Code fields for all records where the vendor code is AW. Save the query as Lab 2-2 Step 2 Query.

3. Create a query for the Item table that includes the Item Number and Description fields for all items where the description starts with G. Save the query as Lab 2-2 Step 3 Query.

4. Create a query for the Item table that includes the Item Number and Description for all items with a Wholesale Cost greater than $15.00. Save the query as Lab 2-2 Step 4 Query.

5. Create a query for the Item table that includes the Item Number, Description, and Wholesale Cost fields for all items with a Wholesale Cost between $5.00 and $10.00. Save the query as Lab 2-2 Step 5 Query.

6. Create a query for the Item table that includes the Item Number, Description, On Hand, and Wholesale Cost fields for all items where the number on hand is less than 5 and the wholesale cost is less than $15.00. Save the query as Lab 2-2 Step 6 Query.

7. Create a query for the Item table that includes the Item Number, Description, Wholesale Cost, and Vendor Code for all items that have a Wholesale Cost greater than $20.00 or a Vendor Code of SD. Save the query as Lab 2-2 Step 7 Query.

8. Create a query that joins the Vendor and the Item tables. Include the Vendor Code and Vendor Name from the Vendor table and the Item Number, Description, Wholesale Cost, and Retail Price fields from the Item table. Sort the query in ascending order by Description within Vendor Code. Save the query as Vendor-Item Query.

9. Create a form for the Vendor-Item Query. Save the form as Vendor-Item Form.

10. If requested to do so by your instructor, rename the form in the Navigation Pane as LastName-Item Form where LastName is your last name.

11. Create the report shown in Figure 2–91. The report uses the Vendor-Item Query but does not use all the fields in the query.

Vendor-Item Report

Vendor Name	Description	Wholesale	Retail
Atherton Wholesalers	Amazing Science Fun	$13.50	$24.99
Atherton Wholesalers	Crystal Growing Kit	$6.75	$12.97
Atherton Wholesalers	Discovery Dinosaurs	$12.35	$19.95
Atherton Wholesalers	Gem Nature Guide	$9.50	$14.95
Atherton Wholesalers	Onyx Jar	$7.50	$13.97
Gift Specialties	Agate Bookends	$16.25	$27.97
Gift Specialties	Dinosaur Egg Ornament	$7.50	$14.99
Gift Specialties	Fibonacci Necklace	$16.75	$29.99
Gift Specialties	Gyrobot	$27.99	$49.99
Gift Specialties	Molecule Necklace	$16.25	$29.95
Smith Distributors	Cosmos Uncovered	$8.95	$15.00
Smith Distributors	Fun with Math	$12.95	$24.95
Smith Distributors	Geek Toys Guide	$5.10	$9.99
Smith Distributors	Paper Planes	$7.10	$13.97
Smith Distributors	Slime Time	$15.35	$24.99

Figure 2–91

Continued >

In the Labs *continued*

12. Create a query for the Item table that includes the Item Number, Description, Wholesale Cost, and Retail Price. Calculate the difference between Retail Price and Wholesale Cost (Retail Price – Wholesale Cost). Assign the alias Mark Up to the calculated field. Save the query as Lab 2-2 Step 12 Query.

13. Create a query for the Item table that displays the average Wholesale Cost and the average Retail Price of all items. Save the query as Lab 2-2 Step 13 Query.

14. Create a query for the Item table that displays the Item Number, Description, On Hand, and Retail Price for the 5 items with the lowest retail price. Save the query as Lab 2-2 Step 14 Query.

15. Submit the revised database in the format specified by your instructor.

16. ✳ How could you modify the query in step 2 to find all vendors where the vendor code is AW or GS? If there is more than one way to perform this query, list all ways.

Lab 3: **Consider This: Your Turn**

Querying the Camshay Marketing Database

Instructions: Open the Lab 3 Camshay Marketing database you created in Module 1. If you did not create this database, contact your instructor for information about accessing the required files.

Part 1: Use the concepts and techniques presented in this module to create queries for the following. Save each query.
   a. Find all marketing analysts who started between June 1, 2015 and September 30, 2015. Show the marketing analyst's first name, last name, salary YTD, and incentive YTD.
   b. Find the client name and street address of all clients located in a city that starts with Bu.
   c. Find the client number, client name, amount paid and current due of all clients whose amount paid is $0.00 or whose current due is $0.00.
   d. Find the client number, client name, amount paid, current due, and total amount for all clients located in North Carolina (NC).
   e. Create a parameter query for the Client table that will allow the user to enter a different city each time the query is run. The user should see all fields in the query result.
   f. Create a crosstab query that groups the amount paid total by city and marketing analyst.
   g. Find the marketing analyst for each client. List the marketing analyst number, first name, last name, client number, client name, and current due. Sort the results by client number within marketing analyst number.
   h. Open the query you created in Step g above and restrict retrieval to only those clients whose current due amount is greater than $5,000.00.
   i. Change the organization of the Navigation Pane so that all objects associated with the Client table are grouped together and all objects associated with the Marketing Analyst are grouped together.

Submit your assignment in the format specified by your instructor.

Part 2: You made several decisions while creating the queries in this assignment, including the parameter query in Step e. What was the rationale behind your decisions? There are two ways to create the query in step e. What are they? Which one did you use?

3 | Maintaining a Database

Objectives

You will have mastered the material in this module when you can:

- Add, change, and delete records
- Search for records
- Filter records
- Update a table design
- Use action queries to update records
- Use delete queries to delete records
- Specify validation rules, default values, and formats

- Create and use single-value lookup fields
- Create and use multivalued lookup fields
- Add new fields to an existing report
- Format a datasheet
- Specify referential integrity
- Use a subdatasheet
- Sort records

Introduction

Once you have created a database and loaded it with data, you must maintain it. **Maintaining the database** means modifying the data to keep it up to date by adding new records, changing the data for existing records, and deleting records. Updating can include mass updates or mass deletions (i.e., updates to, or deletions of, many records at the same time).

Maintenance of a database can also involve the need to **restructure the database** periodically. Restructuring can include adding new fields to a table, changing the characteristics of existing fields, and removing existing fields. Restructuring also includes the creation of validation rules and referential integrity. Validation rules ensure the validity of the data in the database, whereas referential integrity ensures the validity of the relationships between entities. Maintaining a database can also include filtering records, a process that ensures that only the records that satisfy some criterion appear when viewing and updating the data in a table. Changing the appearance of a datasheet is also a maintenance activity.

BTW
Organizing Files and Folders
You should organize and store files in folders so that you easily can find the files later. For example, if you are taking an introductory computer class called CIS 101, a good practice would be to save all Access files in an Access folder in a CIS 101 folder. For a discussion of folders and detailed examples of creating folders, refer to the Office and Windows module at the beginning of this book.

Project — Maintaining a Database

PrattLast Associates faces the task of keeping its database up to date. As the company takes on new accounts and account managers, it will need to add new records, make changes to existing records, and delete records. PrattLast believes that it can serve its

Microsoft Access 2016

PrattLast Associates : Database- C:\Users\Owner\Documents\C

File   Home   Create   External Data   Database Tools   Tell me what you want to do...

accounts better by changing the structure of the database to categorize the accounts by type. The company will do this by adding an Account Type field to the Account table. Account managers also believe they can provide better customer service if the database includes the list of human resource services that are of interest to each account. The company will do so by adding a Services Needed field to the Account table. Because accounts may need more than one service, this field will be a multivalued field, which is a field that can store multiple values or entries. Along with these changes, PrattLast staff wants to change the appearance of a datasheet when displaying data.

PrattLast would like the ability to make mass updates, that is, to update or delete many records in a single operation. It wants rules that make sure users can enter only valid, or appropriate, data into the database. PrattLast also wants to ensure that the database cannot contain the name of an account that is not associated with a specific account manager.

Figure 3–1 summarizes some of the various types of activities involved in maintaining the PrattLast Associates database.

Figure 3–1

In this module, you will learn how to maintain a database by performing the tasks shown in Figure 3–1. The following roadmap identifies general activities you will perform as you progress through this module:

1. **UPDATE RECORDS** using a form.

2. **FILTER RECORDS** using various filtering options.

3. **CHANGE** the **STRUCTURE** of a table.

4. Make **MASS CHANGES** to a table.

5. Create **VALIDATION RULES**.

6. **CHANGE** the **APPEARANCE** of a datasheet.

7. Specify **REFERENTIAL INTEGRITY**.

8. **ORDER RECORDS** in a datasheet.

Updating Records

Keeping the data in a database current requires updating records in three ways: adding new records, changing the data in existing records, and deleting existing records. In Module 1, you added records to a database using Datasheet view; that is, as you added records, the records appeared on the screen in a datasheet. The data looked like a table. When you need to add additional records, you can use the same techniques.

In Module 1, you used a simple form to view records. You can also use a **split form**, a form that allows you to simultaneously view both simple form and datasheet views of the data. You can use either portion of a split form to add or update records. To add new records, change existing records, or delete records, you use the same techniques you used in Datasheet view.

BTW

The Ribbon and Screen Resolution
Access may change how the groups and buttons within the groups appear on the ribbon, depending on the computer or mobile device's screen resolution. Thus, your ribbon may look different from the ones in this book if you are using a screen resolution other than 1366 x 768.

To Create a Split Form

1 UPDATE RECORDS | 2 FILTER RECORDS | 3 CHANGE STRUCTURE | 4 MASS CHANGES | 5 VALIDATION RULES
6 CHANGE APPEARANCE | 7 REFERENTIAL INTEGRITY | 8 ORDER RECORDS

The following steps create a split form. **Why?** *With a split form, you have the advantage of seeing a single record in a form, while simultaneously viewing several records in a datasheet.*

①

- Run Access and open the database named PrattLast Associates from your hard disk, OneDrive, or other storage location.

- Open the Navigation Pane if it is currently closed.

- If necessary, click the Account table in the Navigation Pane to select it.

- Click Create on the ribbon to display the Create tab.

- Click the More Forms button (Create tab | Forms group) to display the More Forms menu (Figure 3–2).

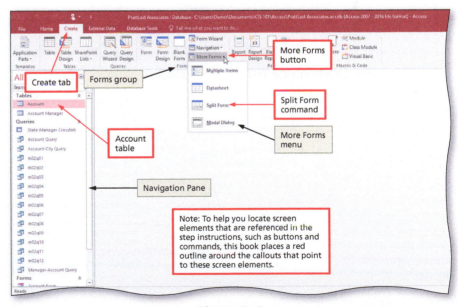

Figure 3–2

2

- Click Split Form to create a split form based on the Account table.

- Close the Navigation Pane (Figure 3–3).

Q&A Is the form automatically saved?
No. You will take specific actions later to save the form.

Q&A A field list appeared when I created the form. What should I do?
Click the 'Add Existing Fields' button (Design tab | Tools group) to remove the field list.

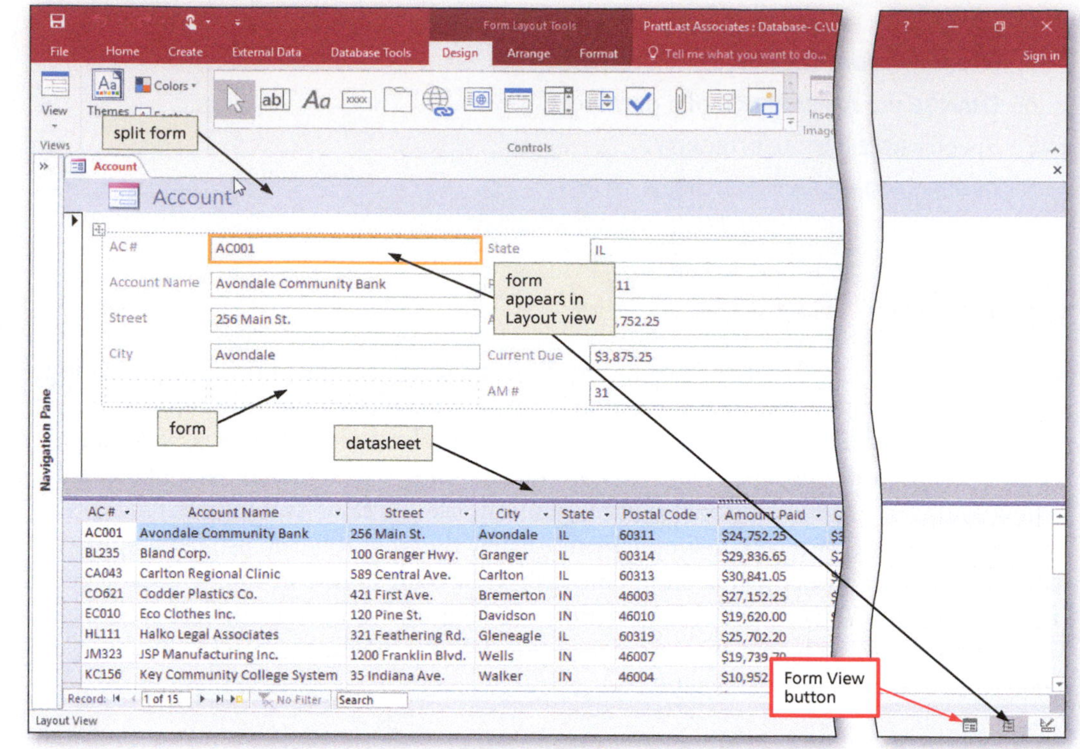

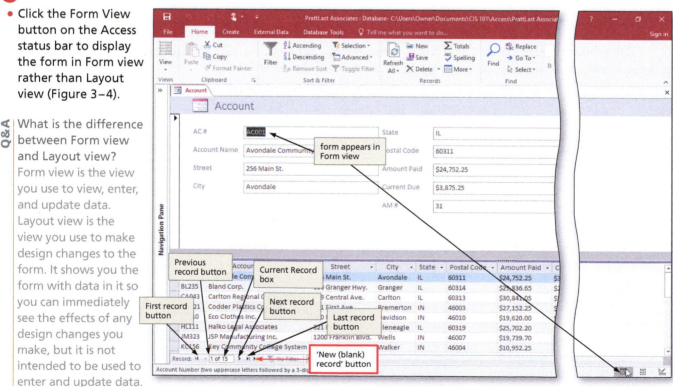

Figure 3–3

3

- Click the Form View button on the Access status bar to display the form in Form view rather than Layout view (Figure 3–4).

Q&A What is the difference between Form view and Layout view?
Form view is the view you use to view, enter, and update data. Layout view is the view you use to make design changes to the form. It shows you the form with data in it so you can immediately see the effects of any design changes you make, but it is not intended to be used to enter and update data.

Figure 3–4

🔎 **Experiment**

- Click the various Navigation buttons (First record, Next record, Previous record, Last record, and 'New (blank) record') to see each button's effect. Click the Current Record box, change the record number, and press the ENTER key to see how to move to a specific record.

4

- Click the Save button on the Quick Access Toolbar to display the Save As dialog box.

- Type **Account Split Form** as the form name (Figure 3–5).

5

- Click the OK button (Save As dialog box) to save the form.

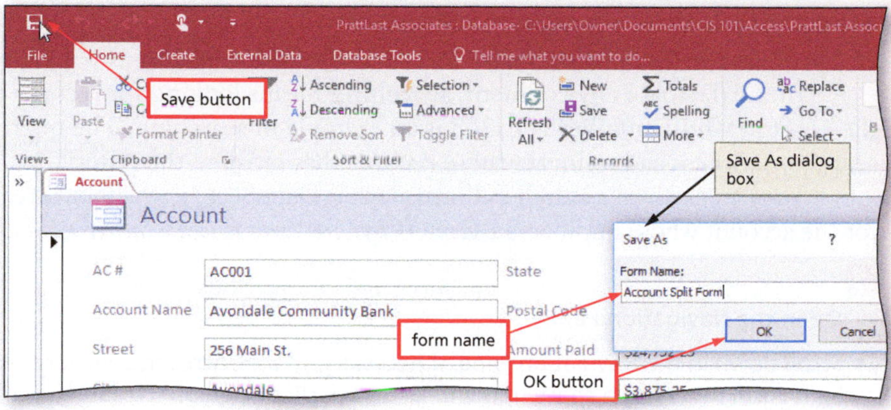

Figure 3–5

Other Ways

1. Right-click tab for form, click Form View on shortcut menu

---

To Use a Form to Add Records

1 UPDATE RECORDS | 2 FILTER RECORDS | 3 CHANGE STRUCTURE | 4 MASS CHANGES | 5 VALIDATION RULES
6 CHANGE APPEARANCE | 7 REFERENTIAL INTEGRITY | 8 ORDER RECORDS

Once a form or split form is open in Form view, you can add records using the same techniques you used to add records in Datasheet view. In a split form, the changes you make on the form are automatically made on the datasheet. You do not need to take any special action. The following steps use the split form that you just created to add records. **Why?** *With a split form, as you add a record, you can immediately see the effect of the addition on the datasheet.*

1

- Click the 'New (blank) record' button on the Navigation bar to enter a new record, and then type the data for the new record, as shown in Figure 3–6. Press the TAB key after typing the data in each field, except after typing the data for the final field (Account Manager Number).

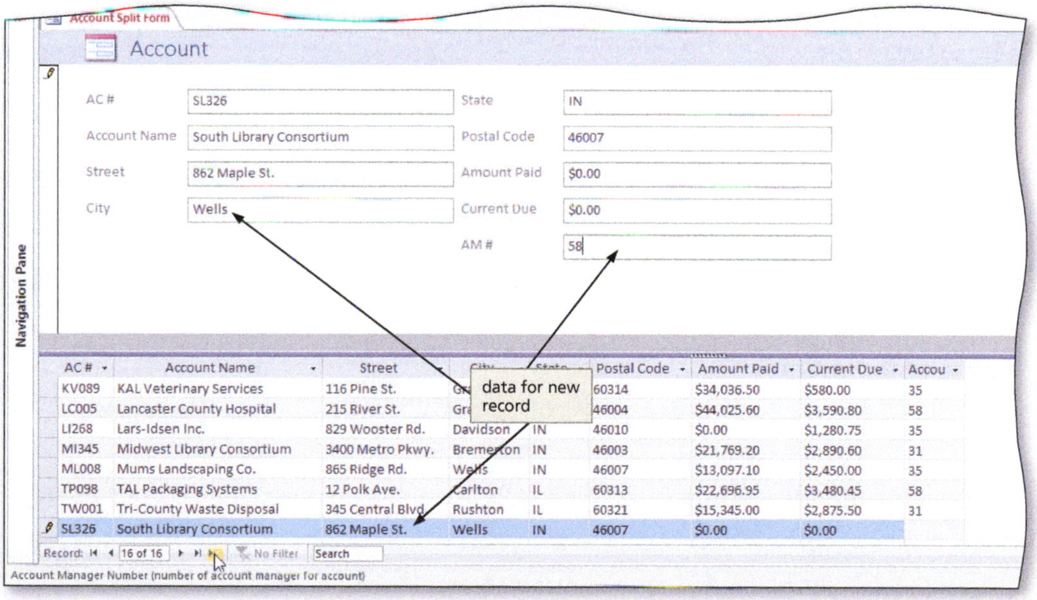

Figure 3–6

2

- Press the TAB key to complete the entry of the record.

- Close the form.

Other Ways

1. Click New button (Home tab | Records group)   2. Press CTRL+PLUS SIGN (+)

To Search for a Record

1 UPDATE RECORDS | 2 FILTER RECORDS | 3 CHANGE STRUCTURE | 4 MASS CHANGES | 5 VALIDATION RULES
6 CHANGE APPEARANCE | 7 REFERENTIAL INTEGRITY | 8 ORDER RECORDS

In the database environment, **searching** means looking for records that satisfy some criteria. Looking for the account whose number is LI268 is an example of searching. The queries in Module 2 were also examples of searching. Access had to locate those records that satisfied the criteria.

You can perform a search in Form view or Datasheet view without creating a query. The following steps search for the account whose number is LI268. *Why? You want to locate the record quickly so you can update this account's record.*

1

- Open the Navigation Pane.

- Scroll down in the Navigation Pane, if necessary, so that Account Split Form appears on your screen, right-click Account Split Form to display a shortcut menu, and then click Open on the shortcut menu to open the form in Form view.

Q&A
Which command on the shortcut menu gives me Form view? I see both Layout View and Design View, but no option for Form View.
The Open command opens the form in Form view.

- Close the Navigation Pane (Figure 3–7).

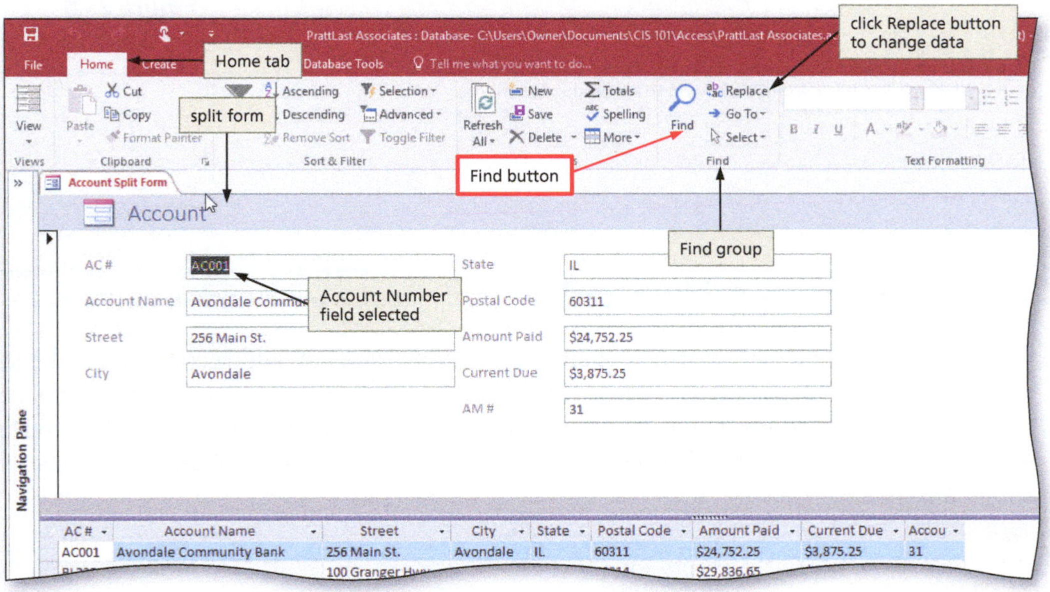

Figure 3–7

2

- Click the Find button (Home tab | Find group) to display the Find and Replace dialog box.

- Type **LI268** in the Find What text box (Find and Replace dialog box).

- Click the Find Next button to find account LI268 and display the record in the form (Figure 3–8).

Q&A
Can I find records using this method in both Datasheet view and Form view?
Yes. You use the same process to find records whether you are viewing the data with a split form, in Datasheet view, or in Form view.

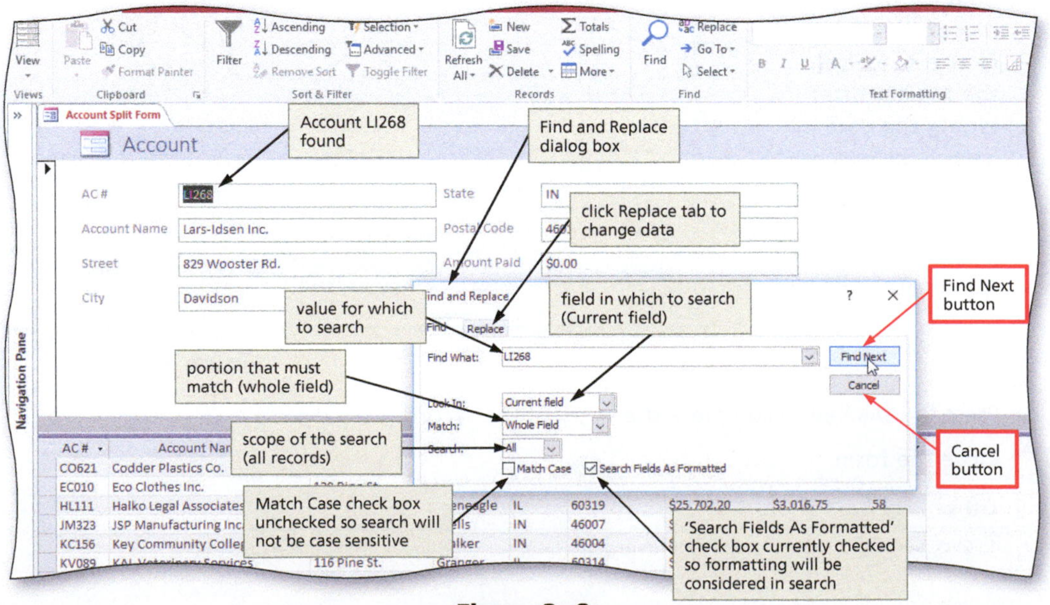

Figure 3–8

3

- Click the Cancel button (Find and Replace dialog box) to remove the dialog box from the screen.

Q&A

Why does the button in the dialog box read, Find Next, rather than simply Find?

In some cases, after locating a record that satisfies a criterion, you might need to find the next record that satisfies the same criterion. For example, if you just found the first account whose account manager number is 31, you might then want to find the second such account, then the third, and so on. To do so, click the Find Next button. You will not need to retype the value each time.

Other Ways

1. Press CTRL+F

CONSIDER THIS

Can you replace one value with another using the Find and Replace dialog box?

Yes. Either click the Replace button (Home tab | Find group) or click the Replace tab in the Find and Replace dialog box. You can then enter both the value to find and the new value.

To Update the Contents of a Record

1 UPDATE RECORDS | 2 FILTER RECORDS | 3 CHANGE STRUCTURE | 4 MASS CHANGES | 5 VALIDATION RULES
6 CHANGE APPEARANCE | 7 REFERENTIAL INTEGRITY | 8 ORDER RECORDS

The following step uses Form view to change the name of account LI268 from Lars-Idsen Inc. to Lars-Idsen-Fleming Inc. **Why?** *PrattLast determined that this account's name was incorrect and must be changed.* After locating the record to be changed, select the field to be changed by clicking the field. You can also press the TAB key repeatedly until the desired field is selected. Then make the appropriate changes. (Clicking the field automatically produces an insertion point. If you use the TAB key, you will need to press the F2 key to produce an insertion point.)

1

- Click in the Account Name field in the form for account LI268 immediately to the right of the n in Idsen.

- Type a hyphen (-) and then type **Fleming** after Idsen.

- Press the TAB key to complete the change and move to the next field (Figure 3–9).

Q&A

Could I have changed the contents of the field in the datasheet portion of the split form?

Yes. You first need to ensure the record to be changed appears in the datasheet. You then can change the value just as in the form.

Q&A

Do I need to save my change?

No. Once you move to another record or close this form, the change to the name will become permanent.

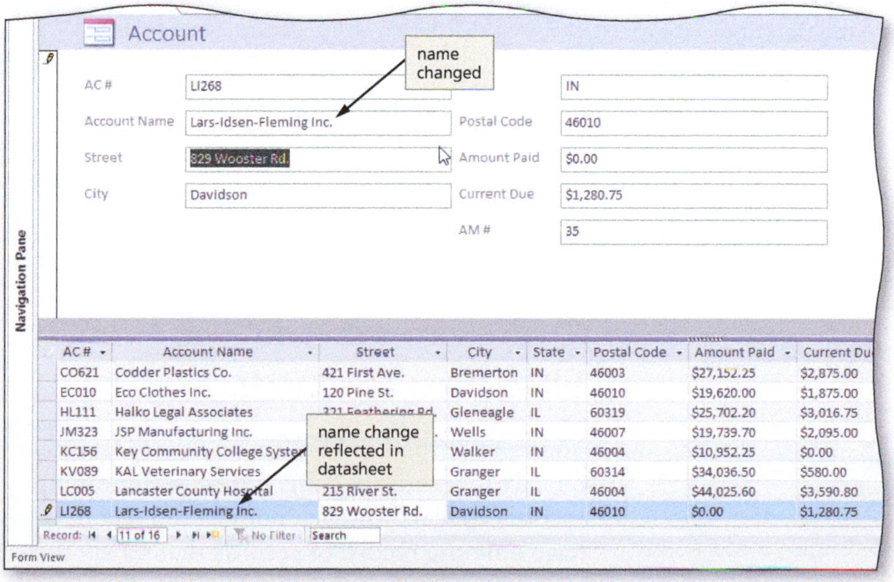

Figure 3–9

To Delete a Record

When records are no longer needed, you should delete the records (remove them) from the table. The following steps delete account JM323. *Why? Account JM323 is no longer served by PrattLast Associates and its final payment has been received, so the record can be deleted.*

1

- With the Account Split Form open, click the record selector in the datasheet for account JM323 to select the record (Figure 3–10).

Q&A That technique works in the datasheet portion. How do I select the record in the form portion?
With the desired record appearing in the form, click the record selector (the triangle in front of the record) to select the entire record.

Q&A What do I do if the record I want to delete does not appear on the screen?
First search for the record you want to delete using the Find and Replace dialog box.

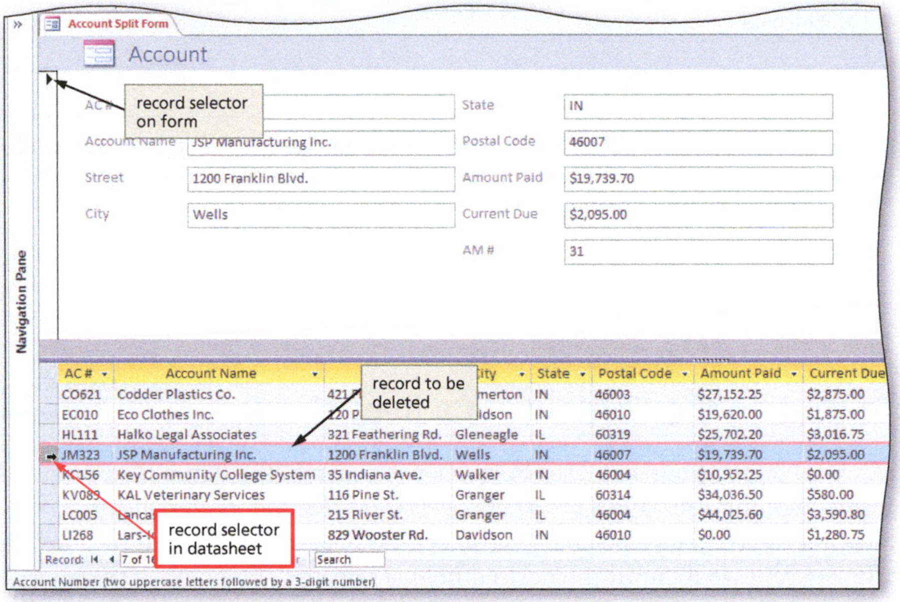

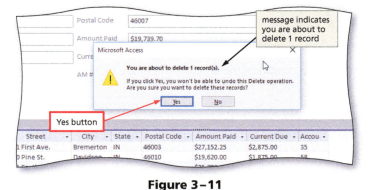

Figure 3–10

2

- Press the DELETE key to delete the record (Figure 3–11).

3

- Click the Yes button to complete the deletion.
- Close the Account Split Form.

Figure 3–11

Other Ways

1. Click Delete arrow (Home tab | Records group), click Delete Record on Delete menu

BTW

Touch Screen Differences
The Office and Windows interfaces may vary if you are using a touch screen. For this reason, you might notice that the function or appearance of your touch screen differs slightly from this module's presentation.

Filtering Records

You can use the Find button in either Datasheet view or Form view to locate a record quickly that satisfies some criterion (for example, the account number is LI268). All records appear, however, not just the record or records that satisfy the criterion. To have only the record or records that satisfy the criterion appear, use a **filter**. Four types of filters are available: Filter By Selection, Common Filters, Filter By Form, and Advanced Filter/Sort. You can use a filter in either Datasheet view or Form view.

To Use Filter By Selection

1 UPDATE RECORDS | **2 FILTER RECORDS** | 3 CHANGE STRUCTURE | 4 MASS CHANGES | 5 VALIDATION RULES
6 CHANGE APPEARANCE | 7 REFERENTIAL INTEGRITY | 8 ORDER RECORDS

To use Filter By Selection, you give Access an example of the data you want by selecting the data within the table. You then choose the option you want on the Selection menu. The following steps use Filter By Selection in Datasheet view to display only the records for accounts in Granger. **Why?** *Filter by Selection is appropriate for displaying these records and is the simplest type of filter.*

1

- Open the Navigation Pane.

- Open the Account table, and close the Navigation Pane.

- Click the City field on the second record to specify Granger as the city (Figure 3–12).

Q&A
Could I have selected the City field on another record where the city is also Granger to select the same city?
Yes. It does not matter which record you select as long as the city is Granger.

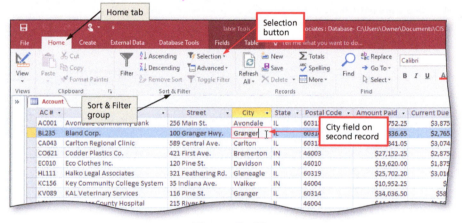

Figure 3–12

2

- Click the Selection button (Home tab | Sort & Filter group) to display the Selection menu (Figure 3–13).

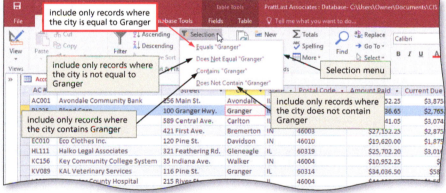

Figure 3–13

3

- Click Equals "Granger" to select only those accounts whose city is Granger (Figure 3–14).

Q&A
Can I also filter in Form view?
Yes. Filtering works the same whether you are viewing the data with a split form, in Datasheet view, or in Form view.

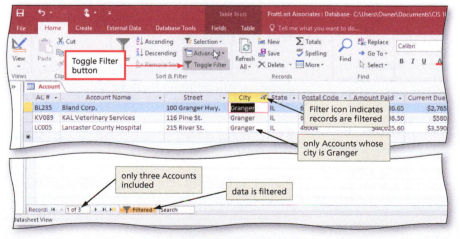

Figure 3–14

To Toggle a Filter

1 UPDATE RECORDS | **2 FILTER RECORDS** | 3 CHANGE STRUCTURE | 4 MASS CHANGES | 5 VALIDATION RULES
6 CHANGE APPEARANCE | 7 REFERENTIAL INTEGRITY | 8 ORDER RECORDS

The Toggle Filter button toggles between filtered and unfiltered displays of the records in the table. That is, if only filtered records currently appear, clicking the Toggle Filter button will redisplay all records. If all records are currently displayed and there is a filter that is in effect, clicking the Toggle Filter button will display only the filtered records. If no filter is active, the Toggle Filter button will be dimmed, so clicking it would have no effect.

The following step toggles the filter. ***Why?*** *PrattLast wants to once again view all the records.*

1

- Click the Toggle Filter button (Home tab | Sort & Filter group) to toggle the filter and redisplay all records (Figure 3–15).

Q&A
Does that action clear the filter?
No. The filter is still in place. If you click the Toggle Filter button a second time, you will again see only the filtered records.

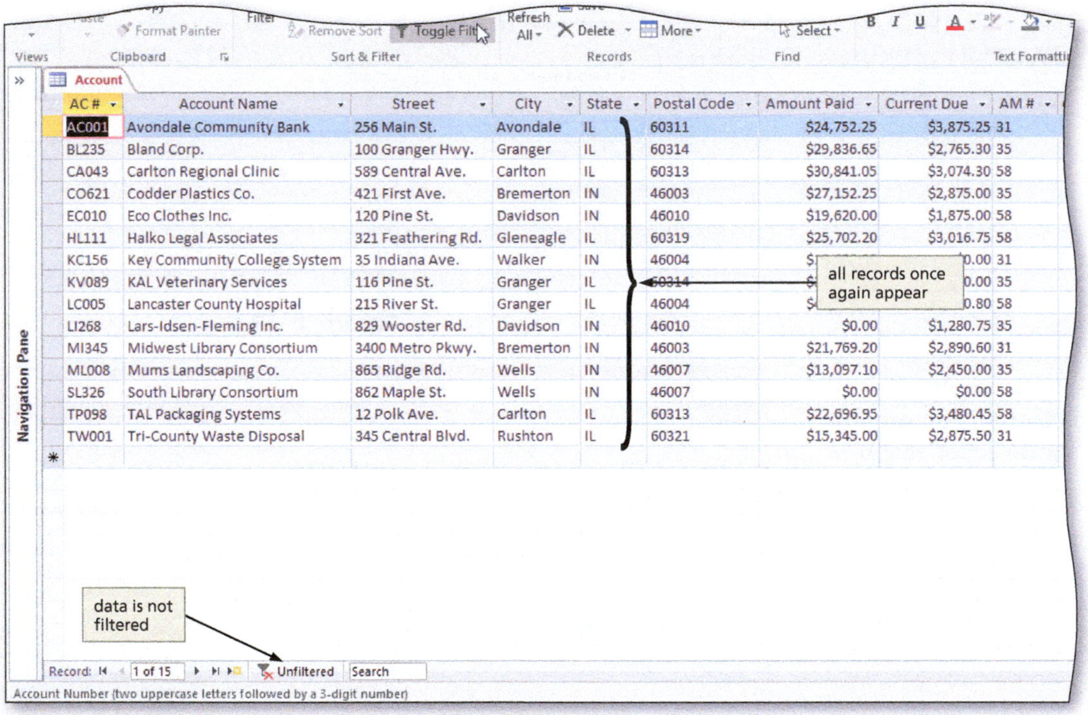

Figure 3–15

BTW
Access Screen Resolution
If you are using a computer or mobile device to step through the project in this module and you want your screens to match the figures in this book, you should change your screen's resolution to 1366 x 768. For information about how to change a computer's resolution, refer to the Office and Windows module at the beginning of this book.

To Clear a Filter

Once you have finished using a filter, you can clear (remove) the filter. After doing so, you no longer will be able to use the filter by clicking the Toggle Filter button. The following steps clear the filter.

1. Click the Advanced button (Home tab | Sort & Filter group) to display the Advanced menu.
2. Click 'Clear All Filters' on the Advanced menu.

To Use a Common Filter

1 UPDATE RECORDS | **2 FILTER RECORDS** | 3 CHANGE STRUCTURE | 4 MASS CHANGES | 5 VALIDATION RULES
6 CHANGE APPEARANCE | 7 REFERENTIAL INTEGRITY | 8 ORDER RECORDS

If you have determined you want to include those accounts whose city begins with G, Filter By Selection would not be appropriate. ***Why?*** *None of the options within Filter by Selection would support this type of criterion.* You can filter individual fields by clicking the arrow to the right of the field name and using one of the **common filters** that are available for the field. Access includes a collection of filters that perform common filtering tasks; you can modify a common filter by customizing it for the specific field. The following steps customize a common filter to include only those accounts whose city begins with G.

1

- Click the City arrow to display the common filter menu.
- Point to the Text Filters command to display the custom text filters (Figure 3–16).

Q&A I selected the City field and then clicked the Filter button on the Home tab | Sort & Filter group. My screen looks the same. Is this right?
Yes. That is another way to display the common filter menu.

Q&A If I wanted certain cities included, could I use the check boxes?
Yes. Be sure the cities you want are the only ones checked.

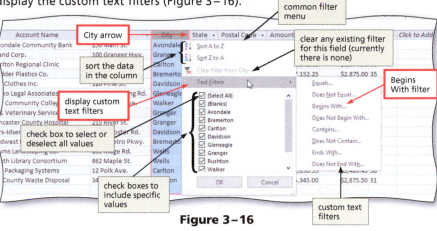

Figure 3–16

2

- Click Begins With to display the Custom Filter dialog box.
- Type G as the 'City begins with' value (Figure 3–17).

Experiment

- Try other options in the common filter menu to see their effects. When done, once again select those accounts whose city begins with G.

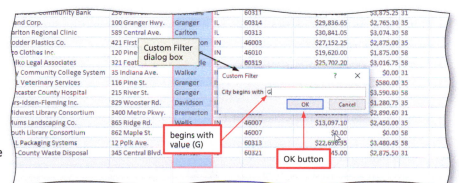

Figure 3–17

3

- Click the OK button to filter the records (Figure 3–18).

Q&A Can I use the same technique in Form view?
In Form view, you would need to click the field and then click the Filter button to display the Common Filter menu. The rest of the process would be the same.

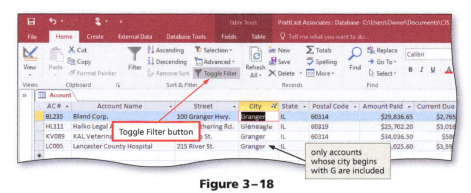

Figure 3–18

4

- Click the Toggle Filter button (Home tab | Sort & Filter group) to toggle the filter and redisplay all records.

Other Ways

1. Right-click field, click Text Filters on shortcut menu

To Use Filter By Form

Filter By Selection and the common filters method you just used are quick and easy ways to filter by the value in a single field. For filters that involve multiple fields, however, these methods are not appropriate, so you would use Filter By Form. **Why?** *Filter By Form allows you to filter based on multiple fields and criteria.* For example, Filter By Form would allow you to find only those accounts whose current due amounts are less than $2,000.00 and whose account manager number is 35. The following steps use Filter By Form to restrict the records that appear.

1
- Click the Advanced button (Home tab | Sort & Filter group) to display the Advanced menu (Figure 3–19).

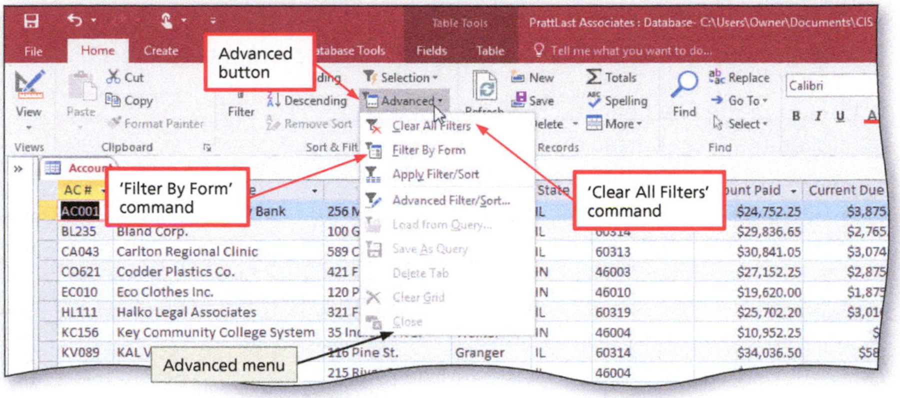

Figure 3–19

2
- Click 'Clear All Filters' on the Advanced menu to clear the existing filter.
- Click the Advanced button again to display the Advanced menu a second time.
- Click 'Filter By Form' on the Advanced menu.
- Click the blank row in the Current Due field, and then type `<2000` to enter a criterion for the Current Due field.
- Click the Account Manager Number (AM #) field, click the arrow that appears, and then click 35 (Figure 3–20).

Q&A Could I have clicked the arrow in the Current Due field and then made a selection rather than typing a criterion?
No. Because your criterion involves something other than equality, you need to type the criterion rather than selecting from a list.

Q&A Is there any difference in the process if I am viewing a table in Form view rather than in Datasheet view?
In Form view, you will make your entries in a form rather than a datasheet. Otherwise, the process is the same.

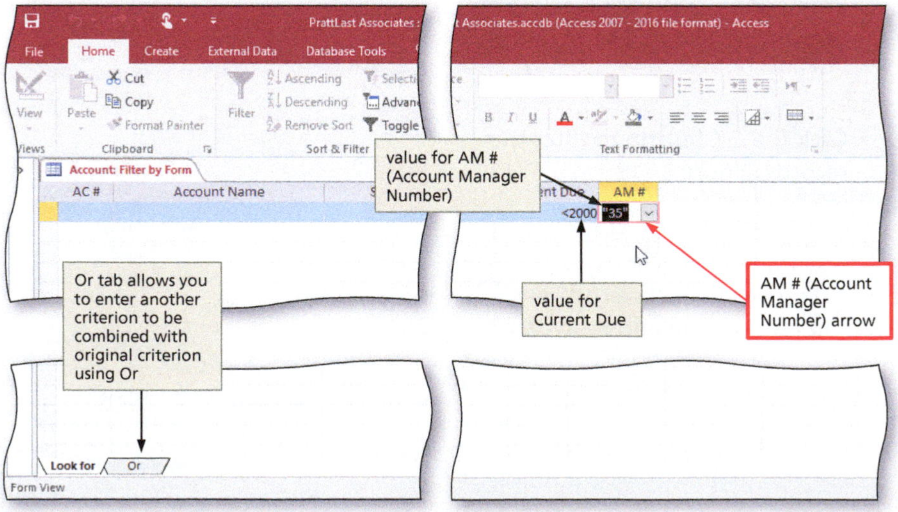

Figure 3–20

3

- Click the Toggle Filter button (Home tab | Sort & Filter group) to apply the filter (Figure 3–21).

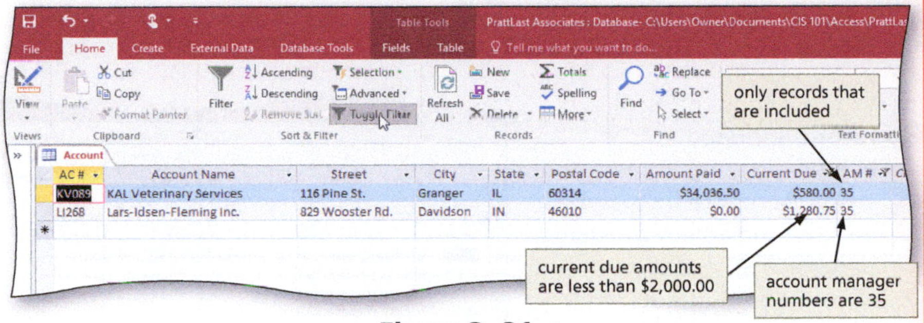

Experiment

- Select 'Filter by Form' again and enter different criteria. In each case, toggle the filter to see the effect of your selection. When done, once again select those accounts whose Current Due amounts are less than (<) 2000 and whose account manager number is 35.

Figure 3–21

Other Ways

1. Click the Advanced button (Home tab | Sort & Filter group), click Apply Filter/Sort on Advanced menu

To Use Advanced Filter/Sort

1 UPDATE RECORDS | **2 FILTER RECORDS** | 3 CHANGE STRUCTURE | 4 MASS CHANGES | 5 VALIDATION RULES
6 CHANGE APPEARANCE | 7 REFERENTIAL INTEGRITY | 8 ORDER RECORDS

In some cases, your criteria will be too complex even for Filter By Form. You might decide you want to include any account whose current due amounts are greater than $3,000 and whose account manager number is 58. Additionally, you might want to include any account whose current due amount is $0, no matter who the account's manager is. Further, you might want to have the results sorted by account name. The following steps use Advanced Filter/Sort to accomplish this task. *Why? Advanced Filter/Sort supports complex criteria as well as the ability to sort the results.*

1

- Click the Advanced button (Home tab | Sort & Filter group) to display the Advanced menu, and then click 'Clear All Filters' on the Advanced menu to clear the existing filter.

- Click the Advanced button to display the Advanced menu a second time.

- Click 'Advanced Filter/Sort' on the Advanced menu.

- Expand the size of the field list so all the fields in the Account table appear.

- Add the Account Name field and select Ascending as the sort order to specify the order in which the filtered records will appear.

- Include the Account Manager Number field and enter **58** as the criterion.

- Include the Current Due field and enter **>3000** as the criterion in the Criteria row and **0** as the criterion in the or row (Figure 3–22).

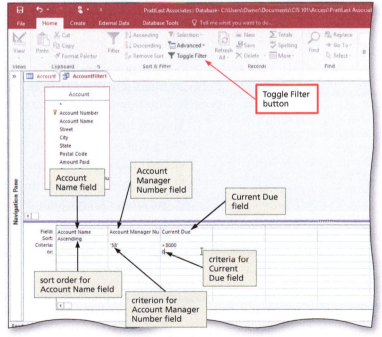

Figure 3–22

2

- Click the Toggle Filter button (Home tab | Sort & Filter group) to toggle the filter so that only records that satisfy the criteria will appear (Figure 3–23).

Q&A Why are those particular records included?
The first, second, fourth, and sixth records are included because the account manager number is 58 and the current due amount is greater than $3,000. The other records are included because the current due amount is $0.00.

Experiment

- Select 'Advanced Filter/Sort' again and enter different sorting options and criteria. In each case, toggle the filter to see the effect of your selection. When done, change back to the sorting options and criteria you entered in Step 1.

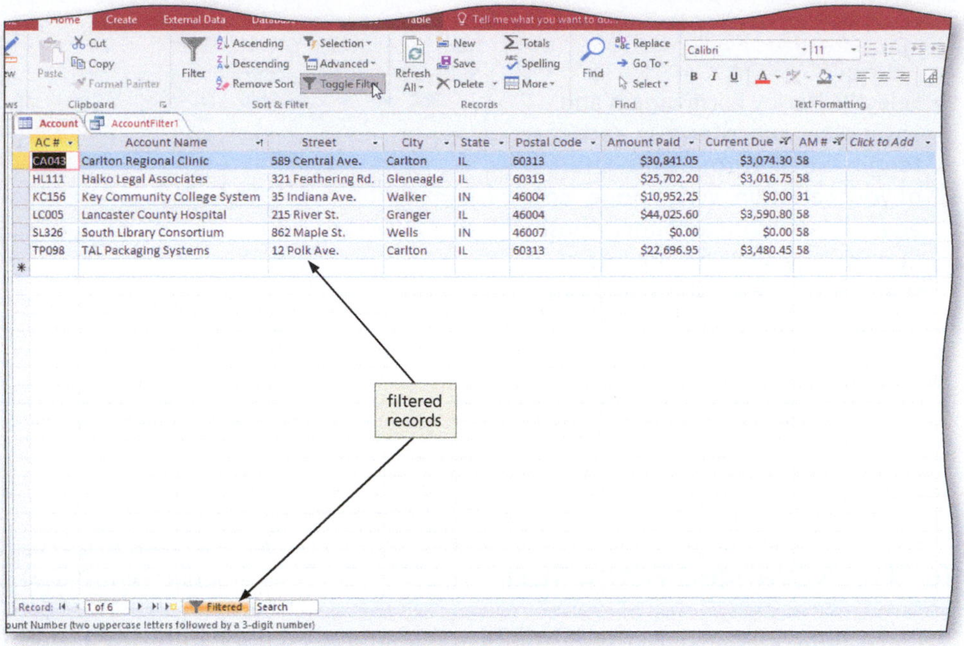

Figure 3–23

3

- Close the Account table. When asked if you want to save your changes, click the No button.

Q&A Should I not have cleared all filters before closing the table?
If you are closing a table and not saving the changes, it is not necessary to clear the filter. No filter will be active when you next open the table.

Filters and Queries

Now that you are familiar with how filters work, you might notice similarities between filters and queries. Both objects are used to locate data that meets specific criteria. Filters and queries are related in three ways.

1. You can apply a filter to the results of a query just as you can apply a filter to a table.
2. Once you create a filter using Advanced Filter/Sort, you can save the filter settings as a query by using the 'Save as Query' command on the Advanced menu.
3. You can restore filter settings that you previously saved in a query by using the 'Load from Query' command on the Advanced menu.

BTW
Using Wildcards in Filters
Both the question mark(?) and the asterisk (*) wildcards can be used in filters created using Advanced Filter/Sort.

CONSIDER THIS

How do you determine whether to use a query or a filter?
The following guidelines apply to this decision.

- If you think that you will frequently want to display records that satisfy this exact criterion, you should consider creating a query whose results only contain the records that satisfy the criterion. To display those records in the future, simply open the query.
- If you are viewing data in a datasheet or form and decide you want to restrict the records to be included, it is easier to create a filter than a query. You can create and use the filter while you are viewing the data.
- If you have created a filter that you would like to be able to use again, you can save the filter as a query.

Once you have decided to use a filter, how do you determine which type of filter to use?

- If your criterion for filtering is that the value in a particular field matches or does not match a certain specific value, you can use Filter By Selection.

- If your criterion only involves a single field but is more complex (for example, the criterion specifies that the value in the field begins with a certain collection of letters) you can use a common filter.

- If your criterion involves more than one field, use Filter By Form.

- If your criterion involves more than a single And or Or, or if it involves sorting, you will probably find it simpler to use Advanced Filter/Sort.

Break Point: If you wish to take a break, this is a good place to do so. You can quit Access now. To resume at a later time, run Access, open the database called PrattLast Associates, and continue following the steps from this location forward.

Changing the Database Structure

When you initially create a database, you define its **structure**; that is, you assign names and types to all the fields. In many cases, the structure you first define will not continue to be appropriate as you use the database.

Perhaps a field currently in the table is no longer necessary. If no one ever uses a particular field, it is not needed in the table. Because it is occupying space and serving no useful purpose, you should remove it from the table. You would also need to delete the field from any forms, reports, or queries that include it.

More commonly, an organization will find that it needs to add data that was not anticipated at the time the database was first designed. The organization's own requirements may have changed. In addition, outside regulations that the organization must satisfy may change as well. Either case requires the addition of fields to an existing table.

Although you can make some changes to the database structure in Datasheet view, it is usually easier and better to make these changes in Design view.

To Delete a Field

If a field in one of your tables is no longer needed, you should delete the field; for example, it may serve no useful purpose, or it may have been included by mistake. To delete a field, you would use the following steps.

1. Open the table in Design view.
2. Click the row selector for the field to be deleted.
3. Press the DELETE key.
4. When Access displays the dialog box requesting confirmation that you want to delete the field, click the Yes button.

To Move a Field

If you decide you would rather have a field in one of your tables in a different position in the table, you can move it. To move a field, you would use the following steps.

1. Open the table in Design view.
2. Click the row selector for the field to be deleted.
3. Drag the field to the desired position.
4. Release the mouse button to place the field in the new position.

BTW

Using the Find Button
You can use the Find button (Home tab | Find group) to search for records in datasheets, forms, query results, and reports.

BTW

Changing Data Types
It is possible to change the data type for a field that already contains data. Before doing so, you should consider the effect on other database objects, such as forms, queries, and reports. For example, you could convert a Short Text field to a Long Text field if you find that you do not have enough space to store the data that you need. You also could convert a Number field to a Currency field or vice versa.

To Add a New Field

1 UPDATE RECORDS | 2 FILTER RECORDS | **3 CHANGE STRUCTURE** | 4 MASS CHANGES | 5 VALIDATION RULES
6 CHANGE APPEARANCE | 7 REFERENTIAL INTEGRITY | 8 ORDER RECORDS

You can add fields to a table in a database. The following steps add the Account Type field to the Account table immediately after the Postal Code field. **Why?** *PrattLast Associates has decided that it needs to categorize its accounts by adding an additional field, Account Type. The possible values for Account Type are SER (which indicates the account is a service organization), NON (which indicates the account is a nonprofit), or IND (which indicates the account is an industrial/manufacturing company).*

1

- If necessary, open the Navigation Pane, open the Account table in Design view, and then close the Navigation Pane.

- Right-click the row selector for the Amount Paid field, and then click Insert Rows on the shortcut menu to insert a blank row above the selected field (Figure 3–24).

2

- Click the Field Name column for the new field to produce an insertion point.

- Type **Account Type** as the field name and then press the TAB key.

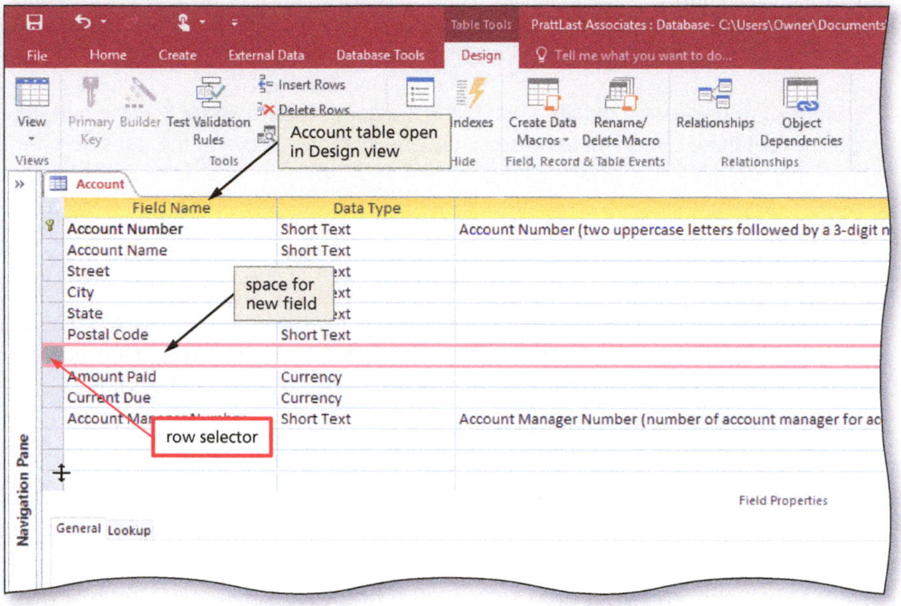

Figure 3–24

Other Ways

1. Click Insert Rows button (Table Tools Design tab | Tools group)

To Create a Lookup Field

1 UPDATE RECORDS | 2 FILTER RECORDS | **3 CHANGE STRUCTURE** | 4 MASS CHANGES | 5 VALIDATION RULES
6 CHANGE APPEARANCE | 7 REFERENTIAL INTEGRITY | 8 ORDER RECORDS

A **lookup field** allows the user to select from a list of values when updating the contents of the field. The following steps make the Account Type field a lookup field. **Why?** *The Account Type field has only three possible values, making it an appropriate lookup field.*

1

- If necessary, click the Data Type column for the Account Type field, and then click the Data Type arrow to display the menu of available data types (Figure 3–25).

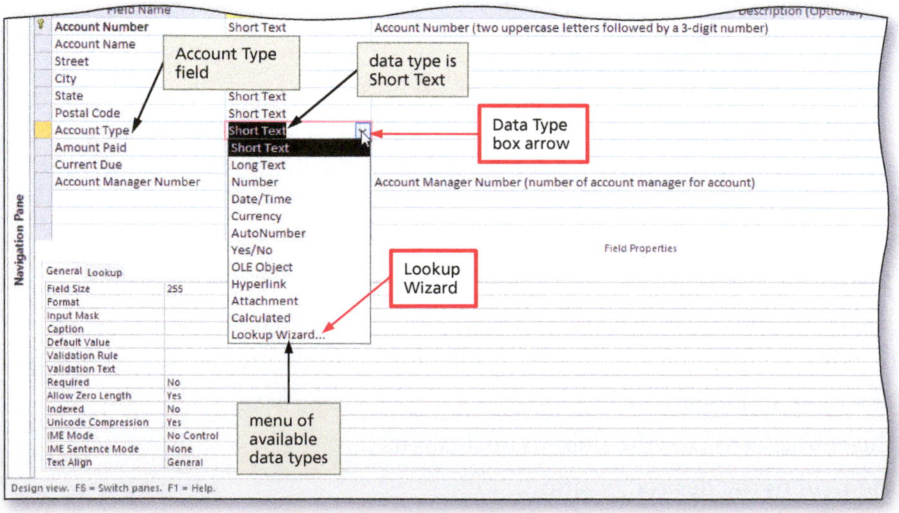

Figure 3–25

2

- Click Lookup Wizard, and then click the 'I will type in the values that I want.' option button (Lookup Wizard dialog box) to indicate that you will type in the values (Figure 3–26).

Q&A When would I use the other option button?
You would use the other option button if the data to be entered in this field were found in another table or query.

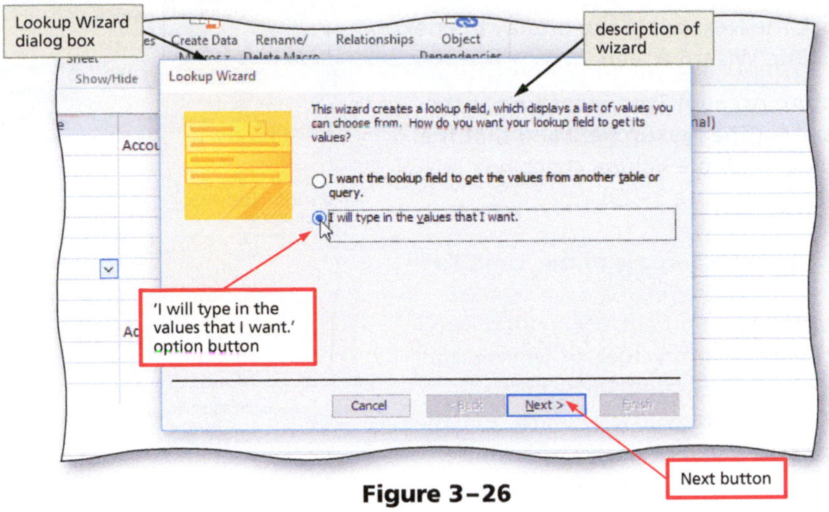

Lookup Wizard dialog box

description of wizard

Lookup Wizard

This wizard creates a lookup field, which displays a list of values you can choose from. How do you want your lookup field to get its values?

○ I want the lookup field to get the values from another table or query.

● I will type in the values that I want.

'I will type in the values that I want.' option button

Cancel   < Back   Next >   Finish

Next button

Figure 3–26

3

- Click the Next button to display the next Lookup Wizard screen (Figure 3–27).

Q&A Why did I not change the field size for the Account Type field?
You could have changed the field size to 3, but it is not necessary. When you create a lookup field and indicate specific values for the field, you automatically restrict the field size.

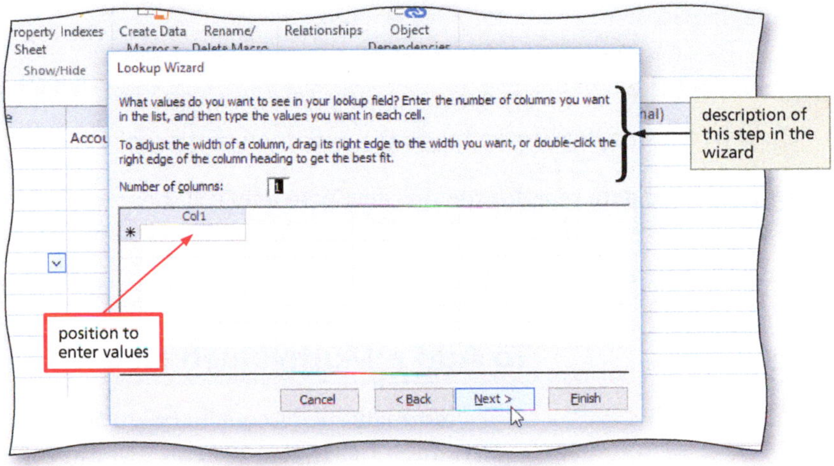

Lookup Wizard

What values do you want to see in your lookup field? Enter the number of columns you want in the list, and then type the values you want in each cell.

To adjust the width of a column, drag its right edge to the width you want, or double-click the right edge of the column heading to get the best fit.

Number of columns: 1

Col1

position to enter values

description of this step in the wizard

Cancel   < Back   Next >   Finish

Figure 3–27

4

- Click the first row of the table (below Col1), and then type **SER** as the value in the first row.

- Press the DOWN ARROW key, and then type **NON** as the value in the second row.

- Press the DOWN ARROW key, and then type **IND** as the value in the third row (Figure 3–28).

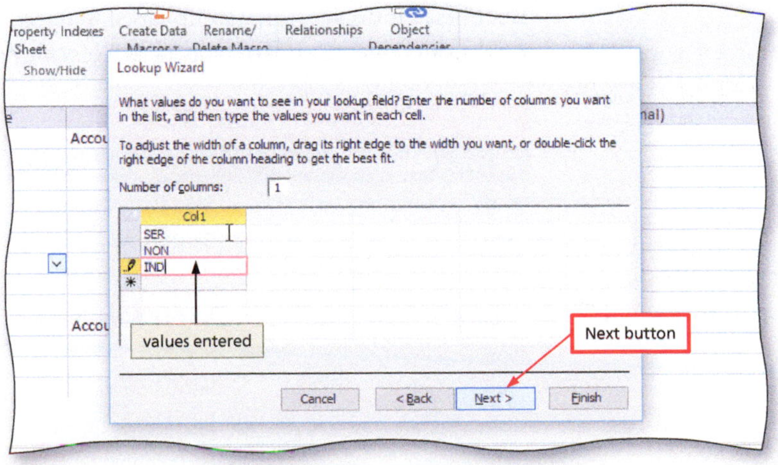

Lookup Wizard

What values do you want to see in your lookup field? Enter the number of columns you want in the list, and then type the values you want in each cell.

To adjust the width of a column, drag its right edge to the width you want, or double-click the right edge of the column heading to get the best fit.

Number of columns: 1

Col1

SER
NON
IND

values entered

Next button

Cancel   < Back   Next >   Finish

Figure 3–28

5

- Click the Next button to display the next Lookup Wizard screen.

- Ensure Account Type is entered as the label for the lookup field and that the 'Allow Multiple Values' check box is NOT checked (Figure 3–29).

Q&A What is the purpose of the 'Limit To List' check box?

With a lookup field, users can select from the list of values, in which case they can only select items in the list. They can also type their entry, in which case they are not necessarily limited to items in the list. If you check the 'Limit To List' check box, users would be limited to items in the list, even if they type their entry. You will accomplish this same restriction later in this module with a validation rule, so you do not need to check this box.

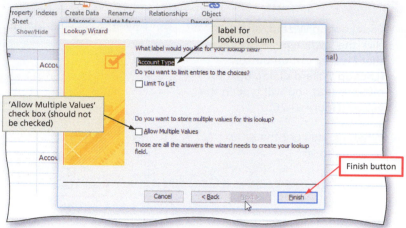

Figure 3–29

6

- Click the Finish button to complete the definition of the lookup field.

Q&A Why does the data type for the Account Type field still show Short Text?

The data type is still Short Text because the values entered in the wizard were entered as text.

To Add a Multivalued Field

BTW
Multivalued Fields
Do not use multivalued fields if you plan to move your data to another relational database management system, such as SQL Server at a later date. SQL Server and other relational DMBSs do not support multivalued fields.

Normally, fields contain only a single value. In Access, it is possible to have **multivalued fields**, that is, fields that can contain more than one value. PrattLast Associates wants to use such a field to store the abbreviations of the various services its accounts need (see Table 3–1 for the service abbreviations and descriptions). Unlike the Account Type, where each account had only one type, accounts can require multiple services. One account might need Bck, Ben, Com, Pay, and Rsk (Background Checks, Benefits Administration, Compliance, Payroll, and Risk Management). Another account might only need Rec, Trn, and Wrk (Recruiting, Training, and Workman's Compensation).

Table 3–1 Service Abbreviations and Descriptions	
Service Abbreviation	**Description**
Bck	Background Checks
Ben	Benefits Administration
Com	Compliance (Regulatory)
Mgt	HR Management
Pay	Payroll
Rec	Recruiting
Rsk	Risk Management
Tch	HR Technology
Trn	Training
Wrk	Workman's Compensation

Creating a multivalued field uses the same process as creating a lookup field, with the exception that you check the 'Allow Multiple Values' check box. The following steps create a multivalued field.

1 Right-click the row selector for the Amount Paid field, and then click Insert Rows on the shortcut menu to insert a blank row.

2 Click the Field Name column for the new field, type **Services Needed** as the field name, and then press the TAB key.

3 Click the Data Type arrow to display the menu of available data types for the Services Needed field, and then click Lookup Wizard in the menu of available data types to start the Lookup Wizard.

4 Click the 'I will type in the values that I want.' option button to indicate that you will type in the values.

5 Click the Next button to display the next Lookup Wizard screen.

6 Click the first row of the table (below Col1), and then type **Bck** as the value in the first row.

7 Enter the remaining values from the first column in Table 3–1. Before typing each value, press the DOWN ARROW key to move to a new row.

8 Click the Next button to display the next Lookup Wizard screen.

9 Ensure that Services Needed is entered as the label for the lookup field.

10 Click the 'Allow Multiple Values' check box to allow the user to enter multiple values.

11 Click the Finish button to complete the definition of the Lookup Wizard field.

TO MODIFY SINGLE VALUED OR MULTIVALUED LOOKUP FIELDS

At some point you might want to change the list of choices in a lookup field. If you need to modify a single value or multivalued lookup field, you would use the following steps.

1. Open the table in Design view and select the field to be modified.
2. Click the Lookup tab in the Field Properties pane.
3. Change the list in the Row Source property to the desired list of values.

To Add a Calculated Field

1 UPDATE RECORDS | 2 FILTER RECORDS | **3 CHANGE STRUCTURE** | 4 MASS CHANGES | 5 VALIDATION RULES
6 CHANGE APPEARANCE | 7 REFERENTIAL INTEGRITY | 8 ORDER RECORDS

A field that can be computed from other fields is called a **calculated field** or a **computed field**. In Module 2, you created a calculated field in a query that provided total amount data. In Access 2016, it is also possible to include a calculated field in a table. Users will not be able to update this field. *Why? Access will automatically perform the necessary calculation and display the correct value whenever you display or use this field in any way.* The following steps add to the Account table a field that calculates the sum of the Amount Paid and Current Due fields.

1

- Right-click the row selector for the Account Manager Number field, and then click Insert Rows on the shortcut menu to insert a blank row above the selected field.
- Click the Field Name column for the new field.
- Type **Total Amount** as the field name, and then press the TAB key.

BTW

Modifying Table Properties
You can change the properties of a table by opening the table in Design view and then clicking the Property Sheet button. To display the records in a table in an order other than primary key (the default sort order), use the Order By property. For example, to display the Account table automatically in Account Name order, change the Order By property setting to Account.Account Name in the property box, close the property sheet, and save the change to the table design. When you open the Account table in Datasheet view, the records will be sorted in Account Name order.

BTW

Calculated Fields
You can use the Result Type field property to format the calculated field values.

- Click the Data Type arrow to display the menu of available data types (Figure 3–30).

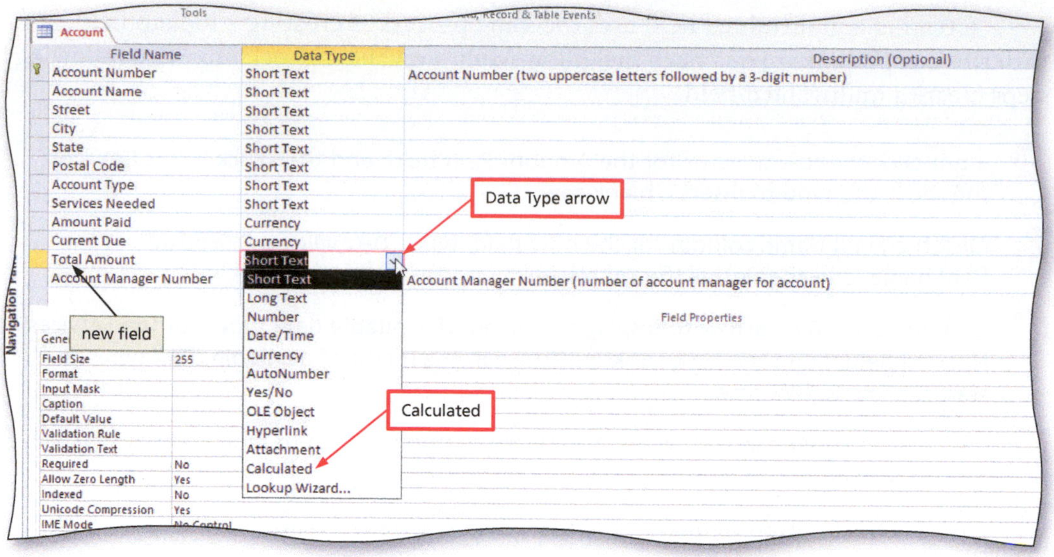

Figure 3–30

②

- Click Calculated to select the Calculated data type and display the Expression Builder dialog box (Figure 3–31).

Q&A I do not have the list of fields in the Expression Categories area. What should I do? Click Account in the Expression Elements area.

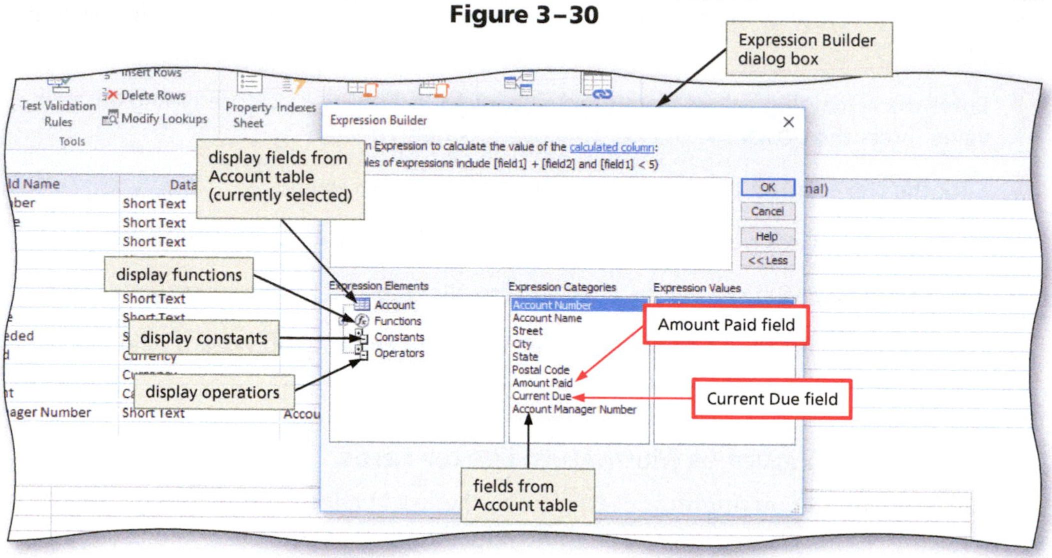

Figure 3–31

③

- Double-click the Amount Paid field in the Expression Categories area (Expression Builder dialog box) to add the field to the expression.

- Type a plus sign (+).

Q&A Could I select the plus sign from a list rather than typing it? Yes. Click Operators in the Expression Elements area to display available operators, and then double-click the plus sign.

- Double-click the Current Due field in the Expression Categories area (Expression Builder dialog box) to add the field to the expression (Figure 3–32).

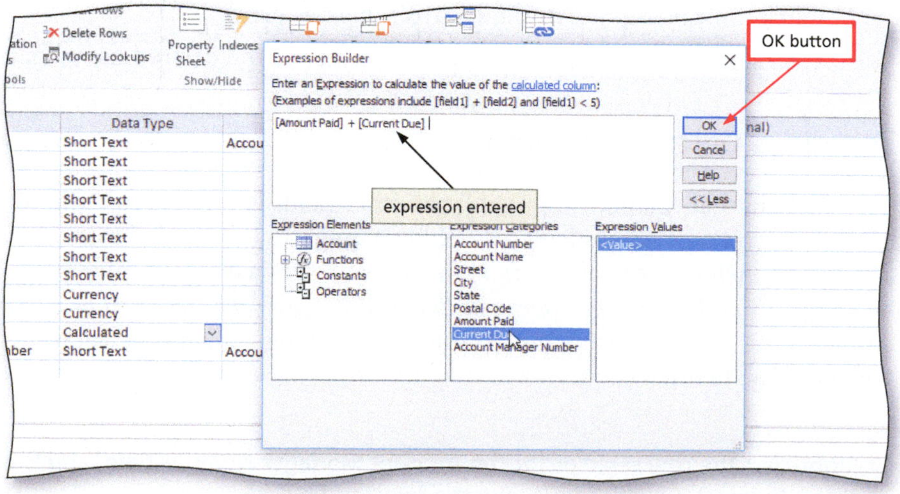

Figure 3–32

4

- Click the OK button (Expression Builder dialog box) to enter the expression in the Expression property of the Total Amount (Figure 3–33).

Q&A Could I have typed the expression in the Expression Builder dialog box rather than selecting the fields from a list?
Yes. You can use whichever technique you find more convenient.

Q&A When I entered a calculated field in a query, I typed the expression in the Zoom dialog box. Could I have used the Expression Builder instead?
Yes. To do so, you would click Build rather than Zoom on the shortcut menu.

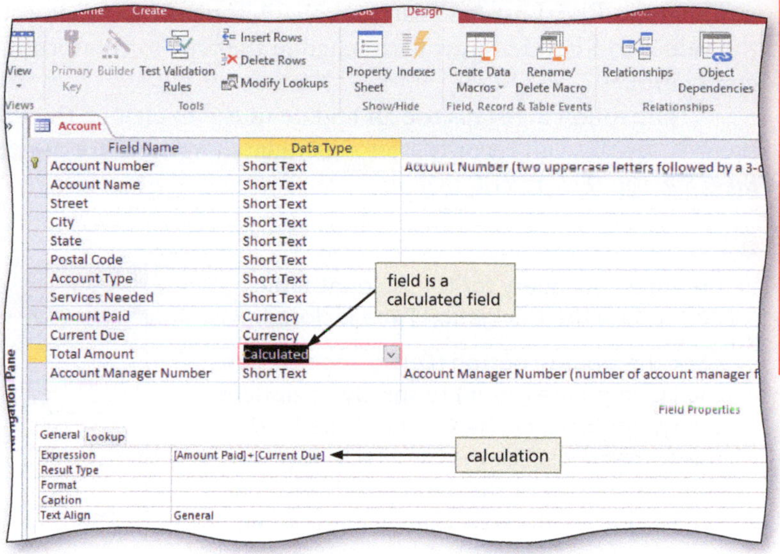

Figure 3–33

To Save the Changes and Close the Table

The following steps save the changes; that is, they save the addition of the new fields and close the table.

1 Click the Save button on the Quick Access Toolbar to save the changes.

2 Close the Account table.

Mass Changes

In some cases, rather than making individual changes to records, you will want to make mass changes. That is, you will want to add, change, or delete many records in a single operation. You can do this with action queries. Unlike the select queries that you created in Module 2, which simply presented data in specific ways, an **action query** adds, deletes, or changes data in a table. An **update query** allows you to make the same change to all records satisfying some criterion. If you omit the criterion, you will make the same changes to all records in the table. A **delete query** allows you to delete all the records satisfying some criterion. You can add the results of a query to an existing table by using an **append query**. You also can add the query results to a new table by using a **make-table query**.

BTW

Database Backup
If you are doing mass changes to a database, be sure to back up the database prior to doing the updates.

To Use an Update Query

1 UPDATE RECORDS | 2 FILTER RECORDS | 3 CHANGE STRUCTURE | 4 MASS CHANGES | 5 VALIDATION RULES
6 CHANGE APPEARANCE | 7 REFERENTIAL INTEGRITY | 8 ORDER RECORDS

The new Account Type field is blank on every record in the Account table. One approach to entering the information for the field would be to step through the entire table, assigning each record its appropriate value. If most of the accounts have the same type, it would be more convenient to use an update query to assign a single value to all accounts and then update the Account Type for those accounts whose type differs. An update query makes the same change to all records satisfying a criterion.

In the PrattLast Associates database, for example, many accounts are type SER. Initially, you can set all the values to SER. Later, you can change the type for nonprofit organizations and industrial/manufacturing companies.

The following steps use an update query to change the value in the Account Type field to SER for all the records. Because all records are to be updated, criteria are not required. *Why? If there is a criterion, the update only takes place on those records that satisfy the criterion. Without a criterion, the update applies to all records.*

1

- Create a new query for the Account table, and ensure the Navigation Pane is closed.

- Click the Update button (Query Tools Design tab | Query Type group) to specify an update query, double-click the Account Type field to select the field, click the Update To row in the first column of the design grid, and then type **SER** as the new value (Figure 3–34).

Q&A If I change my mind and do not want an update query, how can I change the query back to a select query?
Click the Select button (Query Tools Design tab | Query Type group).

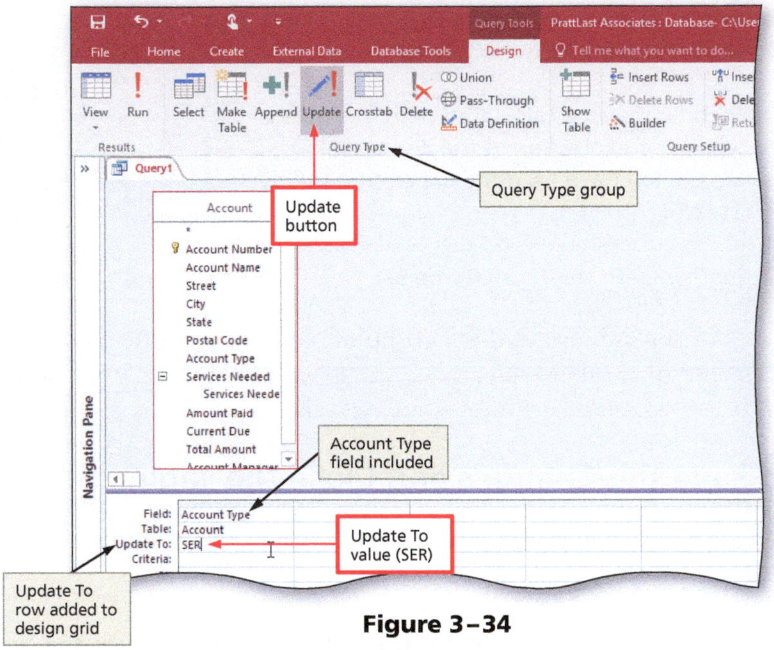

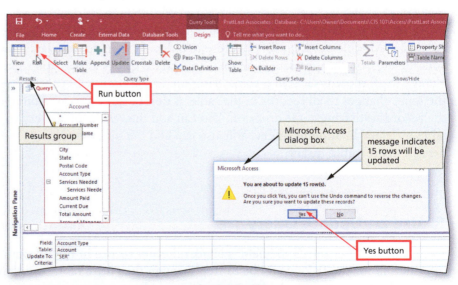

Figure 3–34

2

- Click the Run button (Query Tools Design tab | Results group) to run the query and update the records (Figure 3–35).

Q&A The dialog box did not appear on my screen when I ran the query. What happened?
If the dialog box did not appear, it means that you did not click the Enable Content button when you first opened the database. Close the database, open it again, and enable the content. Then, create and run the query again.

3

- Click the Yes button to make the changes.

Experiment

- Create an update query to change the account type to COM. Enter a criterion to restrict the records to be updated, and then run the query. Open the table to view your changes. When finished, create and run an update query to change the account type to SER on all records.

- Close the query. Because you do not need to use this update query again, do not save the query.

Figure 3–35

Other Ways

1. Right-click any open area in upper pane, point to Query Type on shortcut menu, click Update Query on Query Type submenu

To Use a Delete Query

In some cases, you might need to delete several records at a time. If, for example, PrattLast no longer services accounts in Indiana (IN), the accounts with this value in the State field can be deleted from the PrattLast Associates database. Instead of deleting these accounts individually, which could be very time-consuming in a large database, you can delete them in one operation by using a delete query, which is a query that deletes all the records satisfying the criteria entered in the query. To create a delete query, you would use the following steps.

1. Create a query for the table containing the records to be deleted.
2. In Design view, indicate the fields and criteria that will specify the records to delete.
3. Click the Delete button (Query Tools Design tab | Query Type group).
4. Run the query by clicking the Run button (Query Tools Design tab | Results group).
5. When Access indicates the number of records to be deleted, click the Yes button.

To Use an Append Query

An append query adds a group of records from one table, called the Source table, to the end of another table, called the Destination table. For example, suppose that PrattLast Associates acquires some new accounts; these new accounts are accompanied by a related database. To avoid entering all this information manually, you can append it to the Account table in the PrattLast Associates database using the append query. To create an append query, you would use the following steps.

1. Create a query for the Source table.
2. In Design view, indicate the fields to include, and then enter any necessary criteria.
3. View the query results to be sure you have specified the correct data, and then return to Design view.
4. Click the Append button (Query Tools Design tab | Query Type group).
5. When Access displays the Append dialog box, specify the name of the Destination table and its location. Run the query by clicking the Run button (Query Tools Design tab | Results group).
6. When Access indicates the number of records to be appended, click the OK button.

To Use a Make-Table Query

In some cases, you might want to create a new table that contains only records from an existing table. If so, use a make-table query to add the records to a new table. To create a make-table query, you would use the following steps.

1. Create a query for the Source table.
2. In Design view, indicate the fields to include, and then enter any necessary criteria.
3. View the query results to be sure you have specified the correct data, and then return to Design view.
4. Click the Make Table button (Query Tools Design tab | Query Type group).
5. When Access displays the Make Table dialog box, specify the name of the Destination table and its location. Run the query by clicking the Run button (Query Tools Design tab | Results group).
6. When Access indicates the number of records to be inserted, click the OK button.

Break Point: If you wish to take a break, this is a good place to do so. You can quit Access now. To resume at a later time, run Access, open the database called PrattLast Associates, and continue following the steps from this location forward.

Validation Rules

BTW
Using Wildcards in Validation Rules
You can include wildcards in validation rules. For example, if you enter the expression, like T?, in the validation rule for the State field, the only valid entries for the field will be TN or TX.

You now have created, loaded, queried, and updated a database. Nothing you have done so far, however, restricts users to entering only valid data, that is, data that follows the rules established for data in the database. An example of such a rule would be that account types can only be SER, NON, or IND. To ensure the entry of valid data, you create **validation rules**, or rules that a user must follow when entering the data. When the database contains validation rules, Access prevents users from entering data that does not follow the rules. You can also specify **validation text**, which is the message that appears if a user attempts to violate the validation rule.

Validation rules can indicate a **required field**, a field in which the user *must* enter data; failing to enter data into a required field generates an error. Validation rules can also restrict a user's entry to a certain **range of values**; for example, the values in the Current Due field must be between $0 and $10,000. Alternatively, rules can specify a **default value**, that is, a value that Access will display on the screen in a particular field before the user begins adding a record. To make data entry of account numbers more convenient, you can also have lowercase letters appear automatically as uppercase letters. Finally, validation rules can specify a collection of acceptable values.

To Change a Field Size

BTW
Using the Between Operator in Validation Rules
You can use the BETWEEN operator to specify a range of values. For example, to specify that entries in the Current Due field must be between $0 and $10,000, type BETWEEN 0 and 10000 as the rule.

The Field Size property for text fields represents the maximum number of characters a user can enter in the field. Because the field size for the Account Number field is five, for example, a user would not be able to enter a sixth character in the field. Occasionally, you will find that the field size that seemed appropriate when you first created a table is no longer appropriate. In the Account table, there is a street name that needs to be longer than 20 characters. To allow this name in the table, you need to change the field size for the Street field to a number that is large enough to accommodate the new name. The following step changes the field size for the Street field from 20 to 25.

1 Open the Account table in Design view and close the Navigation Pane.

2 Select the Street field by clicking its row selector.

3 Click the Field Size property to select it, delete the current entry (20), and then type **25** as the new field size.

To Specify a Required Field

1 UPDATE RECORDS | 2 FILTER RECORDS | 3 CHANGE STRUCTURE | 4 MASS CHANGES | **5 VALIDATION RULES**
6 CHANGE APPEARANCE | 7 REFERENTIAL INTEGRITY | 8 ORDER RECORDS

To specify that a field is to be required, change the value for the Required property from No to Yes. The following step specifies that the Account Name field is a required field. *Why? Users will not be able to leave the Account Name field blank when entering or editing records.*

1

- Select the Account Name field by clicking its row selector.
- Click the Required property box in the Field Properties pane, and then click the down arrow that appears.
- Click Yes in the list to make Account Name a required field (Figure 3–36).

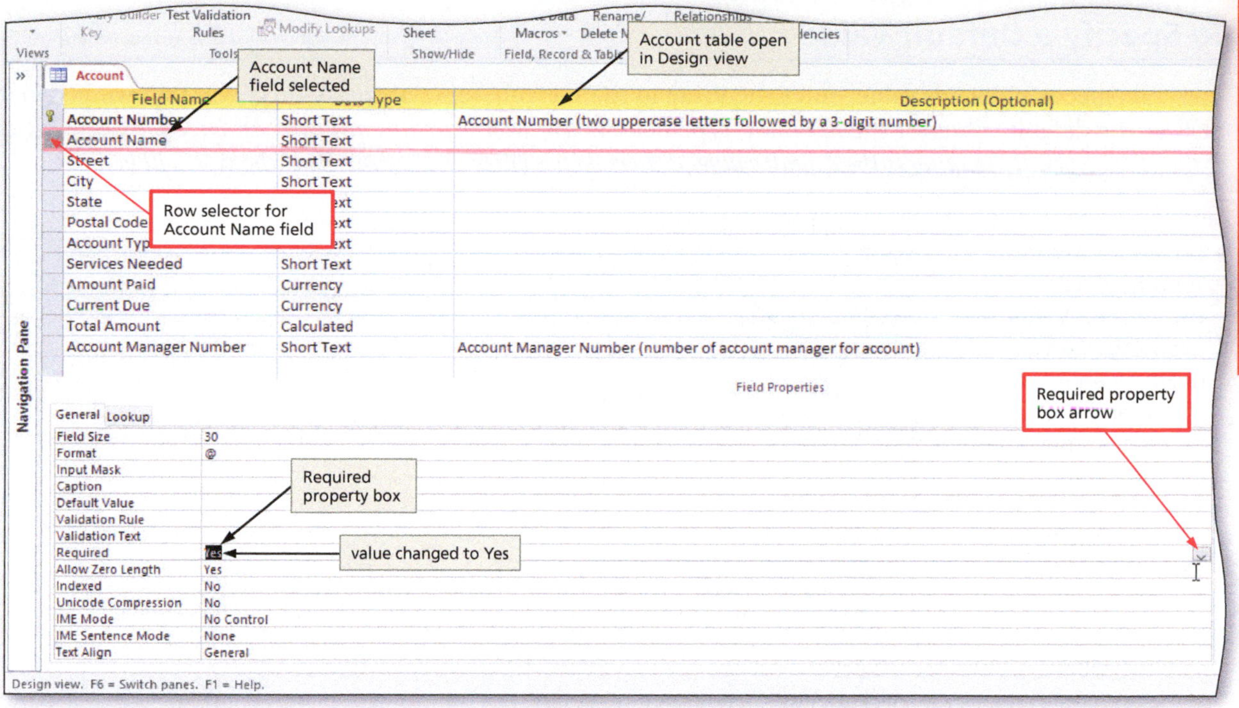

Figure 3–36

To Specify a Range

1 UPDATE RECORDS | 2 FILTER RECORDS | 3 CHANGE STRUCTURE | 4 MASS CHANGES | 5 VALIDATION RULES
6 CHANGE APPEARANCE | 7 REFERENTIAL INTEGRITY | 8 ORDER RECORDS

The following step specifies that entries in the Current Due field must be between $0 and $10,000. To indicate this range, the criterion specifies that the Current Due amount must be both >= 0 (greater than or equal to 0) and <= 10000 (less than or equal to 10,000). *Why? Combining these two criteria with the word, and, is logically equivalent to being between $0.00 and $10,000.00.*

1

- Select the Current Due field by clicking its row selector, click the Validation Rule property box to produce an insertion point, and then type `>=0 and <=10000` as the rule.

- Click the Validation Text property box to produce an insertion point, and then type `Must be at least $0.00 and at most $10,000.00` as the text (Figure 3–37).

Q&A

What is the effect of this change? Users will now be prohibited from entering a Current Due amount that is either less than $0.00 or greater than $10,000.00 when they add records or change the value in the Current Due field.

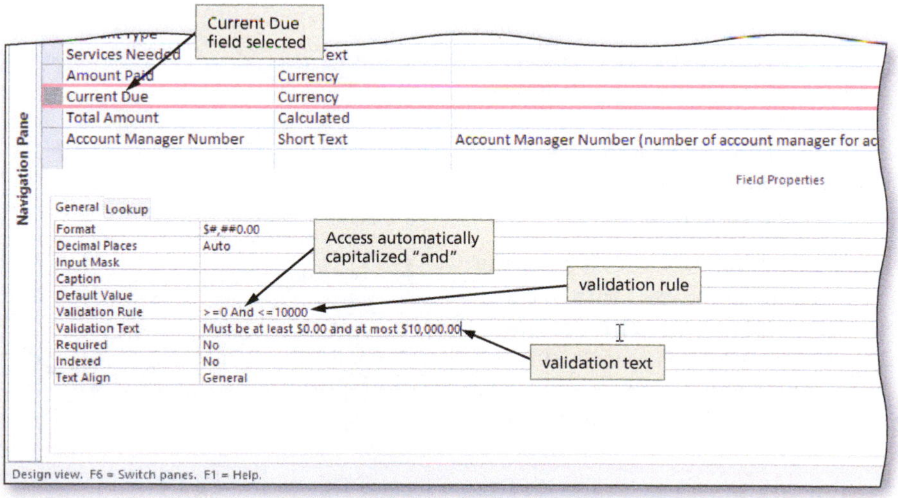

Figure 3–37

To Specify a Default Value

To specify a default value, enter the value in the Default Value property box. The following step specifies SER as the default value for the Account Type field. *Why? More accounts at PrattLast have the type SER than either of the other types. By making it the default value, if users do not enter an Account Type, the type will be SER.*

1

- Select the Account Type field, click the Default Value property box to produce an insertion point, and then type **=SER** as the value (Figure 3–38).

Q&A Do I need to type the equal (=) sign? No. You could enter just SER as the default value.

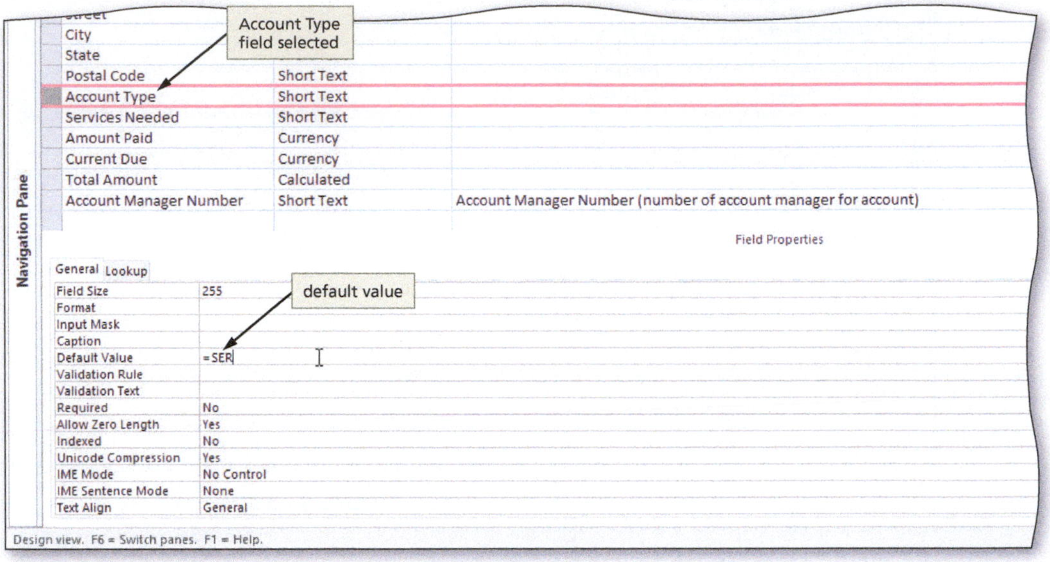

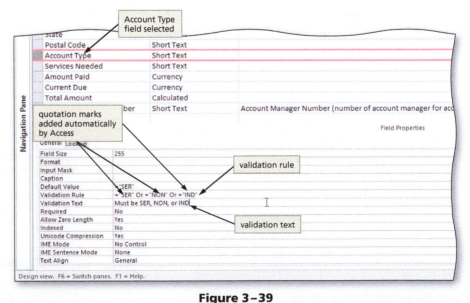

Figure 3–38

To Specify a Collection of Legal Values

The only **legal values**, or **allowable values**, for the Account Type field are SER, NON, and IND. The following step creates a validation rule to specify these as the only legal values for the Account Type field. *Why? The validation rule prohibits users from entering any other value in the Account Type field.*

1

- With the Account Type field selected, click the Validation Rule property box to produce an insertion point and then type **=SER or =NON or =IND** as the validation rule.

- Click the Validation Text property box, and then type **Must be SER, NON, or IND** as the validation text (Figure 3–39).

Q&A What is the effect of this change? Users will now only be allowed to enter SER, NON, or IND in the Account Type field when they add records or make changes to this field.

Figure 3–39

To Specify a Format

To affect the way data appears in a field, you can use a **format**. To use a format with a Short Text field, you enter a special symbol, called a **format symbol**, in the field's Format property box. The Format property uses different settings for different data types. The following step specifies a format for the Account Number field using the > symbol. *Why? The > format symbol causes Access to display lowercase letters automatically as uppercase letters, which is appropriate for the Account Number field.* There is another symbol, the < symbol, which causes Access to display uppercase letters automatically as lowercase letters.

1

- Select the Account Number field.

- Click the Format property box, erase the current format (@), if it appears on your screen, and then type > (Figure 3–40).

Q&A

Where did the current format (@) come from and what does it mean?

Access added this format when you created the table by importing data from an Excel workbook. It simply means any character or a space. It is not needed here.

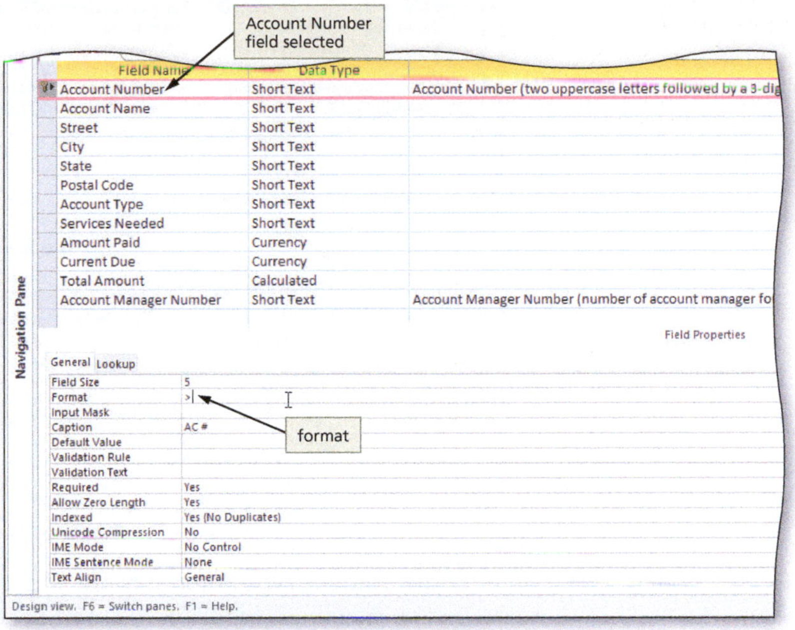

Figure 3–40

To Save the Validation Rules, Default Values, and Formats

The following steps save the validation rules, default values, and formats.

1 Click the Save button on the Quick Access Toolbar to save the changes (Figure 3–41).

2 If a Microsoft Access dialog box appears, click the No button to save the changes without testing current data.

Q&A

When would you want to test current data?

If you have any doubts about the validity of the current data, you should be sure to test the current data.

3 Close the Account table.

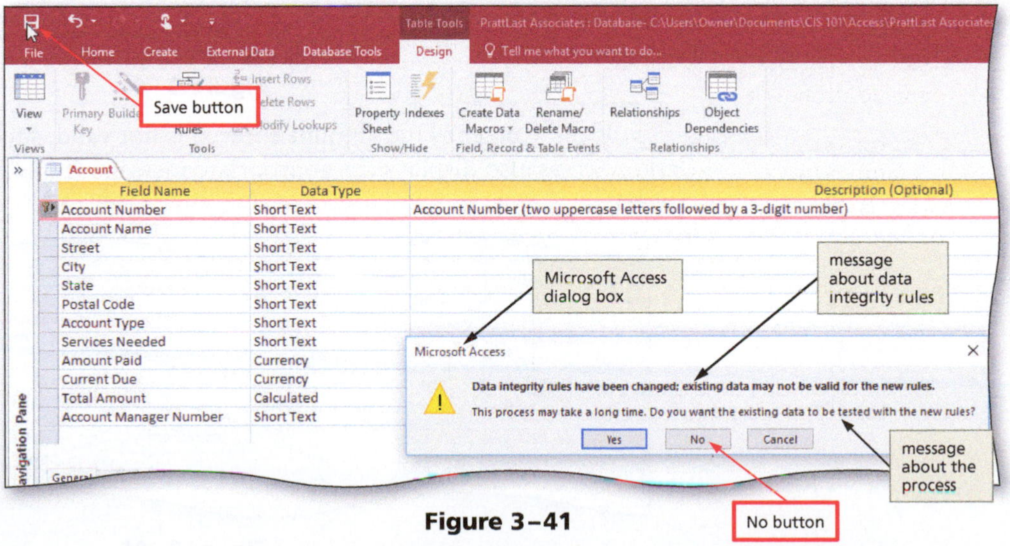

Figure 3–41

Updating a Table that Contains Validation Rules

Now that the PrattLast database contains validation rules, Access restricts the user to entering data that is valid and is formatted correctly. If a user enters a number that is out of the required range, for example, or enters a value that is not one of the possible choices, Access displays an error message in the form of a dialog box. The user cannot update the database until the error is corrected.

If the account number entered contains lowercase letters, such as bc486 (Figure 3–42), Access will display the data automatically as BC486 (Figure 3–43).

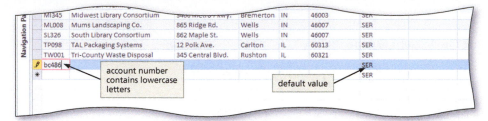

Figure 3–42

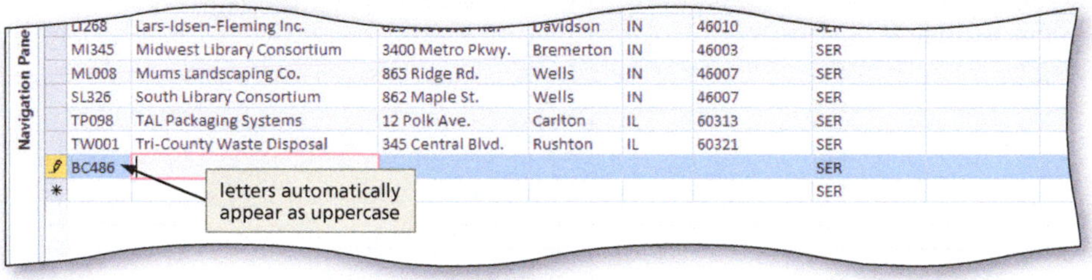

Figure 3–43

If the account type entered is not valid, such as xxx, Access will display the text message you specified (Figure 3–44) and prevent the data from being entering into the database.

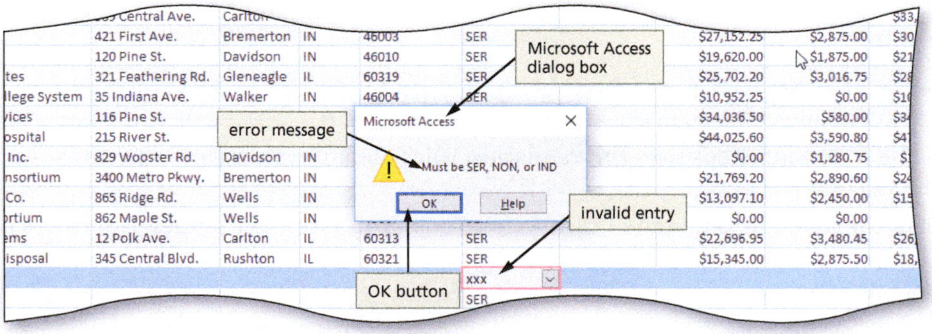

Figure 3–44

If the Current Due amount entered is not valid, such as 50000, which is too large, Access also displays the appropriate message (Figure 3–45) and refuses to accept the data.

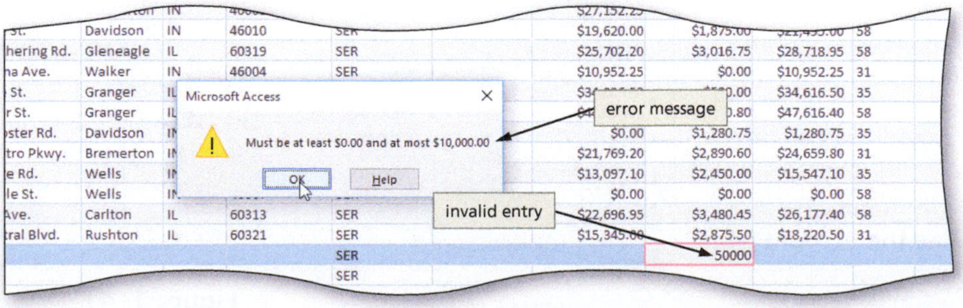

Figure 3–45

If a required field contains no data, Access indicates this by displaying an error message as soon as you attempt to leave the record (Figure 3–46). The field must contain a valid entry before Access will move to a different record.

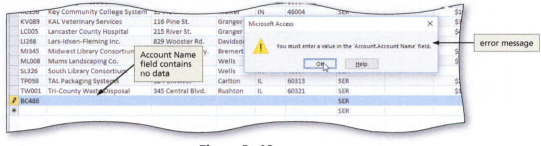

Figure 3–46

When entering invalid data into a field with a validation rule, is it possible that you could not enter the data correctly? What would cause this? If it happens, what should you do?

If you cannot remember the validation rule you created or if you created the rule incorrectly, you might not be able to enter the data. In such a case, you will be unable to leave the field or close the table because you have entered data into a field that violates the validation rule.

If this happens, first try again to type an acceptable entry. If this does not work, repeatedly press the BACKSPACE key to erase the contents of the field and then try to leave the field. If you are unsuccessful using this procedure, press the ESC key until the record is removed from the screen. The record will not be added to the database.

Should the need arise to take this drastic action, you probably have a faulty validation rule. Use the techniques of the previous sections to correct the existing validation rules for the field.

CONSIDER THIS

Making Additional Changes to the Database

Now that you have changed the structure and created validation rules, there are additional changes to be made to the database. You will use both the lookup and multivalued lookup fields to change the contents of the fields. You will also update both the form and the report to reflect the changes in the table.

To Change the Contents of a Field

1 UPDATE RECORDS | 2 FILTER RECORDS | 3 CHANGE STRUCTURE | 4 MASS CHANGES | 5 VALIDATION RULES
6 CHANGE APPEARANCE | 7 REFERENTIAL INTEGRITY | 8 ORDER RECORDS

Now that the size for the Street field has been increased, you can change the Street name for account BL235 from 100 Granger Hwy. to 100 South Granger Hwy. and then resize the column, just as you resized columns in Module 1. *Why? Changing the field size for the field does not automatically increase the width of the corresponding column in the datasheet.* The following steps change the Street name and resize the column in the datasheet to accommodate the new name.

1

- Open the Account table in Datasheet view and ensure the Navigation Pane is closed.

- Click in the Street field for account BL235 immediately to the left of the letter, G, of Granger to produce an insertion point.

- Change the name of the street from 100 Granger Hwy. to 100 South Granger Hwy. by typing `South` and a space, and then pressing the TAB key.

Q&A I cannot add the extra characters. Whatever I type replaces what is currently in the cell. What happened and what should I do?
You are typing in Overtype mode, not Insert mode. Press the INSERT key and correct the entry.

• Resize the Street column to best fit the new data by double-clicking the right boundary of the field selector for the Street field, that is, the column heading (Figure 3–47).

• Save the changes to the layout by clicking the Save button on the Quick Access Toolbar.

• Close the Account table.

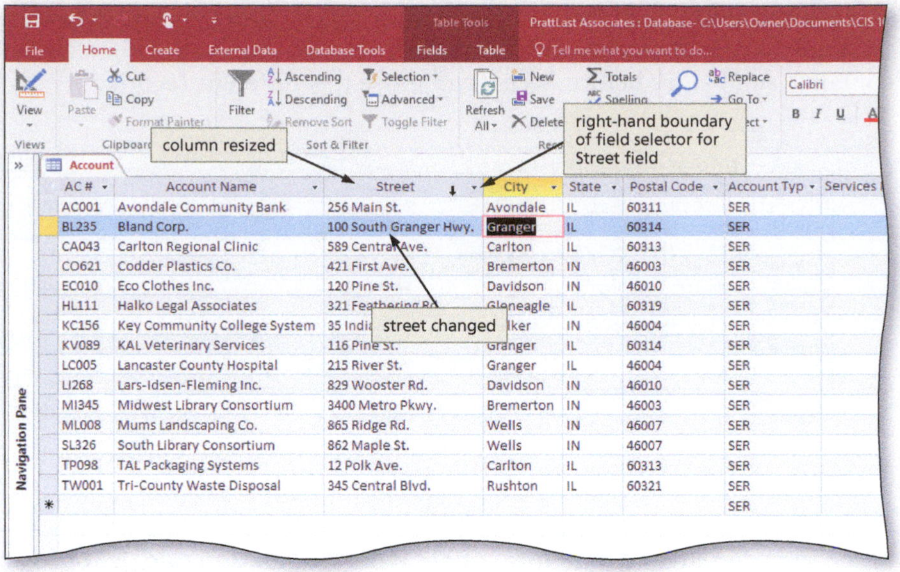

Figure 3–47

To Use a Lookup Field

1 UPDATE RECORDS | 2 FILTER RECORDS | 3 CHANGE STRUCTURE | 4 MASS CHANGES | 5 VALIDATION RULES
6 CHANGE APPEARANCE | 7 REFERENTIAL INTEGRITY | 8 ORDER RECORDS

Earlier, you changed all the entries in the Account Type field to SER. You have created a rule that will ensure that only legitimate values (SER, NON, or IND) can be entered in the field. You also made Account Type a lookup field. **Why?** *You can make changes to a lookup field for individual records by simply clicking the field to be changed, clicking the arrow that appears in the field, and then selecting the desired value from the list.* The following steps change the incorrect Account Type values to the correct values.

1

• Open the Account table in Datasheet view and ensure the Navigation Pane is closed.

• Click in the Account Type field on the second record (BL235) to display an arrow.

• Click the arrow to display the drop-down list of available choices for the Account Type field (Figure 3–48).

Q&A I got the drop-down list as soon as I clicked. I did not need to click the arrow. What happened?
If you click in the position where the arrow would appear, you will get the drop-down list. If you click anywhere else, you would need to click the arrow.

Q&A Could I type the value instead of selecting it from the list?
Yes. Once you have either deleted the previous value or selected the entire previous value, you can begin typing. You do not have to type the full entry. When you begin with the letter, I, for example, Access will automatically add the ND.

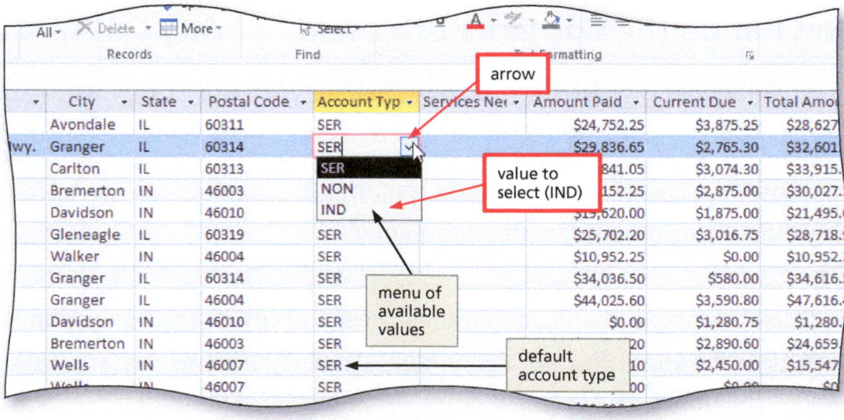

Figure 3–48

2

- Click IND to change the value.

- In a similar fashion, change the values on the other records to match those shown in Figure 3–49.

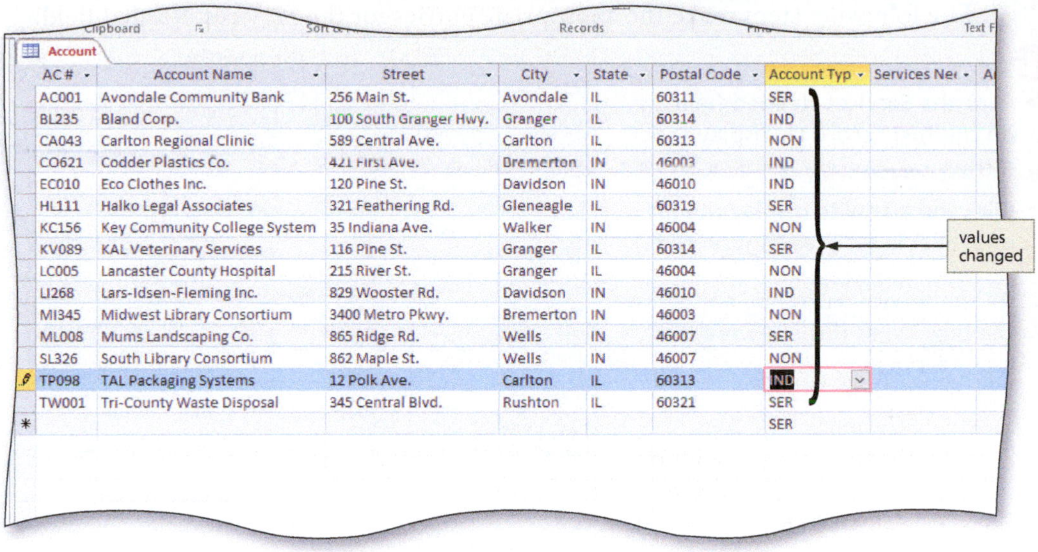

Figure 3–49

To Use a Multivalued Lookup Field

1 UPDATE RECORDS | 2 FILTER RECORDS | 3 CHANGE STRUCTURE | 4 MASS CHANGES | 5 VALIDATION RULES
6 CHANGE APPEARANCE | 7 REFERENTIAL INTEGRITY | 8 ORDER RECORDS

Using a multivalued lookup field is similar to using a regular lookup field. The difference is that when you display the drop down list, the entries will all be preceded by check boxes. *Why? Having the check boxes allows you to make multiple selections. You check all the entries that you want.* The appropriate entries are shown in Figure 3–50. As indicated in the figure, the services needed for account AC001 are Bck, Ben, Com, Pay, and Rsk.

Account Number	Account Name	Services Needed
AC001	Avondale Community Bank	Bck, Ben, Com, Pay, Rsk
BL235	Bland Corp.	Bck, Mgt, Rsk, Tch, Wrk
CA043	Carlton Regional Clinic	Mgt, Pay, Rsk, Tch
CO621	Codder Plastics Co.	Ben, Pay, Rsk, Trn, Wrk
EC010	Eco Clothes Inc.	Rec, Trn, Wrk
HL111	Halko Legal Associates	Ben, Com, Pay, Rsk, Tch, Trn
KC156	Key Community College System	Ben, Com, Mgt, Rsk, Wrk
KV089	KAL Veterinary Services	Ben, Com, Tch, Trn
LC005	Lancaster County Hospital	Ben, Mgt, Pay, Rsk, Tch, Wrk
LI268	Lars-Idsen-Fleming Inc.	Ben, Pay, Wrk
MI345	Midwest Library Consortium	Bck, Ben, Com, Pay, Tch, Trn
ML008	Mums Landscaping Co.	Bck, Pay, Wrk
SL326	South Library Consortium	Bck, Ben, Com, Pay, Tch, Trn
TP098	TAL Packaging Systems	Ben, Com, Pay, Trn, Wrk
TW001	Tri-County Waste Disposal	Bck, Pay, Rec, Wrk

Figure 3–50

The following steps make the appropriate entries for the Services Needed field.

1

- Click the Services Needed field on the first record to display the arrow.
- Click the arrow to display the list of available services (Figure 3–51).

Q&A

All the services currently appear in the box. What if there were too many services to fit?

Access would automatically include a scroll bar that you could use to scroll through all the choices.

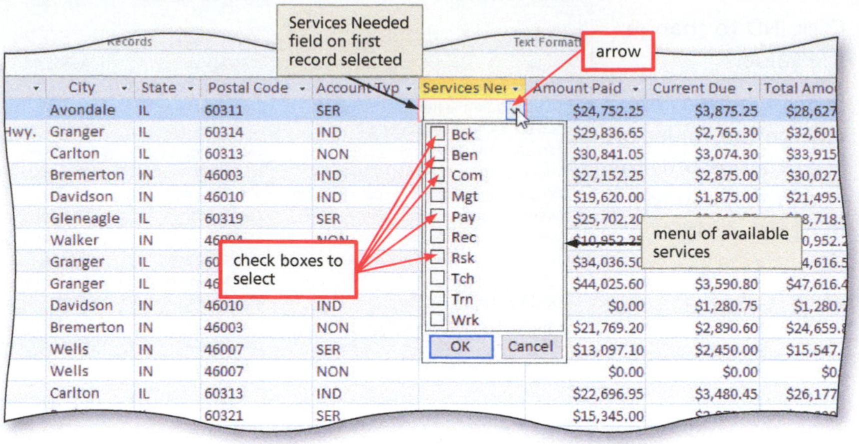

Figure 3–51

2

- Click the Bck, Ben, Com, Pay, and Rsk check boxes to select the services for the first account (Figure 3–52).

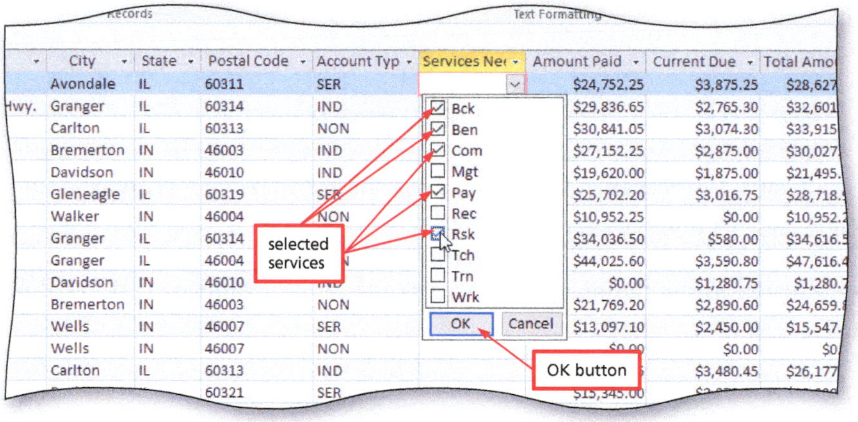

Figure 3–52

3

- Click the OK button to complete the selection.
- Using the same technique, enter the services given in Figure 3–50 for the remaining accounts.
- Double-click the right boundary of the field selector for the Services Needed field to resize the field so that it best fits the data (Figure 3–53).

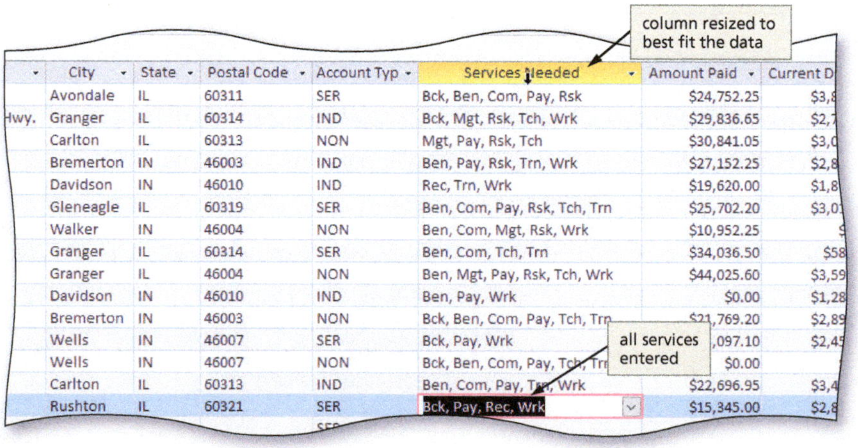

Figure 3–53

4

- Save the changes to the layout by clicking the Save button on the Quick Access Toolbar.
- Close the Account table.

Q&A

What if I closed the table without saving the layout changes?

You would be asked if you want to save the changes.

To Update a Form to Reflect Changes in the Table

Earlier, you clicked the Form button (Create tab | Forms group) to create a simple form that contained all the fields in the Account table. Now that you have added fields, the form you created, Account Form, no longer contains all the fields in the table. The following steps delete the Account Form and then create it a second time.

1 Open the Navigation Pane, and then right-click the Account Form in the Navigation Pane to display a shortcut menu.

2 Click Delete on the shortcut menu to delete the selected form, and then click the Yes button in the Microsoft Access dialog box to confirm the deletion.

3 Click the Account table in the Navigation Pane to select the table.

4 If necessary, click Create on the ribbon to display the Create tab.

5 Click the Form button (Create tab | Forms group) to create a simple form (Figure 3–54).

6 Click the Save button on the Quick Access Toolbar to save the form.

7 Type **Account Form** as the form name, and then click the OK button to save the form.

8 Close the form.

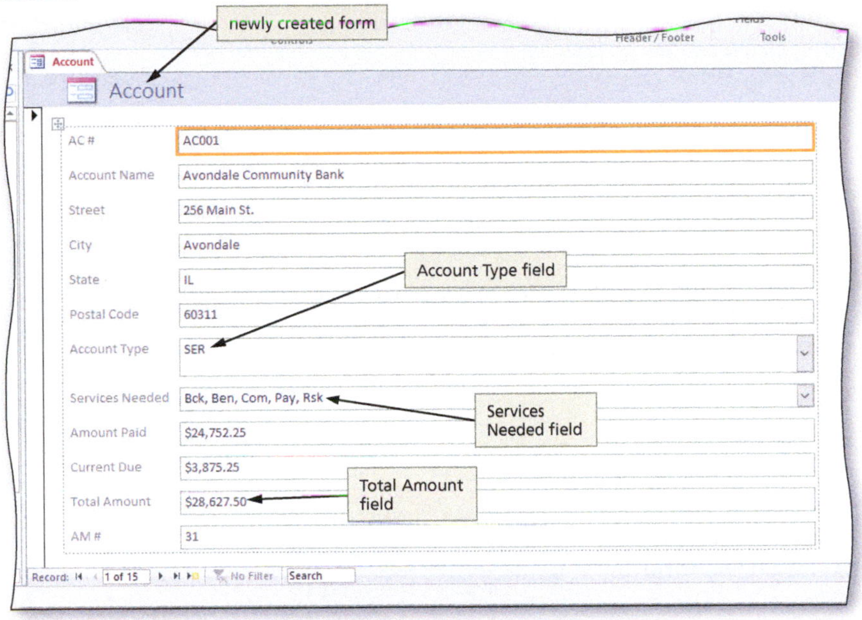

Figure 3–54

To Update a Report to Reflect Changes in the Table

1 UPDATE RECORDS | 2 FILTER RECORDS | 3 CHANGE STRUCTURE | 4 MASS CHANGES | 5 VALIDATION RULES
6 CHANGE APPEARANCE | 7 REFERENTIAL INTEGRITY | 8 ORDER RECORDS

You also might want to include the new fields in the Account Financial Report you created earlier. Just as you did with the form, you could delete the current version of the report and then create it all over again. It would be better, however, to modify the report in Layout view. **Why?** *There are several steps involved in creating the Account Financial report, so it is more complicated than the process of re-creating the form.* In Layout view, you easily can add new fields. The following steps modify the Account Financial Report by adding the Account Type and Total Amount fields. To accommodate the extra fields, the steps also change the orientation of the report from Portrait to Landscape.

1

- Open the Navigation Pane, if necessary, and then right-click the Account Financial Report in the Navigation Pane to display a shortcut menu.

- Click Layout View on the shortcut menu to open the report in Layout view.

- Close the Navigation Pane.

- Click the 'Add Existing Fields' button (Report Layout Tools Design tab | Tools group) to display a field list (Figure 3–55).

Q&A Why are there two Services Needed fields in the list?

They serve different purposes. If you were to select Services Needed, you would get all the services for a given account on one line. If you were to select Services Needed. Value, each resource would be on a separate line. You are not selecting either one for this report.

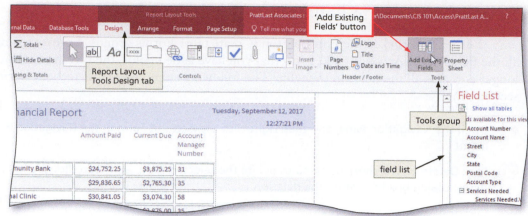

Figure 3–55

2

• Drag the Account Type field in the field list into the report until the line to the left of the pointer is between the Account Name and Amount Paid fields on the form (Figure 3–56).

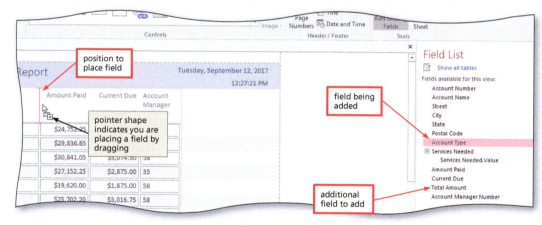

Figure 3–56

3

• Release the mouse button to place the field.

Q&A What if I make a mistake?

You can delete the field by clicking the column heading for the field, clicking the Select Column command (Report Layout Tools Arrange tab | Rows & Columns group), and then pressing the DELETE key. You can move the field by dragging it to the correct position. As an alternative, you can close the report without saving it and then open it again in Layout view.

• Using the same technique, add the Total Amount field between the Current Due and Account Manager Number fields.

• Click the 'Add Existing Fields' button (Report Layout Tools Design tab | Tools group) to remove the field list from the screen.

Q&A What would I do if the field list covered the portion of the report where I wanted to insert a new field?

You can move the field list to a different position on the screen by dragging its title bar.

• Click Page Setup on the ribbon to display the Report Layout Tools Page Setup tab.

- Click the Landscape
button (Report
Layout Tools Page
Setup tab | Page
Layout group)
to change the
orientation of the
report to Landscape
(Figure 3–57).

4

- Click the Save button
on the Quick Access
Toolbar to save your
changes.

- Close the report.

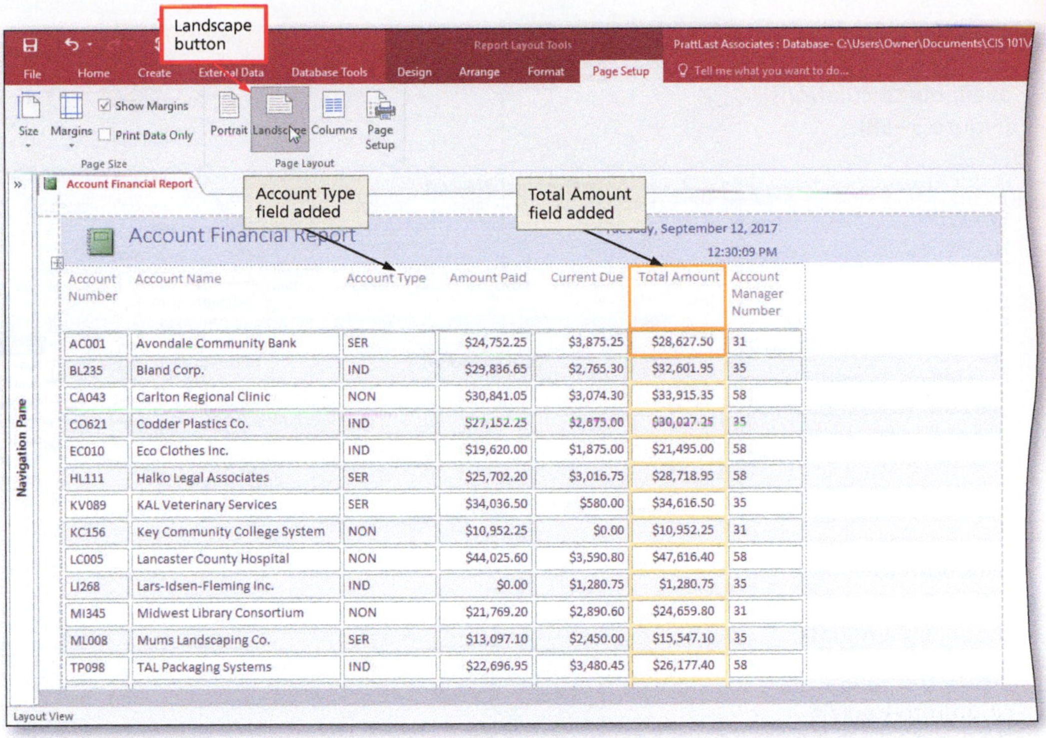

Figure 3–57

To Print a Report

The following steps print the report.

1 With the Account Financial Report selected in the Navigation Pane, click File on the
ribbon to open the Backstage view.

2 Click the Print tab in the Backstage view to display the Print gallery.

3 Click the Quick Print button to print the report.

Changing the Appearance of a Datasheet

You can change the appearance of a datasheet in a variety of ways. You can include
totals in the datasheet. You can also change the appearance of gridlines or the text
colors and font.

To Include Totals in a Datasheet

1 UPDATE RECORDS | 2 FILTER RECORDS | 3 CHANGE STRUCTURE | 4 MASS CHANGES | 5 VALIDATION RULES
6 CHANGE APPEARANCE | 7 REFERENTIAL INTEGRITY | 8 ORDER RECORDS

The following steps first include an extra row, called the Total row, in the datasheet for the Account
Manager table. **Why?** *It is possible to include totals and other statistics at the bottom of a datasheet in the Total row.* The
steps then display the total of the salaries for all the account managers.

1

- Open the Account Manager table in Datasheet view and close the Navigation Pane.

- Click the Totals button (Home tab | Records group) to include the Total row in the datasheet.

- Click the Total row in the Salary column to display an arrow.

BTW

**Distributing a
Document**
Instead of printing and
distributing a hard copy of a
document, you can distribute
the document electronically.
Options include sending the
document via email; posting
it on cloud storage (such as
OneDrive) and sharing the
file with others; posting it
on social media, a blog, or
other website; and sharing a
link associated with an online
location of the document.
You also can create and
share a PDF or XPS image of
the document, so that users
can view the file in Acrobat
Reader or XPS Viewer instead
of in Access.

- Click the arrow to display a menu of available calculations (Figure 3–58).

Q&A

Will I always get the same list?

No. You will only get the items that are applicable to the type of data in the column. You cannot calculate the sum of text data, for example.

2

- Click Sum to calculate the total of the salary amounts.

- Resize the Salary column to best fit the total amount (Figure 3–59).

🔎 **Experiment**

- Experiment with other statistics. When finished, once again select the sum.

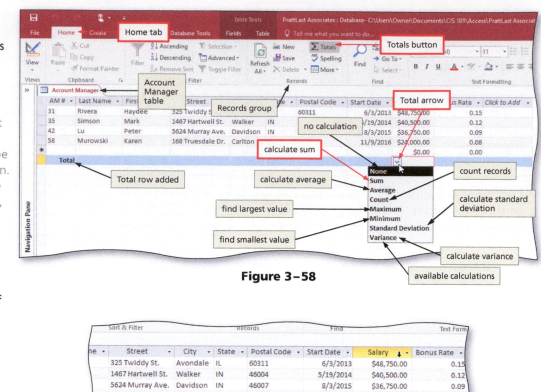

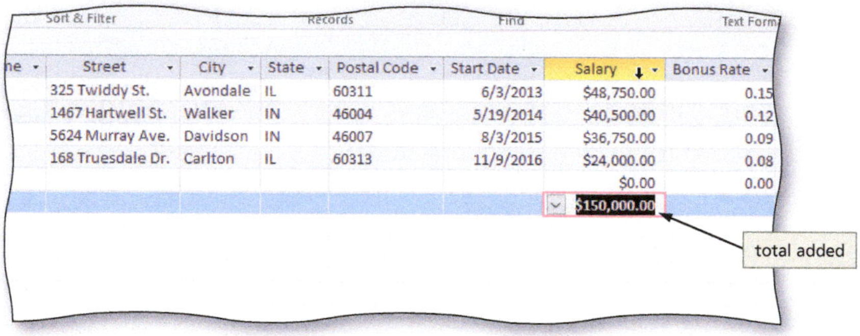

Figure 3–58

Figure 3–59

To Remove Totals from a Datasheet

If you no longer want the totals to appear as part of the datasheet, you can remove the Total row. The following step removes the Total row.

1 Click the Totals button (Home tab | Records group), which is shown in Figure 3–58, to remove the Total row from the datasheet.

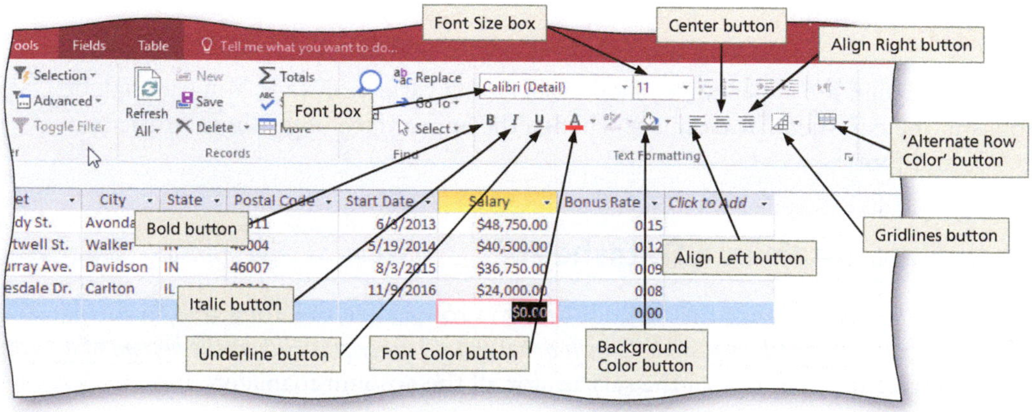

Figure 3–60

Figure 3–60 shows the various buttons, found in the Text Formatting group on the Home tab, that are available to change the datasheet appearance. The changes to the datasheet will be reflected not only on the screen, but also when you print or preview the datasheet.

To Change Gridlines in a Datasheet

1 UPDATE RECORDS | 2 FILTER RECORDS | 3 CHANGE STRUCTURE | 4 MASS CHANGES | 5 VALIDATION RULES
6 CHANGE APPEARANCE | 7 REFERENTIAL INTEGRITY | 8 ORDER RECORDS

The following steps change the datasheet so that only horizontal gridlines are included. *Why? You might prefer the appearance of the datasheet with only horizontal gridlines.*

1

- Open the Account Manager table in Datasheet view, if it is not already open.

- If necessary, close the Navigation Pane.

- Click the datasheet selector, the box in the upper-left corner of the datasheet, to select the entire datasheet (Figure 3–61).

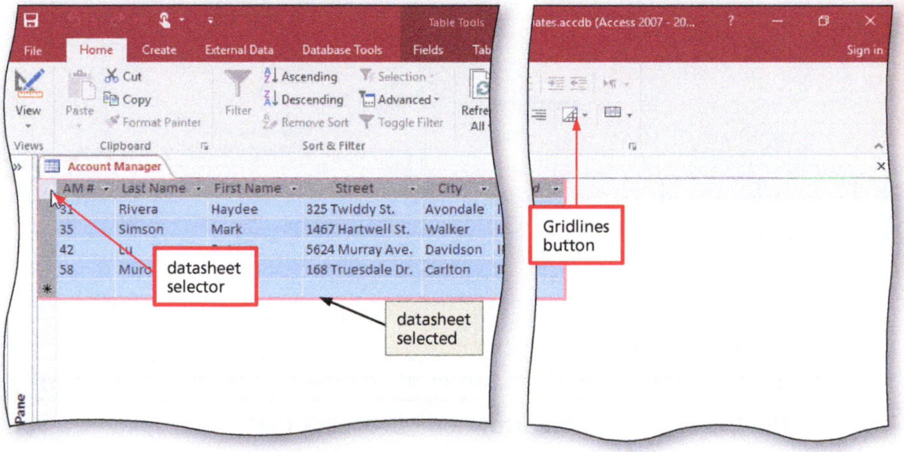

Figure 3–61

2

- Click the Gridlines button (Home tab | Text Formatting group) to display the Gridlines gallery (Figure 3–62).

Q&A Does it matter whether I click the button or the arrow?
In this case, it does not matter. Either action will display the gallery.

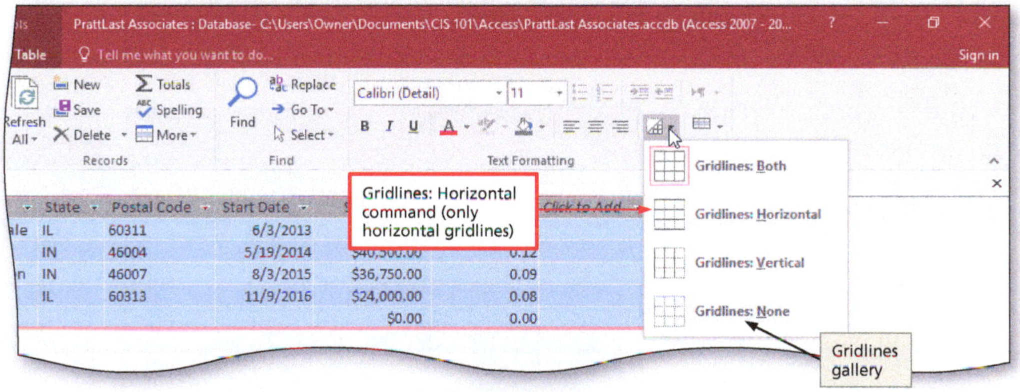

Figure 3–62

3

- Click Gridlines: Horizontal in the Gridlines gallery to include only horizontal gridlines.

Experiment

- Experiment with other gridline options. When finished, once again select horizontal gridlines.

To Change the Colors and Font in a Datasheet

1 UPDATE RECORDS | 2 FILTER RECORDS | 3 CHANGE STRUCTURE | 4 MASS CHANGES | 5 VALIDATION RULES
6 CHANGE APPEARANCE | 7 REFERENTIAL INTEGRITY | 8 ORDER RECORDS

You can also modify the appearance of the datasheet by changing the colors and the font. The following steps change the Alternate Fill color, a color that appears on every other row in the datasheet. *Why? Having rows appear in alternate colors is an attractive way to visually separate the rows.* The steps also change the font color, the font, and the font size.

1

- With the datasheet for the Account Manager table selected, click the 'Alternate Row Color' button arrow (Home tab | Text Formatting group) to display the color palette (Figure 3–63).

Does it matter whether I click the button or the arrow?
Yes. Clicking the arrow produces a color palette. Clicking the button applies the currently selected color. When in doubt, you should click the arrow.

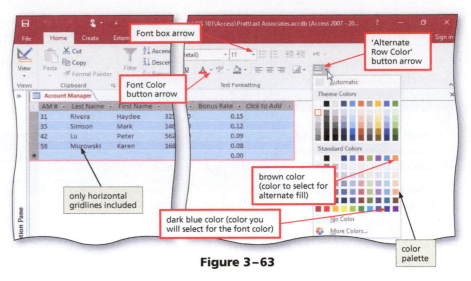

Figure 3–63

2

- Click Brown in the upper-right corner of Standard Colors to select brown as the alternate color.

- Click the Font Color button arrow, and then click the dark blue color that is the second color from the right in the bottom row in the Standard Colors to select the font color.

- Click the Font arrow, scroll down in the list until Bodoni MT appears, and then select Bodoni MT as the font. (If it is not available, select any font of your choice.)

- Click the Font Size arrow and select 10 as the font size (Figure 3–64).

Does the order in which I make these selections make a difference?
No. You could have made these selections in any order.

Experiment

- Experiment with other colors, fonts, and font sizes. When finished, return to the options selected in this step.

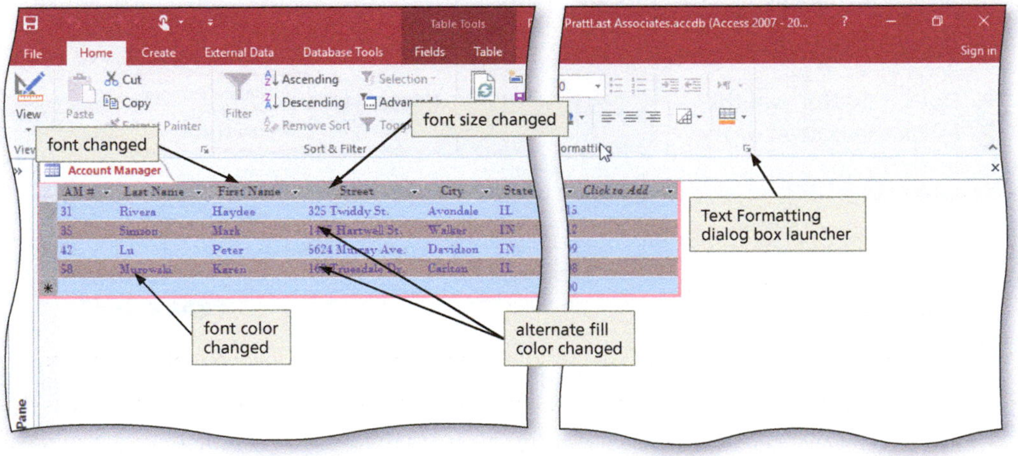

Figure 3–64

Using the Datasheet Formatting Dialog Box

As an alternative to using the individual buttons, you can click the Datasheet Formatting dialog box launcher, which is the arrow at the lower-right of the Text Formatting group, to display the Datasheet Formatting dialog box (Figure 3–65). You can use the various options within the dialog box to make changes to the datasheet format. Once you are finished, click the OK button to apply your changes.

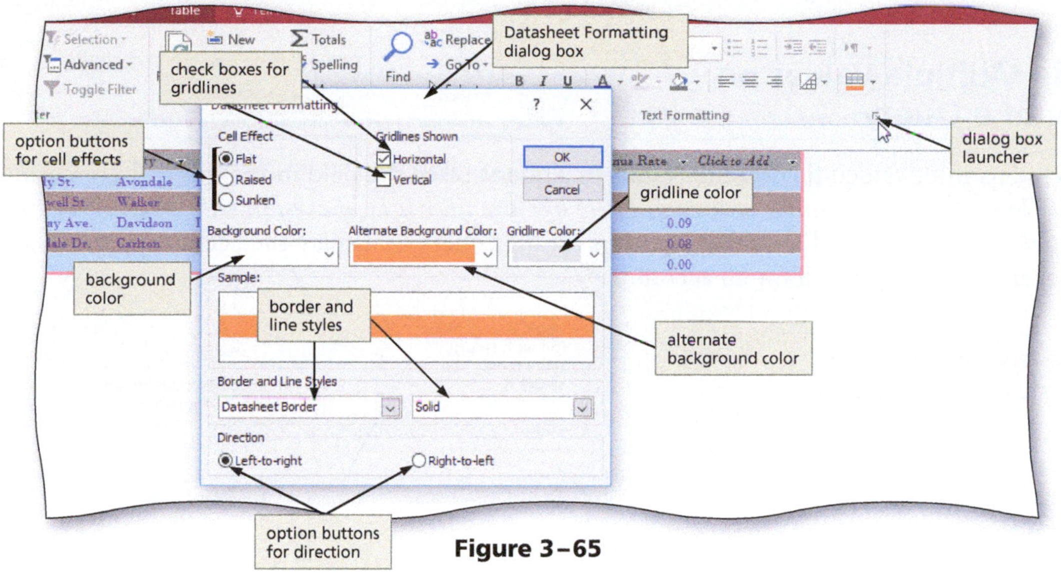

Figure 3-65

To Close the Datasheet without Saving the Format Changes

The following steps close the datasheet without saving the changes to the format. Because the changes are not saved, the next time you open the Account Manager table in Datasheet view it will appear in the original format. If you had saved the changes, the changes would be reflected in its appearance.

1 Close the Account Manager table.

2 Click the No button in the Microsoft Access dialog box when asked if you want to save your changes.

What kind of decisions should I make in determining whether to change the format of a datasheet?

- Would totals or other calculations be useful in the datasheet? If so, include the Total row and select the appropriate computations.

- Would another gridline style make the datasheet more useful? If so, change to the desired gridlines.

- Would alternating colors in the rows make them easier to read? If so, change the alternate fill color.

- Would a different font and/or font color make the text stand out better? If so, change the font color and/or the font.

- Is the font size appropriate? Can you see enough data at one time on the screen and yet have the data be readable? If not, change the font size to an appropriate value.

- Is the column spacing appropriate? Are some columns wider than they need to be? Do some columns not display all the data? Change the column sizes as necessary.

As a general guideline, once you have decided on a particular look for a datasheet, all datasheets in the database should have the same look, unless there is a compelling reason for a datasheet to differ.

CONSIDER THIS

Multivalued Fields in Queries

You can use multivalued fields in queries in the same way you use other fields in queries. You can choose to display the multiple values either on a single row or on multiple rows in the query results.

To Include Multiple Values on One Row of a Query

To include a multivalued field in the results of a query, place the field in the query design grid just like any other field. **Why?** *When you treat the multivalued field like any other field, the results will list all of the values for the multivalued field on a single row.* The following steps create a query to display the account number, account name, account type, and services needed for all accounts.

1

- Create a query for the Account table and close the Navigation Pane.

- Include the Account Number, Account Name, Account Type, and Services Needed fields (Figure 3–66).

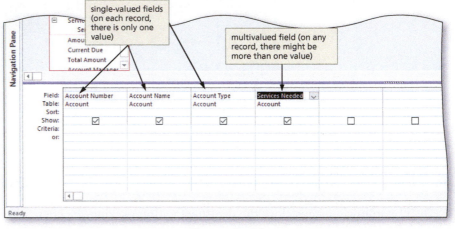

Figure 3–66

2

- Run the query and view the results (Figure 3–67).

Q&A

Can I include criteria for the multivalued field?

Yes. You can include criteria for the multivalued field.

3

- Save the query as m03q01.

Figure 3–67

To Include Multiple Values on Multiple Rows of a Query

You might want to see the multiple services needed for an account on separate rows rather than a single row. **Why?** *Each row in the results will focus on one specific service that is needed.* To do so, you need to use the Value property of the Services Needed field by following the name of the field with a period and then the word, Value. The following steps use the Value property to display each service on a separate row.

1

- Return to Design view and ensure that the Account Number, Account Name, Account Type, and Services Needed fields are included in the design grid.
- Click the Services Needed field to produce an insertion point, press the RIGHT ARROW key as necessary to move the insertion point to the end of the field name, and then type a period.
- If the word, Value, did not automatically appear after the period, type the word `Value` after the period following the word, Needed, to use the Value property (Figure 3–68).

Q&A I do not see the word, Services. Did I do something wrong?
No. There is not enough room to display the entire name. If you wanted to see it, you could point to the right boundary of the column selector and then either drag or double-click.

Q&A I see Services Needed.Value as a field in the field list. Could I have deleted the Services Needed field and added the Services Needed.Value field?
Yes. Either approach is fine.

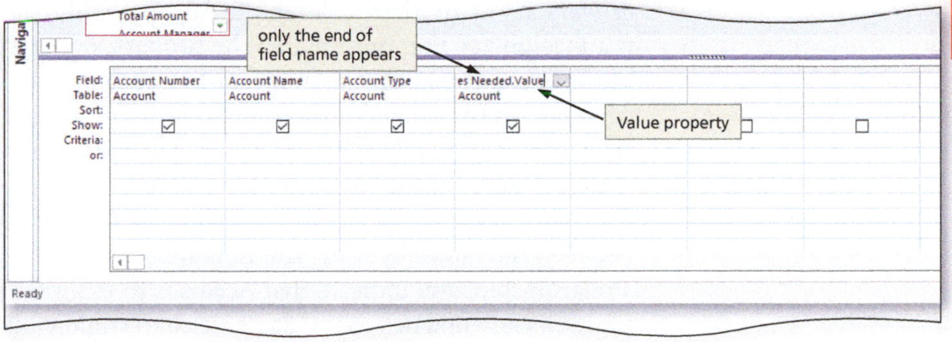

Figure 3–68

2

- Run the query and view the results (Figure 3–69).

Q&A Can I now include criteria for the multivalued field?
Yes. You could enter a criterion just like in any other query.

Q&A Could I sort the rows by account number?
Yes. Select Ascending as the sort order just as you have done in other queries.

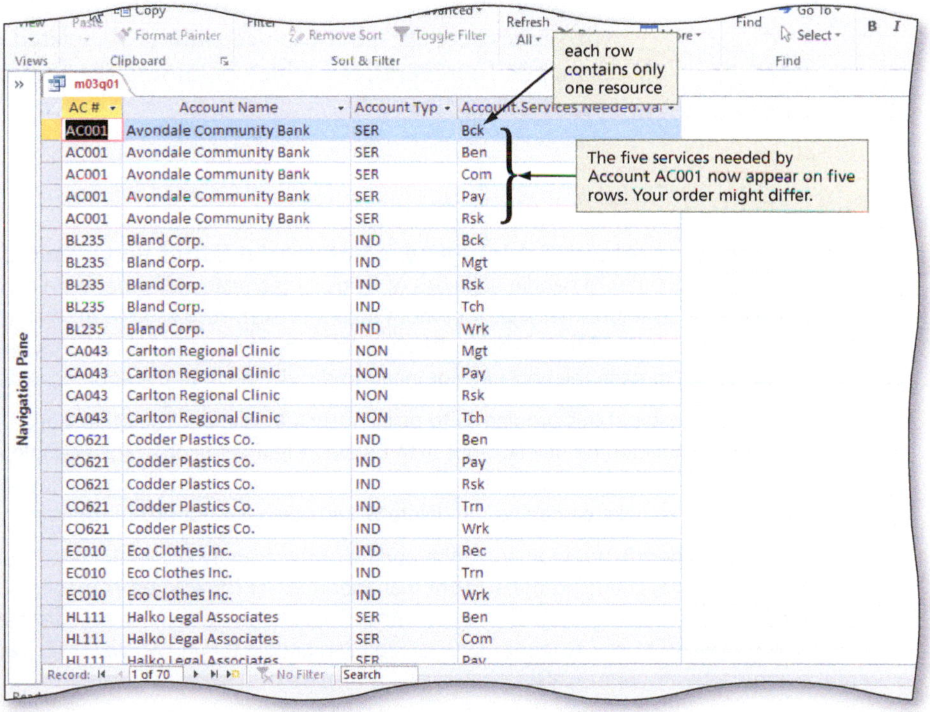

AC #	Account Name	Account Typ	Account.Services Needed.Va
AC001	Avondale Community Bank	SER	Bck
AC001	Avondale Community Bank	SER	Ben
AC001	Avondale Community Bank	SER	Com
AC001	Avondale Community Bank	SER	Pay
AC001	Avondale Community Bank	SER	Rsk
BL235	Bland Corp.	IND	Bck
BL235	Bland Corp.	IND	Mgt
BL235	Bland Corp.	IND	Rsk
BL235	Bland Corp.	IND	Tch
BL235	Bland Corp.	IND	Wrk
CA043	Carlton Regional Clinic	NON	Mgt
CA043	Carlton Regional Clinic	NON	Pay
CA043	Carlton Regional Clinic	NON	Rsk
CA043	Carlton Regional Clinic	NON	Tch
CO621	Codder Plastics Co.	IND	Ben
CO621	Codder Plastics Co.	IND	Pay
CO621	Codder Plastics Co.	IND	Rsk
CO621	Codder Plastics Co.	IND	Trn
CO621	Codder Plastics Co.	IND	Wrk
EC010	Eco Clothes Inc.	IND	Rec
EC010	Eco Clothes Inc.	IND	Trn
EC010	Eco Clothes Inc.	IND	Wrk
HL111	Halko Legal Associates	SER	Ben
HL111	Halko Legal Associates	SER	Com
HL111	Halko Legal Associates	SER	Pay

Figure 3–69

3

- Save the query as a new object in the database named m03q02.
- Close the query.

Break Point: If you wish to take a break, this is a good place to do so. You can quit Access now. To resume at a later time, run Access, open the database called PrattLast Associates, and continue following the steps from this location forward.

Referential Integrity

BTW

Using Criteria with Multivalued Fields
To enter criteria in a multivalued field, simply enter the criteria in the Criteria row. For example, to find all accounts who need payroll services, enter Pay in the Criteria row.

When you have two related tables in a database, it is essential that the data in the common fields match. There should not be an account in the Account table whose account manager number is 31, for example, unless there is a record in the Account Manager table whose number is 31. This restriction is enforced through **referential integrity**, which is the property that ensures that the value in a foreign key must match that of another table's primary key.

A **foreign key** is a field in one table whose values are required to match the *primary key* of another table. In the Account table, the Account Manager Number field is a foreign key that must match the primary key of the Account Manager table; that is, the account manager number for any account must exist as an account manager currently in the Account Manager table. An account whose account manager number is 92, for example, should not be stored in the Account table because no such account manager exists in the Account Manager table.

In Access, to specify referential integrity, you must explicitly define a relationship between the tables by using the Relationships button. As part of the process of defining a relationship, you indicate that Access is to enforce referential integrity. Access then prohibits any updates to the database that would violate the referential integrity.

The type of relationship between two tables specified by the Relationships command is referred to as a **one-to-many relationship**. This means that *one* record in the first table is related to, or matches, *many* records in the second table, but each record in the second table is related to only *one* record in the first. In the PrattLast Associates database, for example, a one-to-many relationship exists between the Account Manager table and the Account table. *One* account manager is associated with *many* accounts, but each account is associated with only a single account manager. In general, the table containing the foreign key will be the *many* part of the relationship.

CONSIDER THIS

When specifying referential integrity, what special issues do you need to address?

You need to decide how to handle deletions of fields. In the relationship between accounts and account managers, for example, deletion of an account manager for whom accounts exist, such as account manager number 31, would violate referential integrity. Accounts for account manager 31 would no longer relate to any account manager in the database. You can handle this in two ways. For each relationship, you need to decide which of the approaches is appropriate.

The normal way to avoid this problem is to prohibit such a deletion. The other option is to **cascade the delete.** This means that Access would allow the deletion but then delete all related records. For example, it would allow the deletion of the account manager from the Account Manager table but then automatically delete any accounts related to the deleted account manager. In this example, cascading the delete would obviously not be appropriate.

You also need to decide how to handle the update of the primary key. In the relationship between account managers and accounts, for example, changing the account manager number for account manager 31 to 32 in the Account Manager table would cause a problem because some accounts in the Account table have account manager number 31. These accounts no longer would relate to any account manager. You can handle this in two ways. For each relationship, you need to decide which of the approaches is appropriate.

The normal way to avoid this problem is to prohibit this type of update. The other option is to **cascade the update.** This means to allow the change, but make the corresponding change in the foreign key on all related records. In the relationship between accounts and account managers, for example, Access would allow the update but then automatically make the corresponding change for any account whose account manager number was 31. It will now be 32.

To Specify Referential Integrity

The following steps use the Relationships button on the Database Tools tab to specify referential integrity by explicitly indicating a relationship between the Account Manager and Account tables. The steps also ensure that updates will cascade, but that deletes will not. *Why? By indicating a relationship between tables, and specifying that updates will cascade, it will be possible to change the Account Manager Number for an account manager, and the same change will automatically be made for all accounts of that account manager. By not specifying that deletes will cascade, it will not be possible to delete an account manager who has related accounts.*

1

- Click Database Tools on the ribbon to display the Database Tools tab. (Figure 3–70).

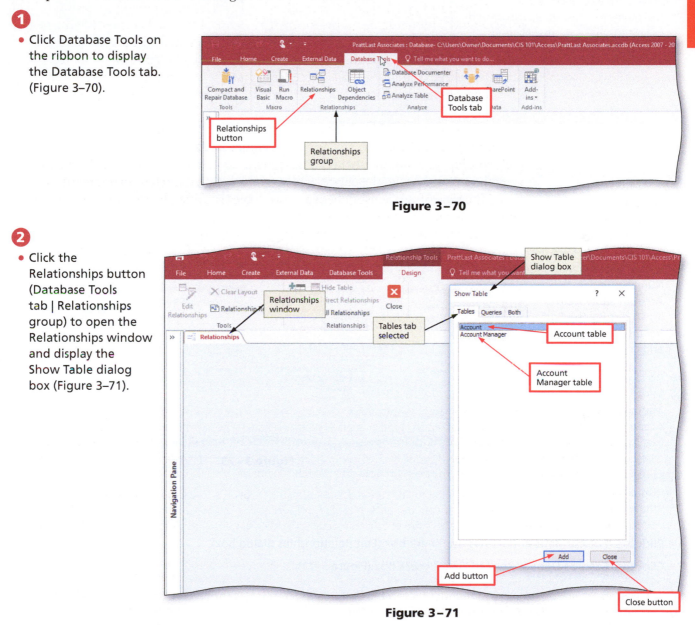

Figure 3–70

2

- Click the Relationships button (Database Tools tab | Relationships group) to open the Relationships window and display the Show Table dialog box (Figure 3–71).

Figure 3–71

3

- Click the Account Manager table (Show Table dialog box), and then click the Add button to add a field list for the Account Manager table to the Relationships window.

- Click the Account table (Show Table dialog box), and then click the Add button to add a field list for the Account table to the Relationships window.

- Click the Close button (Show Table dialog box) to close the dialog box.

- Resize the field lists that appear so all fields are visible (Figure 3–72).

Q&A

Do I need to resize the field lists?
No. You can use the scroll bars to view the fields. Before completing the next step, however, you would need to make sure the Account Manager Number fields in both tables appear on the screen.

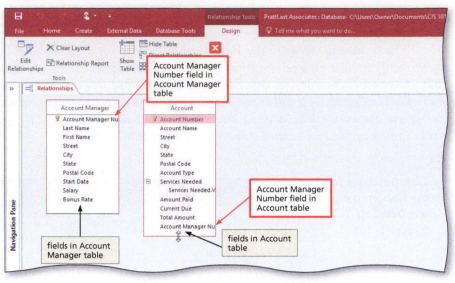

Figure 3–72

4

- Drag the Account Manager Number field in the Account Manager table field list to the Account Manager Number field in the Account table field list to display the Edit Relationships dialog box and create a relationship.

Q&A

Do I actually move the field from the Account Manager table to the Account table?
No. The pointer will change shape to indicate you are in the process of dragging, but the field does not move.

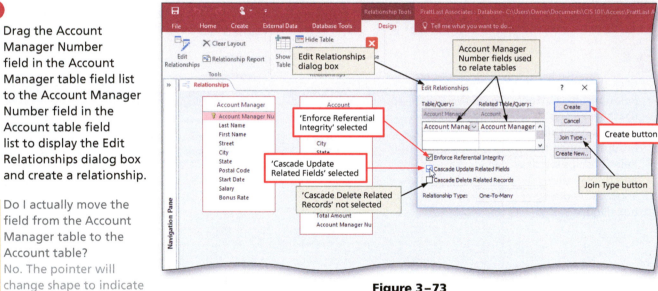

Figure 3–73

- Click the 'Enforce Referential Integrity' check box (Edit Relationships dialog box).

- Click the 'Cascade Update Related Fields' check box (Figure 3–73).

Q&A

The Cascade check boxes were dim until I clicked the 'Enforce Referential Integrity' check box. Is that correct?
Yes. Until you have chosen to enforce referential integrity, the cascade options are not applicable.

5

- Click the Create button (Edit Relationships dialog box) to complete the creation of the relationship (Figure 3–74).

Q&A

What is the symbol at the lower end of the join line?
It is the mathematical symbol for infinity. It is used here to denote the "many" end of the relationship.

Q&A Can I print a copy of the relationship?
Yes. Click the Relationship Report button (Relationship Tools Design tab | Tools group) to produce a report of the relationship. You can print the report. You can also save it as a report in the database for future use. If you do not want to save it, close the report after you have printed it and do not save the changes.

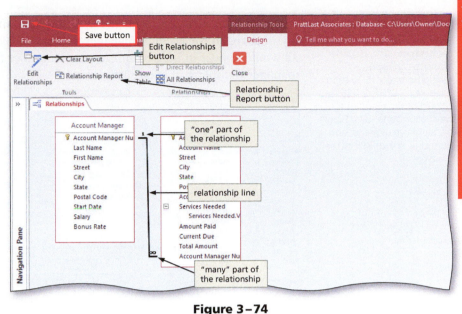

Figure 3–74

6

- Click the Save button on the Quick Access Toolbar to save the relationship you created.

- Close the Relationships window.

Q&A Can I later modify the relationship if I want to change it in some way?
Yes. Click Database Tools on the ribbon to display the Database Tools tab, and then click the Relationships button (Database Tools tab | Relationships group) to open the Relationships window. To add another table, click the Show Table button on the Design tab. To remove a table, click the Hide Table button. To edit a relationship, select the relationship and click the Edit Relationships button.

Can I change the join type as I can in queries?
Yes. Click the Join Type button in the Edit Relationships dialog box. Click option button 1 to create an INNER join, that is, a join in which only records with matching values in the join fields appear in the result. Click option button 2 to create a LEFT join, that is, a join that includes all records from the left-hand table, but only records from the right-hand table that have matching values in the join fields. Click option button 3 to create a RIGHT join, that is, a join that includes all records from the right-hand table, but only records from the left-hand table that have matching values in the join fields.

CONSIDER THIS

BTW

Relationships
You also can use the Relationships window to specify a one-to-one relationship. In a one-to-one relationship, the matching fields are both primary keys. If PrattLast Associates maintained a company car for each account manager, the data concerning the cars might be kept in a Car table, in which the primary key is Account Manager Number — the same primary key as the Account Manager table. Thus, there would be a one-to-one relationship between account managers and cars.

Effect of Referential Integrity

Referential integrity now exists between the Account Manager and Account tables. Access now will reject any number in the Account Manager Number field in the Account table that does not match an account manager number in the Account Manager table. Attempting to change the account manager number for an account to one that does not match any account manager in the Account Manager table would result in the error message shown in Figure 3–75. Similarly, attempting to add an account whose account manager number does not match would produce the same error message.

Access also will reject the deletion of an account manager for whom related accounts exist. Attempting to delete account manager 31 from the Account Manager table, for example, would result in the message shown in Figure 3–76.

Access would, however, allow the change of an account manager number in the Account Manager table. It would then automatically make the corresponding change

BTW

Exporting a Relationship Report
You also can export a relationship report. To export a report as a PDF or XPS file, right-click the report in the Navigation Pane, click Export on the shortcut menu, and then click PDF or XPS as the file type.

to the account manager number for all the account manager's accounts. For example, if you changed the account manager number of account manager 31 to 32, the number 32 would appear in the account manager number field for accounts whose account manager number had been 31.

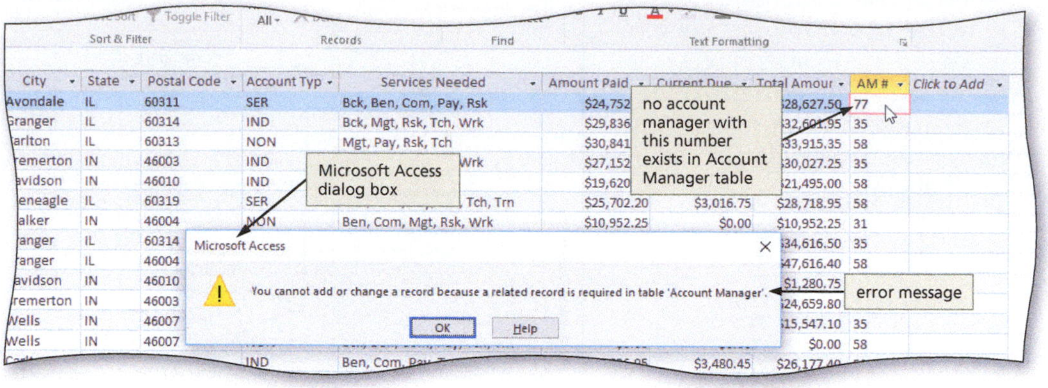

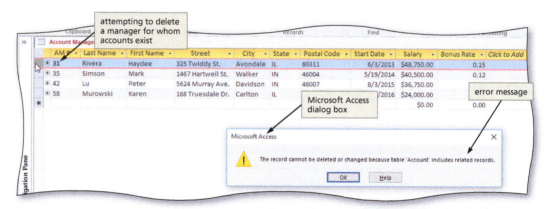

Figure 3–75

Figure 3–76

To Use a Subdatasheet

1 UPDATE RECORDS | 2 FILTER RECORDS | 3 CHANGE STRUCTURE | 4 MASS CHANGES | 5 VALIDATION RULES
6 CHANGE APPEARANCE | 7 REFERENTIAL INTEGRITY | 8 ORDER RECORDS

One consequence of the tables being explicitly related is that the accounts for an account manager can appear below the account manager in a **subdatasheet**. *Why is a subdatasheet useful? A subdatasheet is useful when you want to review or edit data in joined or related tables.* The availability of such a subdatasheet is indicated by a plus sign that appears in front of the rows in the Account Manager table. The following steps display the subdatasheet for account manager 35.

1

- Open the Account Manager table in Datasheet view and close the Navigation Pane (Figure 3–77).

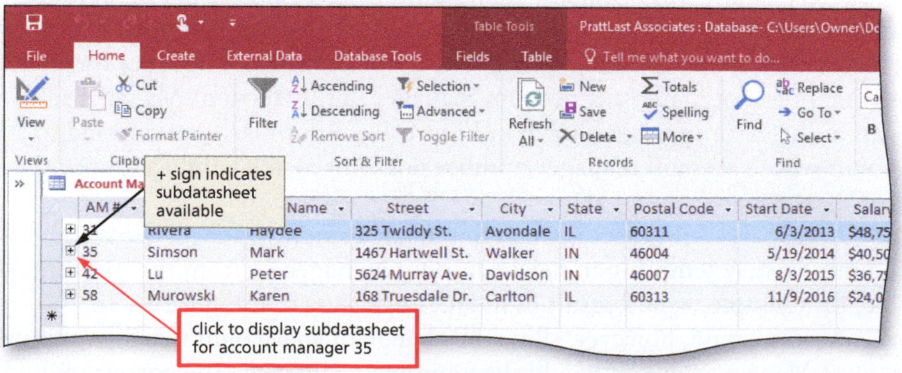

Figure 3–77

②

- Click the plus sign in front of the row for account manager 35 to display the subdatasheet (Figure 3–78).

Q&A

How do I hide the subdatasheet when I no longer want it to appear?
When you clicked the plus sign, it changed to a minus sign. Click the minus sign.

Experiment

- Display subdatasheets for other account managers. Display more than one subdatasheet at a time. Remove the subdatasheets from the screen.

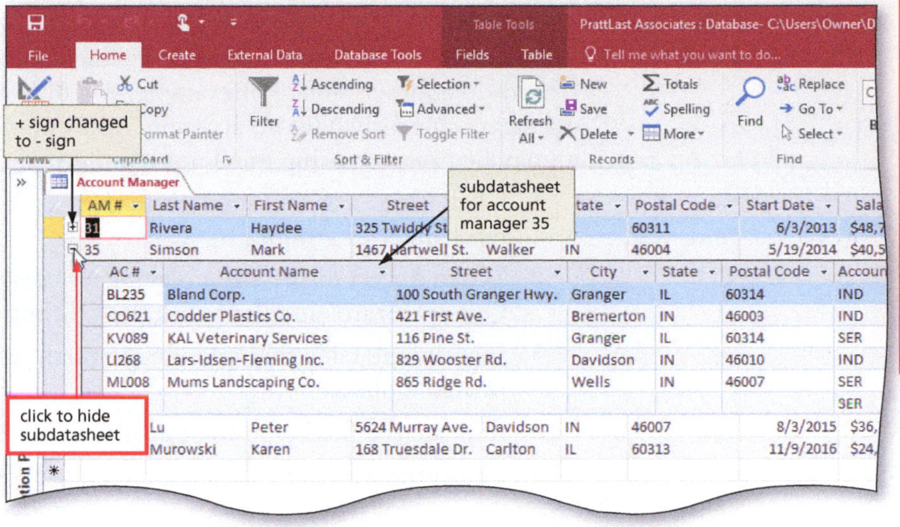

Figure 3–78

③

- If requested by your instructor, replace the city and state for account manager 35 with your city and state.

- Close the Account Manager table.

Handling Data Inconsistency

In many organizations, databases evolve and change over time. One department might create a database for its own internal use. Employees in another department may decide they need their own database containing much of the same information. For example, the Purchasing department of an organization might create a database of products that it buys and the Receiving department may create a database of products that it receives. Each department is keeping track of the same products. When the organization eventually merges the databases, they might discover inconsistencies and duplication. The Find Duplicates Query Wizard and the Find Unmatched Query Wizard can assist in clearing the resulting database of duplication and errors.

BTW

Database Design: Validation

In most organizations, decisions about what is valid and what is invalid data are made during the requirements gathering process and the database design process.

TO FIND DUPLICATE RECORDS

One reason to include a primary key for a table is to eliminate duplicate records. A possibility still exists, however, that duplicate records can get into your database. You would use the following steps to find duplicate records using the 'Find Duplicates Query Wizard'.

1. Click Create on the ribbon, and then click the Query Wizard button (Create tab | Queries group).

2. When Access displays the New Query dialog box, click the 'Find Duplicates Query Wizard' and then click the OK button.

3. Identify the table and field or fields that might contain duplicate information.

4. Indicate any other fields you want displayed.

5. Finish the wizard to see any duplicate records.

To Find Unmatched Records

Occasionally, you might need to find records in one table that have no matching records in another table. For example, you may want to determine which account managers currently have no accounts. You would use the following steps to find unmatched records using the 'Find Unmatched Query Wizard'.

1. Click Create on the ribbon, and then click the Query Wizard button (Create tab | Queries group).
2. When Access displays the New Query dialog box, click the 'Find Unmatched Query Wizard' and then click the OK button.
3. Identify the table that might contain unmatched records, and then identify the related table.
4. Indicate the fields you want displayed.
5. Finish the wizard to see any unmatched records.

Ordering Records

Normally, Access sequences the records in the Account table by account number whenever listing them because the Account Number field is the primary key. You can change this order, if desired.

To Use the Ascending Button to Order Records

1 UPDATE RECORDS | 2 FILTER RECORDS | 3 CHANGE STRUCTURE | 4 MASS CHANGES | 5 VALIDATION RULES
6 CHANGE APPEARANCE | 7 REFERENTIAL INTEGRITY | **8 ORDER RECORDS**

To change the order in which records appear, use the Ascending or Descending buttons. Either button reorders the records based on the field in which the insertion point is located. The following steps order the records by city using the Ascending button. **Why?** *Using the Ascending button is the quickest and easiest way to order records.*

1

- Open the Account table in Datasheet view.
- Click the City field on the first record to select the field (Figure 3–79).

Q&A Did I have to click the field on the first record?
No. Any other record would have worked as well.

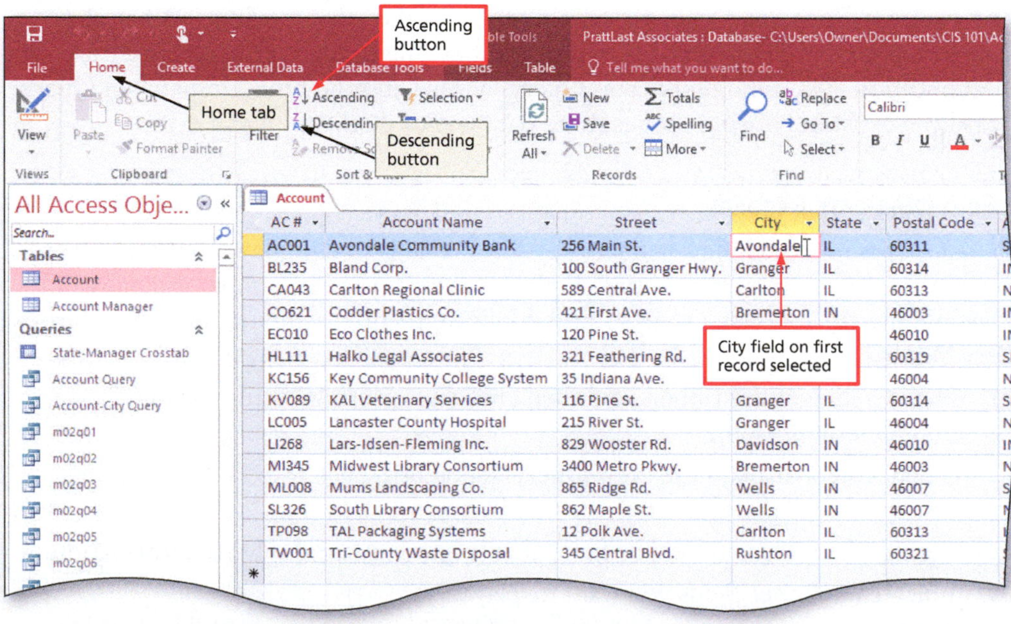

Figure 3–79

2

- Click the Ascending button (Home tab | Sort & Filter group) to sort the records by City (Figure 3–80).

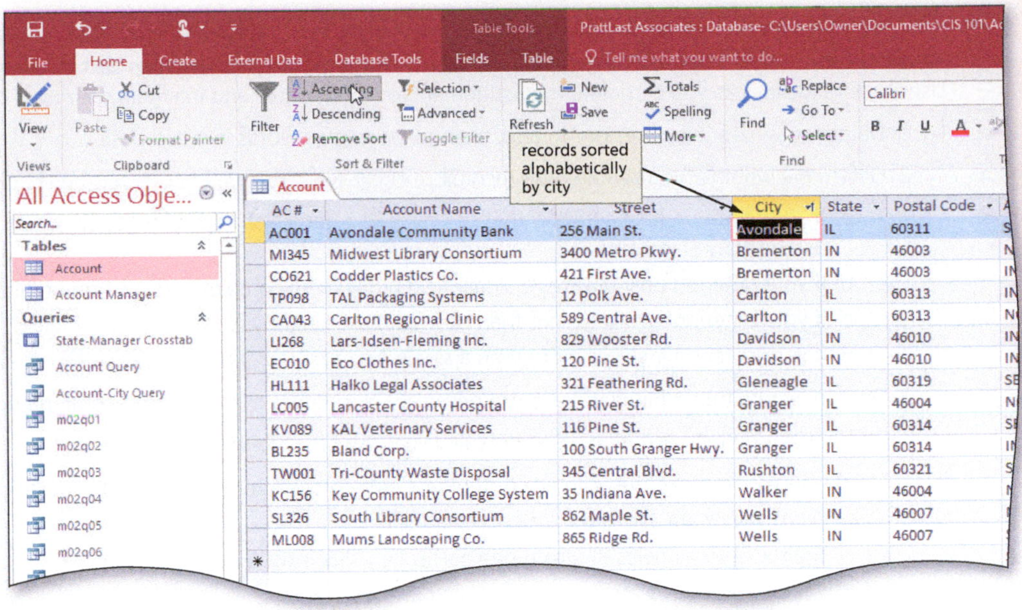

3

- Close the Account table.
- Click the No button (Microsoft Access dialog box) when asked if you want to save your changes.

Q&A

What if I saved the changes?
The next time you open the table the records will be sorted by city.

Figure 3–80

- If desired, sign out of your Microsoft account.
- Exit Access.

Other Ways

1. Right-click field name, click Sort A to Z (for ascending) or Sort Z to A (for descending)

2. Click the field selector arrow and click Sort A to Z or Sort Z to A

TO USE THE ASCENDING BUTTON TO ORDER RECORDS ON MULTIPLE FIELDS

Just as you are able to sort the answer to a query on multiple fields, you can also sort the data that appears in a datasheet on multiple fields. To do so, the major and minor keys must be next to each other in the datasheet with the major key on the left. If this is not the case, you can drag the columns into the correct position. Instead of dragging, however, usually it will be easier to use a query that has the data sorted in the desired order.

To sort on a combination of fields where the major key is just to the left of the minor key, you would use the following steps.

1. Click the field selector at the top of the major key column to select the entire column.

2. Hold down the SHIFT key and then click the field selector for the minor key column to select both columns.

3. Click the Ascending button to sort the records.

BTW

Access Help
At any time while using Access, you can find answers to questions and display information about various topics through Access Help. Used properly, this form of assistance can increase your productivity and reduce your frustrations by minimizing the time you spend learning how to use Access. For instructions about Access Help and exercises that will help you gain confidence in using it, read the Office and Windows module at the beginning of this book.

Summary

In this module you have learned how to use a form to add records to a table, search for records, delete records, filter records, change the database structure, create and use lookup fields, create calculated fields, create and use multivalued fields, make mass changes, create validation rules, change the appearance of a datasheet, specify referential integrity, and use subdatasheets.

What decisions will you need to make when maintaining your own databases?

Use these guidelines as you complete the assignments in this module and maintain your own databases outside of this class.

1. Determine when it is necessary to add, change, or delete records in a database.

2. Determine whether you should filter records.

   a) If your criterion for filtering is that the value in a particular field matches or does not match a certain specific value, use Filter By Selection.

   b) If your criterion only involves a single field but is more complex, use a common filter.

   c) If your criterion involves more than one field, use Filter By Form.

   d) If your criterion involves more than a single And or Or, or if it involves sorting, use Advanced Filter/Sort.

3. Determine whether additional fields are necessary or whether existing fields should be deleted.

4. Determine whether validation rules, default values, and formats are necessary.

   a) Can you improve the accuracy of the data entry process by enforcing data validation?

   b) What values are allowed for a particular field?

   c) Are there some fields in which one particular value is used more than another?

   d) Should some fields be required for each record?

   e) Are there some fields for which special formats would be appropriate?

5. Determine whether changes to the format of a datasheet are desirable.

   a) Would totals or other calculations be useful in the datasheet?

   b) Would different gridlines make the datasheet easier to read?

   c) Would alternating colors in the rows make them easier to read?

   d) Would a different font and/or font color make the text stand out better?

   e) Is the font size appropriate?

   f) Is the column spacing appropriate?

6. Identify related tables in order to implement relationships between the tables.

   a) Is there a one-to-many relationship between the tables?

   b) If so, which table is the one table?

   c) Which table is the many table?

7. When specifying referential integrity, address deletion and update policies.

   a) Decide how to handle deletions. Should deletion be prohibited or should the delete cascade?

   b) Decide how to handle the update of the primary key. Should the update be prohibited or should the update cascade?

How should you submit solutions to questions in the assignments identified with a symbol?

Every assignment in this book contains one or more questions identified with a symbol. These questions require you to think beyond the assigned database. Present your solutions to the questions in the format required by your instructor. Possible formats may include one or more of these options: write the answer; create a document that contains the answer; present your answer to the class; discuss your answer in a group; record the answer as audio or video using a webcam, smartphone, or portable media player; or post answers on a blog, wiki, or website.

Apply Your Knowledge

Reinforce the skills and apply the concepts you learned in this module.

Adding Lookup Fields, Specifying Validation Rules, Updating Records, Updating Reports, and Creating Relationships

Instructions: Run Access. Open the Apply Friendly Janitorial Services database that you modified in Apply Your Knowledge in Module 2. (If you did not complete the exercise, see your instructor for a copy of the modified database.)

Perform the following tasks:

1. Open the Client table in Design view.

2. Add a Lookup field called Client Type to the Client table. The field should appear after the Postal Code field. The field will contain data on the type of client. The client types are IND (industrial, manufacturing), RET (retail stores), and SER (service, nonprofit). Save the changes to the Client table.

3. Create the following validation rules for the Client table.

    a. Specify the legal values IND, RET, and SER for the Client Type field. Enter **Must be IND, RET, or SER** as the validation text.

    b. Format the Client Number field to ensure that any letters entered in the field appear as uppercase.

    c. Make the Client Name field a required field.

4. Save the changes and close the table. You do not need to test the current data.

5. Create an update query for the Client table. Change all the entries in the Client Type field to SER. Run the query and save it as Client Type Update Query.

6. Open the Client table in Datasheet view, update the following records, and then close the table:

    a. Change the client type for clients CC25, CP03, MM01, and TE15 to IND.

    b. Change the client type for clients AZ01, BL24, and HC17 to RET.

7. Create a split form for the Client table. Save the form as Client Split Form.

8. Open the Client Split Form in Form view, find client HC17, and change the client name to Hilltop Crafters. Close the form.

9. Open the Client Financial Report in Layout view and add the Client Type field to the report as shown in Figure 3–81. Save the report.

Client Number	Client Name	Client Type	Amount Paid	Current Due	Supervisor Number
AT13	Atlas Repair	SER	$5,400.00	$600.00	103
AZ01	AZ Auto	RET	$9,250.00	$975.00	110
BB35	Babbage Bookkeeping	SER	$8,820.00	$980.00	110

Figure 3–81

10. Establish referential integrity between the Supervisor table (the one table) and the Client table (the many table). Cascade the update but not the delete. Save the relationship.

11. If requested to do so by your instructor, rename the Client Split Form as Split Form for First Name Last Name where First Name Last Name is your name.

12. Submit the revised database in the format specified by your instructor.

13. The values in the Client Type field are currently in the order IND, RET, SER. How would you reorder the values to SER, IND, RET in the Client Type list?

Extend Your Knowledge

Extend the skills you learned in this module and experiment with new skills. You may need to use Help to complete the assignment.

Creating Action Queries, Changing Table Properties, and Adding Totals to a Datasheet

Note: To complete this assignment, you will be required to use the Data Files. Please contact your instructor for information about accessing the Data Files.

Continued >

Extend Your Knowledge *continued*

Instructions: Babbage Bookkeeping is a small company that provides bookkeeping services to small businesses. PrattLast Associates has been approached about buying Babbage Bookkeeping. PrattLast is interested in knowing how many clients the companies have in common. Babbage also needs to do some database maintenance by finding duplicate records and finding unmatched records.

Perform the following tasks:

1. Run Access and open the Extend Babbage Bookkeeping database. Create a make-table query to create the Potential Accounts table in the Babbage Bookkeeping database shown in Figure 3–82. Run the query and save it as Make Table Query.

Client Numt ▾	Client Name ▾	Street ▾	City ▾	State ▾	Postal Code ▾	Amount Pai ▾	Balance Due ▾	Bookkeeper ▾
A54	Afton Manufac	612 Revere Rd.	Granger	IL	60311	$575.00	$315.00	22
A62	Atlas Distribut	227 Dandelion	Burles	IN	46002	$250.00	$175.00	24
B26	Blake-Scryps	557 Maum St.	Georgetown	IN	46008	$875.00	$250.00	24
D76	Dege Grocery (	446 Linton Ave	Burles	IN	46002	$1,015.00	$325.00	22
G56	Grandston Clea	337 Abelard Rd	Buda	IL	60310	$485.00	$165.00	24
H21	Hill Country Sh	247 Fulton St.	Granger	IL	60311	$0.00	$285.00	34
J77	Jones Plumbin	75 Getty Blvd.	Buda	IL	60310	$685.00	$0.00	22
M26	Mohr Art Suppl	665 Maum St.	Georgetown	IN	46008	$125.00	$185.00	24
S56	SeeSaw Indust	31 Liatris Ave.	Walburg	IN	46006	$1,200.00	$645.00	22
T45	Tate Repair	824 Revere Rd.	Granger	IL	60311	$345.00	$200.00	34
W24	Woody Sportin	578 Central Ave	Walburg	IN	46006	$975.00	$0.00	34
C29	Catering by Jer	123 Second St.	Granger	IL	60311	$0.00	$250.00	34

Figure 3–82

2. Open the Potential Accounts table and change the font to Arial with a font size of 10. Resize the columns to best fit the data. Save the changes to the table and close the table.

3. Open the Bookkeeper table and add the Totals row to the table. Calculate the average hourly rate and the total Earnings YTD. Save the changes to the table layout and close the table.

4. Use the Find Duplicates Query Wizard to find duplicate information in the City field of the Client table. Include the Client Name in the query. Save the query as City Duplicates Query and close the query.

5. Use the Find Unmatched Query Wizard to find all records in the Bookkeeper table that do not match records in the Client table. Bookkeeper Number is the common field in both tables. Include the Bookkeeper Number, Last Name, and First Name in the query. Save the query as Bookkeeper Unmatched Query and close the query.

6. If requested to do so by your instructor, change the client name in the Client table for client number B26 to First Name Last Name where First Name Last Name is your name. If your name is longer than the space allowed, simply enter as much as you can.

7. Submit the revised database in the format specified by your instructor.

8. What differences, if any, are there between the Client table and the Potential Accounts table you created with the make-table query?

Expand Your World

Create a solution, which uses cloud and web technologies, by learning and investigating on your own from general guidance.

Problem: You own a small business that employs college students to do odd jobs for homeowners in the college town where you live. You created an Access database to keep track of your customers and workers and have been teaching yourself more about database design and how best to use Access to promote and manage your business.

Perform the following tasks:

1. Run Access and open the Expand Odd Jobs database. Edit the relationship between the Worker table and the Customer table to cascade the updates. Save the change to the relationship.

2. Create a relationship report for the relationship and save the report as First Name Last Name Relationship Report where First Name Last Name is your name.

3. Export the relationship as an RTF/Word document to a cloud-based storage location of your choice. Do not save the export steps.

4. Research the web to find a graphic that depicts a one-to-many relationship for a relational database. (*Hint:* Use your favorite search engine and enter keywords such as ERD diagram, entity-relationship diagram, or one to many relationship.)

5. Insert the graphic into the relationship report using an app of your choice, such as Word Online, and save the modified report.

6. Share the modified report with your instructor.

7. Submit the revised database in the format specified by your instructor.

8. ✳ Which cloud-based storage location did you use? How did you locate your graphic? Which app did you use to modify the report?

In the Labs

Design, create, modify, and/or use a database following the guidelines, concepts, and skills presented in this module. Labs are listed in order of increasing difficulty. Labs 1 and 2, which increase in difficulty, require you to create solutions based on what you learned in the module. Lab 3 requires you to apply your creative thinking and problem–solving skills to design and implement a solution.

Lab 1: Maintaining the Garden Naturally Database

Problem: Garden Naturally is expanding rapidly and needs to make some database changes to handle the expansion. The company needs to know more about its customers, such as general types of products needed. It also needs to add validation rules and update records in the database.

Note: Use the database modified in Lab 1 of Module 2 for this assignment, or see your instructor for information on accessing the files required for this book.

Instructions: Perform the following tasks:

1. Open the Lab 1 Garden Naturally database and open the Customer table in Design view.

2. Add a multivalued lookup field, Product Types Needed, to the Customer table. The field should appear after the Postal Code field. Table 3–2 lists the product type abbreviations that management would like in the multivalued field as well as a description. Save the change to the table.

Table 3–2 Product Type Abbreviations and Descriptions	
Product Type Abbreviations	**Product Type Descriptions**
Comp	Composting Needs
Frtl	Fertilizers
Grdn	Garden Supplies
Grnh	Greenhouse Supplies
Lawn	Lawn and Landscaping
Seed	Seeds
Soil	Soils and Nutrients
Watr	Watering Equipment

Continued >

In the Labs *continued*

3. Add a calculated field named Total Amount (Amount Paid + Balance Due) to the Customer table. The field should follow the Balance Due field. Save the change to the table.

4. Create the following rules for the Customer table and save the changes:
   a. Ensure that any letters entered in the Customer Number field appear as uppercase.
   b. Make Customer Name a required field.
   c. Ensure that only the values DE, NJ, and PA can be entered in the State field. Include validation text.
   d. Assign a default value of NJ to the State field.

5. Use Filter By Form to find all records where the city is Gaston and the balance due is $0.00. Delete the record(s). Do not save the filter.

6. Open the Customer table in Datasheet view and add the data shown in Figure 3–83 to the Product Types Needed field. Resize the field to best fit and save the changes to the layout of the table.

Customer Table		
Customer Number	**Customer Name**	**Product Types Needed**
AA30	All About Gardens	Grdn, Seed, Soil, Watr
CT02	Christmas Tree Farm	Comp, Frtl, Seed, Soil, Watr
GG01	Garden Gnome	Frtl, Grdn, Lawn
GT34	Green Thumb Growers	Frtl, Grnh, Seed
LH15	Lawn & Home Store	Comp, Frtl, Grdn, Lawn
ML25	Mum's Landscaping	Frtl, Soil, Watr
OA45	Outside Architects	Grdn, Watr
PL10	Pat's Landscaping	Frtl, Grdn, Watr
PN18	Pyke Nurseries	Comp, Frtl, Grnh, Seed, Soil
SL25	Summit Lawn Service	Grdn, Lawn, Watr
TW34	TAL Wholesalers	Comp, Frtl, Seed, Soil
TY03	TLC Yard Care	Lawn, Watr
YS04	Yard Shoppe	Grdn, Lawn, Watr
YW01	Young's Wholesalers	Comp, Frtl, Grdn, Lawn, Seed, Soil

Figure 3–83

7. Open the Sales Rep table in Design view and change the field size for the Address field to 25. Save the changes and close the table.

8. Open the Sales Rep table in Datasheet view, find the record for sales rep 32, and change the address to 982 Victoria Station Rd. Resize the column to best fit.

9. If requested to do so by your instructor, change the last name for sales rep 35 to your last name. If your last name is longer than 15 characters, simply enter as much as you can.

10. Save the changes to the layout of the table and close the Sales Rep table.

11. Establish referential integrity between the Sales Rep table (the one table) and the Customer table (the many table). Cascade the update but not the delete.

12. Submit the revised database in the format specified by your instructor.

13. ✳ The State field currently has three possible values. How would you add MD to the State field list?

Lab 2: **Maintaining the Museum Gift Shop Database**

Problem: The manager of the Science Museum gift shop needs to change the database structure, add validation rules, and update records. Also, a volunteer at the gift shop was asked to add some items to the database. By mistake, the volunteer created a new database in which to store the items. These items need to be added to the Museum Gift Shop database.

Note: To complete this assignment, you will be required to use the Data Files. Please contact your instructor for information about accessing the Data Files. Use the database modified in Lab 2 of Module 2 for this assignment or see your instructor for information on accessing the files required for this book.

Instructions: Perform the following tasks:

1. Open the Lab 2 Museum Gift Shop database, and then open the Item table in Design view.

2. Add a lookup field, Item Type, to the Item table. The field should appear after the Description field. The field will contain data on the type of item for sale. The item types are ACT (activity, game), BKS (book), and NOV (novelty, gift).

3. Add the following validation rules to the Item table and save the changes:
   a. Make Description a required field.
   b. Specify the legal values ACT, BKS, and NOV for the Item Type field. Include validation text.
   c. Assign ACT as the default value for the Item Type field.
   d. Specify that the number on hand must be between 0 and 50, inclusive. Include validation text.

4. Using a query, assign the value ACT to the Item Type field for all records. Save the query as Update Query.

5. Create a split form for the Item table and save it as Item Split Form.

6. Use the split form to change the item type for items 6234, 6345, and 7123 to BKS. Change the item type for items 3663, 4583, 6185, 8196, and 8344 to NOV.

7. Open the Lab 2 Additional Items database from the Data Files.

8. Create and run a query to append the data in the Additional Items table to the Item table in the Lab 2 Museum Gift Shop database. Save the query as Append Query and close the Lab 2 Additional Items database.

9. Open the Lab 2 Museum Gift Shop database and then open the Item table. The result of the append query will be the table shown in Figure 3–84.

Item Number	Description	Item Type	On Hand	Wholesale	Retail	VC	Click to Add
3663	Agate Bookends	NOV	4	$16.25	$27.97	GS	
3673	Amazing Science Fun	ACT	8	$13.50	$24.99	AW	
3873	Big Book of Why	BKS	12	$7.99	$14.95	AW	
4553	Cosmos Uncovered	ACT	9	$8.95	$15.00	SD	
4573	Crystal Growing Kit	ACT	7	$6.75	$12.97	AW	
4583	Dinosaur Egg Ornament	NOV	12	$7.50	$14.99	GS	
5923	Discovery Dinosaurs	ACT	3	$12.35	$19.95	AW	
6185	Fibonacci Necklace	NOV	5	$16.75	$29.99	GS	
6234	Fun with Math	BKS	16	$12.95	$24.95	SD	
6325	Fun Straws	ACT	20	$4.55	$8.99	SD	
6345	Geek Toys Guide	BKS	20	$5.10	$9.99	SD	
7123	Gem Nature Guide	BKS	12	$9.50	$14.95	AW	
7934	Gyrobot	ACT	24	$27.99	$49.99	GS	
8196	Molecule Necklace	NOV	6	$16.25	$29.95	GS	
8344	Onyx Jar	NOV	2	$7.50	$13.97	AW	
8590	Paper Planes	ACT	22	$7.10	$13.99	SD	
9201	Sidewalk Art and More	ACT	15	$9.35	$16.95	GS	
9458	Slime Time	ACT	15	$15.35	$24.99	SD	
*		ACT					

Figure 3–84

Continued >

In the Labs *continued*

10. Create an advanced filter for the Item table. Filter the table to find all items with fewer than 10 items on hand. Sort the filter by Item Type and Description. Save the filter settings as a query and name the filter Reorder Filter. Clear the filter from the Item table.

11. Using a query, delete all records in the Item table where the description starts with the letter M. Run the query and save it as Delete Query.

12. If requested to do so by your instructor, right-click the Item table in the Navigation Pane, click Table Properties, and add a description for the Item table that includes your first and last name and the date you completed this assignment. Save the change to the table property.

13. Specify referential integrity between the Vendor table (the one table) and the Item table (the many table). Cascade the update but not the delete.

14. Add the Item Type field to the Item Status Report. It should follow the Description field.

15. Submit the revised database in the format specified by your instructor.

16. ✳ There are two ways to enter the validation rule in Step 3d. What are they? Which one did you use?

Lab 3: Consider This: Your Turn

Maintaining the Camshay Marketing Database

Instructions: Open the Lab 3 Camshay Marketing database you used in Module 2. If you did not use this database, contact your instructor for information about accessing the required files.

Part 1: Use the concepts and techniques presented in this module to modify the database according to the following requirements:

a. Grant Auction House is no longer a client of Camshay. Use Find or Filter By Selection to delete this record.

b. A Total Amount field that summed the Amount Paid and Current Due fields would be beneficial for the reports that Camshay needs.

c. Camshay could better serve its clients by adding a field that would list each client's type of business or organizations. Businesses are nonprofit (NON), service (SER), or retail (RET).

d. Most businesses are service organizations. Buda Community Clinic, Hendley County Hospital, and Granger Foundation are nonprofit organizations. The Bikeshop and Woody Sporting Goods are retail stores.

e. The Client Financial Report must show the Total Amount.

f. An entry should always appear in the Client Name field. Any letters in the Client Number field should appear in uppercase.

g. A client's current due amount should never exceed $10,000.00.

h. Camshay has acquired a new client and needs to add the data to the database. Fine Wooden Crafts is a retail store located at 24 Oakley in Buda, NC 27032. Its client number is FW01 with zero amount paid and current due. The client has been assigned to Jeff Scott.

i. Specify referential integrity. Cascade the update but not the delete.

j. Camshay would like the records in the Client table to be sorted by client name, not client number.

Submit your assignment in the format specified by your instructor.

Part 2: You made several decisions while including adding a calculated field, Total Amount, to the database. What was the rationale behind your decisions? Does the calculated field actually exist in the database? Are there any issues that you need to consider when you create a calculated field?

Index